TERROR

Terroir (tair-wahr)
a French term meaning
total elements of the vineyard

UNIVERSITY OF CALIFORNIA PRESS
BERKELEY · LOS ANGELES · LONDON
in association with
THE WINE APPRECIATION GUILD
SAN FRANCISCO

Dedication

To Elloie

Terroir
The Role of Geology, Climate, and Culture in the Making of French Wines
by James E. Wilson

First published in the United States in 1999 by the University of California Press in association with The Wine Appreciation Guild. Published by arrangement with Mitchell Beazley.

University of California Press
Berkeley and Los Angeles, California

University of California Press, Ltd
London, England

The Wine Appreciation Guild
360 Swift Avenue, Unit 34
So. San Francisco, California 94080
1-650-866-3020

ISBN 0-520-21936-8

9 8 7 6 5 4 3 2 1

Commissioning Editor: Sue Jamieson
Executive Art Editor: Fiona Knowles
Editor: Stephanie Horner
Wordprocessing and manuscript research: Marguerite Bradford
Design: Watermark Communications Limited
Illustration: LCT Graphics, Adrian Waddington
Picture Research: Cee Weston-Baker
Production: Rachel Lynch
Index: Angie Hipkin

Typeset in Granjon and Frutiger

Printed and bound by Toppan Printing Company in China

Contents

Foreword by Hugh Johnson

A few years ago, and in some places still, it was considered somewhere between foolish eccentricity and serious heresy to talk about where wine comes from.

I don't mean its address, geography, and postcode. The price, the prestige of the name, its very saleability depend on that above all. I mean the unseen dankness where the vineroots suck; where the liquid in your glass is teased out of the soil. A tiny shoot nudges downward through soil, sand, close-packed clay, even into hairline fissures in rock. The fuel that drives it is produced by leaves in the sunlight above. But they in turn depend on the capacity of roots to keep sipping successfully, sometimes where there seems almost no moisture at all.

Grape varieties, their training, cultivation, ripening, picking, and processing have all been under the spotlight. The fruit itself has recently been given the starring role, sometimes almost as though the difference between Cabernet and Syrah were all there was to say about a wine.

As far as I know this book is the first to investigate the primary source of fine wines: rocks and soil. Even recent technical publications in wine countries outside Europe give only fleeting mention to the soil. If it keeps the plant upright and lets excess rainfall drain away its duty, we are led to believe, is done.

Yet soils are more various than vines. They form by an infinity of processes from raw materials as contrasting as sea shells and lava. In their physical make-up, chemical reactions, their interactions, in whether they are willing or grudging to release their elements, from water to metals, they encompass wide, sometimes contradicting, differences. If Chablis tastes different from Meursault, Margaux from Pauillac, the first place we must look for the difference is underground.

Terroir, of course, means much more than what goes on below the surface. Properly understood, it means the whole ecology of a vineyard: every aspect of its surroundings from bedrock to late frosts and autumn mists, not excluding the way the vineyard is tended, nor even the soul of the vigneron.

Jim Wilson's obsession with rocks, soil, and vegetation grew from early curiosity about the contrast of these elements around the family farm in north Texas to those of the surrounding area. Geology and Jim found each other at Texas A&M University. His training as a petroleum geologist was put first to mapping for the Shell Oil Company. In World War II he was wounded in Normandy and turned his knowledge to instruction at the General Staff College. After the war, he resumed the subterranean search for oil and gas but the question why great wines grow where they do proved almost as exciting. Besides, you could drink on the job.

Jim and I started to discuss the influence of geology on wine over a decade ago. I was ready to learn, but found it hard to understand. Now, it seems to me, this geologist-with-glass in hand has succeeded in breaking down, as weathering does rock to soil, the components of the relationship between vines and their context — not just mineral but vegetable and human, too. In a word, their terroir.

This is not to say that all can be explained, but something tells me that Jim Wilson's questioning mind is marking another stage in our understanding of the mysterious substance that unites us, in celebration and in wonder: wine.

Introduction

Why do the fine wines of France grow where they do? How is it that one vineyard yields superior wine, while its neighbor that appears the same does not? Answering these questions is what this book is about. The answers are found in the interaction of the elements of the vineyard habitat. The French for this is *terroir*, a defined place, that grows wines both great and small.

In this totality of elements, geology dictates the overall landscape, rock type, the landform, the exposure, soil, subsoil, and drainage. The climate invites distribution of the vine, the selection of the variety, and its cultivation by man.

Why France? Because this "land of a thousand wines," not quite the size of Texas, has vines growing on the most varied geology and landscapes of any wine country in the world. Its 2000 years of history play a vital role, too.

You should be warned, perhaps, that the author is a geologist, and geologists have a fraternal feeling about rocks – they like to call them by name, know what they are made of, how old they are, and how they became involved in the landscape. You will be introduced to these "rock families" and will get to feel at home with them. But *Terroir* is not a technical book. You can understand and enjoy it without having to reach for anything more than the glass of wine on your side table – French, of course.

The *why*, *where*, and *how* were not compelling questions, but came frequently to mind when I happened to be enjoying a glass of fine wine. Being a geologist I assumed, with due respect to the climate, that the answers would be found in the varied geology and soils of France.

Musing about these questions was about as far as things went, until the early seventies, when I saw Hugh Johnson's *World Atlas of Wine* with its detailed maps of vineyards on a topographic (contour) base. Moreover, the quality classification of the vineyards was indicated by color code and print style. I sensed exciting possibilities to answers to the questions of *why* and *where*. Would not such maps, combined with the geologic map, suggest why some vineyards produce outstanding wines and their neighbors might not? That approach turned out to be overly simplified, but it was the impetus that led to my writing this book.

A few years later, in preparing for a visit to France, I looked for a book on the geology of the vineyards. I could find no such publication, either in the U.S. or London. Somewhat frustrated, I remarked to my wife, "Well, I guess I'll have to write the book." At the time, it was in no way a serious threat.

It was in Burgundy that the realization came to me that it was not the surface geology alone that decided the better vineyards, but the combination of the elements of the vineyard habitat. I quickly learned that the natural history of wine would be a complex study, but the key factor would be geology.

In Burgundy, I met Noël Leneuf, professor of geology at the University of Dijon. Leneuf is convinced that geology and its soils are the critical factors in the terroirs of Burgundy. He was to provide me with many useful publications on the soils and wine, plus enjoyable time in the field. Then, on a trip to London, I met Hugh Johnson who had, in earlier correspondence, been very encouraging about my idea for the book, saying a clear explanation of the relationship between soil and winegrowing was overdue. Could I write about rocks for a non-specialist audience? That challenge has proved to be a lasting one.

Back home, word of my interest in the geology of wine got around, and I was invited to give slide-talks to groups in several cities and states in the U.S. The important result of these talks was finding genuine interest in the subject among a diverse audience.

In 1984, I received a letter from Dr. Robert Lautel, then Deputy Director of the Bureau de Recherches Géologiques et Minières (B.R.G.M.), saying he had learned that I looked for a book on the geology of French vineyards but couldn't find one. He said that he was co-editor of the book *Terroirs et Vins de France, Itinéraires Oenologiques et Géologiques*, and that he would send me a copy.

Was this not the book I had sought? It would have been, seven years earlier. But by now I had beome convinced that there was real interest not only in the geology of *where* wines grow but in *how* the terroirs function. I began to concentrate on research, translations, and map studies for my own book, in which I was generously assisted by Dr. Lautel and his team of contributors.

The first part of my book is an elaboration on the components of the French terroirs. The geologic map (Color Plate 1) shows the distribution of the "rock families" – older, "hard" rock types in the mountains, "younger" ones in basins and valleys. Color Plate 3 identifies the wine districts, relief and main climate zones of France. Rock weathering produces soils – the soul of the vineplant. Erosion and other geologic processes create the vineyard sites and growing zones. Climate aids weathering, influences distribution of the wine areas, the choice of grape, and the type of wine.

But the quality of wine is not simply geologic good fortune. France has been blessed with a population that has an inherent love of the land and its cultivation. Over the centuries, vignerons learned through trial and error how to bring out the best from their land. In the first half of the 20th century France survived two great wars and overcame a near fatal blight to become the greatest and most diverse wine-producing country in the world.

Part two of *Terroir* is a journey through scenic winelands across the diverse geology of France: slopes of chalk, glacial valleys, gravel mounds, granite outcrops, and limestone cuestas. Individual chapters describe the wine areas, the formation of their landscapes, why some vineyards are superior to others and how elements of the terroirs interact. For fine wines, though, it is not the scenery that counts but what is *not* seen, down where the roots grow. The roots have explored this unseen zone; their vineyard products tell us there is a difference. When the soil that sticks to our shoes or is turned by the plow looks the same from one terroir to another, how do we know the nature of this difference. Seldom is the anatomy of this sub-surface zone exposed in the vineyard. It is through the combination of small-scale geologic maps and knowledge of geologic processes that this underground functioning can be interpreted. That is the uniquenes of this book.

As you contemplate the wine in your glass, recognize it has a personality – it comes from a place with a name and a history. It has relatives and a family, possibly very distinguished. Refill your glass and let's go visit the land of its birth.

Part One:

Elements of the French terroirs

1 The habitat: what makes good grapes

Prologue

From time to time, when it was my good fortune to enjoy a glass of fine French wine, I would ponder the question why the great wines of France grow where they do. It was not a compelling question, and as a geologist, I assumed the answer was geology. After all, aren't rocks and soils at the roots of all grapevines? With due regard for climate, would not the greatly varied geology of France account for an even greater variety of wines?

Contemplation in a vineyard

On a spring morning in 1977, it was in the Côte d'Or that I stood with some reverence in a famed terroir – a place, a name, a history. The vineyard soil I was scuffing about with my shoe was a rich, reddish-brown. This was my first visit to Burgundy, but somehow this soil seemed curiously familiar. In a mental flash-back, I was a young field geologist standing on the reddish-brown soil of a particular geologic formation in south-central Texas that I had mapped over half a lifetime ago. Soils and their colors are useful tools in geologic mapping.

The Burgundy and Texas soils were similar in appearance, but I knew the French soil was from Jurassic rocks, 100 million years older than its Texas look-alike. There were other differences as well as similarities. The narrow outcrop band of the Texas formation was cotton land. I had fervently hoped it might overlie deeper reservoirs of oil and gas. (It didn't.) The soils where I now stood yield wines that some prize more highly than crude oil from the Texas plains.

The mother rocks of both of these soils were born of the sea. The fossil shells in each tell us that. I picked up one of the fragments of slabby limestone in the vineyard soil and saw that it was a mass of broken ancient oyster shells. Would you believe that after all these millions of years, the inside of the shells still retained their pearly luster? I later learned that this fragment was from a formation called the *Dalle nacrée*, meaning pearly flagstone.

The Texas formation has an equally odd name, Weches, after a little village in east Texas where the formation typically outcrops. Although the Weches itself is 40 million years old, its fossils closely resemble many of the sea shells found today along the beaches of the Gulf of Mexico.

This exercise in recall stimulated my geologic curiosity about this Burgundian vineyard in which I stood on a brisk spring morning. What was the sub-soil, down where the roots live? How deep was it to bedrock and what was it like?

Looking up the sweeping slope to the top of the long, low scarp half a mile away, I pondered the geologic processes that had created this landscape. What was so special about these slopes and soils of the Côte d'Or that they produce some of the world's most renowned wines? Why were some vineyards classified top quality, while others nearby that appeared the same were of lesser fame? The answer undoubtedly involved a number of factors, but would not a constant in the wine equation be the habitat, the rocks and soils – the geology?

The vinestocks here were quite thick and gnarled. I knelt down to examine one more closely. They appeared to be very old. How old – twenty, thirty years? I wondered how many bottles of marvelous red Pommard had come from the vines within my view. Had I ever had any wine from this particular vineyard? I could not remember. Probably not.

With all due respect to the nobility of these Pinot Noir vines and the loving care they had received, I knew that the vines here and elsewhere had been grafted on rootstocks of crude American ancestry – possibly the originals had come from Texas. How did I dare such a brazen thought? Because, toward the end of the 19th century, the French vineyards had been all but annihilated by a root pest. The ultimate solution for arresting the devastation and allowing the vineyards' recovery was the grafting of French vines on American rootstocks which had long ago developed immunity to the pest. The tiny root louse, given the imposing name of *Phylloxera vastatrix*, had unknowingly been imported from America on a gift of rooted vineplants.

Thomas Volney Munson, a plant scientist from Denison in northeast Texas, had been of great assistance to the French in identifying phylloxera-resistant rootstocks which were compatible both with French soils and scions of the aristocratic *vinifera* (*see* page 47). Denison was only an hour from my boyhood home. As a lad I had made several trips to Munson's nursery with my father to buy grapevines and fruit trees. At that time, I knew nothing about wine, phylloxera, or geology. I was, however, a "rock collector," even though I had not the slightest idea that I would spend my entire professional career trying to discover the relationship between rocks and oil. And now, years on, here I was eager to discover the relationship between rocks and wine!

At the time of this visit to Burgundy, I knew little specifically about the geology of French wine areas. I did know that the wines of France grew on rocks of every geologic type and age. Such diversity could have nothing less than fascinating stories of how habitat influences the character of wine – the chalk of Champagne, the gravel mounds of Médoc, the glaciated valleys of Haute-Savoie, the granite hillocks of Beaujolais. Here was a challenge almost as exciting as exploring for oil.

In my geologic mapping in south-central Texas, I had observed and made use of the natural preference of wild vegetation for soils of certain geologic formations – pine trees for sandy soils, particularly those with iron. Poast oaks grow in ordinary sandy soils, the majestic Live oaks in limy, sandy soils, *mesquite* (a mimosa) in clayey soils.

The problem of vineplant/soils matching in France had been worked out by the vignerons by trial and error over hundreds of years. Habitat is indeed a constant in the wine equation; integral variables are man and climate.

The climate of France was determined when the geologic processes were arranging the landmasses and oceans. The 45° parallel of north latitude passes just north of the city of Bordeaux, placing the top two-thirds of France in the north temperate zone. The Gulf Stream of the Atlantic moderates the climate of France, otherwise it would be more like that of northeast Canada. As a consequence, France has a favorable mix of oceanic and continental influences (*see* Color Plate 3). Regional and local variations in turn affect both the character and style of wine. Man has the first say on what he plants and where; and the last say on how he makes his wine. In between, through soil and climate, nature has much to say. But winegrowers appear to have a spiritual love of the land like few other planters.

On that April morning there was still a "bite" in the air. Budding was just around the corner, and the vignerons would be worried about frost until well into May. For the remainder of the growing season they would be concerned about getting the right balance of sunshine and rain, hopefully without hail. They would worry, but they would also pray. There are no atheists among vignerons. The many calvaries and shrines in vineyards, and holidays honoring patron saints, testify to the deep respect winegrowers have for the Almighty.

On my way out from Beaune to Pommard I watched a family at work in a vineyard. (All French vignerons seem to drive those funny little panel trucks.) The husband was tightening the vine-training wires and pounding back into the ground posts that had been loosened by frost-heave. Other members of the family were tying canes to the wires and doing some final pruning. Winegrowing is hard work – "peasant labor." A great deal of France's preeminence as a wine country is due to its having a population dedicated to the soil and not afraid of hard work.

Was this love of the land inherited from the Celts? Or from the Gallo-Romans? The Celts were fabled for their love of battle, but they were also stock-raisers and farmers. Then there were the Burgundians, Franks, and injections of raw barbarian vigor. Land was very much a part of the life of those days.

The Christian cross quickly followed the Roman eagle into Gaul. Christianity showed the barbarians and pagans a new way of life that caught on and spread like an infection. The monks of several religious orders worked the vineyards with care and patience, setting high standards for viticulture. I was later to learn that the vineyard where I was standing in Pommard was the Petits Epenots, which had once been owned by the abbey of Cîteaux.

As I returned to my car and started north toward the old Cistercian château of Clos de Vougeot, I reflected that it was great good fortune for French viticulture that the Benedictine abbey of Cluny and the Cistercians' Cîteaux had been established in Burgundy with its responsive soils and sun-trapping slopes. These monastic orders did not locate in Burgundy because it was good wine country; it was made so by their diligent and perceptive husbandry. The monks raised viticulture to the level of an agronomic art form.

At the Clos de Vougeot, I compared the map of Côte d'Or vineyards which I had purchased at a wine shop in Beaune with the published geologic map. I had assumed that the geology of the different vineyards would reveal why some grew superior wines and others did not. It was quickly evident that this approach was greatly oversimplified. To my dismay, the geologic map showed most of the vineyard areas were covered with "Terres du Pied de la Côte" or *éboulis* – rubble or scree – the soils at the foot of the hill.

It was clear that I needed to know a great deal more about vines, soils, and how they were formed to begin to answer the question of why great wines grow where they do.

From my petroleum exploration background, I instinctively wanted to "see through the soil" into the habitat where the roots lived. Questions which came to me in the Pommard vineyard repeated themselves here at the Clos de Vougeot. How thick was this "Terres du Pied de la Côte," slope wash? Of what was it composed? In what way are the sub-strata involved in the habitat? A few years later I would commission a shallow-depth seismograph survey that would give a "bone-scan" of the anatomy of the slope wash and bedrock. For now I could only reflect that the geologic aspect of viticulture is almost as complicated as oil exploration. A very agreeable difference, however, is that in working on the geology of wine, one can drink on the job.

Although I was disappointed to realize that finding the geologic solution to why fine wines grow where they do was far more involved than I had imagined. There was, however, a bright spot on this occasion. As a convenience, I had a set of French government geologic maps sent to Jacques Chevignard, Executive Director of the Confrérie des Chevaliers du Tastevin, the famous wine fraternity which is headquartered in Nuits-St.-Georges. When Jacques learned of my interest in the geology of wine, he said I should meet Noël Leneuf, professor of geology and pedology at Dijon University. Professor Leneuf speaks no more English than I do French, but we hardly needed an interpreter. The language of geology is conveyed well by hand motions and drawings in the dirt. (On a subsequent visit, it would be my good fortune to have as mentors on a field trip Noël Leneuf and Dr. Robert Lautel, both experts not only on the geology and wines of Burgundy but on the remainder of France as well.) On this first encounter, Leneuf's knowledge of and enthusiasm for the critical role of soil in Burgundy's vineyards reassured me that the geology of wine was a fascinating story. Could I make it interesting for the non-technical reader? I was eager to try.

The remainder of Part One develops the nature and functioning of the elements of the vineyard habitat which came to mind that day in the Pommard vineyard and the Clos de Vougeot. Part Two discusses how elements of the habitat – man and history included – function in the various wine districts of France.

The geologic map of France

The geologic map of France (*see* Color Plate 1) may appear to the non-geologist as colorful, abstract art, or the work of a pre-schooler possessing a full set of Crayolas. It is art in a way. The map could be called a portrait of the "rock families" of France – the stratigraphic units and rock types. It represents one of nature's masterworks: all the rock time-units and most all rock types known to geology are found in France. What is more, all the major earth movements are recorded in its mountain uplifts – a country not quite the size of Texas.

Conventionally, units of strata and rock types are represented on geologic maps by patterns, shading, or colors. These rocks on the surface may be covered by soil or vegetation, but the color key says "scratch the ground and you will find below the rock which my color represents." The "rock families" can be identified in the "portraits," by the legend on Color Plate 1. Color Plate 2 shows the family tree, the geologic column, giving the names and ages of the major stratigraphic units. Their family characteristics are described in the following paragraphs.

Referring to the geologic map, the pinks and reds are crystalline rocks – granites, gneisses, and schists. These are very old rocks, generally termed the "basement," which crystallized from the molten state at great depths, later to be brought to the earth's surface by uplift. They are more resistive and become exposed by erosion of softer, surrounding areas to form the massifs or mountain masses, such as the Massif Central.

The splashes of deep blue within the Massif Central are lava flows (basalts) that welled up through vents in this carbuncle of granite during the late Tertiary and Quaternary. The eruptions were not violent explosions like Mt. St.-Helens or Vesuvius, but relatively quiet "bleeding" of lava and "belching" of ash similar to that going on today in Hawaii.

Along with the reds and pinks of the massifs are streaks and dabs of tan and olive, particularly in the Massif Armoricain and the Ardennes. These are Paleozoic strata which have been metamorphosed to varying degrees by physical and chemical changes in original rocks due to heat and pressure of deep burial. In this process, for example, shales become slates, or schists; sandstones become quartzites; limestones may be marbleized.

Most of the wine areas are on rocks of the Mesozoic or younger eras. The Mesozoic opened with the Triassic about 230 million years ago. The Triassic represents a three-fold division of rocks whose family color on the map is lavender. At the beginning of the Triassic, the western portion of France was a desolate, hard-rock, red desertland resembling the area in Arizona today around the Petrified Forest. The lower sandstones and conglomerates are pink, as they derived from erosion of the pink granite terrain. Under the desert conditions, extensive saline lakes and playas developed in which beds of salt and gypsum were deposited. This sequence of strata became the weak "breakaway zones" when horizontal stresses buckled the crust during formations of the Jura and sub-Alpine ranges. Later, as the seas deepened, shales, marls, and dolomites accumulated, which form vineyard soils particularly in Alsace and the Jura.

The red sandstone environment covered an extensive area of northeast France, now the northern Vosges and Lorraine Plateau. When the Vosges were uplifted, the rise was strongest in the southern area where erosion peeled the red sandstones completely away, exposing bare granites of the Crystalline Vosges. In the northern area, erosion left the Triassic beds like "reverse shingles." These are the Low or Sandstone Vosges.

Along the eastern margin of the Crystalline Vosges, a few remnants of the basal conglomerates and sandstones remained perched on the granite heights. These rock tables provide building sites with impressive panoramic views of the Rhine Valley. Faulted downward almost half a mile into the valley, marls, shales, dolomites, and sandstones of the Middle and Upper Triassic are bedrocks for many important Alsace terroirs.

The even-bedded, pink Vosges sandstones provide attractive building stones found in many edifices, such as Strasbourg's gothic cathedral, and its splendid citadel built by Louis XIV's brilliant military engineer, Sébastien Vauban.

The Jurassic, the blue color framing the Paris Basin and the north rim of the Aquitaine Basin, was named for the Jura mountains which form a crescent along the Franco-Swiss borders. The Jurassic could be said to be France's "national rock;" it has seen much of war and peace in the country's history. Its limestones are the sheer cliffs back of the landing beaches of Normandy of World War II. The historical fortresses of Sedan, Verdun, Longwy, and Toul, built on Jurassic promontories, witnessed heroic stands and disastrous defeats. Jurassic stones are in the magnificent cathedrals, churches, châteaux, and humble dwellings. Its excellent soils grow abundant crops, forests, and wine. Two miles (3 km) deep in the Aquitaine Basin it provides reservoirs in the giant Lacq gas field and in the shallow, pint-sized oil fields southeast of Paris.

The Jurassic was deposited during what someone has called "the noblest of geologic time." Extensive, warm, quiet seas were festooned by chains of small reefs. Underwater gardens of sea lilies (crinoids) flourished in the shallow waters while banks of shells piled up along the shore. Mud-bottom shallows and lagoons were carpeted with oyster beds. Stretching for miles in the outer clear waters were sub-sea dunes of oolites (fish-egg carbonate pellets). What a terrific travel poster the Jurassic would have made – a "Jurassic Park" without dinosaurs!

An exceptional amount of the fine wines of France grow on the Jurassic: the products of the Côte d'Or, Chablis, Sancerre, Cahors, Alsace, the Aube. The big, sprawling north half of Cognac is underlain by Jurassic limestones.

The map of the Paris Basin is like a big green eye with a yellow pupil. The green is the Cretaceous, the yellow-orange is the Tertiary of the Ile de France plateau. The thick Upper Cretaceous chalks form the plains of Champagne, Picardy, and Artois. Across the English Channel, they are the white cliffs of Dover, which dared first Napoleon then Hitler to invade their island.

Off the south flank of the Massif Central-Limousin, the Cretaceous dips gently at first, then becomes deeply buried in the Aquitaine Basin. From great depths, it along with other strata were dramatically thrust upward by the Pyrenees with huge slabs breaking off and sliding down the mountain side. South of Lake Geneva, massive Lower Cretaceous limestones create the spectacular scenery of the sub-alpine ranges. In the lower Rhône Valley erosional remnants support interesting vineyards.

The 19th-century French scientists Cuvier and Brongniart recognized distribution of the chalk in northeast France as an important formation, but it was Thomas Huxley, the articulate English lecturer, who put romance in this nondescript, white rock in the early 20th century. In "On a Piece of Chalk," Huxley described how magnification revealed the chalk to be an aggregate of shells of tiny, floating microorganisms numerous beyond the counting.

Soils of the Champagne vineyards are a unique mixture of Tertiary sands and clays from the plateau that have washed down over the underlying chalk. Beneath Reims and Epernay miles of tunnels have been excavated in the chalk, providing workrooms and storage tunnels for millions of bottles of champagne. In the Loire Valley, gritty, micaceous chalk, also soft enough to be easily excavated, has full-size homes and storage caves dug far back into the rock. Only the facades of these cave-homes are visible along the cliff-side valleys of Touraine. The choice vineyards for the brandy grapes of Cognac are located on chalky soil of the Cretaceous. (The terms for two of the sub-regions of Cognac, Grande and Petite Champagne, recall that Cognac and Champagne lie on similar chalky outcrops.)

The end of the Mesozoic (Cretaceous) and beginning of the Cenozoic (Tertiary) marked a significant change in both depositional environments and plant and animal life – such as disappearance of the dinosaurs.

The Tertiary (the yellow and orange colors) witnessed the last invasions of the seas before they retreated to their present positions. The low areas of the Paris and Aquitaine Basins and the lower Rhône Valley were the scenes of important struggles between the marine and continental environments, resulting in an interfingering of strata of these types.

It was also a time of great mountain building the world over – the Alps and Pyrenees in Europe, the Rockies of North America, the Andes of South America, and the Himalayas of Asia. As the Alps and Pyrenees rose, they shed to the surrounding areas great sheets of flysch – soft, fine-grained sediments. As the mountains rose faster the deposits became coarse sand, gravel, and clay called molasse. Many vineyards are now found on these broadcast deposits – in the Haute-Savoie, for example, and on the slopes of the southern Aquitaine Basin.

As the seas reluctantly retreated, they launched several limited invasions, but none reached very far or stayed very long. The rivalry between the seas and rivers and lakes in the Paris Basin left notable geologic legacies. The Brie limestone, cap rock of the eastern Ile de France plateau, was precipitated in a large freshwater lake. Dairy farms on the plateau produce Brie cheese, the *roi des fromages*, a marvelous companion to champagne. In the northern part of the Ile de France is the *Calcaire grossier*, a marine limestone known as the "stone of the Gothic." The compact limestone was the favorite of cathedral builders because it "took a good edge."

South of Paris, the fairyland forest of Fontainebleau grows on fossil sand dunes of an ancient shoreline. In what is now the Montmartre area of Paris, a dried-up lagoon left a powdery deposit (anhydrite) which, mixed with water, formed a paste which hardened to become what is known as plaster of Paris.

In the Aquitaine Basin a particularly aggressive marine incursion left the *Calcaire à astéries*, starfish limestone, so named for its abundant fragments of a fossil starfish. Cap rock for the plateau of Bourg-Blaye, St.-Emilion, Fronsac, and Entre-Deux-Mers, the *Calcaire* is the "rock bottom" on which the Garonne and Gironde (the common estuary of both the Garonne and the Dordogne) built the gravel terraces of the Médoc, Graves, and Sauternes. An old Bordeaux saying is that the best vines are those that can see the river – meaning, in effect, those on the gravel terraces. (Graves in French means gravel.)

As the Pyrenees grew from a low welt to their picturesque heights, a series of molassic fans coalesced to form an immense apron known as the Lannemezan Cone. Streams radiating down this cone give it the appearance on maps of an open ladies fan. The ridges and east-facing sides of the rills contain much of the Armagnac vineyards and other ancient wine areas.

Toward the end of the Tertiary, the earth began to grow very cold introducing the Quaternary, last of the major geologic time periods. The gray colors representing this period are obvious in only a few places on the map – valleys of major streams and outwash areas. The first part of the Quaternary is the Pleistocene, the Great Ice Age. The last is the Holocene, more commonly referred to as the Recent (a capitalized geologic noun), dating from about 10,000 years ago, a millisecond in geologic time. The Pleistocene Ice Age, beginning about two million years ago, was of tremendous importance to the wines of France. This is when the landscape got its final "face lift." France was south of the continental ice cap, but much of the country was in the periglacial zone, a peripheral area of extreme cold.

The Ice Age was not one long "freeze-up," but five major glacial periods alternating with six interglacials or warm periods, the last of which we are enjoying today. These freeze-thaw periods "stirred" the ground and chiseled the rocky face of the land. The interglacials, several thousands of years in duration, were in effect growing seasons for man and animals and certain plants. Underground solution of Jurassic and Cretaceous limestones created caves which provided prehistoric people with protection from the very severe elements. Prehistoric animals which roamed among the lakes and rivers in the Aquitaine Basin were illustrated with amazing accuracy by the cave-dwelling artists of Pech-Merle and Lascau.

The crown-jewels of the Quaternary are the chain of gravel terrace-mounds of the Garonne–Gironde deposited by floods of the warm periods. Starting in the high Pyrenees and the Massif Central, frost-shattered rocks were ground by stream action to walnut-size gravel, which, along with loads of sand and mud were dumped on successive terraces along the riverbanks of the Garonne and Gironde. These deposits of waste-rock are the sites of the proud châteaux and world-renowned vineyards of the Médoc and Graves-Sauternes.

The high Alps developed their own ice cap which poked glacial fingers down the surrounding valleys. Many of the vineyards in Haute-Savoie are located on soils derived from broken and ground-up rocks which these valley glaciers scraped from the sides and bottoms of the valleys. These vineyards look over beautiful lakes or up to Mont Blanc and some of the most spectacular scenery in the world.

As the continental ice cap grew, it took up vast quantities of water, causing a lowering of sea level by several hundred feet. Winds whipped up dust and sand from the broad beaches of western Aquitaine and spread a layer over the low area inland which is the delta-shaped Les Landes. Phalanxes of sand dunes driven onshore by the Westerlies threatened to overwhelm the vineyards of Médoc until, in 1788, their progress was arrested by the planting of maritime pines and special grasses.

As the last glacial stage came to a close about 10,000 years ago, evolving vegetation began to flourish, aiding weathering and development of the soils of today. As shown on Color Plate 3, the wine areas are well distributed over the southern three-quarters of France, where they grow on rocks of every geologic age and type. Geology had prepared the land. It would be up to man in his good time to make France a wine country.

Development of the science of geology

Geologic processes have been at work since the earth began some four billion years ago, but geology as an earth science was not developed until the 19th century. It was fathered by the intellectual curiosity of people of various scientific disciplines and classical education who came into frequent contact with rocks and fossils. From their trained observation and logical reasoning grew theories and explanations for the various rock formations and how they became involved in the landscape.

Scientists of that day were broad in their interests, especially of natural phenomena. They were doctors, chemists, physicists, mathematicians, botanists, and surveyors of various nationalities, each contributing in various ways to the development of geology as a science. Ironically, it was a churchman, Abbé Giraud-Soulavi, whose observations along the middle Rhône inaugurated the concept of "evolutionary geology" by noting how fossil forms changed with time in a succession of older to younger strata.

Two French scientists, Georges Cuvier, an anatomist, and Alexandre Brongniart, a mineralogist, became intrigued by the repeated occurrence of a soft, white chalk north of Paris. They produced a map showing its continuity between ravines and along the river banks. A massive, white rock they termed the Upper Chalk. A dirty, gray chalk occurring below it, containing beds of greenish sand and clay, they called the Lower Chalk. As the world-wide system of stratigraphic nomenclature was developed, these strata were given status as the Upper and Lower Cretaceous (Latin: *creta* = chalk).

Gradually, facts and well-reasoned theories gave rise to accumulated axioms and guiding principles. For example, Cuvier and Brongniart made similar observations as did the Abbé Giraud-Soulavi. They noted that in a sequence of layers, fossil shells and animal remains in older (lower) strata had few recognizable present-day relatives, whereas those in younger (upper) strata had a close resemblance to marine life and animals living today. This line of reasoning led to the principle of dividing rock sequences on the basis of plant and animal life that lived at the time of their deposition. Thus a geologic "life column" was developed.

The major sequences were given names with Greek or Latin prefixes representative of the characteristics of life of the time. In layers with only vague resemblance to present-day forms, they gave the name *paleo*, meaning old or ancient. This prefix was added to the word *zoe*, life, plus the English suffix, *ic*, meaning of, or pertaining to. Thus Paleozoic, meant "ancient life." Mesozoic was "middle-life" followed by the Cenozoic, "recent life." Some early workers preferred the terms Primary, Secondary, Tertiary, and Quaternary. Only Tertiary and Quaternary are in common usage today.

Major rock sub-divisions (systems) within the "life eras" were named for localities where they were first studied and described (type localities). Type localities for the Jurassic were the Jura Mountains of France and Switzerland, Devonian from Devonshire, England, and Permian from the province of Perm in the western Urals of Russia.

Sub-divisions of the systems (epochs, series, and stages) grew out of detailed studies – generally upper, middle and lower, but sometimes with names such as Bathonian and Bajocian for the Middle Jurassic of western Europe. Names for yet smaller sub-divisions within the epochs, however, proliferated as different geologists studied and described local areas. The generally accepted principal European divisions of the geologic column and time scale correlated with their North American equivalents are indicated in Color Plate 2.

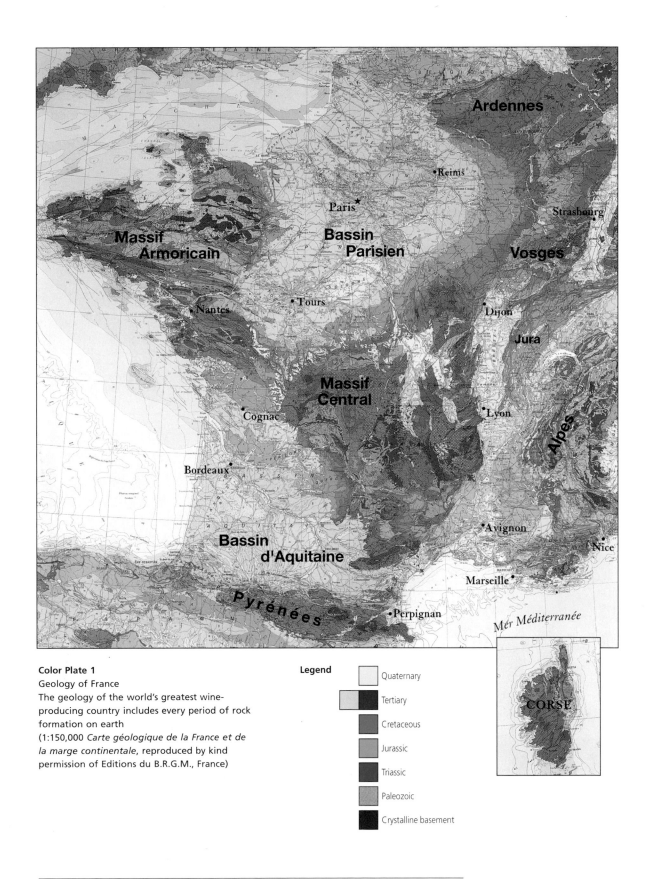

Color Plate 1
Geology of France
The geology of the world's greatest wine-producing country includes every period of rock formation on earth
(1:150,000 *Carte géologique de la France et de la marge continentale*, reproduced by kind permission of Editions du B.R.G.M., France)

Legend

Quaternary

Tertiary

Cretaceous

Jurassic

Triassic

Paleozoic

Crystalline basement

Millions of years before present (note scale change below)	Life Eras	Systems (of rocks) Periods (of time)	Series (of rocks) Epochs (of time)		Age (smallest universal unit of rocks)	Orogenies (periods of mountain building)	Wine areas (general age group of main vineyards of wine districts)
—0.01— (10,000 years)	Cenozoic (recent life)	Quaternary	Holocene		Post-Glacial to Present		Savoie, Médoc, Graves-Sauternes, Pomerol
—1.8—			Pleistocene		Glacial stages and interglacial flooding. See Table 5.1 in the Aquitaine Basin Chapter		
		Tertiary	Pliocene	Villefranchian		Alpine	Frontonnais, Gaillac Bergerac, Duras, Buzet, Brulhois Southern Rhône Jurançon, Béarn, Tursan, Madiran-Vic Bilh Armagnac, Alsace Provence, Quincy, and Reuilly Champagne Languedoc-Roussillon Auvergne
			Miocene	Not divided on this chart			
			Oligocene	Lattorfian			
			Eocene	Not divided on this chart		Pyrenean	
			Paleocene			Laramide of North America	
—67—	Mesozoic (middle life)	Cretaceous	Upper (Gulfian of North America)	Maastrictian		From end of Permian to beginning of Tertiary, the continent was relatively stable. This was the time of widespread, shallow seas in which extensive deposits of limestones, marls, chalks, and shell beds accumulated	Chalks of Champagne Southern half of Cognac Touraine and Anjou (Middle Loire) Languedoc
				Campanian			
				Santonian			
				Coniacian			
				Turonian			
				Cenomanian			
			Lower (Comanchian of North America) (Coahuilan of North America)	Albian			Savoie, Southern Rhône Diois Provence N. of Marseille
				Aptian			
				Barremian			
				Hauterivian			
				Valanginian			
				Berriasian			
—137—		Jurassic	Malm	Upper	Portlandian		*Kimmeridgian Chain:* Aube, Chablis, Pouilly-sur-Loire, Sancerre, Menetou-Salon Burgundy: Côte d'Or, Chalonnais, Mâconnais and Bas-Beaujolais Northern half of Cognac Cahors sub-Vosgian hills - Alsace Savoie Diois
					Kimmeridgian		
					Oxfordian		
			Dogger	Middle	Callovian		
					Bathonian		
					Bajocian		
			Lias	Lower	Not divided on this chart		
—195—		Triassic	Keuper	Upper			sub-Vosgian hills - Alsace Irouléguy (Pays Basque) Basal conglomerates and sandstones perched on granite, Alsace, overlook Rhine Valley
			Muchel-kalk	Middle			
			Bunter	Lower			
—230—		Scale change as Paleozoic outcrops have fewer vineyards than Mesozoic and Cenozoic					
—285—	Paleozoic (Ancient life)	Permian	Not divided on this chart			Variscan (Hercynian)	Alsace - Flank of Vosges Lower Carboniferous metamorphosed volcanics - Alsace Central Corsica Irouéguy (Pays Basque) Anjou Muscadet Languedoc-Roussillon
		Carboniferous	Upper	North American Pennsylvanian			
—350—			Lower	North American Mississippian			
		Devonian	Not divided on this chart				
—405—		Silurian	Not divided on this chart				
—440—		Ordovician	Not divided on this chart			Caledonian	
—500—		Cambrian	Not divided on this chart				
—570— To approx. 4.6 billion years		Precam-brian	For simplification of wine terrain, complexes of granite and metamorphics are grouped as Crystalline basement.				Haut-Beaujolais - Burgundy Flank of Vosges - Alsace Muscadet - Pays Nantais and Anjou Northern Côtes de Provence, Northern Rhône Western Corsica

Color Plate 2
Geologic column and timescale

18

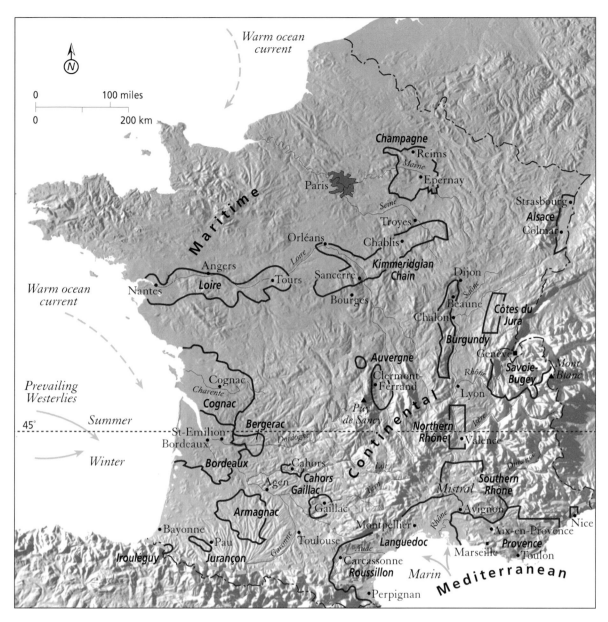

Warm ocean current

N

0	100 miles
0	200 km

Maritime

Champagne
•Reims
Marne
•Epernay

Paris•

Strasbourg•
Alsace
Colmar•

•Troyes
Chablis•

Warm ocean
current

Orléans•
Loire
•Tours
Sancerre•
•Bourges

*Kimmeridgian
Chain*

Dijon•
Saône
•Beaune
Chalon•
Burgundy

*Côtes du
Jura*

Angers•
Nantes•

Loire

Auvergne
Clermont-
Ferrand•
▲
Puy
de Sancy

Geneve•
*Savoie-
Bugey*
Mont
Blanc
▲

Prevailing
Westerlies

Cognac
Charente
Cognac

Rhône
Lyon•

45°
Summer

Bergerac•

Continental

St-Emilion•
Bordeaux•

Dordogne

*Northern
Rhône*
Valence•

Winter

Bordeaux

Cahors•
Cahors
Agen•
Gaillac
Isère

Lot

Rhône
Durance

*Southern
Rhône*
Avignon•

Armagnac•
Armagnac

Gaillac•

Mistral

Aix-en-Provence•
Nice•

•Bayonne
•Pau
Jurançon

Toulouse•
Garonne

Montpellier•
Languedoc

Marseille•
Provence
•Toulon

Irouléguy

Aude
Carcassonne•
Roussillon

Marin

Mediterranean

•Perpignan

Color Plate 3
Principal wine districts, relief, and climatic
zones
The boundaries between climatic zones,
particularly maritime and continental, are
transitional
(Relief supplied by Mountain High Maps®,
© 1995 Digital Wisdom, Inc.)

Legend

☐ *Wine districts*

- - - **Climatic zones**

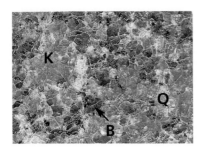 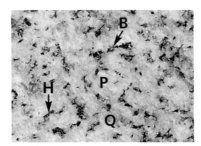 

Color Plate 4
Crystallography of granites
As various minerals crystallize when the molten granite "soup" begins to cool, they interfere with each other in developing their crystal shapes, resulting in the runic pattern. Chemical weathering attacks the weak minerals. Water seeps into the cracks and contacts between mineral grains. Freeze–thaw aids disintegration of the solid rock to form soil.

The lettering identifies the mineral components. The precise combination of minerals determines the type of granite. The left photograph, magnified x 1, is a pink granite, the coloration deriving from mineral impurities in the potassium feldspar. The middle one is a white variety. The right is a cross polarized light micrograph, magnified x 2.5, of a thin section of granite

Q = Quartz, silicon oxide, a hard mineral resistant to weathering
B = Biotite, "black mica," (which shows as bright green, blue, and yellow on the micrograph) a potassium, magnesium, iron, aluminum silicate which weathers easily
H = Hornblende, a fibrous mineral of calcium-magnesium silicate with other elements
K = Orthoclase feldspar, a potassium aluminum silicate, which weathers easily to clay minerals
P = Plagioclase, a sodium-calcium feldspar, characteristically lacking in color, which dominates white granites. It too weathers to clay minerals

Color Plate 5
Puy de Sancy, part of the ancient volcanic landscape of the Auvergne

The total thickness of strata in France is perhaps over 6000 feet (1800 m) Mesozoic and younger with more than twice that amount in the Paleozoics of the Massif Armoricain. The geologic column of Color Plate 2 is a composite. Nowhere in the world does a complete sequence of all the stratigraphic units exist. The symphony of the earth over geologic time had seas and topographically low areas accumulating sediments and high areas providing those sediments. The time it takes to accumulate sediments, especially very thick shales and limestones, has always been a question in geology.

Geologic processes such as an earthquake happen in seconds; sandbars may appear or disappear almost overnight; coastlines may be dramatically altered during a storm. But it took 35 million years for the 1000 feet (300 m) of Cretaceous chalk to accumulate.

The addition of age-dating to the geologic column is recent. It might be considered something of a geologic frill, as it makes no difference to grapevines whether rocks on which they grow are five million or fifty million years old.

The radiometric "clock"

Age-dating of rocks is made possible by radiometric or isotope geology. Nearly all rocks contain at least a tiny amount of some radioactive mineral. Such minerals are in a continuous process of "decaying" – emitting energy particles. Highly sensitive measuring devices allow the geochemist to convert the amount of radiometric decay into a time-scale of years. The radiometric "clock" is started when the mineral becomes a part of the host rock. Age-dating of rocks introduces big numbers like the national debt and major business transactions, but it is difficult to grasp duration of events measured by a time scale greater than one's own lifetime. My suggestion is just to respect nature for the long hours she has put in and deal with the big numbers without batting an eye – as do politicians, economists, and geologists.

About slopes

The better wines of France all grow on a hillslope of some description – cuesta faces, glaciated valleys, granite knobs, gravel mounds, tilted fault blocks – the landform styles are almost endless. With such a variety, no slope can be considered really typical; although, I often refer to cap-rock slope (*see* Figure 1.1) as "classic." The model serves to identify components of the slope profile developed to various degrees on all slopes.

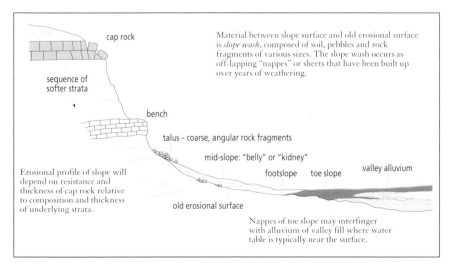

cap rock

Material between slope surface and old erosional surface is *slope wash*, composed of soil, pebbles and rock fragments of various sizes. The slope wash occurs as off-lapping "nappes" or sheets that have been built up over years of weathering.

sequence of softer strata

bench

talus – coarse, angular rock fragments

mid-slope: "belly" or "kidney"

footslope   toe slope   valley alluvium

Erosional profile of slope will depend on resistance and thickness of cap rock relative to composition and thickness of underlying strata.

old erosional surface

Nappes of toe slope may interfinger with alluvium of valley fill where water table is typically near the surface.

Figure 1.1
Cap-rock slope and terminology

The best part of the slope for vineyards is the mid-slope, which is given the colloquial term of "belly," or sometimes "navel." The French seem to prefer "kidney." Take your choice of the visceral analogies, but it is this concave part of the slope that concentrates slope wash for soil, traps the sun, and normally offers good drainage.

Although the soil may be thick in the "foot" and "toe" of the slope, it may also interfinger with alluvium of the low land in front of the scarp where the water table tends to be high. Vineplants themselves may do well in this zone of damp soil, but "leafy" vines produce grapes that are too "flabby" for fine wine.

With so much of the quality grape-growing area of France north of 45° latitude (*see* Color Plate 3), the angle of the sun for these areas is relatively low, even in summer. This makes orientation of the slope important – southeast to easterly being the preferred direction. This catches the early morning sun to begin to warm the plants after a cool or dewy night.

Vineyards of the Mediterranean zone have almost too much sun, but vineplants north of the Midi welcome all the sun they can get. (The Midi is the term referring generally to the south of France, particularly Languedoc-Roussillon, from the Rhône delta to the Spanish border.) In Champagne, we have an anomalous situation where north-facing slopes produce excellent wines – champagne grapes are best when tart, not "sun-luscious."

Slope wash tends to be in offlapping nappes (*see* diagram in Glossary, page 61) which helps distribute percolating waters more evenly. A sloping bedrock also helps bottom drainage. If the bedrock is fractured or has appreciable porosity, it will help with water storage and proper feeding of the vineplant.

Clearly, soil in the habitat of wine has a role more important than simply holding the plant upright.

Soil, soul of the vineplant

Soils are simply rotted rocks with a mixture of organic matter. In reality, of course, rocks do not "rot" in the manner of plant and animals; they weather. What weathers is the "parent material," a term used by soil scientists in preference to original rock.

Weathering is a "one-two" punch process: *mechanical* or physical weathering cracks the rock mass; *chemical* weathering "rots" the pieces into soil. God's given mission to weathering is to see that every rock on the surface of the earth is returned to dust.

The agents of mechanical weathering are water, ice, heat, roots, and gravity. The broken rock presents multiple surfaces which chemical weathering can attack. When water freezes, it expands 9 percent. This may not seem like much expansion, but burst water pipes attest to the tremendous pressure exerted when confined water freezes. The same thing happens when water seeps into pores and cracks of a rock then freezes. (You who live in northern climes know how freeze-thaw develops chuckholes, otherwise known as frost-heave holes.) From rock outcrops, large, angular pieces are pried loose. Many fall into streams where they are banged into smaller and smaller pieces. Depending on how far they travel, the pieces are worn down to gravel, sand, and silt. Whatever the size, they are mineral particles or aggregates in some sedimentary rock somewhere.

Chemical weathering is as relentless as rusting. All that is needed to get either process started is moisture and air. As soon as a fresh surface of rock shows its face, it is immediately attacked by chemical weathering. The process works exceedingly slowly, but it is inexorable and thorough. It takes only a minute, rough spot on a rock's surface to support tiny, clinging wisps of lichens or mosses. These miniature colonies accumulate dust and produce debris of their own. Moisture reacting with this plant matter produces organic acids. The acids are weak and skimpy, but give them time. Mute witnesses to the affects of chemical weathering over time are old tombstones, statues, bricks, and glass bottles.

Both mechanical and chemical weathering are aided by climate, topography, organisms, and time.

Climate ranks very close in importance to parent material in soilmaking. From high-school chemistry we learned that many chemical reactions require water as a reagent, and that they proceed best with heating. It is the exactly the same in rock weathering. France, located in the temperate zone with strong variations in heat and cold plus ample moisture, is ideally situated for reduction of rocks to soil.

Topography (surface relief) aids the mechanical process by downhill movement of debris, breaking rocks, and exposing fresh surfaces to weathering. Whether by creep, viscous flow of freeze-thaw material or torrential washing, pebbles, rock fragments, and old soils are moved downslope and mixed to become parent material. In a few cases, such as on the plateau of St.-Emilion and in the Massif Armoricain, deep soils develop *in situ*.

The soil in a vineyard may look dead, but not far beneath the surface it is a hotbed of activity. Organisms work the soil night and day, most generally for the vineplant's benefit. Larger organisms, such as moles, mice, and other burrowing creatures push the soil around but are usually more harmful than helpful. The lowly, blind earthworm, which ingests only dead matter, is a welcome volunteer. But the real activity is carried on by the very tiniest of creatures – microorganisms such as bacteria. Sub-microscopic in size, like clay particles, these organisms live only a few hours. One shovelful of topsoil is estimated to contain as many microorganisms as there are people on earth. As the organisms die, they release ammonium and nitrate ions beneficial to the plant-feeding process. The pungency of freshly plowed ground is due to the ammonia given off in the mass extinction of soil bacteria.

Soil microorganisms include fungi (molds and yeasts), algae, actinomycetes, and bacteria which are both aerobic (needing oxygen) and anaerobic (living without oxygen). Fungi and actinomycetes are particularly useful as their bacterial "glue," the web-like fabric they create, helps build soil aggregates by sticking particles together. The actinomycetes are single-celled creatures whose main function is to decompose organic matter. Microorganisms function best under alkaline soil conditions. They work the vineyard soil thoroughly and for free – they live, work, and die there – although unfortunately, certain fungi and other microorganisms are pathogenic (disease-causing).

Most of the soils of France began their life toward the end of the Great Ice Age – 10,000 years ago, give or take a millennium or so. France, being in the "periglacial zone," the term used by geologists for the region adjacent to the

The importance of moisture and frost action (freezing) in weathering is well illustrated by an obelisk of Syene granite brought to New York's Central Park from Egypt in 1880. By 1950, the deep-cut hieroglyphics of the "Cleopatra's Needle" were all but obliterated. The humidity and winter frosts caused more weathering of the rock in 70 years than had occurred in the previous 3500 years in warm, dry Egypt.

Another example, albeit not a standard one, serves to illustrate the length of time it takes for rocks to become soil. In southern Russia, the top of a limestone tower developed a foot (30 cm) of soil in only 200 years.

What about CA? Italy

Photograph 1.1
Frost action, cryoturbation (Gr. *Kryma*, frost and Lat. *turbidue*, stirring). This freeze-thaw phenomenon shown here from Champagne was commonplace in the periglacial zone as far south as Bordeaux. The fragmentation affect extends 3–6 feet (1–2 m) below the cryoturbation pockets. The pockets and chimneys are filled with chalk fragments, old soil, and occasionally some reworked Tertiary strata

continental ice sheet, was subjected to periods of extreme cold and freezing, alternating with warm periods. This freeze-thaw process on a grand scale helped to sculpt the landforms, accelerated movement of slope wash, and "stirred the ground," as illustrated in Photograph 1.1, above.

Soil texture and structure

These terms may appear synonymous – and they are very much related – but they define quite different physical properties of the soil. Texture comes from the proportions of different size particles – the way the soil "feels" – fine, coarse or gritty. Structure is the way the particles are stuck together – platy, blocky, or granular. Texture in combination with the kind of clay, the amount of organic matter, and chemistry of the ground fluids influence the structure. Of the two, structure is the more important property for it influences the movement and storage of ground water. The structural fabric also influences the ease of root penetration, granular being the most favorable.

Different rock types yield to the soil's characteristic particles – granite and sandstones form gritty shales, and limestones silt and clay. As most vineyards are located on a slope of some description, its soils will be a mixture of source material. Whatever the parent material, the quality of life for the vine largely depends upon texture and structure of the soil. Granular structure, which is best for vineplants, develops most easily when there is about 25 percent sandy or coarse material in the mix. Pebbles or rock fragments help break up the tendency of soils to compact.

It is seldom that we know anything of the structure and mineral composition of soil zones below plow depth, down where the roots live. However, we can make some useful interpretations if we know the nature of the parent material of the slope wash and the bedrock. This is where geology helps hark back to the *éboulis* (slope wash) at the Côte d'Or, and my disappointment about interpreting the geology of vineyards (*see* page 10). Inasmuch as the soils are a combination of slope wash and weathered bedrock, a knowledge of the overall geology allows for a reasonable estimate of the soil mix.

Grapevines by preference are deep-rooted. If conditions are favorable, their roots may go as deep as 20 feet (6 m) or more. Where the bedrock is shallow and the soil thin, rooting will of necessity be shallow, making the vineplant susceptible to drought during dry spells.

Light, sandy soils are easy to till and easily wetted but also dry rapidly. Heavy, clay soils are difficult to wet through and through, difficult to drain, and difficult to till. It is fairly obvious that ideal for the vineyard is a pebbly, sandy-clayey soil with considerable organic matter. Good soil structure is influenced by limy waters and the type of clay minerals.

The evolution of soils may be complex, but the parent rock of most strata and soils is granite or volcanic rock.

Granite – the rock of ages?

We think of granites as nearly indestructible, but from birth their doom is written in the hieroglyphics of their mineral texture. This characteristic runic pattern is the random orientation of different minerals as they crystallized from the molten state. The mineralogy of some commonly occurring granites is illustrated in the photographs in Color Plate 4.

Certain of the minerals that are found in granite, such as the micas, feldspars, and some "dark" minerals, are far more susceptible to chemical weathering than quartz and other "hard" minerals. (Feldspars, the most widespread minerals on earth, are complex aluminum silicate compounds containing varying amounts of such elements as potassium, sodium, and calcium.) As the "weak" minerals weather, the fabric of the granite begins to break down with the micas and feldspars undergoing remarkable chemical alteration to clay minerals. Clays appear to be formless substances, but they have a platy mineral structure which is described in the following section.

New clays weathered from granite minerals are easily removed from the rock-mass (matrix), allowing the rock fabric to disintegrate, or "rot." The erstwhile "rock of ages" becomes an earthy crust and crumbles to sandy "granite wash." Although the newly formed clays may be transported, they are never destroyed. However far they travel or however old they become, the clay minerals are destined to be forever in a stratigraphic rock or soil somewhere.

Granites were probably the "Mother Rock" of the earliest stages of the planet. It was the eons of weathering of the granites that started the cycle of clastics – sands and clays. The chemical compounds from the weathering began to be concentrated in the sea water, some later to be precipitated in the shells of sea creatures and as limestones or silica rocks. Life on earth owes much to the fact that granite is not indestructible.

Sandstones are formed of grains of sand that are stuck together by some form of natural cement. When the bonding is loosened or dissolved, the rock crumbles to sandy soil. If the cement is clay or carbonate, it is easily broken down chemically as well as mechanically. However, if the cement is an iron oxide or a silicate (a glass-like compound containing silicon), the rock is very resistant and weathers slowly. Such hard sandstones stand out as topographic benches or the backbones of ridges.

Neutral to alkaline soils

Plants in soils that are too acid are like people with acid stomachs, the digestive system just doesn't work well. Figure 1.2 shows graphically that, although a few minerals are more available under acid conditions, overall, the plants are better served when the pH is neutral or on the alkaline side. The symbol pH with a number represents the change from acidity to alkalinity on a scale from 0 to 14 with 7 being neutral, the pH of pure water. (The pH of lemon juice is 2.3, vinegar is 3.1, and bicarbonate of soda is 8.2.) Vineplants like the "Alka-Seltzer side."

Limestones weather primarily by solution. Their basic chemical compound, calcium and/or magnesium carbonate, is readily attacked by natural organic acids. The loosening of fossils or disaggregation of oolites by freeze-thaw aid the work of acidic waters. Generally, carbonate rocks are "impure" and as they weather they leave a residue of clay, silt, or sand to accumulate as soil particles. On flat limestone terrains in semi-arid climates, soils are typically thin – for example, the Quercy plateau on the southeast flank of the Massif Central and the Garrigues north of Montpellier. If the climate is more moist, as for instance in the St.-Emilion and Cognac areas, weathering proceeds more aggressively and the soils are deeper.

The "lime" solution from dissolved limestones, chalk, or shell beds becomes active calcium carbonate. The term "active" means that the solution readily reacts with carbon dioxide of the air and organic acids in the soil. Besides neutralizing acids and imparting alkalinity in the soils, the calcium carbonate re-precipitates in a webby fashion to form good soil structure. Under some conditions re-precipitation may form a very hard layer, "hardpan" or caliche as it is known in the southwestern U.S., which is the bane of grapegrowers and agriculturists in general.

Figure 1.2
The availability of mineral nutrients (adapted from N. C. Brady *The Nature and Properties of Soils*, 1974, Macmillan Publishing Co.)

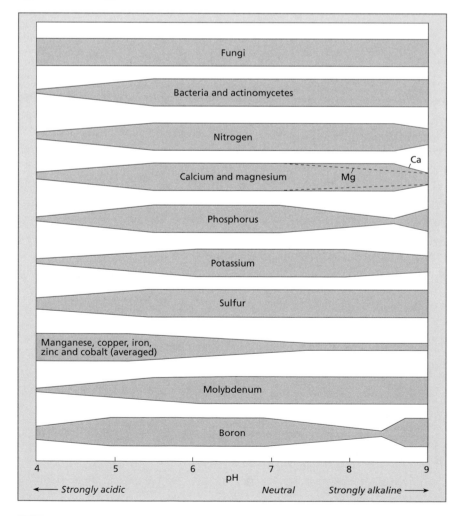

26   ELEMENTS OF THE FRENCH TERROIRS

According to Dr. Gérard Seguin at the University of Bordeaux, active calcium carbonate is the one chemical soil constituent generally associated with wine quality. The quality factor is due to the soil structure organized by the carbonate solution which favors moisture retention, and hence the feeding of the vineplant.

Biological activity in decomposition of plant litter works best in an alkaline (basic) environment due to carbonates. However, in one of nature's ironies, as Professor Philippe Duchaufour notes, calcium carbonate solutions form a skin around fresh or slightly altered organic matter, thus slowing its decomposition. Approximately two-thirds of France is underlain by carbonate rocks producing excellent agricultural soils, so this skin cannot be too serious.

Neutral to alkaline soil conditions also favor chemical availability of mineral nutrients (see Figure 1.2). The extensive outcropping of calcareous rocks in France ensures that most soils inherit a parental immunity from acidity. This is not to say that acidic soils do not produce some fine wines: the granitic soils of Alsace and Haut-Beaujolais are two examples. Granitic and sandy soils tend to be acidic because of the absence of carbonates (limestones) in the parent material. Early-day vignerons did not have litmus paper, so it was by trial and error that they found which grape varieties were most adaptable to which soil conditions.

Clay, the wonder substance

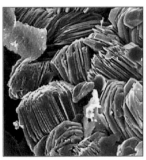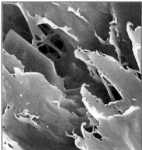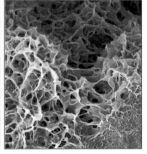

Clay is the principal glue that sticks soil particles together. Loose, sandy soil has little clay; "gumbo" (not the soup) is all clay. A lump of clay may look like a formless hunk of thick mud, but believe it or not, clays are a mass of crystals. Under powerful magnification, clays are seen indeed to be tiny, plate-like minerals. The molecular structure of clay minerals has strong bonds within the plates but weak attraction between them. That is what makes clay slippery – the platelets slide easily, like a new deck of playing cards. Molecular structure also plays an integral role in the feeding of mineral nutrients to the plant.

The extent of the crystal surfaces of the mineral plates in a chunk of clay is absolutely unbelievable. The molecular structure of the plates resembles a lattice, whose "holes" attract or release anions and cations. The soil must be sufficiently moist, however, for this movement to take place. (Cations are atoms or molecules with a positive electrical charge. Those negatively charged are anions.) The extensive molecular lattice gives clay a great capacity for "cation exchange." A familiar example of cation exchange is in the action of chemical water softeners. Mineral cations which make the water "hard" are exchanged in the process for "soft" cations found in a chemical softener such as zeolite.

Photograph 1.2
Clay mineral characteristics revealed by scanning electron microscope imagery. On the left is kaolinite magnified x 1400. The field of imagery is about the size of a pinhead. The crystals are from weathered feldspars. The center photograph shows illite-smectite (about 70% illite), magnified x 4100. Crystals are growing into the tiny pore space of a rock. In the right-hand photograph the white material is the contorted crystal plates of montmorillonite, magnified x 9500. The honeycomb pattern is typical of the way the mineral from weathering solution precipitates around solid nuclei. It is evident from the extremely high magnification that the clay mineral crystals are very small indeed (imagery and interpretation courtesy Dr. Thomas Tieh, Texas A&M University)

This cation-exchange capability is as vital to the life functioning of the vineplant as oxygen is to the human bloodstream. It is how plants get their nutrients and neutralize toxic chemicals. Of the several clay minerals, certain ones are more effective in the exchange process than others. Dominance of the kind of clay in the soil is why some vineyard plots may be better than others mere paces apart. How clay minerals function in the soil is worth knowing more about.

Clay minerals are classified according to their crystal structure. The most widely distributed clay mineral in soils is kaolinite, the end product of long-time weathering of feldspars and micas. Unfortunately, for winegrowing, this most abundant clay mineral has a low cation-exchange capability; the reason being, the plates as seen in the electron microscope imagery (Photograph 1.2) stick together tightly, plate to plate. Exchange molecules have a difficult time getting in or out of the lattice between the plates. This plate-to-plate attraction is why kaolinite can be molded into thin-walled forms which do not shrink or crumble when kiln-fired. Kaolinite is therefore ideal for pottery, but not so desirable as the dominant clay in a soil. Clay minerals that are products of less severe weathering than kaolinite and much better for soils are chlorite and illite.

The best clay minerals for agricultural soils are montmorillonite (smectite) and vermiculite, products of even less severe weathering than illite. Molecular attraction is very strong horizontally within their plates, but is notoriously weak between them. As a consequence, water and other molecules readily enter between the plates and find places in the lattice. These are the "swelling clays" or "heaving shales," so-called because of the readiness and high degree to which they expand when wetted. Weak plate-to-plate attraction gives montmorillonite a tremendous cation-exchange capacity (vermiculite has considerably less). Soils made of these clays are wonderful for agriculture but disastrous for road beds and building foundations. However, the expansion feature has other useful applications. As the commercial product Bentonite, montmorillonite makes a very slick "mud" and excellent "plastering agent" in oil-well drilling fluid. Also known commercially as Fuller's Earth, the clay is an excellent absorbent used especially for fulling (shrinking and thickening) woolen fabric. In vineyards, montmorillonite "thickens" soils composed of silt, sand, and broken rock.

Bentonite has another use in winemaking: it fines or clarifies wine which has developed a haziness during fermentation. The clay absorbs the precipitates causing the cloudiness, but, unfortunately, also some of the preferred flavors.

If clay forms the body of agricultural soils, montmorillonite is its spirit – a free spirit at that. This mineral is a real chemical "flirt." However, it is a selective flirt. Being negatively charged, it takes up only with positively charged ions or cations. With its very large exchange capacity, montmorillonite does a supermarket business by hosting and trading cations of the various mineral nutrients in the plant-feeding process to be described in the following section.

Mineral-feeding the vineplant

Plants don't eat rocks *per se*, but sip on mineral concoctions dissolved from them. Different rocks offer different menus of mineral constituents. Balance in the nutrient diet is undoubtedly one of the factors in the mystery of why the wines of one vineyard plot may be judged superior to its look-alike neighbor.

Kaolinite is "china clay," named for Kao Ling or "high hill" near Jiaxian in the Hunan Province of China. Montmorillonite was named for Montmorillon near the city of Limoges in west-central France. Limoges is famous for its china which utilizes local deposits of kaolinite.

Weathering puts the minerals in edible form, but they have to be in solution in the soil to be "swallowed." (A "soil solution" only needs to be damp, not saturated.) It is water in the ground that puts wine in the bottle. Too much water is as bad as not enough. Since irrigation is not permitted in France's *appellation contrôlée* vineyards (the officially delimited areas), the water supply depends on nature's blessings.

The "meat and potatoes" of the working plant's diet are the macro-nutrients (those needed in quantity): oxygen, nitrogen, phosphorus, calcium, magnesium, potassium, sulfur. Other staples are carbon and hydrogen from the air and the soil. Then there are little side dishes that, although needed only in small portions, are critical for a healthy, grape-making diet. These are the micro-nutrients: iron, zinc, manganese, copper, boron, molybdenum, and chlorine.

The plant's underground food-processing factory, the soil, is not just one big, happy workplace. There are competitions, slowdowns, lockouts, and shortages. For example, as shown in Figure 1.2, iron, zinc, manganese, and copper are most easily assimilable in acidic soils (low pH), whereas the macronutrients prefer neutral to alkaline conditions. Phosphorus, after nitrogen, is the most critical element for total plant growth and grape development. When it is in its soluble form as a phosfate, it also readily combines with other metallic elements to form an insoluble compound, a chemical "lock-out."

Normally, in most soils there exists sufficient iron for the plant's needs, but having it in a digestible form may be a problem. Unfortunately, in limy (alkaline) conditions iron tends to become an oxide that is poorly soluble. "Lime-induced chlorosis" (loss of normal green color in the leaves) indicates where highly alkaline soils have caused a chemical "lock-out" of iron. This problem is particularly vexing in the chalky soils of the Touraine region of the Loire where iron gets latched onto by oxygen as soon as it weathers from the mineral glauconite, a complex iron-rich mica. The source of iron in the chalk terrain of Champagne is pyrite (iron sulfide) found in lignites of the Tertiary slope wash. The slope wash of sands, clays, lignites, and marls is mixed with chalk from the underlying Cretaceous. Although roots commonly plunge to considerable depths, the chalk is fractured and does not "pond" super-saturated lime water.

Normally, calcium and magnesium are chemically quite congenial, but when calcium is the more abundant mineral in soils, it combines in compounds at the expense of magnesium. This competition is unfortunate, for each molecule of chlorophyll in the leaves requires one atom of magnesium.

The really puzzling question is: how do these mineral elements get from the soil into the plant system? The response that they are taken up through the roots does not explain how they got into the roots. The answer varies from complicated to mysterious to essentially unknown. Any attempt to explain the process has to get down to some pretty fine points – down to the atomic level, as a matter of fact.

I have already indicated, for the process to function, that there must be sufficient moisture for the nutrient substances to be diffused in solution throughout the soil. (Diffusion is the way whiskey mixes with water in a highball glass.) The "feeding" takes place through root hairs which are fine, tubular growths on the outer wall of a root cell.

Figure 1.3
Mechanism of absorption of nutrients by root hairs
(Diagram a modified from N.C. Brady, *The Nature and Properties of Soils,* 1974, Macmillan Publishing Co.; Diagrams b and c from R.L. Donahue, R.W. Miller, and J.C. Schickluna, *Soils: An Introduction to Soils and Plant Growth,* 6th edn, © 1990, p. 254. Adapted by permission of Prentice-Hall, Inc, Englewood Cliffs, NJ 07632)

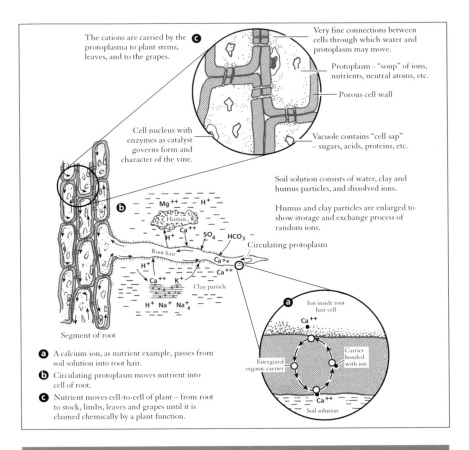

The cations are carried by the protoplasma to plant stems, leaves, and to the grapes. **c**

Very fine connections between cells through which water and protoplasm may move.

Protoplasm - "soup" of ions, nutrients, neutral atoms, etc.

Porous cell wall

Cell nucleus with enzymes as catalyst governs form and character of the vine.

Vacuole contains "cell sap" – sugars, acids, proteins, etc.

Soil solution consists of water, clay and humus particles, and dissolved ions.

Humus and clay particles are enlarged to show storage and exchange process of random ions.

Mg^{++} H^+ **b**
Humus
H^+ Ca^{++} SO_4 HCO_3^-
Ca^{++} Circulating protoplasm
Root hair
H^+ Ca^{++}
Ca^{++} K^+ Clay particle
H^+ Na^+ Na_4^+

Segment of root

a A calcium ion, as nutrient example, passes from soil solution into root hair.

b Circulating protoplasm moves nutrient into cell of root.

c Nutrient moves cell-to-cell of plant – from root to stock, limbs, leaves and grapes until it is claimed chemically by a plant function.

a Ion inside root hair cell
Ca^{++}
Carrier bonded with ion
Energized organic carrier
Ca^{++}
Soil solution

How plants absorb minerals

Authorities on plant physiology admit that just how mineral ions are selectively absorbed through the cell wall of the root into the plant system is still largely unknown. (An ion is an atom or group of atoms which may be either positively or negatively charged.) In *Introduction to Plant Physiology*, Professor B. S. Meyer and his co-authors describe one possible way in which this absorption may take place. With apologies to Dr. Meyer and his colleagues, I have rewritten their theory to read like a little skit.

The extremely thin membranes of root hairs are permeable to water, and allow the water molecules to pass through without challenge. But molecules of the other mineral nutrients are held up at the border. They have to have a passport and an escort. Remember negatively charged montmorillonite and her cation-exchange capacity? She also runs a travel agency linked with an escort service. Clay particles and humus (partially decomposed plant or animal matter) swap, borrow, or store ions from the soil solution and position them to "get through customs" into the plant. For some happy reason, most of the nutrient ions are positively charged and are attracted to the negatively charged root surfaces (unlikes attract, likes repel).

One of the positively charged nutrient ions shows up at the cell wall, but is halted by the membrane. An escort molecule of opposite electrical charge residing in the inner space as part of the plant tissue unites with the ion wanting to gain entrance. The fee for this escort service is paid by the vineplant with a bit of energy resulting from the chemical reaction in respiration (evaporation) in the leaves. The carrier molecule, now joined to the candidate ion, escorts it to inner space. Once inside, this little marriage of convenience is broken, freeing the ion. The wandering ion now "captured" inside the cell resumes its positive electrical charge. The escort molecule can go back to help other ions wishing to gain entrance.

The itinerant nutrient ions now inside the plant cell are no longer vagabonds. They are put to work. Some of the macronutrients such as nitrogen, potassium, calcium, and sulfur build plant tissue. The micronutrients, being highly skilled, are given high-tech jobs. Some are assigned to the chlorophyll laboratory; some activate the enzymes which act as catalysts making carbohydrates in the sugar factory.

The mechanism of absorption, the complicated and mysterious part, is described opposite. While science may not fully understand how plant physiology works, the plants signal with their leaves when their diet of nutrients is deficient – or when they have had too much of one thing. Deficiencies are indicated when leaves become faded, discolored, or brown around the edges. Brown speckling and leaf-cupping indicate mineral toxicity – an excess of a particular nutrient.

Soils of the various rock types seem to contain most of the nutrient elements that are needed by the vine. Those with the better balanced menu are most likely to grow the finer wines. Nitrogen, potassium, and phosphorus are nearly always deficient because they are removed in solution (leached) so readily. Although nitrogen is in excess in the air, it is the most universally deficient nutrient in the soil because it must be in the ammonium or nitrate form in the soil solution to be absorbed. Requirements for these nutrients have to be supplied by chemical additives and fertilizers along with some natural mulching and manuring.

I have already pointed out that climate ranks right along with parent material in the weathering process and soil formation. Its sunshine and rain are the seasonal variants that directly affect the wine.

Climate

Climate is the long-term result of temperature, moisture, and winds. Weather is what is going on outside and in the five-day forecast. Our climatic temperature and its seasonal variations come from the sun, in particular the angle with which it strikes the earth. It was the difference in the angle of the sun at different north–south locations that led to the development of the word *climate*. The Greeks had a word for it, *klimata*. Observations by Eratosthenes at Alexandria, Egypt, were to the affect that there were differences in the length of shadows at the same time of day and season between southern Egypt, Alexandria, and Greece. Eratosthenes correlated these differences with the angle of the sun. He drew equally spaced lines which he called *klimata* representing the inclination of the sun above the earth at a given time. Eratosthenes' *klimata* were later converted to degrees of latitude, with the equator being zero and the north and south poles being 90 degrees.

Climate in concert with geologic processes began when the world was young, varying over time as the seas and landmasses evolved. The climatic cycle that we are experiencing today began about 10,000 years ago as a warm period following the last glacial stage of the Pleistocene. The climate of western Europe had some readjusting to do. Much of France was tundra-like and treeless. Tage Nilsson, a Swedish geologist who is expert on the Pleistocene, thinks this was due more to dryness than to extreme cold.

The Gulf Stream, western Europe's giant radiator system, resumed its former northward circulation path, after having been diverted much further south by the icecap. As temperatures became warmer (during the Boreal and Atlantic climatic periods), plants and animals that had retreated south, migrated northward. As vegetation flourished, it aided rock weathering and soil formation. It was the freeze-thaw climate of the periglacial zone that "stirred" the ground and chiseled at rock faces during the Ice Age phases.

As the continental ice cap melted, the tremendous volume of water formerly impounded was released, raising the sea level some 400 feet (120 m). The land bridge between Dover and Calais that had connected England with the mainland for at least two million years was flooded, and the English Channel joined the North Sea and the mid-Atlantic. The rise in sea level also "drowned" the valleys of major rivers, turning the outlets of the Gironde, Loire, and the Seine into estuaries. (A similar thing happened to the Hudson River, Chesapeake Bay, and other rivers in North America.)

By Greco-Roman times, sea level had reached its current norm, and the climatic patterns of today had developed. Then, about 1000 years ago, after a very warm period, the climate began to get cold again. Mountain glaciers stopped receding and began to grow. The ensuing period, known as the Little Ice Age, extended into the mid-19th century (some scientists say up to the early 20th century.) An interesting record of the past few centuries is shown in Figure 1.4. The onset of the grape harvest in France, 1500–1980, originally published by Emmanuel Le Roy Ladurie, is shown by ten-year averages. The higher the bars of the graph, the later the harvest, meaning several years of inclement weather. (The vertical scale creates the appearance of considerable fluctuation between the ten-year periods, but the greatest difference is only about ten days.)

Figure 1.4
Commencement of *vendange* since 1500
(adapted from original graph by E. Le Roy Ladurie, *Histoire du climat depuis l'an mil*, vol. 1, 1983, p. 81, by kind permission of Flammarion. Trends A–F added by author)

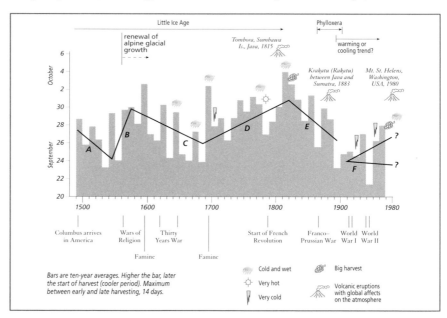

Historical and natural events have been added to Ladurie's original graph. He correlates several of the periods of late harvests with historical wet, cold springs resulting in disastrous wheat harvests, famines, and rebellions in western Europe. Although the variations are not strong, warmer and cooler trends have been added to the graph. These are only "eye-averages," not mathematically derived. These suggestions only emphasize that long-term trends can only be interpreted from a look back, or "hind-cast," of 50 years or more. There is considerable debate today as to whether or not the world is experiencing global warming. Only time will tell.

The vintage year on the wine label is of utmost importance to the wine lover. This is an index to how the weather treated the grapes for the wine that season. It is, however, only a general indicator. Expertise of the winemaker apart, it is the rain, sunshine, frost or hail at a particular vineyard that is the critical, but seldom known, information to the buyer.

The geologic processes that shaped the European peninsula of the great Euro-Asian landmass place France in a very privileged position. Color Plate 3 shows the three climatic zones influenced by the Atlantic and the Mediterranean that affect the country.

To emphasize the affects of oceans on the climate, let's move France along the 45° parallel to the U.S., making Bordeaux a triplet of the twin cities of Minneapolis-St.-Paul, Minnesota. Paris would be a Canadian city, with the northern third of France in Manitoba and Ontario. Despite the fine wines of the latter province, such a "North American France" would not be the great wine country that it is.

Happily for the real France, the entire western border is over 600 miles (almost 1000 km) along the Atlantic. The prevailing Westerlies pass over the warm Gulf Stream, pick up moisture and come ashore with a full cargo of water-laden clouds. Major relief features and impinging weather systems influence where and how this cargo will be dumped. The plateaux surrounding the massifs begin to wedge the moisture currents upward, giving the high mountains 60–90 inches (1500–2300 mm) of precipitation per year. Except for the margin along the Atlantic coast, the rainfall map for France would make a good replica of the relief map of the country.

The maritime or oceanic climate in northwestern Europe is "woolen-weather" year-round: summers are generally cool and damp; winters rainy, often with high wind velocities, but dust-free air. In France, the boundary between maritime and continental zones is broadly transitional, modified to fit around the massifs and plateau regions.

The climatic boundaries are frequently ruptured by a strong penetration of one into the other – such as snow in the flower gardens of Nice in February, 1985. Champagne, the most northerly of the French wine regions, lies far enough inland to experience the generally clear skies of the continental climate, yet it remains within the moderating influence of the maritime zone. Warm, dry, pleasant summer days in Bordeaux and southwestern France occur when the Azores ridge of high pressure is centered off the coast of Spain and has pushed the westerly cyclonic tracks farther north.

The continental zone exhibits more extreme temperature variations than the maritime, and its air is drier. It has its heaviest rainfall in summer, usually as thunderstorms, as rapidly moving depressions create unstable atmospheric conditions. With the storms all too frequently comes hail with its devastation.

Forecasting the trooping of low-pressure systems moving on western Europe played the decisive role in the high drama of first postponement, then the momentous decision to go ahead with the D-Day invasion of Normandy on June 6, 1944. Today we in the U.S. have the opportunity to see daily weather satellite pictures of Europe on television and to imagine what is happening to our friends and their grapes in France. The satellite imagery

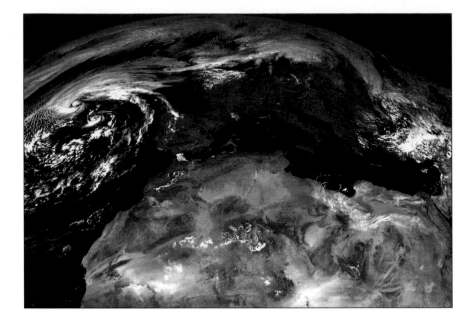

captured in Photograph 1.3 shows how the air masses affecting the northern part of France, including much quality vineyard, are previewed by the British Isles.

Although more than a third of all French wine is grown in the Midi, primarily in Languedoc, this vast region still has only a few wines of distinction. The Mediterranean climatic influence extends up the Rhône Valley to Valence and sometimes pushes as far as Lyon. The Mediterranean coast is famous for its warm, dry summers, but winters here may be wet and sometimes stormy. The oft-quoted Doctor Guyot, writing in the 1860s, praised France's temperate climate (north of the Midi) as the only one to father good table wines. He believed the climate of Burgundy, the Loire, and Bordeaux endowed the grape with "sweet perfection, excellent aroma, and flavor." Pierre Bréjoux, formerly head of the Institut National de la Recherche Agronomique (I.N.R.A.), also recognized that in the southern, hotter regions it is difficult to obtain white wines which are fresh and fruity. Bréjoux observes that the traditional grapes of the Midi have more juice and a stronger aroma than the middle (temperate) zone, but when made into wine, they do not sustain those qualities for long.

> Jules Guyot, born in 1807 in the Aube (Champagne) region, became a doctor of medicine at age of 26. His knowledge and interest, however, were as much in physics and agriculture as in medicine. In 1860 he was commissioned to study all vineyards in France and to suggest better methods of viticulture and wine-making. These studies were published in 1868 in three volumes.

Microclimate

Wild things – animals, birds, insects and plants – find the places where they are most comfortable. So do your domestic pets. They are all identifying micro-climates. But planted vines are not able to choose their habitat; they are stuck where man puts them. In time, they tell him whether or not they like the place he has chosen. The wine literature makes frequent reference to microclimate, but details are mostly lacking, and surprisingly, there are few published technical studies on the subject. Nevertheless, the vignerons know where these little climate bands exist in their vineyards.

How "micro" is a microclimate? It appears to run the scale from a few rows of vines to an entire vineyard and possibly larger. Professor Rudolf Geiger, an authority on microclimate, reminds us that instrument stations generally record meteorologic data at the height at which man breathes and senses; temperature differences can vary as much as 10°F (6°C) from the ground to the height of a man. So, what man senses and records and what many of his vines feel may be significantly different. Furthermore, T. Bedford Franklin, author of *Climates in Miniature*, bemoans the fact that most meteorological data are reported in mean values which he says are of very little use in studies of microclimates.

Pierre Bréjoux suggests that in the hot climate of the Midi, maturity can be delayed by choosing a northerly and hence cooler exposure. This is what is done in the small appellation of Palette on the outskirts of Aix-en-Provence. It is surprising, however, that a few years ago when special appellations such as St.-Chinian and Pic-St.-Loup were being delineated in Languedoc, northern exposures for particular appellations were not emphasized.

An alternative to north-slope planting to obtain a cooler microclimate is to locate vineyards at higher altitudes. This is done to some extent in both Languedoc and Provence. In America, Professor Gordon Dutt of the University of Arizona did just that with his experimental vineyards, locating them at elevations to upwards of 5000 feet (1500 m) above the hot, desert valley in the "Sun Belt" of Arizona.

The nature of the surface of the soil influences the microclimates. The hottest point on the bare ground is its surface. (Remember how sand on the beach can be uncomfortably hot to bare feet but bearable if we "squiggle" down an inch or so.) A moist (not wet) soil absorbs heat about 15 percent more efficiently than a perfectly dry soil. This is important in vine terms because the rate at which soils warm up has a bearing on the rate of ripening: long, slow maturation tends to mean more concentrated fruit flavors. Daily fluctuations of temperatures penetrate no more than a few inches below the surface and have little affect on root growth. The cumulative of seasonal changes, however, penetrates much deeper, helping to regulate the growing and dormant periods.

Stony soil is extolled as being ideal for vineyards. What rocky surfaces often indicate is a texture and structure of soils that are well drained. Stones themselves on the surface serve particular functions. Here's how. The rock surfaces reflect and diffuse sunlight to the lower leaves shaded by the canopy. Also the rocks absorb heat during the day, then act as miniature radiators to give it back during the cooler evening hours. Stones are also helpful in a more obscure way. Who hasn't turned over a stone and seen the bugs busy in the damp ground beneath? This micro-reserve of moisture isn't enough to contribute to the water-feeding of the plant, but it harbors a very large microorganism population that helps physical and chemical working of the soil.

It is a well-known fact that it takes longer for the ground to warm up and cool off than it does a lake or river. This is because water is such a good heat conductor (as in cooking). We observe the moderating of lakes and rivers on the local microclimate in such areas as Lake Geneva and Lake Bourget in the Savoie, the Gironde estuary of Bordeaux, and the Marne River in Champagne. (The Finger Lakes of west central New York State moderate the extremes of temperature along their shores so that a very good winegrowing area exists. The region may experience 18–20° below zero Fahrenheit (–28°C) in winter, but warms up rapidly in the spring.)

Sunshine and temperature

It is obvious from the sunshine and temperature graphs that some wine districts get more of each than others – Champagne gets enough for tart grapes – ideal for producing wines with a sparkle; Languedoc has problems keeping its grapes from being cooked. Temperature is, of course, a function of the amount of sunshine, but, as we shall learn, sun rays bring more than heat to the living plant.

The further north of the 45° parallel, the lower the angle of the sun and more critical the orientation of the vineyard. In Champagne, northernmost of the wine areas, the maximum angle of the summer sun is only 65°; by the autumnal equinox the angle is down to 49°. For obvious reasons, the northern vineyards of France prefer southeast- or south-facing exposures to catch the first rays of the sun to warm the vines after a cool or foggy night.

Figure 1.5
Climatic elements of key wine regions of France
The graphs show the average climatic factors for the five principal French wine areas
(compiled and modified from various sources)

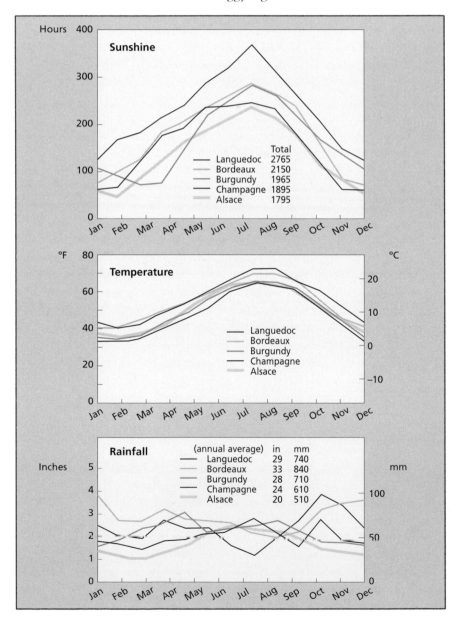

In early spring when the mean daily temperature reaches 50°F (10°C), the vineplant, which has been dormant since November, begins to come to life. Budbreak occurs in late March or early April. Leaf buds come first, then fruit buds. Frost damage to the fruit buds may wipe out an entire crop, whereas leaf buds may get a second chance. As the weather continues to warm, leaves, new growth, flowering, and grape development follow.

For maximum utilization of the sun, the direction and width of rows, density of planting, methods of training and pruning have all been studied and are part of appellation regulations. The first layer of leaves in the canopy enjoys maximum light saturation. Sunlight reaching the layer below is reduced by at least a third, and the next layer receives only enough for the leaves to pay their way – they may even become, in the words of W. M. Kliewer, a researcher at the University of California in Davis, photosynthesis parasites.

Photosynthesis kicks in for optimum performance at about 77°F (25°C) and, surprisingly, drops off precipitously at temperatures higher than 86°F (30°C). Higher temperatures cause instability of the enzymes, tissue desiccation, and closure of pores in the underside of the leaf, in other words, wilting.

Research during the 1940s by A. J. Winkler and M. A. Amerine, also at Davis, concluded that temperature was the principal factor affecting quality in California wines. The temperature affect on grape maturation the researchers called "heat summation," describing the number of hours the temperature is above 50°F (10°C) during the growing season. The summation is called "degree-days," although in fact it is expressed in hours. On the basis of "degree-days," Amerine and Winkler recognized five zones for California which they correlated with wine quality. However, some growers in the state told me that because the temperature of warm but cloudy days was recorded as "degree-days" the result was often misleading. In terms of quality-grape maturation, direct sunshine is what the growers look for.

The "degree-day" zonation has useful application in California where new vineyards are being created each year. Certain grape varieties are recommended for particular zones. Although temperature zones have been recognized in France for many years, zonation has less practical value as a guide for plant selection as new plantings are primarily limited to extensions within established appellations with already authorized varieties. Considerable research, however, is being done on habitat adaptability, particularly in Languedoc, where the delineation of appellations is relatively recent, and growers are experimenting with non-traditional grape varieties.

Temperature zonation may be useful in California, but breaks down when it comes to explaining the difference in quality between adjacent vineyards within the same zone in France. Nevertheless, it may be of interest to compare the "degree-days" of certain French and California wine districts.

Champagne, Chablis, and the Loire, all with "degree-days" between 1710 and 1980, are cooler than California's coolest region, the Monterey Peninsula, at 2160–2340. The "cool" areas of Monterey, the Santa Clara, and Livermore Valleys are all appreciably warmer than the Côte d'Or and Alsace. Average of the "degree-day" range for California's famous Napa Valley is the same (2475) as the Médoc in Bordeaux.

The saying goes in France, "June makes the wine, August makes the taste." Researchers led by the eminent enologist Emile Peynaud of Bordeaux point out that it is the rate of change of the sugars and acids in the grape during the latter part of the maturation stage that is critical to the strength and quality of wine. It is particularly those warm, sunny days in September and early October that the winegrower prays for.

Professor Peynaud's graph showing sugar–acid development is reproduced in Figure 1.6. It indicates that from the commencement of ripening through maturation (a period of between 45 and 55 days), the sugar concentration in the fruit increases at about the same rate as acidity decreases. (The critical importance of sugar is that during fermentation it turns to alcohol.) As the grapes near maturity, the sugar curve begins to flatten. The plant decides it is time to start storing some carbohydrates elsewhere in the system to make ready for next season. That is when the vineyard manager decides it is time to start picking the grapes. Readings of the sugar concentration in the grapes are taken daily and sometimes hourly to determine the optimum time for picking – the proclamation of the *ban de vendange* in France. (The scales for determining sugar concentration by a refractometer or hydrometer are known as Baumé in France and as Brix in America.)

Figure 1.6
Sugar–acid development
When the sugar level has reached its maximum and begins to level off, the "ban de vendange" is sounded
(E. Peynaud, *Connaissance et Travail du Vin*, p. 60, 1984, Dunod/*Knowing and Making Wine*, 1984, Wiley, by kind permission)

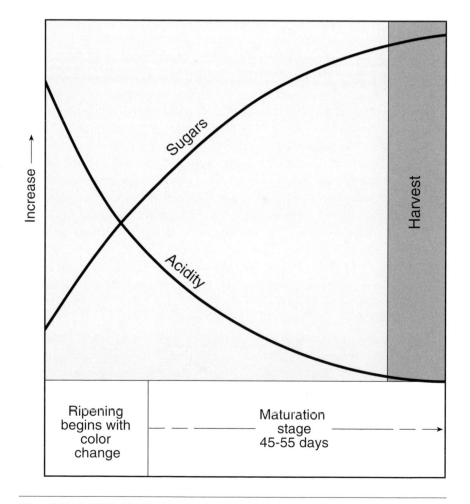

Magic of the sunbeam

There is magic as well as poetry in a sunbeam. Sunlight is a composite of rays of different wavelengths, some of which the eye recognizes as light. Infrared and ultraviolet are well known as heat rays. But heat is only one of the several functions of sunlight.

Chemical reactions in plants are set in motion by a combination of sunbeam waves. The "solar reactors" of a plant are chemical molecules in the green leaf which have the familiar name of chlorophyll. Certain wavelengths excite the molecular components of the chlorophyll, causing light energy to be converted into chemical energy. Thus begins the process of photosynthesis and the manufacture of plant food.

The "fast foods" generated within the plant by the "microwaves" are primarily carbohydrates, which are simply concocted out of air and water with chlorophyll as the catalytic converter. Within the plant when a mixture of carbon dioxide from the air and water drawn from the soil is shot through with sunlight, the chemical bonds of these simple compounds are "shaken up." They reorganize as carbohydrates, mostly sucrose (sugar). Some protein and fatty acids (glycerides, esters, etc.) are also produced. The amount of water utilized in this process is less than 1 percent of the water absorbed by the roots leaving the bulk of the water in the cells and plasma ("bloodstream") of the plant.

T. Bedford Franklin figured the amount of heat energy needed by a green plant to make a pound of sugar was 7200 Btu, enough to raise a 5-gallon (22 liters) tub of ice-cold water to the boiling point. (A Btu, British thermal unit, is the amount of heat applied to 1 pound of water to raise its temperature 1 degree Fahrenheit.) This temperature conversion may seem like an impossible task for a plant, but the pot doesn't boil while you watch – Professor Franklin's number is the heat summation of temperatures over an entire season.

In the chemical manufacture of carbohydrates, some oxygen and water are left over and released into the air by transpiration (evaporation). As soon as the food is created in the foliage, it is moved through the plant's circulatory system from the leaves to other parts of the plant, including the grapes.

Vines, like other deciduous plants, are "warm-blooded." The food manufacturing plant closes for the winter.

Rainfall: welcome or worrisome?

Rain for wine is as necessary as sunshine, but winegrowers, like farmers everywhere, prefer to have it at a chosen time and in just the right amounts. It seldom falls that way on the plains of Spain, France, or anywhere.

Unfortunately, some parts of France have their rainiest weather in the fall, precisely when sunshine is most needed. From Champagne to Beaujolais, yellow slickers and rubber boots are often the uniform of the day during picking time. Too much rain at the beginning of the growing cycle is also bad because it can cause rot and invite other diseases. Nature does at times try the patience of the hearts that want to love her! But on occasions, as in 1978, just as the vignerons were feeling that nature had indeed betrayed them, the rain and clouds that had plagued the entire summer gave way to sunny, warm days that lasted well through the harvest and produced an exceptional vintage.

The rainfall graph (*see* Figure 1.5) shows the average annual precipitation for several wine regions to be about 27 inches (680 mm) per year – only a little better than semi-arid. As irrigation is not allowed in *appellation contrôlée* vineyards, there is much looking to the heavens. Is it any wonder that the French vignerons have such a deep reverence for the Almighty?

Vineyard soils are leaky systems, but they need to be to some extent, as too much water in the soil excludes oxygen and carbon dioxide from the pore spaces. These gases are critical in the nutritional feeding of the roots. If the soil is too permeable, the water drains away before the roots can make much use of it. *Useable* water is what counts. That is the water held in pores, micropores, and capillaries of the soil, and in the fractured bedrock where it is available to be absorbed into the plant system by the rootlets.

What's in the wind?

Sailors, farmers, and other outdoorsmen know that a change of the wind brings a change in the weather – for better or for worse. Winds as such have only limited influence on viticulture. It is the weather changes they bring that emphasize the importance of wind on wine.

Owing to its geographic position and relief, France catches half a dozen or more winds which blow from various directions, and the same wind may be known by different names from one locality to another. The major winds are shown on the map of the climatic zones (*see* Color Plate 3).

The Westerlies, picking up moisture from the Atlantic Gulf Stream, are the most important winds to affect France, but the most famous – or infamous – is the *mistral*, the cold, north wind that funnels down the Rhône Valley. More famed and fabled for its velocity, it may also drop the temperature as much as 50°F (10°C) in 24 hours. Rhône vines are grown as single plants, pruned low to help them withstand the onslaught of the wind. Generation of the *mistral* builds when there is a high-pressure system in the north of France and a low-pressure one in the Mediterranean. As the moving air mass from the north is crowded into the constriction between the Massif Central and the Vercors, its velocity may be increased to as much as 90 miles per hour (145 km/h). (A similar phenomenon occurs along the Front Range, northwest of Denver, where winds of hurricane force are sometimes generated when a frontal system spills down through the canyons opening onto the plains.)

Either the *mistral* is milder today or the stories about it are less exaggerated than times past. Winegrowers in the lower Rhône Valley and Languedoc often welcome this wind as it brings clear, dry weather to their vineyards to offset the lingering rot that sets in when the *marin*, the warm, moist wind that blows in from the Mediterranean, persists.

The *marin* does not penetrate far up the Rhône Valley but veers westward through the Carcassonne Gateway into the Aquitaine Basin. As the warm, moist air rises over the elevated area, it expands and cools, releasing precipitation. Rushing down the slopes on the other side toward Toulouse, it develops tremendous speeds and is heated by compression. The warm, dry air of the converted *marin* becomes the *autan*, also known as the *autan noir*. A similar wind descending from the Pyrenees is the *autan blanc*.

The *föhn* is a warm, down-driving wind of the Alps, generated in the same manner as the *marin–autan* wind. (The chinook, known from Alberta in Canada to the Colorado Rockies, is the North American *föhn*.)

The *bise* or *bise noire* is a cold, dry wind from the Arctic regions. (The *bise* is like the famous "Blue Norther" of Texas that comes out of the northwest as a fast-moving, occluded cold front.) The *bise noire* may persist for days, as it did in Champagne, Burgundy, and Alsace, in 1987, a difficult vintage for growers in all three regions.

Frost and hail, the white perils

Frost and hail are the two most feared weather hazards in wine country. Either can completely devastate a crop. Born of a physical phenomenon – moisture versus air temperature – there is next to nothing man can do to prevent hail, but he can minimize if not prevent frost damage.

Frost happens more subtly than hail, but its destruction can be just as devastating and may be more widespread. The maximum amount of water vapor that can be held by the air at a given temperature is called its dew point. As the air cools, moisture may condense as dew, rain, or snow. If this release occurs when temperatures are below freezing, it will be frost rather than dew. This is white or hoarfrost.

Frosts of late spring which occur during budbreak are potentially the most damaging as they may set back, if not altogether eliminate, the entire grape season for an area. Autumn frosts do less damage, as the leaves offer some protection, and if the grapes are gathered immediately they can be used. The severity of frost damage depends on the temperature preceding the frost, how far the temperature goes below freezing, and how long it stays there. Low-lying areas are the most frost-prone, as cold air is heavy and tends to flow or settle into frost pockets or hollows. There may be as much as 10°F (6°C) difference in temperature between low and high ground in short distances; small changes of a few degrees become critical as temperatures drop toward freezing.

With blessed irony, when water freezes, a slight warming is produced (not enough, however, to save your water pipes in a hard freeze). The change in physical state from liquid to solid releases the energy required by molecular attraction to maintain a liquid state. This energy is given up as "latent heat." This bit of thermodynamics is employed in the sprinkler method of frost protection. It is highly effective. The sprinklers wet the leaves and buds, and as the water begins to freeze, it releases this latent heat, thus momentarily protecting the vines while an insulating coating of ice is formed. It is essential that a film of water be maintained on the ice coating so that the protective temperature does not go below freezing point (*see* Photograph 1.4a). Quite a number of Grand Cru vineyards in frost-prone Chablis and some areas in Champagne have installed overhead sprinkler systems.

Because less initial capital is involved than for sprinklers, the butane heater or smoke pot is still in use in numerous vineyards. Convection created by the heaters mixes the cold and warm air, and provides some direct radiation. Initial cost may be low, but operation of the heaters can be fairly expensive due to the labor involved in lighting and maintaining them throughout the night.

Whatever protective measures are employed, economics is an important factor. Initial cost of equipment plus its operation averaged over several years may be greater than the probabilities of loss from frost damage. (Frost-protection measures are additionally discussed under Chablis in chapter 9.)

Hail is born of atmospheric violence and is usually concentrated in local areas or bands. Snowden Flora, an authority on tornadoes and hailstorms, calls hail the "white plague." The friendly hills and ridges which shield vineyards from the cold, wet, north and west winds may become villains in summer by creating updrafts that trigger thunderstorms. The witches' brew develops when warm, moist air collides with cooler, drier air. Air masses of different densities do not mix easily; an updraft can set these two unfriendly atmospheres off into the devil-dance of a thunderstorm.

Surprisingly, in some parts of Europe hail is more frequent than in "hail centers" of the United States. Can you believe that the city of Paris has a hail frequency about the same as Cheyenne, Wyoming, which has one of the highest in the U.S. with an average of ten occurrences a year.

Considering the overall favorable climate, fertile soil and extensive native vegetation in France, it would seem perfectly logical that grapevines had been domesticated from wild plants. Paleobotanists, however, find little evidence to support such a seemingly logical course.

Lineage of the grapevine
All grapevines, even those we now call noble, had their beginnings somewhere, sometime as wild plants. Evidence points to Transcaucasia as the likely area where man domesticated wild vines. It is equally obscure as to when, by whom, and where wine was developed from grapes. "When" was likely after the end of the Ice Age. As to who or where, it is uncertain as to whether it was the ancient civilizations of Mesopotamia, Egypt, or the Caucasus.

The narrow, high Caucasus range ties the Caspian and Black Seas like a belt with Mt. Elbrus the buckle, rising to the spectacular elevation of 18,481 feet (5600 m) only 70 miles (110 km) from the shores of the Black Sea. Transcaucasia (both sides of the Caucasus) includes the former Soviet states of Georgia, Azerbaijan, and Armenia. It is certain that some of the grapes found uniquely in this region – Georgia has at least 500 indigenous varieties – are very old indeed.

A fertile belt of plateaux and lowlands with a mild, sub-tropical climate lies along the western side of the Caucasus Mountains. Here, the soils are derived from Jurassic and Cretaceous limestones and basaltic lavas, so vines felt quite at home when they got to France. Grapeseeds found in Georgia are reported by the Russians to be carbon-dated at 7000–5000 B.C. Archeological evidence identifies wine to have been in use by the civilizations of Turkey, Greece, the Holy Land, and Egypt as early as 7000 B.C. Apparently, Noah was enjoying his wine even before that period.

As peoples of the eastern Mediterranean moved westward, they took the grape, the fig, and the apricot with them. Several centuries before Christ, the Phocaeans (Greeks) had established grapevines at their colony of Massalia (Marseille) on the southern coast of Gaul, and likewise in Spain. During the ensuing centuries as western Europe was settled, the grapevine would spread by various ways and means – as seeds or rooted plants, by emigrants, merchants, soldiers, and monks (*see* page 45).

It wasn't until the 18th century that the Swedish scientist, Carolus Linnaeus, developed a classification of vines, shown in Figure 1.7. His criteria distinguished grapevines from other vines and ivy. In time, grapevines themselves were further

**Figure 1.7
Lineage of the grapevine**
(compiled from various sources)

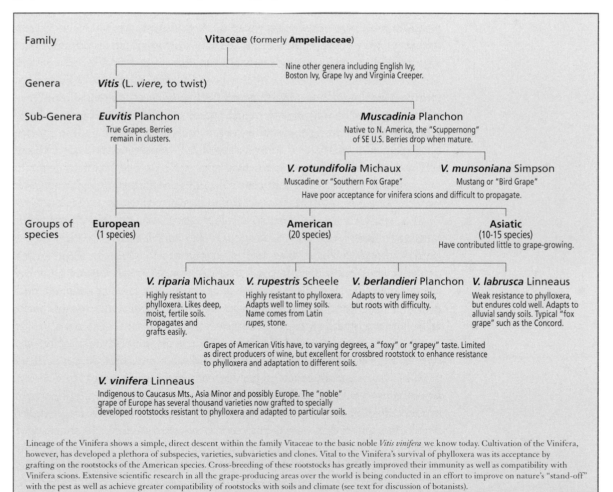

Lineage of the Vinifera shows a simple, direct descent within the family Vitaceae to the basic noble *Vitis vinifera* we know today. Cultivation of the Vinifera, however, has developed a plethora of subspecies, varieties, subvarieties and clones. Vital to the Vinifera's survival of phylloxera was its acceptance by grafting on the rootstocks of the American species. Cross-breeding of these rootstocks has greatly improved their immunity as well as compatibility with Vinifera scions. Extensive scientific research in all the grape-producing areas over the world is being conducted in an effort to improve on nature's "stand-off" with the pest as well as achieve greater compatibility of rootstocks with soils and climate (see text for discussion of botanists).

differentiated. Linnaeus placed all vines in the botanical family of *Vitaceae*. He then differentiated vines which climb by tendrils from ivies which climb by cellular pads that stick to surfaces. Grapevines are in the genera *Vitis*, from the Latin *Viere*, meaning to twist (tendrils).

Jules-Emile Planchon, the eminent French botanist, pharmacologist and entomologist, further separated the *Vitis* into two sub-genera: *Euvitis*, which retains its berries in clusters as they ripen, and the *Muscadinia* which drops its individual berries as they mature.

By some quirk of nature, North America ended up with over 20 species of the *Euvitis*. An equally large number has been identified in the Far East (*Euvitis Asiatic*). Oddly, only one true wine grape ended up in Europe. But what a grape! That lone European species, *Vitis vinifera satavia*, is the "granddaddy of them all." From the *vinifera*, several thousand varieties or sub-species have developed a dozen or more of truly noble character, which are responsible for all the great wines of the world. (*Vinifera*, derived from the Latin, means wine-bearing. *Satavia* is the cultivated *vinifera*; *sylvestris* the woodland or wild one.)

Prior to development of the laws of heredity in the mid-1800s by the Austrian monk and geneticist Gregor Mendel, propagation of grapes was mostly achieved by seedlings. Because of the long and haphazard history of evolution of the grape, seedlings frequently reverted to some prior stage. It was largely luck when a plantlet from seeds was like the parent. After Mendel's principles of genetics or heredity were better understood, propagating by cuttings and layering became the mode. (Layering is burying a living shoot until it develops roots then cutting it loose and planting it.) Those methods gave more assurance of obtaining a plant like the parent. Even with careful propagation, grapevines are notorious for evolving, or mutating, or even reverting to more primitive forms. Viticulturists say it is easier to get a new variety than to keep a classic (noble) one pure or to improve upon it.

Altogether there are over 120 varieties cultivated in France, under a dozen are recognized as classic. Of these, four are red grapes, Cabernet Sauvignon, Pinot Noir, Syrah, and Merlot, and six are white grapes, Riesling, Chardonnay, Gewurztraminer (it yields white juice, even though its skin is colored peach-gold), Muscat, Sauvignon Blanc, and Chenin Blanc.

With understandable parochial pride, the French would like to believe that at least some of their wine grapes were native to Gaul. Although this might be true in some instances, there is no paleontological, paleobotanical, or archeological evidence to support such a fervent wish.

Around 1880, a paleontological discovery containing fossil vineleaf imprints was, according to the author Roger Dion, promoted (by media hype of the day) to the rank of ancestors of the Pinot Noir of Epernay and Reims. The find was in a travertine deposit (calcium carbonate) near Sézanne on the southern edge of the Champagne country. It was an amazing collection of fossil plants, crustaceans, and insects. The flora of willows, magnolias, and ferns indicated a hot and humid climate. Of particular interest were the imprints of three vine leafs and fragments of branches and shoots. In 1886, a study published by several naturalists reported the identification of the leaf imprints as those of *Vitis*. This was enough to set off the fireworks.

One specimen was given the specific name of *sezannensis*, another that of *balbainii*, and the third specimen, *dutilli*. The disappointing conclusion of the research committee, which went largely ignored, was that the vine types were more akin to those currently growing in America than the modern types of Champagne. In the 55 million years that ensued from the time the leaves were entombed in the travertine, no evidence of descendants of the *sezannensis* or its companions has been found in Europe.

In another of nature's ironies, it was undoubtedly a collection of the native American grapevines – *Vitis labrusca*, *riparia*, and the *rotundifolia* – which was sent to botanist friends in France that introduced phylloxera to that country. The American plants had long ago developed immunity to the pest.

The wild *Vitis labrusca* is known locally as the Northern Muscadine, Swamp, Skunk, or Fox Grape. The names reflect a "foxy" taste, as in the odor of an animal cage. My grandmother used to make jams and jellies from the wild "Mustang" (Muscadine) grapes that I would gather for her in the woods. Although a teetotaller, she would also make some wine for "medicinal" purposes. It was worst tasting than the most horrible medicine in the cabinet.

The large, red Concord table grape of the U.S. is reputed to have been developed from the wild *labrusca* growing near Concord, Maine. The equally famous Catawba, also from the *labrusca*, was named for the Catawba River in North Carolina, but was reputedly domesticated in a vineyard which is now part of Rock Creek Park in Washington, D.C.

Unaware of the death-dealing phylloxera in their soils, the American growers tried unsuccessfully to cultivate European *vinifera*. The Europeans also experimented with American hybrids, but found they did not like the characteristic "foxy" taste or other flavors typical of those grapes.

If not native, when and how did the grape get to Gaul?

How the grape got to Gaul

Deferring for the moment that at least some of the grapes may have been domesticated from wild vines in Gaul, the popular notion is that following Caesar, the Rhône corridor became an "Oregon Trail," busy with emigrants, merchants, soldiers, and monks moving into the new frontier. Undoubtedly, these "pioneers" introduced some grapes and winemaking into Gaul.

Advocates of this "frontier days parade" were in for a bit of a shock when an archeological discovery in 1952 indicated the presence of wine in northern Gaul long before the appearance of Caesar's legions. The artifacts were found in the grave of a Celtic princess near Châtillon in Burgundy. The centerpiece of this find is a gigantic bronze vase (265 gallons or 1200 liters) purportedly used as a punch bowl for mixing wine. (Some party!) With it were bronze goblets and wine jugs. The shock was that the bas relief figuring on the vase are of Greek and Etruscan origin, dating from the 6th century B.C. These artifacts do not necessarily mean that the Celts were growing grapes and making wine. Nor do they indicate positively that the Celts were trading in wine. Such a prize might well be loot from one of the Celtic invasions of the Italian peninsula or brought back from a period of residency there.

Raymond Dumay questions whether the Rhône–Saône corridor was the principal route for the grape, doubting that plants brought directly from the Mediterranean climate would have survived a rapid transplant to the rigorous climate of northern Gaul. Dumay suggests that the route from the Adriatic region (Venice, Bologna, etc.) was more likely to have been via the Alto Adige of northern Italy, the Alps, and Rhaetia (referring to the upper Danube basin). Extended residence in the Alto Adige would certainly have acclimatized the plants for a cooler climate. The Brenner Pass (Amber Road) and Resia Pass were well-traveled routes across the Alps. From the Tyrol (north slopes of the Alps) and Rhaetia, it was an easy migration into the cool regions of northwest Gaul and the Rhine Valley.

We know from the Roman historian Livy that from 500 B.C. Celts of the Alps invaded northern Italy several times, with some tribes remaining there for extended periods. We are told that the Celts grew immoderately fond of wine in preference to their mead. Upon returning to northern Gaul, trade with the Etruscans and Greeks included wine. They may also have taken vines with them and produced some wine of their own. According to Bruno Roncarati, author of the book *Viva Vino*, when the Romans, who replaced the Etruscans, occupied Rhaetia in 15 B.C., they found excellent wines already being produced there – possibly by the Celts.

Viticulture is demanding work. Conceivably, by inattention or outright abandonment, Celtic vine imports could have "gone native," reverted to the wild state. Could these be the "native" plants which were later domesticated, such as the Riesling? Might this also be the case for the Chenin Blanc which St.-Martin, Bishop of Tours in A.D. 371, has been credited with domesticating from the wild state?

One thing is certain: that the Celtic Allobroges who occupied the area south of Lake Geneva, a part of Transalpine Gaul, were well into winemaking before the arrival of Caesar. Their grape was the *Allobrogica* whose ancestry was most likely obtained from the Greek colony at Massalia. It has been suggested that the *Allobrogica* in turn was ancestor to the Pinot Noir. The grape became acclimatized in the cool of the Haute-Savoie before moving further north into Burgundy and Champagne.

The truth of the matter is we don't know just how or when the grape first came to Gaul. Neither alone nor in combination does paleobotany, archeology, or history give us more than negative information, a few clues, and interesting speculation on the question.

Grapes were brought from the east, south and southwest in one form or another. In those very early times, viticulture was trial and error, random and haphazard. Although monks contributed significantly to disciplined viticulture, it was the commercial incentive that really drove development to make France become the world's greatest wine country.

This venerable industry with 2000 years of painstaking trial and error and diligent development would seem inured to problems in the vineyard. However, just past the mid-point of the 19th century, the winegrowers of France found that nature can be brutal and devastating.

Phylloxera, the "Trojan bug"

It was the last half of the 19th century. The vignerons had only recently conquered the oidium or powdery mildew, a disease that rots the green parts and prevents the grapes from ripening properly. But now the vines were mysteriously becoming sick and dying, and no one seemed to know why. Eventually it was determined to be a root louse. The venerable French vineyards were now set back to square one by an insect so small that a hand lens is needed to make out any of its details.

The tiny critter that dealt such havoc to the vineyards carries the exalted name of *Phylloxera vastatrix*. The scientific terminology is a combination of Greek and Latin words. In Greek *phyllox* means leaf and *xeros*, dry. In its naming, the entomologist assumed that it was female or hermaphroditic. The Latin word *vastatrix* identifies it as a ravager.

Leaf galls are involved in the complex life-cycle of the insect but it does its real "homicidal" work on the roots. It literally sucks the life out of them, while exuding a poisonous juice into the wound. (No matter that most of the devastators die with their vineplant victim. The pest has provided for perpetuity by a "fail-safe" life-cycle in which an unbelievable number of individuals are produced from a single egg.)

Devastation of the vineyards by the small louse wasn't a season's bad dream, nor did it occur overnight. The epoch spanned 30 years from symptoms, through sickness and widespread death to diagnosis, cure, and eventual restoration to health of the vineyards. It has been over 100 years since the depredation, but the criminal is still at large in vineyards throughout the world and no chemical has been developed to eradicate it.

The eventual solution to the catastrophe that had struck the French wine industry was the grafting of French *vinifera* scions on phylloxera-resistant American rootstocks. It was no easy task to convince the proud French vignerons that their noble vines had to be grafted onto rootstocks of American ancestry. So, the those charged with resolving the problem were even further back than square one; for in addition to finding out which *vinifera* scions were compatible with which grafting stocks, they had to learn which American rootstocks were most adaptable to which French soils. In the desperate search, the value of the work of Thomas V. Munson, a plant scientist in Denison, Texas, proved immeasurable (*see* boxed feature on page 49).

Munson's home was on the high south bank of the Red River which separates Texas and Oklahoma. Munson had located his plant nursery there because the area offered a variety of soils, numerous wild grapevines, and a climate subject to sudden, severe changes. His grapevine collection was planted in a dozen experimental plots of different soils provided by narrow bands of Cretaceous sandstones, marls, and limestones. By his own account, no better location could have been found in which to test varieties of vines against diseases and the elements. (Dr. Roy Renfro, Director of the T. V. Munson Memorial Viticulture and Enology Center, and Millard Brent, professor of geology at Grayson County College in Denison, attempted to locate these experimental grounds for me, but unfortunately the areas are now under shopping centers and housing developments.)

**Photograph 1.5
Thomas Volney Munson, 1843–1913**
The name of the plant scientist from Denison may not be as well known as Burbank, but when you contemplate a glass of fine wine, give a toast to Dr. Munson. He had a lot to do with your having it today

Initially, most of the rootstocks for grafting had been obtained from the sandy soils in the eastern U.S., but these did not match the makeup of the French vineyards; many of the fine-wine areas of France being largely on limestone or chalky soils. Then, in 1887, the French Ministry of Agriculture sent a special delegation to America to identify vines that thrived on chalky soils. Once again the help of Munson was enlisted by Pierre Viala, a professor of viticulture, who was selected to head the French delegation.

Eventually the mission found the vines they sought in the limestone hills around Austin, San Antonio, and along the edge of the chalky limestone forming the "Black Land" cotton belt of Texas. (Interestingly, a young wine industry is developing today in this limestone Hill Country of central Texas.) The *Vitis berlandieri* was found to be doing well in these soils, and Munson's experimental plots showed that the *Vitis rupestris* also did well in limy soils. Munson emphasized that the soil conditions and climate under which each variety thrived must be learned. Not all American rootstocks were phylloxera-proof, and serious errors were made by some French planters who violated Munson's "adaptation" principle.

As phylloxera spread, scions of noble grapevines were being grafted onto rootstocks whose ancestors were crude frontier types from America. The pest was brought under control, but the prize originally offered by the French government was never awarded. George Ordish, in *The Great Wine Blight,* relates that the French horticulturist Léopold Lailman claimed the prize for his work on grafting (*see* opposite), but was denied. The review council admitted that Lailman's work was important, but contended that at no time did he try to destroy the insect.

Phylloxera continues to exist in most of the world's vineyards but the pest has difficulty maintaining its life-cycle in sandy soils. It has no natural enemies, and still no pesticides have been developed to eradicate it. Researchers and growers work continuously to achieve a balance or "threshold of tolerance" between the deadly pest and various, resistant rootstocks.

Dr. Jeffrey Granett of the Department of Entomology, at the University of California in Davis, took his sabbatical in 1987 to work on phylloxera biotypes with Professor D. Doubails at the National Viticultural School in Montpellier, France. In personal correspondence with me, Dr. Granett commented that the European vignerons use only rootstocks with a high level of phylloxera resistance in order to prevent any phylloxera from thriving and growing; whereas in California, the rootstock commonly used is less resistant, but has been satisfactory – until recently.

Phylloxera "die-out" in the vineyards has already reached quite alarming proportions in several areas of California. Dr. Granett is of the opinion that the bug itself has been subtly evolving almost from the beginning. He warns that hardy strains of phylloxera are now beginning to develop in both Europe and North America, and emphasizes the need to redouble the research effort and strengthen exchange and cooperation between winegrowers, researchers, biotechnicians, and involved institutions in the United States and abroad. It will be a race to stay ahead of the "Trojan bug" which now has "fifth columns" under every vineyard.

Phylloxera: scourge of the French vineyards

The first recorded account of the mysterious plant sickness was in November, 1867, in southern France. Soon afterwards a commission was formed which set about investigating the problem. Among those on the commission was Professor Planchon of Montpellier University.

In his privately published dissertation, Professor G. J. Gilbank relates how Planchon reasoned correctly that the origin of the illness was to be found on the living plants, not on the roots of dead ones. Planchon had noticed that all the dying vines had small, yellow insects on their roots, in some cases so numerous they appeared as a yellow varnish. A hand lens showed the insect to have the appearance of an aphid similar to *Phylloxera quercus* found on the underside of oak leaves. It was on this basis that Planchon gave the new insect the name *Phylloxera vastatrix*. He further maintained that this enemy could only be fought if all stages of the insect's life-cycle were known.

To "know the enemy" is a sound maxim for any confrontation whether it be war or insect control. For this enemy, it was more easily advocated than done. Unraveling the life-cycle of vastatrix was enormously complicated because of polymorphism (existance in several forms) and the unbelievable numbers of individuals produced at certain stages.

The rather sudden appearance of the insect was puzzling until it was recalled that in 1858 and 1862 a considerable number of rooted American vines had been imported in personal exchange by growers and plant scientists. The specimens had gone to Bordeaux and to Pujaut in the southern Rhône where phylloxera had been first reported. This "Trojan bug" had gotten into France due to the laxity of controls in shipping botanical specimens without inspections. The friendly act of American horticulturists had been to export a devastating "louse." Again Planchon reasoned, if the pest had come from America, would not the answer to its control be found there?

Meanwhile, the phylloxera continued its inexorable spread. Reaction was slow. France was caught up in events more exciting than bug control: the Great Exhibition in Paris in 1867; the opening of the Suez Canal in 1869, and in 1870, declaration of war on Germany by Louis-Napoleon, the elected president-cum-emperor. However, the government did take enough note of the phylloxera crisis to appoint a new commission within the Ministry of Agriculture and offered a prize of 300,000 francs to be awarded to the "inventor of the cure." Hundreds of charlatans looking for a fast franc offered an unbelievable assortment of absurd cures, including burying a live toad under the vine to draw off the poison. Some clergy were certain that the phylloxera was God's punishment for the vices of the age. In 1873 the French horticulturist Léopold Lailman was the first to suggest grafting French scions on American roots. His suggestion received little notice at the time.

After five years of evaluation of proposed solutions, two schools of attack emerged: a chemical or insecticide treatment and a biological or botanical approach (grafting). The "chemists" used carbon bisulfate, a dangerous chemical, but with some apparent success. Those advocating the grafting of European vines on immune American rootstock were known as the "Americanist" school. The failure of the "chemists" approach was that it offered some control of a phase of phylloxera's life-cycle, but the overwhelming reproduction phase assured the bug's inexorable march of destruction.

Pierre Viala, an expert on fungi diseases and later professor of viticulture at the Institut Agronomique National in Paris, suggested in 1908 that the resistance of American plants to phylloxera was probably the result of natural selection, and therefore a guarantee of the permanence of its resistance. (At that time, the natural selection theory of the English scientist, Charles Darwin, was new and very controversial; 30 years earlier he had been refused admission to the French Academy of Science in 1872 by a vote of over two to one.)

French and American entomologists and viticulturists exchanged visits and engaged in extensive correspondence. Viala was selected by his government to go to America to learn what he could about phylloxera-resistant vines. Viala's mentor in the U.S. was Thomas Volney Munson, the plant scientist in Denison, Texas, who had built up an extensive collection of both wild and domestic grapevines identified with the soils which they preferred and their degree of resistance to phylloxera and other diseases. Munson has been proclaimed as "the Texan who saved the French vineyards." This is an exaggeration by a later fellow Texan, Avery McClurg, but the name Munson is better known in French historical viticultural circles than in America. In recognition of Munson's contribution, the French government had already, in 1889, awarded Munson and the American entomologist C. V. Riley the Chevalier du Mérite Agricole and the Légion d'Honneur for their great assistance with the phylloxera problem.

The part that man played

Pests, the weather, good and bad yearly vicissitudes of the market – growing wine requires patience as well as hard work. Above all, it requires a population with a love of the land. Henri Berr, the French historian and scholar, suggests that it was the Celts who made the France of today. To know something of the population that identified the vineyard sites, improved the soils, and found the grapes best suited to them is an adjunct element to the wines of France.

The Celtic inheritance

Countless generations have come and gone since the Celts and Romans melded into the Gallo-Romans population. It has been 15 centuries since invasions by the Franks, Burgundians, and Visigoths injected that population with the vigor of raw but talented people. Yet Professor Berr says that the blood and bones of France today are mainly composed of Celtic elements.

Despite the Celts being popularly depicted as fierce, war-like barbarians conquered with some difficulty by the Romans, the two adversaries had a mutual admiration for the other's culture. It was the Celtic love of the land that kept alive the spirit of an "undestroyable people of peasants." Professor Berr also points out that it was the Celts who identified and cultivated some of the best soil, and made judicious choices of dwelling-places and location of roads.

Indeed, the Celts have been described as "madly fond of war," but they were first and foremost farmers and stock-raisers. They were also great smithies, and forged the iron plow as well as the two-edged sword. They made seamless iron rims for the wheels of their chariots and wagons, and were the first to shoe horses. They knew how to employ slope farming, as well as cultivate level ground. Camille Jullian, the French historian, says there are those who would have Rome giving Gaul the priceless gift of agriculture, but he contends that what Rome did for agriculture in Gaul was to bring peace and order to the land.

It was certainly the Romans who improved the primitive roadways, creating an impressive network of well-drained and surfaced roads for military control and commerce. The historic development of man and key events in France after the arrival of Caesar is traced in the time chart opposite.

Monks and wine

The great network of Roman roads helped the cross to follow the Roman eagle into Gaul. As Henry and Carol Faul observed in *It Began With a Stone*, Christianity was a way of life which the caesars never dreamed would be their most permanent export. It spread and caught on like nothing else the Romans ever adopted into their culture.

For three centuries the Romans persecuted Christians, then in 313, the Emperor Constantine issued the Edict of Milan making Christianity lawful. Ironically, it became the official religion of the Roman Empire. The church in turn copied the Roman organization of governance and administration. The barbarian "warrior-kings" trained for battle, but were poorly equipped for peaceful administration. Consequently, the church acted as a constructive and stabilizing force. Church and state developed together, sometimes competing, sometimes supporting each other, sometimes being one and the same.

Time Graph of French History (Log Scale)

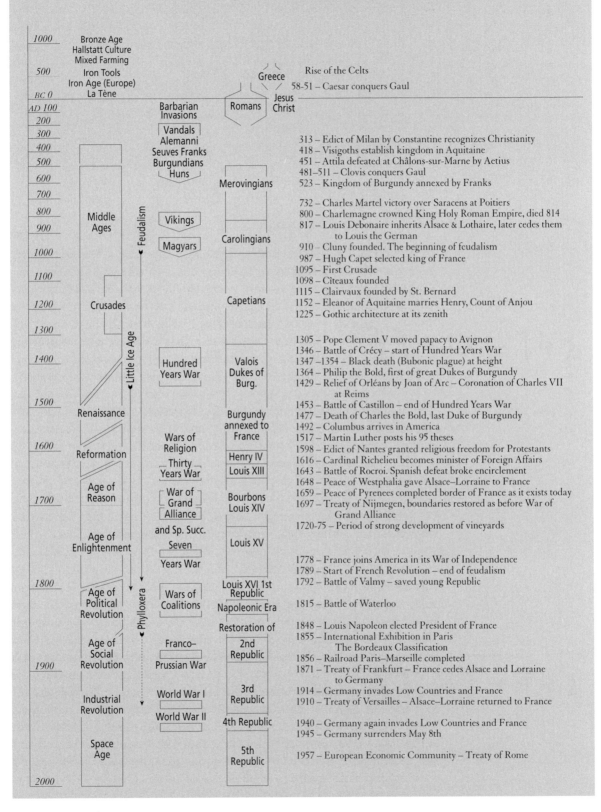

Monasticism was an early development of legalized Christianity. The monastic orders came early to western Europe and spread quickly. It was natural that viticulture became a vocation of the monks, as manual labor, particularly agriculture, was one of the threefold divisions of the daily life of most of the orders. Moreover, wine was needed for liturgical services.

Monasteries were obliged to host travelers of all types, including the entire entourage of high-ranking personages. Keeping wine in stock for such large companies was a serious concern. It was important that well-to-do people look back on a warm and congenial stay. They paid well.

Desmond Seward, in his unique study *Monks and Wine,* asserts that it was the monks who were largely responsible for saving viticulture during the Dark Ages (Middle Ages). He suggests that the monks alone had the security, resources, and patience to improve the quality of their vines. William Younger in *Gods, Men and Wine* questions the pivotal position of the early church in advancing viticulture. Younger, as well as others, contend that it was private enterprise and oral traditions of lay vignerons and not the monasteries that brought winegrowing through the Middle Ages.

Seward and Younger are both right; the efforts were not mutually exclusive. Without question, the Benedictines and Cistercians were excellent viticulturists; their knowledge of good farming methods was multiplied by lay brothers and observant neighbors. The font of monastic viticulture were the Benedictines of Cluny and the Cistercians of Cîteaux, both estates in Burgundy. Viticulture particularly flourished under the Valois dukes of Burgundy in the 15th century (*see* chapter 4).

For the most part, vineyards of the church coexisted peacefully with those of the laity. In Alsace, however, the abbeys were particularly aggressive, and conflicts with nobles and other winegrowers were sometimes violent.

Other ecclesiastical orders as well as the Benedictines and Cistercians owned and developed many fine-wine properties, but by no means did the church have a monopoly on good French vineyards. Members of the nobility, and in time, persons of wealth also owned vineyards as part of their estates. During the early Middle Ages, a social order developed around wealthy land owners that became known as feudalism.

Feudalism

The term feudalism, coined by more recent historians, developed in France out of political unrest and economic uncertainty. In the Middle Ages (approximately A.D. 500–1500), Christianity was the dominant religion in western Europe and feudalism the common form of local and regional government. The kingdom was generally too poor — and often too poorly led — to provide adequate protection for its subjects from local bandits and foreign raiders like the Vikings. Lords of lands of various sizes began to assume responsibility for the protection of their local populations. In return, the people owed the lord fealty and service. For many centuries feudalism proved a satisfactory arrangement — everyone understood the "rules of the game." Although feudalism and Christianity were antithetical in many ways, together they moved civilization forward in France, and with it wine.

The term "Dark Ages" is an alternative term for Middle Ages. Middle Ages is the translation of medieval (or mediaeval) from the Latin, *midi*, middle plus *aevum*, age. The term was coined by Italian writers in the 15th century for the period from the end of the Roman Empire to the time which they thought was going to be a rebirth of the Greco/Roman age.

The root of this term is of Germanic origin: *feh, feo* or *fihu*, relating to cattle. Fief, a variant on the same root was a grant of land with a right of succession. Our word "fee," relating to property, is derived from fief.

In similar ways that wine was essential to the church, so it was to the feudal lords; it was a symbol of hospitality. To have insufficient wine on hand in order properly to receive an important guest, even if his arrival was unexpected, put the entire household in a dither. People of position in the wine regions had vineyards and generally produced wine in excess of castle needs – just to be on the safe side. Wine presses were expensive, and those who could afford them pressed wine for those who could not. Estate winemaking was born of this economic and social system.

Early in the 9th century, the Carolingians were the first to make grants of land (fiefs) in return for service to the Crown such as military support. The land grants were linked with a personal bond (vassalage). Under the principle of feudalism, fealty was pledged by men to lords of various ranks, lords to kings, lords to other lords, and even kings to kings.

Resentment of English kings having to pay homage to the French crown was at the root of the Hundred Years War (1337–1453). The vassalage of English kings to the French crown was inherited from the French expatriates, Henry of Anjou and Eleanor of Aquitaine. As a French count, before becoming king of England, Henry had sworn allegiance to the king of France.

The prolonged conflict involving particularly the region of Bordeaux probably had more lasting affect on wine than any other war in French history. The wine industry of Bordeaux as wine cellar to England grew enormously. The fondness of the English for their Bordeaux "claret" became permanent.

Concurrently, the lavish life-style of the Valois dukes greatly enhanced viticulture in Burgundy, and wine as a symbol of the court. The Valois courts were the trend-setters for the courts of western Europe.

In the feudal system, the majority of the peasants were serfs, a condition of servitude little different from slavery. Serfs had no freedom of movement nor legal rights. On the other hand, there were "free peasants," who were essentially tenant farmers. They gave service or shares of their production in return for protection, land to work, or a place to ply their trade. Feudalism and these forms of servitude would end with the French Revolution in 1789. They were replaced by new social orders and forms of government.

From the Middle to the Modern Ages

As the Middle Ages and feudalism approached their end, our "time machine" goes into fast forward with the Renaissance in France, followed quickly by the Reformation and Wars of Religion. Unfortunately, the particularly bloody Wars of Religion distorted Christianity into personal and permanent biases within the population.

Other wars and boundary struggles kept France in almost constant turmoil for centuries. Viticulture suffered ups and downs with the conflicts, but wine became a vital part of the national economy as well as the social amenity. The wineglass was the emblem of a cultural life-style.

By the 18th century, the population had become more literate and politically more questioning; feudal bonds became fragmented. As in the restlessness of birds before migration, there was a stirring in the land. The peasant was fed up with tithes and taxes. With the stoicism of a peasant, he went to the fields, went to church, went to war for his lord. Now it was time to go to revolution. A revolution not intended to be violent, but as often happens, that is the way it turned out. The revolutionary government confiscated large estates and ecclesiastical properties and put them at the "disposal of the state," that is, they were sold at auction. Thus many formerly large vineyards were fragmented and saw new owners.

As Olivier Bernier describes in the Afterword of his book *Words of Fire, Deeds of Blood*, the country that emerged from the great revolutionary storm had little resemblance to the old France, except geographical location. Much of its population, which had been landless, now owned enough acreage to prosper. This did not mean, however, that everyone had "forty acres and a mule." Often it was the original owners (except the church) who were wealthy enough to buy back at least some of their former vineyard property.

Napoleon's ascendancy was a product of post-revolutionary changes which allowed the rise in military rank on the basis of ability and not title. Importantly, a product of the Napoleonic era was a code of property inheritance in which all heirs share. Accordingly, vineyard tracts of various size began to be divided. The result is that many vineyards have numerous owners, some with only a few rows of vines. For example, the large 125-acre (50 ha) Clos de Vougeot in Burgundy has 90 owners – and counting. In such circumstances of multiple ownership, it is difficult for all the owners to agree on such tasks as fertilizing, pest control, and frost protection. Moreover, each owner may vinify and market his own wine under the name of the property. The result is that only a very few wines solely represent a vineyard of great reputation.

In historical perspective, the French population has evolved since the 6th century with only minor additions to its racial mix. André Maurois, the great French historian, says "There has never been a French race," going on to note that the mixture of peoples saved France from the "eternal provincialism of central Europe," which is so distressingly confusing today.

There were sad and extreme losses of vignerons in two World Wars. There has been a serious exodus of farm workers to city and industrial jobs. Changes will continue in the wine areas, but tradition and pride are steadfastly strong. There are tasks in the vineyard that only the heart and hand can do. That ruddy-faced old vigneron with hands as gnarled as the vines he has tended all his life may have Celtic, Frankish, or Burgundian elements in his blood and bones. What he has for certain is a love of the land and a willingness to work hard. He is a vital element to turn the habitat of the vineplant into the great French wines.

Appendices

Terroir, a unique French term

Terroir has become a buzz word in English language wine literature. This lighthearted use disregards reverence for the land which is a critical, invisible element of the term. The true concept is not easily grasped but includes physical elements of the vineyard habitat – the vine, subsoil, siting, drainage, and microclimate. Beyond the measurable ecosystem, there is an additional dimension – the spiritual aspect that recognizes the joys, the heartbreaks, the pride, the sweat, and the frustrations of its history. Because terroir is so meaningful, let's help to define it by considering how some of the wine experts have described the concept.

To understand the wines of the Côte d'Or, Matt Kramer maintains that one must understand the concept of terroir. He points out that the physical attributes are not too difficult to comprehend, but there is what he calls the "mental aspect." Kramer's explanation of "mental aspect" is that winegrowers feel each terroir should be allowed to be itself and produce the wine for which nature endowed it. The winemaker's "signature" (vinification style) is permissible, so long as it does not substitute for terroir. That is, vinification should not make the wine taste significantly different than the "natural" wine that would be produced from a particular tract.

In the *Wine Atlas of France*, Hugh Johnson expresses essentially the same interpretation: "the land itself chooses the crop that suits it best." Otherwise, he says, "Why have all French growers not settled for the same grapes, the same techniques, the same ideal of what a good wine should be?" For Johnson, a sense of place, an awareness of terroir, is the key to understanding the wines of France. He suggests that knowing sidestreets, lanes, and history, intensifies this sense of place. (I would suggest that knowing the geology of a vineyard also gives it a special identity.)

Gérard Seguin, the Bordeaux enologist, laments that there are no in-depth studies of the ecosystem of terroir, and suggests it is because of the many factors involved. This lack of studies is particularly regrettable, says Séguin, for terroir plays an important role in the quality of wines. By his definition, quality terroirs are where the habitat permits complete but slow maturation of the grapes.

Daniel Querre, a grower in St.-Emilion and onetime General Attorney for the Jurade de Saint-Emilion, questions any attempt to explain a particular terroir, if only its obvious physical conditions are described. He points out that grapevines find something "precious – almost sacred" in their deep rooting. He compares the deep rooting of vines to the incense (gum) tree in the arid lime-stone country of Somaliland. He admits that many might shrug their shoulders at this "something," but he asks how else can we explain the sensory differences between two wines grown under the same physical conditions. Without the mystery of the "unknown something," Querre says, "I cannot explain how, simply by smelling it, one can distinguish a 'Cheval' from a 'Figeac'."

The writers of Larousse's *Wines and Vineyards of France* emphasize the mental aspect of terroir, it being the link visualized by a consumer between his wine and the winegrower who produced it.

In a commercial example, the British magazine *The Economist* describes how the concept of terroir has been used by the French to counter efforts by the European Union (the E.U., formerly E.C.) to deal with wine simply as a "brand" (a class of goods) in international trade. The French contend that good (and great) wine can come only from certain severely limited environments – the terroirs. The terroir pinpoints the geographical location of a vineyard with a specific climate, soil, and exposure. In other words, a wine is not just a commodity like sugar beet, but a distinct product from a unique place.

In the commodity sense, U.S. wine writer and critic Robert Parker says, "Think of *terroir* as you do salt, pepper, and garlic. In many dishes these flavorings represent an invaluable component, imparting wonderful aromas and character. But if consumed alone, they are usually difficult to swallow." Among other factors beyond *terroir* that influence the style of the wine, Parker suggests discovering the producers who make wines worth drinking and enjoying.

In all honesty, some question whether it is a valued term at all. I puzzle at their real appreciation of wine. The name slips easily into – or through – one's silent reading vocabulary, but if one wishes to pronounce it, it is *tair-wahr*.

Terroir may sound pedantic, strange, and certainly "foreign." Why not just use the more familiar word "vineyard" – especially in a book avowed to be easily readable? As a matter of fact, I confess that I am inconsistent in the use of terroir and vineyard. My intent has been to reserve the use of terroir for specifically named quality vineyards. I trust there will be a mutual Franco-American tolerance for my lack of consistency. Hopefully, this explanation will acquaint the reader with the term and its meaning so that it slips comfortably into, rather than through the reader's vocabulary.

Glossary of geologic, geographic, and wineland terms

Throughout the text a special effort has been made to put technical and unfamiliar terms into everyday language or explain them parenthetically. Nevertheless, a glossary allows elaboration and illustration of certain terms. Terms are listed alphabetically and identified as to category by an applicable abbreviation: (Geol) for geologic and landform terms; (FrTopo) for French topographic terms; and (WnT) for wineland terms.

Alluvium (Geol) general term for unconsolidated erosional material deposited in comparatively recent (q.v.) geologic time: gravel, sand, mud. Ancient alluvium may often become conglomerate (q.v.).

Ampelography (WnT) (Gr, *ampelos*, vine and *graphe*, description)the scientific description and identification of grapevines.

Appellation (WnT) French designation or identifying name of a defined (delimited) wine area.

Appellation d'Origine Contrôlée (A.O.C.) (WnT) the controlled or guaranteed place-name of origin. The concept came into being about 55 years ago and is the highest rank of three categories of delimitation classification in France. Below A.O.C. are "Vin Délimité de Qualité Supérieure" (V.D.Q.S., q.v.) and "Vin de Pays" (q.v.), the latter in reality the most dynamic of the two tiers. Wines within a broad appellation, but not otherwise classified are *appellation communale*. – *.commune* (q.v.) wines.

Appellation boundaries are precisely outlined on land survey maps (*see* cadastre) and regulated by the I.N.A.O. (q.v.). Legally, one may grow grapes anywhere in France, but if the wine is marketed to the public as a "Product of France," it must conform to very restrictive regulations.

Arkose (Geol) coarse-grained sandstone composed primarily of feldspars (q.v.), pink or reddish in color. The grains, usually derived from nearby granite, are typically angular and poorly sorted. (*See also* Graywacke.)

Basalt (Geol) (typically lava)a dark-colored igneous rock (q.v.) composed of fine-grained crystals of feldspars (q.v.). Basalts normally weather rapidly into good soil.

Basement (Geol) general term for very old rocks associated with the earth's crust. An undifferentiated rock complex which has been exposed by uplift and erosion.

Bioherm (Geol) mound, lens, or reef-like mass of corals, algae, and other marine animals and plants that attach themselves to rock surfaces, to each other or to accumulated debris.

Block diagram (Geol) three-dimensional drawing showing the surface and cross-sectional views of the front and side of a segment of the earth's crust. Most of the illustrations in this glossary are block diagrams.

Breccia (Geol) coarse-grained, clastic rock (q.v.) composed of angular fragments cemented together by a ground-water precipitate. Breccia differs from a conglomerate (q.v.) whose fragments are more rounded like gravel.

Butte (Geol) an isolated hill usually an erosional separation from a mesa or plateau. The top may be flat or rounded depending on the nature of the rocks. *See* sketch under cap rock. Butte is also a French term, but coteau (q.v.) is the more commonly used.

Cadastre (FrTopo) the French term for the local land survey or registry. (The term has the same meaning in the United States although it is seldom used.) The cadastre is a very precise instrument survey showing boundaries and ownership of all properties including vineyards. The originals are kept by the I.N.A.O. with copies lodged in each *mairie* (town hall) of the respective communes (q.v.).

Canton and Arrondisement (FrTopo) territorial terms which seldom enter the wine vocabulary. These are administrative units for various civil and police functions.

Cap rock (Geol) a hard rock layer overlying weaker, more easily eroded strata. The cap rock may be flat as indicated in the sketch.

If it is steeply tilted, the cap rock forms a hogback – a sharp ridge like the backbone of a wild hog. *See* sketch under dip.

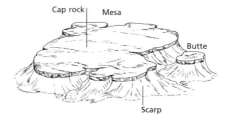

Causse (FrTopo) limestone plateau generally deeply pitted with sink holes caused by dissolution of the limestone (geological topography known as karst).

Cépage (WnT) meaning vineplant or variety of grapevine. The root stem Cep is a more restrictive term meaning vinestock. Cépage and grape variety (vineplant) are used interchangeably in this book.

Château (WnT) in wine parlance, château does not necessarily mean a great castle; it may be a modest farmhouse. If the term is used on the wine label, it must comply with specific I.N.A.O. regulations: a building and winemaking apparatus must exist with a bona fide vineyard from which wine has been produced and sold for some period of time. *Mis en bouteille au Château* means wine bottled by the Château from grapes grown on properties of the château. The statement is one guarantee of authenticity of origin, but not necessarily of quality.

Chert (Geol) dense, compact sedimentary rock composed of microscopic crystals of quartz. It typically forms in pockets and nodules rather than layers.

Clastic(s) (Geol) general term for a rock or sediments derived from preexisting rocks and transported some distance from the source. The fragments may be small or large, sharp or rounded. Reference is usually to sandstones, silts, and shales, but may include conglomerates, arkoses, etc.

Clay (Geol) in physical appearance, an earthy, extremely fine-grained, soft rock. Microscopically, it is composed of platy minerals that require ultra high magnification such as electron imagery (illustrated in Part One, page 27). (*Also see* shale and marl.)

Cluse (FrTopo) an Alpine term meaning a sharp valley transverse to the long axis of a structural fold or ridge.

Col (FrTopo) mountain pass, e.g., the Col du Somport.

Colline(s) (FrTopo) hill (*see* the more comonly used term, coteau).

Combe (FrTopo) deep, narrow notch normally along the edge of a plateau or scarp (*see* sketch of alluvial fan under Fan).

Commune (FrTopo) the smallest civic administrative unit in France and the basic geographic wine reference. It comprises a village and the surrounding land. The name of the chief town is often used synonymously for commune. Communes were originally ecclesiastical subdivisions, designed to allocate the local population according to the size of the parish churches. The commune is governed by an elected council and a mayor (*Maire*) who is in turn elected by the council. Napoleon recognized the efficacy of communes and reaffirmed them as part of the civic structure. Smaller settlements which rate a road sign are *hameaux* (hamlets).

Conglomerate (Geol) coarse-grained, poorly sorted sedimentary rock composed of rounded or sub-round fragments. The fragments may vary in size from small pebbles up to cobbles or boulders. The mass may also contain sand and silt and be cemented with calcium carbonate, iron oxide, silica or clay.

Contours (Geol) lines on topographic map joining points of equal elevation. The interval chosen between the levels will depend on the amount of relief or differences in elevations within an area (*see also* hachures.)

Côte (FrTopo) ridge or edge of plateau, e.g. Côte d'Or, or plural Côtes du Rhône. May be single, prominent hill, e.g. Côte de Brouilly.

Coteau (FrTopo) hill or knoll (*colline*) used most commonly in the plural, e.g. Coteaux de Touraine.

Cru and Growth (WnT) terms frequently used interchangeably, but are not truly synonymous. Cru applies to a specific vineyard and the wine it produces – traditionally one of superior quality. In Burgundy, "cru" is normally combined with an adjective or modifier such as Grand Cru or Premier Cru. The term growth has a more complicated definition with different meanings in different parts of France. When it is referring to the growing area of a specific wine, it is the equivalent of cru. For example, in Bordeaux, growth designates a single estate (château) and can only be applied to the wines produced from it, such as Château Latour, First Growth. "Classed" or "classified growths" can only be used in a title in Bordeaux and refer to a wine in one of the five classifications of 1855.

In 1954, a hierarchal classification for St.-Emilion was approved with the top grade combining the terms Premier Grand Cru Classé.

In Cognac, "growth" refers to large areas of production such as Fin-Bois, or in Armagnac, Tenaréze. In Champagne, it corresponds to commune rating; in southwest France, the term generally relates to a châteaux.

Cuvette (FrTopo) a topographic bowl.

Dark minerals (Geol) refer to the color of a group of minerals such as biotite (black mica), hornblende, and augite (complex ferro-magnesium compound), found in granites and other igneous rocks. Typically these minerals weather easily along with feldspars (q.v.).

Degree (Geol) *see* Gradient.

Degree (WnT) measure of alcoholic strength: one degree of alcohol is equivalent to its percentage by volume.

Département (FrTopo) the largest administrative sub-division in France. Involved with wine primarily in a political way. It is governed by a préfet appointed by the central government, but with a locally elected council. Départements were created by the Revolutionary Assembly in the 1790s to replace the old traditional provinces and help eradicate the feudal system.

Detritus (noun) or **detrital** (adjective) (Geol) "waste rock" – a general term applied to erosional material derived from outside their site of deposition – usually applied to rapidly formed accumulations in basins or rivers or at the foot of a mountain.

Dip and Strike (Geol) companion terms. Dip is the angle at which a layer or strata are inclined from the horizontal. Strike is the lateral direction at right angles to the dip. Strike is also applied to the long direction of a fault or shoreline.

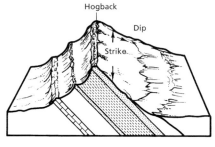

Dolomite (Geol) sedimentary rock of which more than half is calcium-magnesium carbonate.

Dome (Geol and FrTopo) the English term for a partial sphere describing a similar uplift of strata or topographic feature.

Enology (WnT) *see* Oenology.

Eolian (from Aeolus, god of the winds) (Geol) the term applied to deposits that are moved or have been carried by the wind, e.g. sand dunes, loess (q.v.) often found in residual pockets or coverings on plateaux.

Facies, (fay-sheez) (L., *face*) (Geol) an environmental condition. The appearance of a rock unit as it differs from an adjacent unit with which it is associated. The time lines in the diagram indicate that, although the adjacent (lateral) sedimentation conditions are different, they were deposited at the same time. The sawtooth lines represent **facies change**, the shifting back and forth of environmental conditions, as the sediments accumulated.

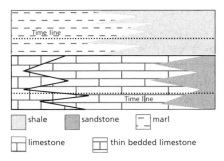

shale sandstone marl limestone thin bedded limestone

Falaise (FrTopo) a cliff or scarp (q.v.), most commonly used in a landscape name. *Faille* is fault in French.

Fan or **alluvial fan** (Geol) the detritus (q.v.) which spreads out from a narrow source into a valley or plain in the shape of a flattened cone or ladies' open fan. The French term is "cône de déjection." The surface of the fan flattens at a decreasing rate outward. The soils are normally well drained in the higher parts, but the outer margins may interfinger with valley sediments and be affected

by a shallow water table. The Cone of Lannemezan on the south side of the Pyrenees below Tarbes is a giant alluvial fan.

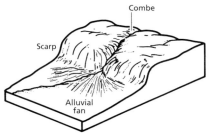

Fault(s) (Geol) a fracture or zone of fractures where the two sides are relatively displaced. Faults are classified according to the manner of displacement and angle of the plane of slippage – the fault plane. A **normal fault** is where the sense of movement is up–down, and the fault plane is at a relatively high angle. In an **overthrust fault** an upper block overrides a lower block on a near horizontal plane (*see* Figure 11.2)

Faulting in the Saône–Rhine graben of Alsace and Burgundy is of the normal type. There may be some lateral movement. Faulting in the Jura, Savoie, Southern Rhône, Provence, and Languedoc is primarily of the overthrust style.

Ancillary terms in faulting are throw, upthrown, and downthrown blocks. The relative direction of movement is indicated by arrows in cross-sections.

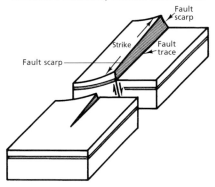

Feldspars (Geol) family of pink or white minerals found in igneous rocks. They are complex silicate compounds containing varying amounts of potassium, sodium, calcium, barium, strontium and iron. On weathering, feldspars decompose to clay minerals releasing most of the accessory elements as mineral nutrients.

Gateway or Gap (Geol) wide, low pass between two basins, e.g. Belfort Gap or Carcassonne Gateway. The French geologic term is *seuil* (q.v.).

Gave (FrTopo) a stream originating as a mountain torrent, local to Pyrenees.

Geography (Geol) the study of all aspects of the earth's surface including its natural and political divisions, the distribution and differentiation of areas created by man.

Geology (Geol) the scientific study of the origin, history, and structure of the earth including the material that composes it.

Geomorphology (Geol) the science that treats with the general configuration of the earth's surface. It includes the classification, description, origin, and development of landforms and their relationship to the underlying geology. The term was coined by the earth-science profession adding geo- to the companion term -morphology to specifically identify earth relationships. Because the term is not familiar outside the earth science field, it is used sparingly in this book.

Graben and Horst (Geol) opposing landforms. A graben is a topographic trough resembling a grave formed by opposing sets of faults whose downthrown sides face each other leaving a central downthrown block or blocks.

In the horst, the downthrown sides of the faults face away from each other, leaving a central upthrown block. The Rhine Valley is a classic example of the graben. A horst is featured in the cross-section of Pouilly-Fuissé in the Burgundy area.

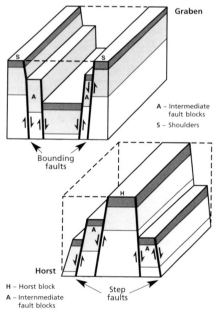

Graben

A – Intermediate fault blocks
S – Shoulders

Bounding faults

Horst

H – Horst block
A – Internmediate fault blocks

Step faults

Gradient (Geol) gradient has two meanings in this book – the angle of slope of the vineyard surface and also applied to the drop of the bed or a stream. Gradient is given in percent which is the number of units (feet or meters) of drop (or vertical rise) of the surface per 100 units in the horizontal direction. A 5-foot drop in 100 feet is a gradient or slope of 5 percent.

The angle of slope may also be given in degrees of arc measured from the horizontal; for example, a 5 percent grade is a slope angle of just under 3 degrees. Stream gradients are usually given in feet per mile or comparative units.

Graywacke (or **Grauwacke**) (Geol) hard, coarse-grained sandstone composed of poorly sorted, angular to subangular grains of quartz and feldspar. It was originally a German miner's term for barren country rock (one containing no minerals).

Growth (WnT) *see* Cru.

Hachures (Geol) convention for indicating terrain relief. The hachure stroke is in the direction of slope; short hachures indicate steep slope, long ones, a more extended slope. Topography of many older maps is indicated by hachures rather than contours.

Horst (Geol) *see* Graben.

Igneous rocks (Geol) have solidified from the molten state such as granites and lavas.

I.N.A.O. (Institut National des Appellations d'Origine des Vins et Eaux-de-Vie) (The National Institute of Appellation Controlled Wines and Spirits) (WnT) a professional-technical body under the Ministry of Agriculture. Its operations and reviews are carried on by a National Committee composed of 24 growers and 12 merchants elected from 10 Regional Committees. The latter are composed of growers and merchants (*see* négociants) in a ratio of two growers to one merchant, and commonly retain technical consultants such as geologists and soil scientists.

I.N.A.O. jurisdiction, extending over all appellations, promulgates regulations almost every aspect of growing, making, and marketing wine: the grape varieties allowed, the method of pruning, the allowable volume of must (q.v.) per hectare, the alcohol content of the wine, etc.

Karst (Geol) limestone plateau with many sink holes caused by underground solution. The term comes from the province of Kars on the Adriatic coast of the former Yugoslavia where this terrain is typically developed.

Landform (Geol) any recognizable physical feature of the earth's surface having a characteristic shape and formed by natural causes, e.g. mounds, plateaux, scarps, etc.

Leached or **leaching** (Geol) results from the dissolving and removal of certain soluble constituents from soil or rock. The leached compounds may be precipitated or concentrated at a lower level in soils, or they may be removed entirely.

Lithology (L-G, *lithos*, stone) (Geol) the physical character or description of a rock, e.g., a dark, hard, sandy limestone.

Loess, pronounced luss (Geol) from German dialect "löss," meaning "loose." The term was applied to deposits of fine-grained, wind-blown silt and sand by the peasants and brickmakers along the Rhine Valley. It is homogenous, porous, and friable, but coherent enough to erode in steep walls.

Loessial soils are some of the most fertile in the world, having a high capacity for holding moisture and are thus known as "cool" soils.

Marl (Geol) somewhat loosely used term for earthy, limy clay. The extensive calcareous clays in France are generally referred to as marls.

Massif (Geol) a topographic or structural feature such as a mountain mass. The massif is generally formed of rocks more rigid and older than those surrounding it. Massifs vary in size from a few square miles to those comprising hundreds of square miles, such as the Massif Central.

Metamorphic or **Metamorphics** (Geol) rocks that have been changed from their original state by heat and pressure within the earth's crust. E.g.: clay or shale to slate (q.v.).

Mont or **Montagne** (FrTopo) mount or mountain. Most usually applied to a singular prominence, e.g. Mont Blanc. Montagne is usually a more complex mass of rocks such as the Montagne Noire.

Moraine(s) (Geol) mounds or ridges of unsorted, unstratified rock and soil deposited by glacial ice. Lateral moraines form along the margins of valley glaciers. Terminal moraines build up where the glacier ceased its forward motion.

Morphology (Geol) several applications dealing with form and structure of earth, soil or paleontology. In soil terms, it is the physical and chemical properties of the different soil horizons. In paleontology, it is concerned with the form and structure of animals and plants. *See* Geomorphology.

Must (WnT) grape juice, or crushed grapes in the early fermenting process.

Nappe (Geol) French geologic loan-word whose actual meaning is sheet or tablecloth. Most frequently used in structural geology to describe the overthrust blocks or sheets (q.v.). Also used to describe depositional layers that have "offlapped" one another. As shown in the diagram below, when slope wash successively overwashes earlier layers, they are described as offlapping nappes.

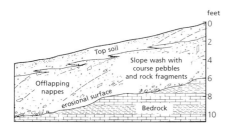

Négociant (WnT) a buyer of wine who cares for, bottles, and ships it. Many négociants are also growers and vice versa. Because of the thousands of small growers in France, the négociant, by collecting wines and merchandising them, is an important link between small growers and consumers.

Nid (FrTopo) topographic pocket or nest.

Oenology (*also* Enology) (WnT) the whole science dealing with wine, its making, its care and its handling. Viticulture (q.v.) has a somewhat similar meaning, but deals more with the cultivation phase.

Orogeny (Geol) literally the process of formation of mountains, including folding, thrusting, and uplift.

Outcrop (Geol) the part of a rock formation that is exposed at the surface.

Pays (FrTopo) country, e.g. *vin de pays*, Haut Pays, upland, or up-country.

Pente (FrTopo) slope or inclination of a hill.

Physiography or **physiographic** (Geol) term earth scientists would like to replace with geomorphology. However, physiography is generally used in this book as it is the more familiar term that refers to the lay of the land. Geomorphology is a more technical sounding term implying origin of the terrain as well as "lay of the land."

Pic (FrTopo) sheer mountain peak, especially in the Pyrenees, e.g., Pic du Midi.

Piedmont (Geol) slightly elevated plain at the foot of a mountain.

Plomb (FrTopo) upright or sheer mountain peak, e.g. Plomb du Cantal.

Puy (FrTopo) prominent remnant of volcanic origin, typically a lava-filled cone, e.g. Puy de Sancy.

Quartzite (Geol) metamorphosed sandstone or chert (q.v.) recrystallized by hot, mineralized ground water and/or regional pressure.

Rau (abbr. for **Ruisseau**) (FrTopo) a small stream or brook.

Recent (Geol) term representing geologic age from the end of the Ice Age to present. Referring specifically to geologic age, the word is capitalized. Otherwise, referring to an indifinite time, it is lower case.

Rift (tectonic) (Geol) zone or system of long, narrow faults of regional extent. Movement is by normal faults. There may also be some lateral slippage (*see* graben).

The combination of faulting and lateral slippage may produce rift valleys, grabens or half grabens. The Rhône, Saône, and Rhine Valleys are sectors of a rift system that extends across western Europe.

Scarp (Geol) abbreviated form for "escarpment" (*see* sketches for cap rock, fan, and fault). Scarp is usually applied to a line of cliffs or steep slopes (*see* falaise).

Schist (Geol) strongly metamorphosed, foliated rock similar to slate (q.v.), usually softer. The original rock is not always identifiable, but may be shale, sandstone, or even granite. It can be readily split or splintered into thin flakes or slabs. Bedrocks of Muscadet and Anjou are largely schists which have weathered into excellent soils.

Scree (Geol) fragments of rocks at the base of a steep slope. Scree and talus (q.v.) are often used interchangeably. Strictly speaking, scree is the material that makes up a talus slope.

Seuil (FrTopo) threshold or sill or broad gateway or watershed between two basins, e.g., Seuil du Poitou between the Loire Valley and the Aquitaine Basin.

Shale (Geol) fine-grained, detrital sedimentary rock; compressed/consolidated clay, silt or mud, typically laminated.

Sheet (Geol) term to describe a relatively thin spreading of sand, gravel, lava, etc. Essentially the same as the French nappe.

Slate (Geol) compact, fine-grained rock, metamorphosed from shale or silt. Slate can be split into thin plates used in roofing.

Slope wash (Geol) non-technical term for "colluvium" or "solifluction." *See* sketch under nappe. The term slope wash is used in this book, as it is clearly suggestive of material that has moved down a slope whether by rain wash (colluvium) or over frozen ground (solifluction).

Talus (Geol) the sloping pile of rock fragments accumulated at the base of a steep slope or scarp (q.v.). By some usages, it is synonymous with scree (q.v.). When talus or scree has been redeposited as strata, it may be referred to as detritus (q.v.).

Tectonics (Geol) branch of geology dealing with the broad architecture of the earth's crust. It is a useful term but because of its formidable appearance is sparingly used in this book.

Terrace (Geol) a long, narrow, relatively level, shelf-like surface or bench bordering a stream or body of water.

Normally a stream will erode or cut a bench, then in a later phase, deposit terrace "fill" on it. The terrace fill is composed of gravel, sands or mud, typically in lenticular and irregular beds. As flood waters which overflowed the banks recede, their carrying capacity weakens and they "drop" their load of sediments as "fill."

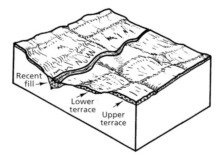

Terrain (Geol) physical features of a geographical area, generally with a descriptive adjective, e.g., chalky terrain, hilly terrain, etc. (*see* Topogeaphy).

Terroir (WnT) *see* definition, page 55.

Topography (Geol) general configuration of a land surface, including relief, natural and man-made features. A topographic map portrays topography or relief and other natural and man-made features. Relief is usually indicated by contours (q.v.), hachures (q.v.), or shading.

Val, Vallée (FrTopo) a valley.

Vendange (WnT) wine harvest. *Vendange tardive*, late-harvested crop. *Ban de vendange* is the official permission or signal issued locally that picking may begin.

Versant (FrTopo) decline or down-grade, similar to pente.

Vigneron (WnT) French vineyardist. Many vignerons are growers, who either own the land or may be working it on a share or tenant basis (*métayer* in French).

Vignoble (WnT) vineyard or wine region; *pays de vignobles* means wine district.

Vin Délimité de Qualité Supérieure (V.D.Q.S.) (WnT) ranks below A.O.C. in quality, but it is strictly regulated by I.N.A.O. with defined boundaries. Although of second rank, there are many fine wines in this category.

Vin de Pays (WnT) third rank of appellation wines. The wines must come from within a general appellation outline and conform to appellation criteria. "Wine of the country" usually goes by the regional name such as Vin de Pays du Jardin de la France (Loire).

Vinification (WnT) broad term applied to the making of wine, from fermentation to bottle-ready.

Viticulture (WnT) the science and business of growing wine grapes. Includes the making of wine, but the common usage implies only the agricultural activity.

Water gap (Geol) narrow pass in a ridge through which a stream flows. Such a gap without a stream is a wind gap, but it may have had a stream at one time.

Water table (Geol) underground surface below which the soil is more or less permanently saturated. Its surface usually slopes with the topography, and the level may fluctuate with the seasons. Because the saturated zone excludes air and carbon dioxide, the roots are smothered and grape production is inhibited.

I would like to acknowledge the immense help of the *Glossary of Geology*, edited by the late Robert L. Bates and Julia A. Jackson and published by the American Geological Institute. Their definitions have in some cases been quoted almost verbatim. (My copy of the A.G.I. Glossary was the third edition, 1987.)
James E. Wilson

Part Two:

Where the wines grow

2 Champagne: chalk country

Less than two hours eastbound out of Paris, the Orient Express had stopped at the Epernay station. This was not a coaling stop, but the provisions being taken on board were as essential as engine fuel – enough champagne for the trip to Istanbul and return. In the early 20th century, international travel, particularly by the Orient Express, was the chic thing for wealthy Europeans. Champagne was the drink of the sinfully rich or of those with sinning on their minds.

No such diversions were on my mind that day in Epernay when my car was suddenly hit from the rear, as I was stopping for a changing signal light. The incident caused me to be late for an appointment with the Countess de Maigret, who, at the time, was grande dame of Moët & Chandon's public relations.

Figure 2.1
Champagne: general geology and wine regions
Vineyards lie along the slopes and spurs of the highly indented eastward projection of the Ile de France. Plantings are discontinuous, utilizing the most favorable exposures and soil conditions. The zone of interfingering is all-important to the wine lover: the majority of the best terroirs lie within the continental facies
(interpreted from 1:150,000 geologic map of France, by kind permission of Editions du B.R.G.M., France)

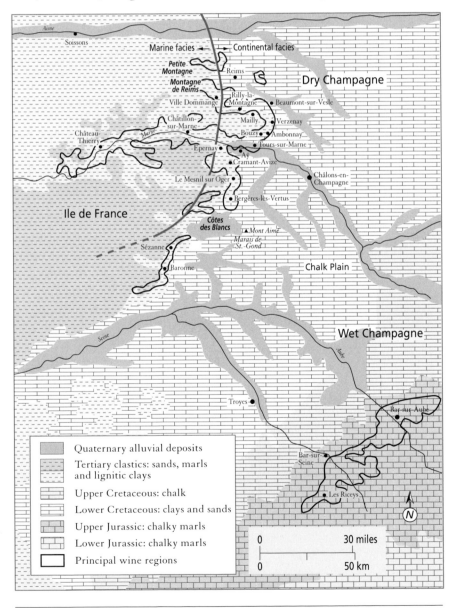

Upon our arrival at the winery, my wife and I were shown to a pleasant garden room while the secretary rescheduled my meeting. Almost immediately a waiter appeared with a tray of champagne and glasses. Until then my "nerves' medicine" had been bourbon. In that garden room on that day, I became a convert to champagne as my analeptic as well as my drink of choice for pleasurable occasions.

This harmonious wine is grown on classic slopes where Tertiary strata capping the Ile de France plateau overlie soft Cretaceous chalk of what is known as Dry Champagne, *see* Figure 2.1. (By the way, it is little "c" for the wine, capital "C" for the province.)

With two or three hours until my rescheduled appointment, my wife and I decided to continue our exploration of the nearby vineyards. As we made our way along the base of the Montagne de Reims across the Marne from Epernay, I stopped to examine a roadside cut, clearly showing the profile of soil and chalk substrata. I was reminded of the apothegm that Champagne's vines "have their heads in the Tertiary and their feet in the Cretaceous" (*see* Color Plate 6). This personification describes the unique geologic relationship of sands, marls, and lignitic clays of the Tertiary which have washed downslope over the underlying Cretaceous chalk. The trunks and branches of the vineplants, the "heads," grow upward from the soils of Tertiary slope wash, while the roots, the "feet," explore the underlying, fractured Cretaceous chalk.

The chalk plain surrounding the Ile de France was for countless years a treeless plain known in early days as *Champagne pouilleuse* (literally lousy), now more charitably referred to as the Dry Champagne. The porous and fractured chalk quickly soaks up the rainfall, leaving a dry and dusty land. That is, until modern farming methods, especially chemical fertilizer, clothed the landscape in a pleasant, agricultural green.

Further south, below Châlons (formerly Châlons-sur-Marne, the town has been renamed Châlons-en-Champagne), the Lower Cretaceous is a series of clays and sands whose poor permeability causes marshy conditions, giving the outcrop belt the name Wet Champagne (*see* Figure 2.1). Champagne owes its greatness as a wine province to the chalk of the Upper Cretaceous.

In addition to the part it plays in the unique soils, underground tunnels in the chalk have a natural refrigeration important in the winemaking process. Miles of these tunnels afford storage for millions of bottles of champagne, while larger excavations provide naturally cooled work rooms. At two levels down the temperature is a constant 50°F (10°C).

Historically, the open terrain of the Dry Champagne was the easy, fateful, passage-way of invasions, first by barbarians, later by major powers. Attila and his hordes got a running start when they pell-melled into northern Gaul in the 5th century, but took time to sack Reims. After an unsuccessful siege of Orléans, Attila retreated to the favored open country of the chalk plain. Near Châlons Attila suffered his first and only defeat and was allowed to slip away eastward.

Numerous battles were fought in Champagne and along its borders, some for the very life of France. Invasions were not always stopped nor the wars always won, but geology decreed that for 20 centuries, Champagne would endure painful fame, and its wine fields would be trampled and torn.

Lay of the land

In cross-section, the Paris Basin is seen as a downwarping of successive geologic formations. The upturned edges of these formations form concentric outward-facing escarpments like a set of nested dishes. The regional cross-section, Figure 2.2, illustrates the geologic relationships of the Paris Basin, the Vosges, and Rhine graben. Back when warfare was conducted by foot and horse, these outward-facing scarps were termed the "natural defenses of Paris." The mechanized and aerial tactics of World War II essentially nullified this protective terrain. The corrugated edge of the Tertiary Ile de France overlying the Upper Cretaceous chalk is where the Champagne vineyards are sited.

Figure 2.2
Geologic cross-section, Paris Basin to the Rhine Graben

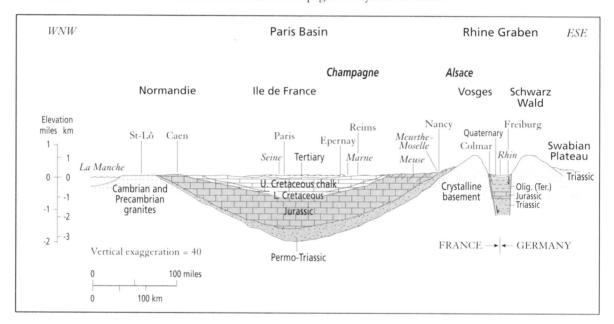

The chalk plain and the plain chalk

The name Champagne is derived from *campania*, by which the Oscan people of Italy knew the dusty, open country north of Mt. Vesuvius. Seeing the open, dusty chalk plain of northeastern Gaul, the Romans called it Campi Catalounici, which eventually was modified to Champagne. Similar terrain, yes, but not similar geology, for the Italian *campania* is carpeted by thick layers of volcanic ash, not chalk.

An interesting coincidence of geology is a belt of chalk in north Texas known as the Grand Prairie. This is rich farming land in soils derived from the Austin chalk, a formation the approximate age equivalent of the chalk of Champagne. It was to Cretaceous limestone hills in Texas around Austin and San Antonio that T. V. Munson (*see* page 47) led the French to find wild phylloxera-resistant rootstocks that would be compatible with French chalky soils of the Charente (Cognac) and Champagne.

It was the continuity of chalk from ravine to ravine and along river banks northeast of Paris that stirred the curiosity of French scientists Cuvier and Brongniart (*see* page 16). Their study of these strata was instrumental in the development of the science of geology during the 19th century. The Champagne vineyards were in existence at that time, but it was many years hence before the significance of the relationship of this lifeless-looking white rock and the soils of Champagne was recognized.

Magnification of the chalk reveals that it is composed of calcareous algae (a form of seaweed) and fragile shells of tiny, floating organisms so numerous that they clouded the Cretaceous seas and settled to the bottom like powder-snow. These seas stretched over the British Isles and most of France, their formations contributing significantly to vineyard terrain and soils. Born as oceanic ooze, chalk as a rock at the surface weathers to dust. The dust is easily blown or washed away – unless, as in the case of the wine slopes of Champagne, it is saved by marriage with Tertiary slope wash. That geologic union is the parentage of the unique soils of Champagne. What really makes for a long and happy marriage of those vineyard soils is the moisture conservation provided by the fractures and porosity of the chalk partner.

Magnification also shows porosity to be uniform in this light, compact, fine-grained rock. This porosity is capable of holding an enormous amount of soil water, which is "leaked" or "drawn" from the rock by capillary action to nourish the roots of the vineplant. Some vine roots have been observed to extend tens of feet through the fractured chalk seeking to tap this moisture supply. The average annual precipitation is only 26 inches (660 mm), near minimum for grape growing, but the vineyards of Champagne seldom suffer stress because of the moisture supply in the pores and fractures of the chalk. The fracturing resulted from deep frost action during the Ice Age, illustrated and described in Part One (*see* pages 23–24).

The geology of the Champagne slopes is relatively simple – classic cap rock – concave slope (*see* Figure 1.1, page 21) with soil accumulated in the mid-slope or "belly." However, misinterpretation of the true viticultural role of the chalk has created a bit of geologic mystery.

The chalk enigma

Certain early observers accorded a magical agronomic property to the upper part of the chalk. Repetition of the erroneous interpretation has elevated the story to a viticultural myth.

The massive Upper Cretaceous chalk, almost 1000 feet (300 m) in thickness, has been subdivided by the paleontologists into "biozones," based on the vertical range of "key" fossils. The key fossil of the uppermost zone is the Belemnite (or Belemnitella) (Gr. *belemon*, dart or arrow), an extinct relative of the modern squid or cuttlefish, and a "straight" cousin of the coiled ammonite. Below the Belemnite is the Micraster biozone named for a fat and puffy sea urchin which belongs to the starfish family.

The Belemnite zone is the one with the presumed magical properties, which the grapevines are reputed to favor. Georges Chappaz, Inspector-General of Agriculture in the mid-1930s, in his extensive study of the vines and wines of Champagne wrote that "The winegrowers of old, although ignorant of the geology, *always* (my emphasis) stopped their vineyards right at the contact between the two chalk formations [the Belemnite and Micraster]." This is apparently how the story got started. Patrick Forbes in his comprehensive book

Champagne, the Wine, the Land and the People makes quite a thing of this apparent preference of the vines. A few other writers repeat this tale of the Belemnite magic as part of the wine lore of Champagne, implying that the grapevine just does not like the Micraster soil. But the basis for this supposed hostility fails to take into account the "geologic geometry" of the slopes which is clearly brought out in the cross-sections in this chapter of some of the best vineyard sites in Champagne.

The apothegm mentioned earlier about vines with their heads in the Tertiary and feet in the Cretaceous, emphasizes that these strata are the two major components to the soils of Champagne. Vines may grow on either one alone, but the two together is the magic formula.

Professor Hubert Guérin of the Laboratoire des Sciences de la Terre, Université de Reims, in personal communication agrees with me that the supposed phenomenon is due to the "geologic geometry," rather than to some mysterious difference in the two chalks. Professor Guérin says there are no significant mineralogic or physical differences in the two zones. Likewise, Tom Stevenson in his book *Champagne* makes reference to Dr. Geoffrey Tresise of the Merseyside County Museum in Liverpool, England, who also finds no physical or chemical properties of the Belemnite chalk which would make it superior to the Micraster for winegrowing.

As to this "geologic geometry," please refer to Figures 2.3 and 2.5. The upper part and belly of the Grand Cru slope are occupied by the Belemnite zone which is about 300 feet (100 m) thick. The Micraster comes in where the slope begins to flatten. The erosional hydraulics was seldom strong enough to carry a significant amount of Tertiary slope wash out as far as the Micraster. The Micraster chalk has nothing against grapevines, it simply does not get enough sands, clays, and lignites for the magical soil mix.

Professor Guérin also points out that during the 18th century there were actually important plantations on the Micraster chalk, around Châlons. Perhaps the soil mix there included river terrace material of the Marne. Furthermore, within the last few years Moët & Chandon has been developing a vineyard near Pontfaverger-Moronvilliers, 15 miles (24 km) northeast of Reims, well out on the Micraster. Also, many villages on the Micraster chalk within the Champagne A.O.C. boundary are requesting authorization to plant vineyards. But without the mix of Tertiary slope wash, the chalk requires an enormous amount of manuring and loads of "borrowed" soil to produce good grape land.

The Tertiary soil ingredients

That the chalk plain was once known as *Champagne pouilleuse*, poor or lousy land, testifies that it lacked something to make it good growing soil. The early-day vignerons found the slope soils below the plateau most conducive to grape vines. What ingredients does the Tertiary bring to this magical mix? The Tertiary clastics themselves seem like a sterile lot, but the sands provide coarse ingredients to the texture helping build good soil structure. The clays, marls, and weathered chalk form a binding with the particles giving the soil body. The subtle, "magical," ingredient is lignite. The lignite itself contributes little to the composition of the soil. It is the minerals that "season" the soil.

In the quick burial which formed the lignite, important minerals (iron, sulfur, and zinc) in the plant material were concentrated. The iron in the form of pyrite (iron sulfide) is a hard mineral but it weathers readily. Iron is particularly critical in this carbonate province as the vineplant is susceptible to chlorosis, a yellowing of the leaves. However, as you, and gardeners especially, will know, iron is a critical element for all plants, particularly roses. Unfortunately, calcium carbonate also has an affinity for iron, forming an insoluble compound, thus denying a significant amount of iron to the plants. Good drainage is important to help prevent the ponding of calcium carbonate solutions, thereby minimizing the chemical reaction.

They may not have understood the chemistry involved, but those early-day vignerons recognized that lignite in the soil was important. Lignite is a soft, low-grade coal which occurs in beds but it also crops up as streaks and flecks in clay and silt. Consequently, around the base of the Champagne plateau, there are numerous open-pit quarries for lignite and lignitic clays called *cendrières*. From ancient times these *cendres noires*, meaning "black ashes," have been spread to enrich and replenish thin and eroded soils.

Unlike the uniform deposition of the chalk, Tertiary sedimentation was an interfingering between marine and non-marine facies as indicated on Figure 2.1. Lignite was a constituent of the continental environment, making that facies the most favorable for viticultural soils – a fact which is recognized in the classification of the communes (*see* page 73).

During the Tertiary, the sea made at least 15 incursions and retreats in the Paris Basin. The maximum advance in this region forms a line approximately through Reims and Epernay, *see* Figure 2.1. Note that most of the Montagne de Reims and the Côte des Blancs, the most favored parts of the Champagne region, lie within the zone of continental facies.

The continental environment was characterized by rivers, swamps, and shallow lakes, which meant that there were frequent lateral and vertical changes in lithology. Sandy shorelines were adjacent to muddy lagoons accumulating red, green, beige, or gray clays; shallow lakes precipitated limestones mixed with clay. The many swamps and lagoons in this semi-tropical climate were overgrown with vegetation, which when quickly buried became the viticulturally important lignite.

Not only did the continental deposits themselves vary within the zone, but their slope wash was not always spread evenly down the slope, while erosion frequently carried away valuable amounts of soil. This in part explains why the plantings are discontinuous as the vignerons seek to utilize the most favorable soil conditions as well as exposures.

In more recent years, a compost of sterilized, organic waste and trash from the local villages, called *gadoues* or *boues de ville*, is spread over the vineyards. This acts as a mulch to help break up heavy clay soils. When I first saw shredded paper and other bits of trash in the vineyard between Champillon and Hautvillers, I was horrified that someone had desecrated the venerable soils within the very sight of Dom Pérignon's abbey. I soon learned that this was not "trash" at all, but the highly prized *boues de ville* – and a far less pungent manure than the barnyard variety.

Climate

In all seasons, Champagne is the coolest of the French vineyards (*see* Figure 1.5, page 36). Interestingly, its remarkable wine comes close to being a caprice of nature, as the viticultural climate is near-marginal. At 49° north latitude, the seasonal coolness slows ripening so that the red grapes Pinots Noir and Meunier and the white Chardonnay do not reach a luscious stage, but retain a tartness (acidity) ideal for champagne. Although the Marne region is 150 miles (240 km) from the English Channel (La Manche) it enjoys the moderating influence of the Atlantic maritime climate. It is far enough inland, however, to lose much of the cloudiness typical of the coastal region. Occasionally, when severe continental conditions prevail, Champagne feels its 49° latitude. Winters are sometimes bitterly cold, but as the vines are dormant they seldom suffer seriously. Nevertheless, when temperatures approach zero Fahrenheit (⁻18°C) there is danger of the branches bursting, as occurred in the winter of 1985, when many vines had to be replaced. In that particular attack, Professor Guérin reports that the Chardonnay best resisted the freeze of the three varieties.

Summers in this part of France are generally very agreeable. Short periods in July and August may be quite hot, but the average temperature for the summer months is in the pleasant mid-70s Fahrenheit (mid-20s Centigrade). The autumns are supposed to be sunny and warm, but sometimes they are wet and cold, resulting in a disastrous *vendange*. Spring is the riskiest time when late frosts may damage early budding. Historically, there are 60–80 days of frost a year, with the Marne Valley and lowermost slopes around the Montagne de Reims being particularly frost-prone. At Reims the midday angle of the sun at summer solstice is only 65°, making every ray of the sun precious. By the autumnal equinox the angle is down to 49°, and in mid-winter is as low as 20°.

Curiously, a number of quality vineyards are on north-facing slopes of the Montagne de Reims, rather than the otherwise preferred southerly exposure. Considering the low angle of the sun at this latitude, how can we account for the quality of so many north-facing slopes? The true-scale profile (same horizontal and vertical scale) in the Verzenay cross-section below shows that, except for very near the cliff-face, the surface slopes away from the sun at a low angle

Figure 2.3
Verzenay, cross-section of Grand Cru slope
The Grand Cru slope of Verzenay is a prototype for the Tertiary–Cretaceous relationships. It is said that the Verzenay vineyards produce the darkest Pinot Noir grapes and the strongest wines

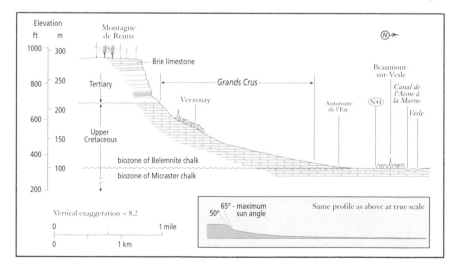

averaging only about 4 degrees. Evidently the reduction of 4 degrees by which sun rays impinge on the slope is not a serious loss. By the law of physics, the angle of reflection equals the angle of incidence (impingement). Could reflection from the bare, white chalk below the vineyards on the north side of the Montagne act as a "radiator belt" warming the air which might then be drawn back up the slopes by aspiration of the prevailing Westerlies?

Undoubtedly microclimates exist in Champagne, but for some reason there is little mention of such phenomena in the literature. An early-day reference reports that vines were closely spaced both in rows and between plants to provide protection from the more severe climatic conditions. Today, planting is more open to allow each plant to obtain as much sun as possible.

Something similar to a microclimate is achieved when grapes from over the region grown under local variations in climate are brought together in the crusher. The vicissitudes of the Champagne weather mean few individual communes can be depended upon to produce a consistent wine year in, year out. As a consequence, "vintage champagnes" are more a response to public demand than the proud product of the winemaker. Not spurning a good marketing opportunity, however, vintage issues sell at a premium. A perfect vintage year in Champagne is an extreme rarity. This situation is recognized by allowing blending of different years, which, incidentally, may produce a champagne with better balance than would be possible from a single terroir in any given year.

The grapes

The authorized grape varieties are the Pinot Noir and Pinot Meunier, red grapes crushed for their white juice, and the white Chardonnay. The Pinot Noir is the main grape planted around the Montagne de Reims and in the Marne Valley, but restricted to locations where the threat of frost is minimal. With an early bud-break the Pinot Noir is very susceptible to spring frosts. Much is being done on clonal selection to improve the plant's hardiness, so that it may be planted in the frost-prone areas now given to the Meunier.

There are significant plantings of Chardonnay in the same plots with the Pinot Noir where growers have found that it does well, especially in places sheltered from the west wind. In such areas the Chardonnay can hold its own in the classification scheme (*see* page 73).

The Pinot Meunier is a "common" relative that complements the noble Pinot Noir with strong floral and fruity aromas. The name derives from the fact that the underside of the leaf is whitish as if dusted with baking flour – *meunier* – meaning a miller of flour. Although the hardiest of the three champagne grapes, its fruitiness tends to peak early and fade fast. In addition to minor plantings in several communes, it is planted down-river in the Aisne district along the valley walls of the Marne beyond where the chalk has disappeared.

The Chardonnay is the exclusive grape of the Côte des Blancs and overall accounts for about 27 percent of all vines planted in Champagne (the Pinot Noir currently occupies 37.5 percent and the Meunier 35 percent.) These planting ratios have changed in the last few years in response to popular preferences in champagne style. When it comes to the wine itself, however, each house will have its own formula of blends.

Champagne, a remarkable wine?

I recall reading somewhere that champagne is the world's most accommodating wine, with the assertion that there is no menu, no gathering, no occasion, and no hour of the day or night for which it is not well-suited. Does this not sound like the "ultimate wine?" From any point of view, champagne is indeed a remarkable wine grown on unique geology and produced by an involved, well-specified *méthode champenoise* (*see* feature below).

Champagne may not be the "ultimate wine," nor have been the first sparkling wine in France, but the name has certainly become the touchstone for fizzy wines. French wine districts other than Champagne produce wines with various degrees of sparkle: *mousseux, pétillant*, etc., some even made by the classic method or *méthode traditionnelle* (meaning the *méthode champenoise*), but the French call none of these champagne. That name is strictly reserved for *Champagne Viticole*. Several countries outside France produce sparkling wines which they call "champagne." Either by treaty or trade agreement, most wine-growing countries recognize that champagne is an *appellation d'origine* of France and that the name cannot be used except for wine produced in Champagne under the classic method. Regrettably, the U.S. does not have such an agreement and most any "fizzy" wine in the U.S. may be represented as "champagne."

Some pleasant, sparkling wines from outside France may indeed have been made according to the classic method. There is, however, only one ethical champagne, and that is produced in the appellation of Champagne under the very specific regulations of the *méthode champenoise*. Somehow, the chalk of the Champagne soils imparts an élan to "true" champagne that is not duplicated elsewhere in the world. Within the *méthode*, however, there is ample freedom for the champagne houses to develop individual styles by the blending of wines from authorized grapes.

The méthode champenoise

True champagne is made by a two-stage process. After the initial fermentation and blending, a small mixture of wine, sugar, and yeast is added before bottling to encourage a second fermentation. The bottles are then stored neck down in the coolest place in the cellar. Almost as uncanny as when birds sense it is time to migrate, a second fermentation commences the following spring. The bottles are gradually tilted, toward the neck, so that the products of fermentation collect above the temporary cork. The sediment collected in the neck is frozen and disgorged (*dégorgement*) as a sludge in a fascinating process done in the larger houses by assembly-line machines. The bottles are then "topped off" by addition of the same wine as in the bottle. A little sugar (*dosage*) is added to the "topping;" otherwise, the champagne would be too dry for most tastes, although Brut Zéro or Nature, meaning without any added sugar, is a style offered by some houses. The bottle is then recorked, wired, labeled, and ready for sale after a mandatory year's storage.

For all the concern about the authenticity of champagne, it is a blend. But it is a blending of wines from authorized grapes. The blending is an art form, and each champagne house has its own secret recipe. No one house grows all the grapes it needs. There are over 15,000 growers in 150 communes with whom they may deal to fill their needs. Potentially, this is a disquieting variable as consistency year-to-year is the prime objective. Consistency is achieved by experience and the patience to "get it right." The reputations of the Champagne houses, large and small, stand on their dependability to produce a consistent champagne.

It is the still wines that are blended. In the larger houses there may be several hundred tanks of still wine from which the blender may choose to craft his art-piece. The permutation possibilities are enormous. Rémi Krug of Krug & Co. is quoted as saying "I don't mind if people don't understand what we do. The hard work is our part, and the enjoyment is yours."

Rémi Krug, interviewed by James Suckling, "Blending champagne in true Krug style," *Wine Spectator*, May 31, 1989.

Delimitation and classification

As the appreciation of champagne grew in the early 20th century so did the demand for grapes and places to grow them, making it imperative to define the boundary of *Champagne Viticole*. Quite naturally – and emotionally – this raised the concerns of who was in and who was out.

Disagreement related primarily to whether or not the regions of Aube and Aisne should be in *Champagne Viticole*. The Aube district is 70 miles (112 km) southeast of the main Marne region, along the Aube and Seine rivers. The Aisne district is down the Marne Valley from Epernay, centering around the town of Château-Thierry, in the Aisne département. The controversy was exacerbated by shortages resulting from the phylloxera devastation and savaging of the land by the battles of World War I.

The root of the problem was geologic. The Marne winegrowers contended that the fame of champagne was based on the chalky soils of the Cretaceous, and that the soils of the Aube were different, hence so too were the wines. Soils of the Aube region are indeed different, and although somewhat chalky, they are from the Kimmeridgian of Jurassic age. (The Aube is included in chapter 9, the Kimmeridgian Chain.) In the Aisne region, the soils are derived entirely from Tertiary sands and clays, the Cretaceous chalk having dipped below the Ile de France into the Paris Basin. (Disappearance of the Cretaceous down-river will be explained shortly.)

The controversy began in 1908, when legislation excluded the Aube as being officially part of Champagne, which, of course, incensed the winegrowers of the Aube. Later, upon word that the law would be rescinded, ugly riots were triggered on the part of the Marne growers. In an effort at compromise, a law in 1911 created a *deuxième zone* for the Aube and Aisne. This was more an insult to the Aube than a solution.

Eventually, in 1927, a new law eliminated the *deuxième zone* and designated by name the communes which were to be included in a delimitation that had been originally set out in 1919. One criterion of the 1919 survey was that only vineyards in existence before phylloxera were eligible for recognition – most of the Aube and Aisne vineyards qualified on that score. The boundaries that exist today for *Champagne Viticole* are almost exactly those of the 1919 survey, that is, the Aube and Aisne are included. Nevertheless, the Aube is still treated as a *deuxième zone,* as is apparent in the classification system.

Because most champagnes are blends of wines from several localities, a terroir classification would have little meaning. A classification based on a percentage rating for the communes developed the *échelle des crus*. The term means "scale" of the vineyards where *cru* = growths = specific vineyards. Communes with the best soil, sun exposure, and history of production were rated 100 percent, other communes being scaled downward to 75 percent, lowest on the scale. There is almost no market for grapes below this rating. Several modifications of the scale have taken place – a drastic one in 1945, another major one in 1971, and a later one in 1985. Grapes at 100 percent are considered the Grands Crus, and those from 99 percent to 90 percent inclusive are Premiers Crus. A dual classification is usually applied where red and white grapes are grown in the same commune.

As the price paid for grapes is pegged to the classification, percentage points mean francs. The commune classification is paramount – up to a point. The commune loses its identity when its grapes are dumped with others into the crusher. It is imperative that the price be arrived at before the *vendange* starts. Picking time cannot be haggling time – grapes crushed in the bottom of the containers in the vineyard start fermenting immediately.

Up to April, 1990, setting prices for grapes was done by the C.I.V.C. (the Comité Interprofessionnel du Vin de Champagne), which had been in effect since 1959. After months of negotiation, growers and négociants failed to renew their contract with the C.I.V.C. Since 1990 the champagne houses have been free to negotiate price and terms directly with growers (but still prior to the harvest). Although prices and sales fluctuated for a time, both appear to be reasonably stabilized. Inasmuch as champagnes are blends and the wines come from different communes of varying classification, the place of origin (the *appellation d'origine*) is not as meaningful as in, say, Burgundy. In Champagne, the guarantee of authenticity is the integrity of the champagne house and the word "champagne" burnt in the cork.

Terroirs and the houses

Don't look for a commune or terroir name on champagne labels in the manner of Burgundy appellations or Bordeaux châteaux. Only in a very few cases can you take your bottle of champagne to a single vineyard and say this is where my wine grew. We can discuss the geology of any particular commune, but the fact is the grapes from that commune go not to one but to a number of champagne houses. For example, the large Grand Cru commune of Verzenay (which has 1000 acres/400 ha planted) has vines owned by 14 of the larger houses and 17 other growers who sell champagne under their own names.

On average, the major houses grow only about 13 percent of the grapes they need. Supplemental grapes are bought from any of thousands of small growers whose properties vary in soils and exposures, and whose farming methods may differ. These facts and blending make it difficult to calibrate the effect of soil with wine quality. The major houses have long-term contracts with growers in highly rated communes, but no one house has a corner on the terroirs carrying an *échelle* of high percentage.

What matters for the consumer is the name and reputation of the house. Back in 1965 Ernest Hornickel made the somewhat irreverent analogy that champagne is sold like soap – the first thing that counts is the name of the company or brand, the second thing is the perfume of the soap, or in this case the taste of the champagne.

For wine areas generally, *appellation contrôlée* on the label guarantees that the wine in the bottle comes from the vineyard or château it says it does, and that the wine was made by the vintner whose name is on the label. For champagne, that name on the label guarantees that the contents come from within the Champagne A.O.C. delimitation, that only specified grapes were used, that it has been made by the *méthode champenoise*, and that it has been stored in bottle at least one year. For quality and consistency, the consumer's greatest assurance is the reputation of the champagne house.

Houses and towns of Champagne

During the quarter century leading up to the French Revolution, half a dozen or more German immigrants, among them Mumm, Heidsieck, Krug, and Bollinger, came to the region and set up champagne wineries that eventually became renowned "houses." The first of these houses was Nicolas Ruinart in 1729. Claude Moët, of Dutch descent, established in 1743 what was to become the most important firm in Champagne, Moët & Chandon. With time, a proliferation of small houses came about in the Revolution and its aftermath, when the monastic and other large estates were broken up. Many growers and merchants began to establish houses bearing their own names, some of which, although remaining small, grew famous.

The largest numbers of houses are in Reims, Epernay, and Aÿ. Reims is the elite university and cathedral city on the autoroute from Paris to Strasbourg. Epernay is the wine city on the Marne. Only 12 miles (20 km) apart, on opposite sides of the Montagne de Reims, these two towns were inconveniently located on the invasion routes of the barbarians and were burned and sacked probably more times than any other towns in France.

Reims became important as an ecclesiastical city in 496 when Clovis, King of the pagan Franks, was baptized there as a Christian by St.-Rémy (Remi). This distinction led to Reims becoming the chosen city for future coronations. During the 13 centuries that followed Clovis, 37 kings and 11 queens and regents of France went to Reims to be crowned. Among these was Charles VII, brought there as the Dauphin by Joan of Arc.

Reims' magnificent cathedral was begun in 1211, and completed a century later – a record in cathedral building. The record was due in large part to the geology of the area: building stone from the limestone of the plateau, including the Brie and *Calcaire grossier*, the "Gothic Stone," which takes a fine edge, and mortar-lime from the chalk. For the artisans there was wine close at hand. The craftsmen cleverly enshrined themselves with their own likenesses among the statues of kings, saints, devils and animals which decorate this great church. Every leaf type in northern France is also depicted.

The city of Reims lies on the chalk plain beyond the actual viticultural slopes, but more than 20 champagne houses have offices and cellars there, including Krug, Lanson, Mumm, Ruinart, Roederer, and the Heidsieck houses. Reims also has miles of tunnels in the underlying chalk in which champagne is stored. Many of these deep cellars were expanded from the bottle-shaped *crayères* of Gallo-Roman times which were excavations for building material. The narrow necks of these *crayères* could be covered to keep out rainwater.

Epernay, located where the Marne cuts into the Ile de France, has always been a wine town. Over 30 of the champagne houses, including Pol Roger, Mercier, Perrier-Jouët, and, largest of all, Moët & Chandon, have wineries and cellars there. The city itself is a collection of odd architectural types, but the Sparnacians are not in the least concerned. (Inhabitants of Epernay are referred to as "Sparnacians," from the Roman name of the town.) The Sparnacians seem to say: think what you wish about the appearance of the town above ground; the one below is priceless. It is three to four levels deep with caverns, work rooms, and a labyrinth of tunnels containing countless bottles of champagne.

An alternate spelling is Rheims, but modern-day usage usually drops the "h." The French pronounce it *Rr-ans* or *Ranss*, but it is frequently anglicized to *Reems* or *Rimz*.

Champagne histrionics

The house of Moët & Chandon makes the most of its historic association with two of the great names in French history: the Benedictine monk, Dom Pérignon (whose story is told on the facing page), and Napoléon Bonaparte. Once religious worship was eventually permitted after the Revolution, members of the families that were to become the Moët & Chandon firm acquired the grounds and restored the abbey where Dom Pérignon had done his "cellar-tasting" and blending. A statue of Dom Pérignon proferring a bottle of champagne greets the visitor at the gate of Moët & Chandon's winery.

On display in the lobby of the winery office are memorabilia of Napoléon who was a personal friend of Jean-Rémy Moët, the grandson of the founder. On numerous occasions on the way to or from campaigns in northeastern Europe, Napoléon stayed with his friend Moët in Epernay. On his last visit, just before his abdication, the Emperor pinned his own Chevalier's Cross of the Légion d'Honneur on Moët, an expression of his appreciation for ten years of gracious hosting and friendship.

Moët's friendship with Napoléon was not punished by the Allies after Waterloo. Quite the contrary. The two identical orangeries which Moët had built across the street from his winery as guest houses for Napoléon and his entourage were continuously occupied by monarchs and V.I.P.s traveling to and from Vienna to the congress on "what to do with France." Kings, princes, grand dukes, and marshals, including the victorious Wellington, availed themselves of Moët's delightful accommodations and ready refreshments. Tsar Alexander of Russia was one of the frequent guests.

In Vienna, Prussia and Austria were pressing plans for dismemberment of France, but Tsar Alexander and the English saw the merits of a strong France – the Tsar trusted Prussia and Austria even less than he did France. Patrick Forbes in his book *Champagne, the Wine, the Land, the People*, tells the engaging story of how the Tsar decided on a little subtle saber-rattling to impress upon his fellow sovereigns that his views were to be considered. He planned to parade his military might of almost 300,000 troops who were still in France and to invite the Prussians and Austrians to the show. But where? Color Plate 8 shows the slopes of Mont Aimé, an outlier butte at the south end of the Côtes des Blancs, 15 miles (24 km) south of Epernay. This was the reviewing stand, the chalk plain below the parade ground. Demands on the local populace for logistical support were unbelievably burdensome, like supplying 100,000 horseshoes, barrels of grease for the wagon wheels, and tons of hay for the horses. Nevertheless, the parade went on; the king of Prussia and emperor of Austria came and got the message. France remained intact.

The officer-corps of the Russian forces who had occupied Reims and Epernay at the time of Waterloo evidently acquired a liking for champagne. In one of history's little ironies, upon their return to Russia, those same officers became the advance guard which the enterprising young widow Clicquot exploited when she "invaded" the country to acquaint the Russian nobility with champagne. By the time of the Russian Revolution in 1917, 30 percent of Champagne's production was going to Russia, with the House of Clicquot far in the lead. Champagne beat vodka, hands down.

Sub-provinces and communes

Champagne Viticole consists of four sub-districts: Marne Champagne comprises the physiographic-geologic provinces of the Montagne de Reims, Petite Montagne, the Marne Valley, and the Côte des Blancs (*see* Figure 2.1). Other sub-districts are Côte de Sézanne, Vignoble de l'Aisne, and the Aube (*see* chapter 9).

The Montagne de Reims, a large eastward projection of the Ile de France, has the largest number of communes as well as the largest number of Grands Crus. The plateau margin is fairly straight along the north side, but the south side is highly indented. The profile at Verzenay (Figure 2.3) typifies the geologic slope relationships along the north side of the Montagne. There is a zone of interfingering between continental and marine environments in the Tertiary (*see* Figure 2.1). Of Champagne's 17 Grands Crus of the Montagne de Reims, 12 lie within the continental facies. The significance of the continental facies is that it contains lignitic clays and beds of lignite. You will recall it is these all-important lignites that have the mineral nutrients which enhance the soils.

The Montagne slopes are planted primarily to Pinot Noir, but with varying amounts of Chardonnay and still smaller plantings of Meunier.

The puzzling anomaly of six Grands Crus on the north slope of the Montagne at this near-marginal latitude was discussed earlier under climate (*see* page 70). As was suggested, whether or not the white chalk may act as a solar element, red table wine is not in the making, so the Pinot Noir does not need to ripen to full pigmentation.

Other communes on the north side are Beaumont-sur-Vesle, Sillery, Puisieux, Mailly, and Rilly-la-Montagne. Only limited areas of production are on the slopes, but the chief towns of the communes gained historical prominence, by virtue of their location on the travel route in the valley.

On the south side of the Montagne, La Livre, a small stream originating on the plateau, has eroded an intricate pattern of lobes and galleys. Vineyards of the communes of Louvois and Tours-sur-Marne within this stream-basin are relatively small. In contrast, the Grands Crus of Bouzy and Ambonnay, lying along the unbroken southern margin of the plateau, have excellent, wide slopes of over 800 acres (320 ha) each.

Aÿ (pronounced "eye"), claimed by both the Montagne and the Marne Valley, is a wide steep slope, somewhat convex upward (*see* Figure 2.4). Normally, such slope profiles are not the best for concentrating slope wash. In the case of Aÿ, the brush-covered margin of the plateau, rather than being very steep, curves into the rounded slope. The brushy slope helps to control an even supply of Tertiary slope wash and also contributes organic matter to the soils.

The still wines of Aÿ had an early and long history as being the favorite of international royalty and popes. Surprisingly, this small village, wedged between the slope and the roadway, is the resident headquarters for 18 champagne houses, including Bollinger and Gosset. Such crowding is accommodated by the "fourth dimension" – extensive tunnels and levels dug into the chalk.

Figure 2.4
Aÿ, cross-section of the Grand Cru slope
Aÿ is one of the oldest and best-known Grands Crus of Champagne, the source of smooth, well-balanced Pinot Noir

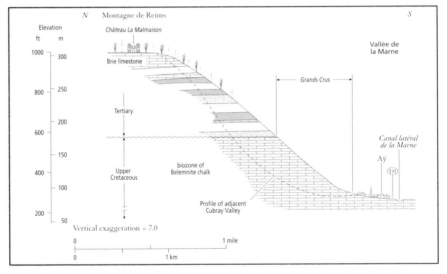

The Petite Montagne is not generally recognized as a sub-unit by wine geographers, but refers to that portion of the Montagne de Reims west of the Reims–Epernay highway. This area lies more in the marine facies so the soil contains more sand and less marl and lignitic clays. An amphitheater-like slope facing Reims supports the well-regarded Premiers Crus of Ville-Dommange and Sacy, recently joined in this classification by Chambery, Jouy-lès-Reims, Parigny-lès-Reims, and Villers-aux-Noeuds.

The Marne Valley is the most pleasant and inviting landscape of *Champagne Viticole*. Although the commune of Hautvillers contains the site of the restored abbey where Dom Pérignon performed his masterful blending, the associated vineyards rank a modest 93 percent on the *échelle*. However, it should be remembered that the cellarmaster's grapes came from many places in the area, not from the Hautvillers vineyards alone.

Below Hautvillers is a hollow known as the Côte-à-Bras, one of the commune's quality terroirs. The accumulation of slope wash is thick here, but the soils tend to be heavy with clay, so they need to be generously composted with *boues de ville*.

About 10 miles (16 km) downstream along the Marne below Epernay is the departmental boundary of Aisne, and the Vignoble de l'Aisne. In this direction two things are happening geologically: the strata are dipping gently westward into the Paris Basin, and the Tertiary strata are becoming more marine. The classification is also dipping, from the mid-90s to the mid-80s on the *échelle*.

Disappearance of the chalk in the vicinity of Châtillon-sur-Marne is again a matter of "geologic geometry" as in the Belemnite vs. Micraster enigma. In this case the Cretaceous and Tertiary strata dip into the Paris Basin in the same direction the Marne is flowing. However, the rate of dip of the strata is steeper than the gradient of the river, so the chalk goes underground while the river flows on younger and younger Tertiary. This geometric disappearance occurs near Châtillon. Vineyards continue to cover the Tertiary valley walls for another 25 miles (40 km) to well below Château-Thierry. The Tertiary soils tend to be heavy with clay or very sandy. The classification for most of the Vignoble de l'Aisne is 77 percent.

The Côte des Blancs is a T-shaped projection of the Ile de France with the head of the "T" facing eastward. The Côte is planted exclusively to the Chardonnay, but it is not known whether the Côte got its name from its white grape or from the prominence of white chalk.

The backbone of the 10-mile (16-km) long Côte is a narrow ridge capped by Brie limestone, illustrated by the profile of Cramant in Figure 2.5. Although slopes of the large Grand Cru communes of Cramant and Avize are heavily cut by rills, their broad east-facing exposures support excellent vineyards. The very large commune of Chouilly (1200 acres/485 ha), which now has Grand Cru

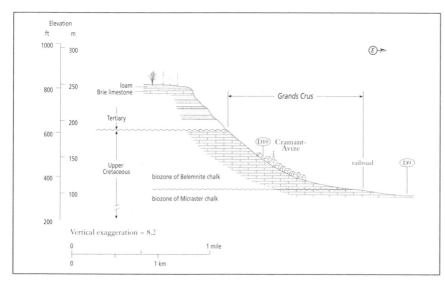

Figure 2.5
The Côtes des Blancs: Cramant–Avize, cross-section of the Grand Cru slope
The slopes of the Côtes des Blancs are somewhat steeper than those of the north-facing slope of the Montagne de Reims and are fed by a slightly reduced thickness of Tertiary. On the Côtes des Blancs the Chardonnay grape reigns supreme. "Blanc de Blancs," champagne made from pure Chardonnay, is currently enjoying a vogue

status for its white grapes (95 percent for red grapes), occupies a wrinkled apron around the Butte de Saran. The butte is an outlier from the plateau with the village of Cramant located in the saddle between the butte and the plateau.

Southward the cap rock of the narrow "T" deteriorates, but a good thickness of Tertiary strata remains to contribute to the soil mix. Vertus (red grapes) and Bergères-lès-Vertus (white) at the southern end of the ridge are both classified 95 percent. (*Bergère* means shepherdess, suggesting that sheep may have at one time been more abundant than vines.) Vineyards of lesser quality continue southward onto the slopes of the detached conical butte of Mont Aimé – Tsar Alexander's reviewing stand.

South of the St.-Gond marshes, the slopes along the eroded edge of the Ile de France continue as the Côte de Sézanne. It was in a Tertiary travertine deposit near Sézanne that the fossil vineleaf was found (*see* page 44). Here the vineyard slopes have less sweep as the plateau has lost some prominence and the Tertiary has become thinner. The clays are more plastic with little or no lignite, so the soil mixture loses some of its magical character as found around the Montagne de Reims. As a consequence, the Sézanne communes are only in the percentage range of the mid-80s.

The historical panorama

As a territorial entity, Champagne first gained importance in 1014 when Eudes, Count of Blois and vassal of Hugh Capet, inherited the large county of Troyes. (A county was the territories ruled by a count. Counties varied greatly in size, some being as large as a mid-sized state of the U.S.)

Thibaut IV, successor to Eudes, created the county of Champagne out of Troyes. It was also Thibaut who established the Fairs of Champagne, at which merchants from over Europe gathered and thus became acquainted with the wines of Champagne, particularly those of Aÿ and Sillery. The wines were still wines, mostly red, but not very red. Nor were the white wines very clear. These too were still wines; "fizzy" wines and their fame were 600 years away.

In spite of many conflicts and interruptions of the Middle Ages, the Champenois went about their business of making wine for lords, soldiers, and a growing population. Royalty liked the wines of Champagne, especially for the fact that the supply was plentiful and close at hand.

Ironically and sadly, this land whose wines came to be synonymous with joy and celebration, was the scene of many of Europe's most devastating and bloody battles, a fate destined by its location and geology – it was "on the road to Paris" and the open country invited rapid maneuver.

In the 5th century, Clovis brought his Franks from the lowlands of Flanders to the more delightful and productive lands of the Paris Basin. Clovis' baptism in Reims gave Christianity an enormous endorsement which allowed it to flourish, and with it, winegrowing.

For 14 centuries, the land and people suffered periodically from wars, some of their making, others from outside. Then in the latter part of the 19th century came devastation of the vineyards by phylloxera. Recovery was scarcely underway when the Great War (World War I) thrust into Champagne. The unbelievably bloody and muddy trench warfare stretched across Champagne to

Extracts from the poem "Champagne, 1914–15" by Alan Seegar, himself killed in the Great War, senses its grim reality:

"To those whose blood,
  in pious duty shed
Hollows the soil where
  wine had birth.
In the slant sunshine of
  October days
Be mindful of the men
  they were, and raise
Your glasses to them in
  one silent toast."

Seeger also wrote "I Have a Rendezvous with Death," an appointment he kept on July 5, 1916 "on some scarred slope of battered hill...."

Gith Clarke, *A Treasury of War Poetry*, New York: Houghton Mifflin, 1917.

the English Channel. Advances were measured in meters, deaths in millions — an appalling loss of life on both sides. Barely a generation later, invasion again broke across the Low Countries and Champagne. This time it was blitzkrieg, "lightning war" and all of France was occupied.

Following peace in 1945, there was considerable despair in Champagne, with the necessity to reorganize the champagne houses, rebuild the vineyards, and develop markets. In an amazing comeback, the shell-pocked, ravaged vineyards were restored to productive use and sales quadrupled in 20 years.

Although competition between the large houses was keen, there was also need for cooperation and accommodation with the very great number of small growers. In 1964, a commercial syndicat changed its name to beome the Comité Interprofessionnel du Vin de Champagne (C.I.V.C.). A committee similar to the commercial syndicate had actually been created in the early days of World War II to present a coordinated front in dealing with the occupation administration. It is the C.I.V.C. which evaluates and recommends classification of the communes, emphasizing particularly the geology and soils. As described earlier, the C.I.V.C. for many years coordinated negotiations for setting the price for grapes prior to the beginning of each harvest.

The geology and geography of Champagne predestined it to be continuously on the front pages of history. From the earliest of times, the winegrowers of Champagne have combined the geologic and climatic factors of their land to make remarkable wines. Whether the winemakers have crafted an "ultimate wine" is for the consumer to decide. I vote yes.

3 Alsace: granite slopes, marly hills

Alsace is irrevocably linked with the Rhine, a river misty with legends, headlined by history, tinctured with blood and wine. The Rhine of Alsace is not the vine-clad gorge of the Lorelei, but a wide, steep-walled, flat valley. This is the Rhine graben, a classic of geologic structures. *Graben* is German for what it sounds like, a grave-like trench, depicted in Figure 3.1. The valley is the result of two systems of parallel faults with a down-dropped block between. It was Alsace's geologic good fortune that an intermediate fault block on the west formed a piedmont on which developed a patchwork of soils supporting a variety of grape vines.

Figure 3.1
Generalized geology of Alsace
(courtesy Professor Claude Sittler, Université Louis Pasteur de Strasbourg)

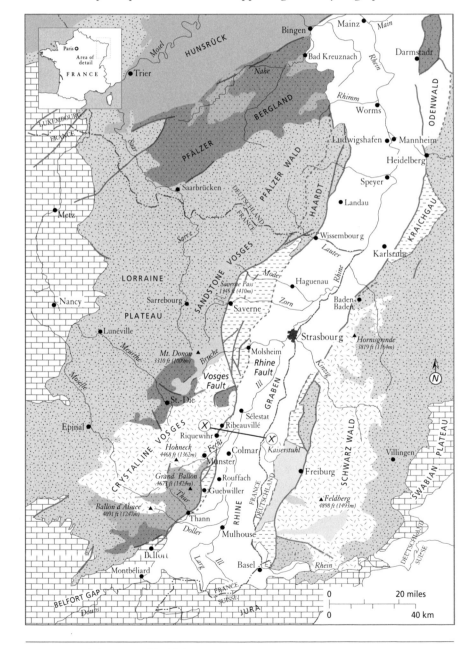

Tertiary and Quaternary

Sub-Vosgian Hills. Triassic, Jurassic, and Tertiary

Jurassic: limestone and marls

Triassic: Upper and Middle: marls, dolomites, and limestones. Lower: sandstones and conglomerates

Permian volcanic detritus, puddingstones, and sandstones

Upper Paleozoic: Devonian, Mississippian, Carboniferous, and Permian – mostly volcanics and graywackes

Devonian slates of Hunsrück and Taunus

Crystalline basement: granites, gneisses, and metamorphic schists

Faults, known and implied

X — X' Figure 3.2

Julius Caesar considered the Rhine the natural boundary between Gaul and the Germanic tribes to the east. During his first engagement in the conquest of northern Gaul, Caesar drove Ariovistus, the Germanic chieftain, from southern Alsace eastward back across the Rhine. This action opened the book of Alsace's poignant history that has seen the nationality of Alsace change six times between Germany and France in the past 300 years.

As the Roman Empire began to crumble in the 5th century, Germanic tribes who had been deterred by Roman presence began to cross into Gaul. Alsace became a mixing ground of Gallic, Roman, and barbaric cultures. André Maurois, the eminent French historian, suggests that the fusion of these cultures was essentially complete by the 9th century, but that the French and German population on either side of the Rhine could be differentiated, not by race, customs, and language so much as by the way men "felt." The way men "felt" would be demonstrated in several distressing ways in the coming centuries. On the occasions when under the German flag, efforts were made to Germanize Alsace, but its heart would always be French.

Although Alsatian culture is largely Germanic in appearance (placenames, architecture), its unique dialect is from the barbarian Alemanni; its spirit and heart are from the Gauls. The variety of soils is the inheritance of the geologic processes which produced the landscape of half mountain-half valley.

Making of the landscape

Formation of the graben began in the early Tertiary about 45 million years ago when the Alps were piling massive blocks 3 miles (nearly 5 km) high, and the Jura were being wrinkled like a caterpillar. This regional deformation was the result of a rift system which zigzagged across western Europe from the Mediterranean to the North Sea.

The region of Alsace had long been a land area bordering Cretaceous seas to the west. Then, after the dinosaurs had disappeared but before the mastodons were brought on, a vast crustal doming of the region began. Like a pudding that has risen too high, cracks appeared in the uplift, and the area between two parallel cracks began to collapse – the beginning of the graben. The Jurassic and Triassic strata overlying the uplift were shed like water off the back of a surfacing whale. Shoulders of the graben were bared to basement granites which became the Vosges of Alsace and the Black Forest (Schwarz Wald) of Germany. The Vosges do indeed suggest the shape of a whale, the body being the High or Crystalline Vosges on the south, the tail being the Low or Sandstone Vosges on the north. Uplift was not so strong in the north, and some of the Triassic sandstone cover remains, *see* Figure 3.1. Remnants of these basal conglomerates and sandstones are apparent along the crests of the eastern margin of the Crystalline Vosges. These small plateaux and rock tables perched on the granite are the sites for the Château du Haut-Barr at Saverne, the convent of Mont-Ste.-Odile, the old castle of Haut-Koenigsbourg, and the village of Trois-Epis.

Fortunately for wine, the western side of the graben was not one clean break but a series of somewhat sinuous faults stepping down to the central gutter. The westernmost fracture is a major break along the base of the mountains known as the Vosges Fault. A second major break, sometimes as much as 2 miles (3 km) east of the Vosges Fault, is known as the Rhine Fault. The sinuosity of these two major displacements forms a braided piedmont. Alsatian geologists call the lens-shaped areas "fault bundles," as they themselves contain step-faults but relatively minor displacements. Numerous cross faults cut the "bundles" into a criss-cross pattern. Differential erosion of these rectangular fault blocks produced low hills or mounds known as the sub-Vosgian Hills, the site of the Alsace vineyards. The cross-section, Figure 3.2, illustrates how successively younger strata – Triassic, Jurassic, Tertiary Oligocene – are brought into place by the step faults across the sub-Vosgian belt. This patchwork of different strata results in a variety of soils, which are the outstanding characteristics of Alsace vineyards and wines.

A significant feature of the wine landscape is the alluvial fans of the larger streams as they debouch from the Vosges. The fans support extensive vineyards but few of exceptional quality. The Thur, Lauch, Fecht, Weiss, and Liepvrette flow not to the Rhine but to the Ill. This last small, slow-moving stream begins where the Alps corner on the Jura south of Basel and parallels the Rhine at a respectful distance before joining it just below Strasbourg.

Figure 3.2
Cross-section of the sub-Vosgian Hills
The cross-section shows how step-faulting introduces successively younger strata on the surface. Of the Grand Cru terroirs, Schoenenbourg lies on Upper Triassic clays, Sporen on Lias marls, Froehn on Upper Lias shaley marls, Sonnenglanz on Tertiary conglomerates (modified from *Sciences Géologiques Bulletin*, Figure 10, p. 163, Université Louis Pasteur de Strasbourg, 1981, Tome 34, Fascicule 3)

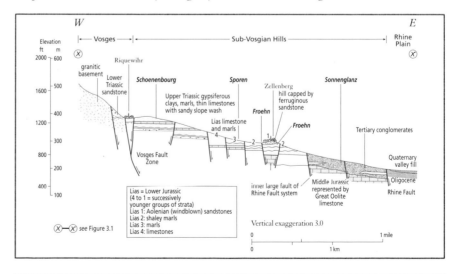

Characteristics of the viticultural terrain

There are three principal viticultural terrains in Alsace: the sub-Vosgian Hills, the lower slopes of the Vosges or crystalline terrain, and the alluvial fans.

The sub-Vosgian Hills

This belt of hills is developed in the three principal fault "bundles" which from north to south are Saverne, Ribeauvillé, and Rouffach. The largest of these is by far the Saverne "bundle," *see* Figure 3.1. Here the weather shield is much less effective than the higher Crystalline Vosges. The surface is extensively covered by loess, a "cool soil" better for hops and fruit than for grapes. (Loess, pronounced *luss*, is dialectal German meaning "loose," and was the name given by the brickmakers along the Rhine Valley to the fine-grained, wind-blown, sandy silt.) The southernmost part of the Saverne bundle is relatively free of loess, consequently several Grands Crus are found around Molsheim on soils from the Jurassic and Triassic.

Although the Saverne "bundle" can boast few quality vineyards, the pink-red, slabby sandstones of the Triassic are marvelous building stones found in the superb gothic cathedral in Strasbourg and at Speyer, down the Rhine in Germany. Massive blocks from the royal quarry north of Molsheim were selected by Sébastien Vauban, military engineer for Louis XIV, to build the equally spectacular citadel at Strasbourg.

Ribeauvillé is the beneficiary of the weather shield of the High Vosges and the diverse geology of the sub-Vosgian Hills. Richest in Grands Crus of the three fault "bundles," approximately half of those of Alsace are found in this small area. The perspective drawing, Figure 3.3, shows the heart of the "bundle" whose entire surface, except for small villages, roads, and a few wooded knolls, is covered with vineyards.

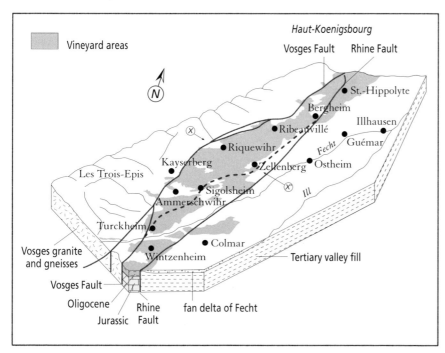

Figure 3.3
Panoramic perspective of Ribeauvillé Fault Bundle
The overall distance, north to south, is approximately 10 miles (16 km). X—X' is the cross-section shown in Figure 3.2

The pattern of geologic formations produced by the faulting is colorfully illustrated by the geologic map (*see* Color Plate 12). If the map were a patchwork quilt, it would win a blue ribbon at a county fair anywhere. On one of my visits to Alsace, Dr. Georges Hirleman, who had mapped this area some years earlier for his university thesis, and I were studying the geologic map. Hubert Trimbach, of the firm F. E. Trimbach, who was listening to the discussion remarked, with tongue in cheek, that his ancestors had mapped the geology of that area in the early 17th century — with their vines.

The Rouffach "cluster" is three times as large as Ribeauvillé, and, although it contains a number of Grands Crus, many of the Triassic sandstone hills are rugged and forest-clad. The Grand Cru Zinnkoepflé above Soultzmatt west of Rouffach averages 16 degrees and extends in a majestic slope from an elevation of 800 feet (240 m) to almost 1400 feet (425 m). Zinnkoepflé is especially noted for Muscat. Domaines Schlumberger's Kitterlé and companion terroirs above Guebwiller have slopes between 32 and 40 degrees, requiring extensive terracing. The narrow terraces can be worked only by hand and horses — the result is rich Riesling, Pinot Gris, and Gewurztraminer.

Lower slopes of the Vosges

Although most of the Alsace vineyards are situated on sedimentary strata of the sub-Vosgian belt, a number of Alsace's most famous terroirs, including the Schlossberg below Kaysersberg, are found on the granites of the lower slopes of the Vosges. Soils of the granites are coarse and sandy but high in mineral nutrients, and yield particularly fine Rieslings.

The variety of granites of the Crystalline Vosges seem like a marble cake, as they are mixed with a dozen or more types of metamorphic and "old rocks." ("Old rocks" are those of Paleozoic age.) In particular three areas of metamorphic rocks support famous terroirs, such as the Kastelberg at Andlau where a band of schist known as the Steige, provides a distinctive soil. (Schists are shales that have been changed by heat and pressure into a foliated rock. The compression has concentrated the minerals and often, if not too crystalline, the schists weather to good soils.)

The Muenchberg terroir at Nothalten north of Dambach-la-Ville is on "old rocks," "puddingstone" conglomerates, and breccias of Permian age. (Breccias are strata of angular pieces of rock.) South in the Rangen at Thann, granites intruded into older volcanic material, resulting in a unique complex of soils.

Alluvial fans

Other vineyards, some of importance with long histories, thrive on the deep, rich soils of alluvial fans. An especially high-quality terroir, the Kaefferkopf, is located on Oligocene strata with a thin covering of alluvium of the Fecht.

Natural instincts, not geologic knowledge, led pioneer winegrowers such as Hubert Trimbach's ancestors to choose their vineyard sites. The great variety of soils and grapes required unbelievable patience and time of trial and error to find the happy match. Of inestimable influence on viticulture in Alsace has been "Mother Vosges" who, like a garden wall, shields the piedmont from the harshness of the Westerlies.

Climate

The skyline of "Mother Vosges" is relatively simple, mountains that are more beckoning than forbidding. Within the higher reaches, however, are cirques and sharp declivities, relics of the Ice Age. Several of the better known peaks such as the Grand Ballon and Ballon d'Alsace are actually rounded summits resembling partially inflated balloons or possibly thatched roofs. The ancient Celtic cult of Bel celebrated its religious rites on these summits. The name ballons, and in turn, the modern word balloon, very possibly derived from *bel*.

From May to October, Alsace is "sunshine valley." This period counts the most in winegrowing. As sunny days of summertime extend well into the fall, they allow slow ripening of the grapes, thus preserving their natural aromas. There may be snow on the High Vosges, while harvesting continues in the valley below – *vendanges tardives*, the late picking of grapes almost bursting with sugar.

As the moisture-bearing Westerlies move onto the Vosges they are deflected upwards, cooling the air which releases moisture, with the heaviest precipitation on the higher elevations of the west side. The weather station at Ballon d'Alsace normally records 90 inches (2280 mm) of precipitation per year. On the lee side above the vineyards, the rainfall decreases as rapidly as the relief falls away. The rain-shield of the mountains is so effective that Colmar is one of the driest places in France, with only 22 inches (550 mm) of moisture per year – about that of Denver, Colorado.

Just because there is much summer sun in Alsace doesn't mean that the winters aren't cold. They can be. The average January temperature in the grape belt is 35°F (1.7°C). The really severe cold occurs when an Arctic air mass slips down from the north and drops the temperature to below zero Fahrenheit (–18°C). On average, however, there are only about 15 days in winter when the weather is continuously below freezing, all day and night.

Colmar, at the edge of the low, flat valley, has an annual average of 60 days of frost – about as many as the mid- to upper Mississippi Valley. But the sub-Vosgian vineyards, higher than the valley, rarely suffer serious frost damage.

During the "Little Ice Age," (15th–late 19th centuries) the winters were long and severe. Chronicles of the Franciscan monks of Thann and Guebwiller, collected by Bruno Stehle, describe the joys and sorrows of the winegrowers of southern Alsace. In the 15th century, the monks wrote that for several years vines and grapes froze on Holy Days in both spring and fall. These men of the cloth must have begun to question whether the Lord really approved of wine. But the recorders also told of joyous times. In 1484, the harvest was so abundant that wine was given away "in the name of God and friendship." In 1530, it was again so plentiful there were not enough barrels for the new wine. Legend has it that barrels were reclaimed by using the not-so-good wine of the previous year to mix mortar for construction in Thann – more a stunt than a necessity.

Alsace still has good and bad growing years, and there is little that can be done about the weather except pray. Numerous calvaries and shrines in the vineyards are evidence that the Alsatian vignerons are constant in their petitions and thanks for divine influence over their climate and crops. To cover any unforeseen contingencies, the cautious Alsatian winegrowers employ not one, but seven patron saints.

The grapes and the soils they prefer

With nine authorized grapes, Alsace has more varieties than almost any other major wine region in France. To offer so many wines rather than concentrate on one or two choice varieties may be confusing and even appear redundant, according to J. Dreyer, a former officer in the Confrérie St.-Etienne, the ancient wine brotherhood of Alsace. Mr. Dreyer concedes there may be an element of tradition involved, but maintains that in reality having a large number of grapes is an agricultural necessity due to the great diversity of geology and soils. If not a necessity, it is one of the things that makes Alsace wines unique.

Of the authorized grapes, the Riesling, Muscat, Pinot Blanc, Auxerrois Blanc, Sylvaner, and Chasselas are white grapes. The Pinot Noir and Pinot Gris are red grapes, but the Pinot Gris is vinified exclusively as a white wine. The Pinot Noir is usually made into a rosé, as the Alsace climate does not normally permit full pigmentation for a true red wine. Ampelographers agree that Pinot Gris is a white mutation of the Pinot Noir and although its skin may be any of several dark shades, its juice is white. The Gewurztraminer grape is a gold to peachy-pink color, but it too yields white juice.

Increasingly in wine districts of France, the grape variety is being shown on the label – except for top wines. In Alsace, A.O.C. rules insist that the grape variety be prominently displayed on the label – and for good reason: 99 percent of the wines are white and can be from any of the varieties but Pinot Noir. The label tells which one. It is also required that the contents in the bottle be 100 percent from the variety shown. The exception is Edelzwicker, a blend mainly of "noble" grapes, usually grown and harvested together in the same vineyard.

For advocates that geology has an influence on the personality of wine if not actual quality, Alsace is an interesting proving ground. With the frequency of faulting in the "bundles," different soils within the same terroir are often found on either side of a fault, but may be planted to the same grape. The grower may harvest and vinify separately the grapes from the two soils. The result is two wines of different character. Most generally, however, where different soils occur within an individual terroir, the separate soils will be planted with grapes known to prefer the specific soils, *see* Table 3.1.

Rémy Gresser of Andlau, formerly Secretary of the Grand Cru Association, and Léonard Humbrecht of Domaine Zind-Humbrecht are convinced that the real character of a wine is due to the soil to which that particular grape has been adapted. (Neither of these gentlemen is a geologist.) Johnnie Hugel of Hugel & Fils in Riquewihr, on the other hand, doubts the practicality of scientific matching of cépage and soil. In a discussion of the subject, he pointed out to me that although a grower might very well wish to plant a certain variety, he may not have a vineyard with soil conditions best suited for it. Hugel takes the position that "the vine can look after itself and struggle for life anywhere." (It might be noted that vines on the Hugel properties have not had to struggle very hard; they are in the heart of the best grapeland in Alsace.)

Hubert Trimbach of Ribeauvillé recognizes there are cases where grape varieties of lesser quality occupy positions in superior terroirs. He points out that uprooting and replanting results in a time delay of several years before new vines yield a return on the investment – an income hiatus few growers can afford.

Professor Claude Sittler and Robert Marocke collaborated in an informative study relating geology to the grapes of Alsace. Sittler is professor of geology at the Institut de Géologie, Université Louis Pasteur, in Strasbourg, and Marocke was at the time enologist at the Station Agronomique in Colmar. Table 3.1, modified from their report, identifies the soils which the several varieties of vineplants seem to favor. With the assistance of Professor Sittler, the terroirs most identified with a particular grape variety have been added to the original table.

Table 3.1 Soil–vine preferences

Vineplant (approx % planting)	Favored soil type	Some noted terroirs*
Riesling (20)	sandy-clayey, loamy soils with abundant coarse material	Brand, Clos Ste.-Hune, Elsbourg, Hengst, Kaefferkopf, Kastelberg, Kirchberg (Ribeauvillé), Kitterlé, Osterberg, Rangen, Schneckelsbourg, Schoenenbourg, Sporen, Zahnacker
Gewurztraminer (20)	marly, deep and rich soils with average calcareous content	Affenberg, Altenberg (Bergheim), Bollenberg, Eichberg, Hengst, Kaefferkopf, Kanzlerberg, Kessler, Kirchberg (Barr), Kitterlé, Mambourg, Schlossberg, Zahnacker, Zinnkoepflé
Pinot Gris (5)	deep, rich, loamy/argillitic or volcanic soils or sandy, stony soils	Clos des Capucins, Clos St.-Landelin, Kahnacker, Spiegel
Muscat family (4)	loamy, more or less calcareous soil. Also sandy, loamy soils	Clos. St.-Landelin (Vorbourg), Mandelberg, Steingrubler
Pinot Noir (6)	sandy, calcareous soils	Clos des Capucins, Clos St.-Landelin
Pinot Blanc (18)	loamy, light and fertile soils, with fine texture	Clos du Strangenberg
Sylvaner (20)	deep, sandy and calcareous soils, rich in fine material	Forst, Wiebelsberg, Zotzenberg
Auxerrois (4)	heavy, marly/argillitic soils.	No Grands Crus (for blending)
Chasselas (3)	various soils of average fertility but with water retention	No Grands Crus

Notes: * The list does not include all of the Grands Crus
Because of the patchwork of soils, several terroirs contain more than one type of soil and hence more than one variety of grape.

The Riesling is the premier grape of Alsace as it is in Germany, but oddly, it is not authorized in A.O.C. vineyards elsewhere in France. Although hailed as "king" by the Alsatians, it occupies only 20 percent of the total planting. One reason is that its preference for sunny, sheltered sitings is self-limiting. With planters holding stubbornly to the tradition of offering several wine varieties, the Riesling has to share good ground in limited space with other grapes.

The Riesling sleeps late in the spring, which means getting a slow start on the growing season and consequently late ripening. But a redeeming feature is that it continues to ripen even as cool weather sets in. When dry weather prevails into late fall, more and more growers are opting for *vendanges tardives*, which allows more sugar to be concentrated in the grapes.

The Riesling's demand for sunshine and shelter is offset to some extent by its adaptability to almost any soil, so long as it is well drained. Its preference, however, is for a light, coarse-grained, sandy-loam which warms up quickly.

The influence of geology on the character of wine was demonstrated in an impromptu tasting in the cellars of Domaine Zind-Humbrecht with Léonard Humbrecht and his son Oliver. (The Zinds and Humbrechts united in 1959. The Domaine is run by Léonard and his son Oliver, a graduate viticulturist and the first French Master of Wine.) Léonard, although not a geologist, is a true believer in the influence of the soil on wine character. The walls of his office are covered with geologic maps and cross-sections. He invited Professor Sittler and me to taste three of his Rieslings, each from different terroirs. One was from the Herrenweg on the rich sandy-loamy soils of the alluvial fan of the Fecht near Wintzenheim. It was light and fruity but lacked body. The one grown on the shallow, sandy soils of the granite slopes of Brand, west of Turckheim, had a finesse, balance, and a particular distinctive fruitiness. The third, from the Clos St.-Urbain, in the famous Rangen at Thann was marvelously balanced, full-bodied, musky-flavored – clearly it did honor to its patron saint. The Rangen has one of the most unique soils in France being composed of old volcanic material and detritus from a granite terrain (see page 104).

Another unusual Riesling terroir already mentioned is the Kastelberg on the Steige schist at Andlau. The schist weathers to a soil akin to the slates of the steep-walled Mosel Valley in Germany. Although the Riesling in Alsace is the same as the German variety, there is no mistaking an Alsace Riesling for a German one. For a start, Alsace Rieslings are normally held longer in the barrel, but more importantly, most of these wines are grown on calcareous, clayey soils which give them a fuller-bodied personality than the Rieslings of the "austere," slate soils of Germany.

If the Riesling is king, then the Gewurztraminer is queen of Alsace cépages. (The French do not use the umlaut over the "u" as in the German spelling, because the French "u" sounds like the German "ü.") Although evidently of Italian descent, the Gewurztraminer as it has evolved in Alsace is considered its most distinctive grape. The *Traminer* part of the name comes from the region of Termeno in the Alto Adige north of Bolzano, Italy (where it is known as Traminer Aromatico). The *Gewürz*, meaning spicy, was added in Germany for the more perfumed growths, Traminer alone being reserved for its less spicy wines. In Alsace, the decree of June 30, 1971 declared Gewurztraminer to be the one and only official name for the pink grape with the aromatic white juice.

The Upper Danube basin is just across the Brenner Pass from Italy's Alto Adige, where grapegrowing existed in pre-Roman times. The Upper Danube basin also lies only 30 miles (48 km) across the Black Forest from the Rhine Valley. The Gewurztraminer as well as the Tokay and Muskat may have come to Alsace, as Raymond Dumay suggests, from Italy by the Upper Danube route.

While the Riesling is not choosey about its bed, the Gewurztraminer, as befits a queen, prefers deep, rich, well-drained soils with a high concentration of mineral nutrients. Its most harmonious qualities are brought out when the soils are moderately calcareous and clayey. Due to its early flowering and weak resistance to frosts, the Gewurztraminer prefers a sunny, southerly or southeasterly exposure and a location in the thick soils found in the "belly" or toward the base of the slope. The Sonnenglanz (sunshine) terroir offers an ideal siting for the Gewurztraminer (the variety seems to have lost some of the hardiness of its Alpine heritage).

The Gewurztraminer is one of the most intriguing wines in France, or perhaps in the world. Its dryness but low acidity, complex fruitiness, and spicy bouquet make it a favorite of beginners as well as aficionados. Just mention of the name is almost enough to recall the exotic, Middle-Eastern aftertaste.

Pierre Huglin, formerly head of the Station Agronomique in Colmar, relates that while on the faculty at l'Ecole Nationale Supérieure d'Agronomie de Montpellier he tasted Gewurztraminers from all over the world and could distinguish whether the wines came from a country other than Alsace. Those which came from a warm climate or a very low altitude were almost totally lacking in the characteristic bouquet of the variety in Alsace. Huglin concluded that the grape's particular aromatic character is due not only to its selective breeding, but also to the climatic environment. Likewise, in the Alto Adige, the Italians recognize that the best Traminer comes from the higher elevations. In Alsace during exceptionally warm years, there is concern that the grape may lose too much of its acidity and lessen the harmony and freshness of the wine.

The Pinot Gris (formerly known as Tokay d'Alsace) is perhaps Alsace's most favored wine to accompany food. The name change imposed by the E.U. was meant to clarify that the grape grown in Alsace is the Pinot Gris and not to be confused with the Tokay (Tokaji) dessert wine of Hungary.

In Alsace the Pinot Gris produces an elegant, heady, full-bodied wine quite unlike other grapes of the region. Marc Beyer of Maison Léon Beyer has been quoted as saying it is the least typical of Alsace wines, being more akin to Burgundy. The Pinot Gris likes a deep, rich, clayey-calcareous soil and because it has the earliest budding of the top varieties, it is cultivated only in sheltered, warm exposures. This opulent, velvety wine is dubbed the "Sultan" by the Confrérie St.-Etienne.

The Muscat (the Muscat Blanc d'Alsace à Petits Grains) is also choosy about its location and soils, and is the least planted (4 percent) of the top quality grapes in Alsace. A sub-variety known as Muscat Ottonel was developed in the Loire Valley about 1852, and later brought to Alsace. The Ottonel ripens earlier than the Muscat d'Alsace, and is therefore planted more often.

Muscat wines are served mostly as aperitifs. Wine-writer Pamela Vandyke-Price suggests that one reason for the lack of popularity of this grape may be the difficulty in finding a place for it in the context of a meal. She says a glass of Muscat is like a mouthful of grapes.

The Pinot Noir is undergoing a resurrection in Alsace, with its planting acreage having nearly doubled in the past ten years, but most winemakers in Alsace still vinify the Pinot Noir as a rosé.

The Pinot Blanc is a white mutation of the Pinot Gris – itself a lighter version of the Pinot Noir. According to Jancis Robinson, plantings of "Clevner" (one of Pinot Blanc's many synonyms) were noted in the early 16th century by Jerôme Bock. Today its appearance is limited to parts of upper (southern) Alsace, where the Riesling and Gewurztraminer would have difficulty ripening.

The Sylvaner (spelled Silvaner in Germany) grape is not a top variety, but it is the one most commonly planted in northern Alsace (about 20 percent) where the soil is cooler. Late ripening, regular in yield, and more or less indifferent to soils, the Sylvaner does well under adverse conditions such as higher altitudes, unfavorable exposures, and infertile ground. However, its acreage has steadily decreased in the last 20 years.

The Chasselas is one of the grapes of mass production which yields only ordinary wine. Its plantation is dwindling (now about 3 percent), as the Alsatians continue to opt for quality. Another secondary white grape is the Auxerrois (Auxerrois Blanc), which yields a rather dull wine that is mostly blended into Edelzwicker. The Auxerrois plus other varieties grown for blending total about 4 percent of the Alsace planting.

A better understanding of the traditions and interplay of landscape, grapes, and wines of Alsace requires more knowledge of its people and history.

The cultural mixing ground

The graben offered the best crossing areas of the Rhine for the barbarian invaders. The stream through the Pfälzer Wald and Hardt was deep and swift. At times of low water, the braided stream of the graben could be crossed by wading or swimming.

One of the barbarian tribes to have crossed the Rhine in the 5th century when the deterrent of Roman presence began to wane was the Alemanni. Rather than press further west into Gaul, the Alemanni liked Alsace and established themselves there.

Professor Sittler says the origin of the name Alsace is probably a combination of the Latin *Ali* meaning "strangers" and *Säss*, Old German for settlers or inhabitants. This definition of Alsace ties with Lillian Langseth-Christensen's suggestion that when the Alemanni flooded into the valley west of the Rhine, those who remained east of the river looked across at their expatriate brothers and called them "elisazones," "those who are sitting over there." The land where they were "sitting" became Elisaza or Elsass – Alsace.

Whatever the origin of the name, the difficult but distinctive Alsatian dialect developed from the Alemanni. These tribal people in Alsace were also known as the Suevi, a loose confederation of several German tribes. In 496, Clovis conquered the area west of the Rhine, bringing Frankish influence to Alsace. Amalgamation of the Alemanni, the Gallo-Romans, and Franks became the foundation of the Alsatian population and culture. An important aspect of the amalgamation was that customarily, when a "barbarian" married a Gallo-Roman woman, the children spoke the language of the mother, a dialectic Latin. However, the naming of places and things was the male privilege. The many Germanic placenames in Alsace come from the Alemanni and Franks.

Although German culture is much in evidence by architecture and placenames, it seems there has always been something intrinsically Gallic about the Alsatian people. The scion of a very old Alsatian wine family said to me, "Yes, we do many things in the German way, but our hearts are eternally French." Similarly, André Halbeisen, a winemaker from Bergheim, was quoted as saying, "I am French in the heart and German in the head."

The ecclesiastical influence

The origin of many Alsace vineyards can be traced back to Roman times and the early 6th century when the church began to acquire a significant number of vineyards. Monasteries, abbeys, and convents acquired properties for commercial purposes in competition with the lay winegrowers, which, understandably, led to considerable resentment.

Ecclesiastical ownership of the Alsace vineyards reads like a book of canonical accounts: the Benedictine bishopric at Murbach just west of Guebwiller, founded in 727, owned a good portion of the Rangen vineyard at Thann. They also had the Wanne (now Kessler) on the foothills at Guebwiller and other properties north along the Rhine in Germany. A sister abbey at Altdorf owned the Grands Crus of Altenberg de Wolxheim and the Kastelberg and Moenchburg at Andlau. The cathedral of Strasbourg owned vineyards in the Rangen, the Engelberg, and Goldert. The monastery at Munster (west of Colmar) had vineyards at Turckheim, while the monastery at Ebersmunster held the best of the hillside at Sigolsheim. The bishopric of Basel and convents in Switzerland owned several properties that became Grands Crus. Finally, the Knights Hospitaller of St.-John of Jerusalem (Order of Malta) owned the choice Kanzlerberg at Bergheim.

The resentful lay winegrowers were happy to see the ecclesiastical properties confiscated at the time of the Revolution. Nevertheless, religion is very much a part of the Alsatian vigneron's life. Ignoring the imperious competition of the Church, André Simon observed that, "In Alsace, as in other famous Benedictine-blessed bacchic regions, wine was made to the glory of God, as good as it could be made by men of goodwill."

The advent of terroir classification

Perhaps due to the frequency of foreign occupation, Alsace did not develop a hierarchical classification as in Burgundy and Bordeaux until relatively recently. The concept of Grands Crus was authorized on November 20, 1975, but it took a number of years for the proposal to gain acceptance within Alsace and recognition abroad. As might be expected, the notion was met originally with criticism on the one hand and apathy and uncertainty as to its intended benefit on the other. With some 10,000 growers tending vineyards spread over diverse geology, the uncertainty on the part of the growers should be no surprise. Alsace viticulture is dominated by the small grower, and changes come slowly with these methodical, traditional people.

Each vineyard proposed for this classification is examined by a panel of experts to determine if it meets the stipulated requirements, *with particular emphasis on the geologic nature of the soil and exposure to the sun* (my emphasis).

Photograph 3.2
Jean-Frédéric ("Johnnie") Hugel and his family operate Hugel & Fils in Riquewihr where the firm has made wine since 1639. Their philosophy is "A wine that is well treated is not treated at all," although there is no hesitation in using the most modern techniques and equipment. They own significant portions of the terroirs of Sporen and Schoenenbourg on southeast-facing slopes overlooking the village of Riquewihr. The soils are from Upper Triassic and Lower Jurassic gypsiferous marls and dolomites rich in mineral nutrients

Only four varieties – Riesling, Gewurztraminer, Pinot Gris, and Muscat – are permitted to be considered for Grand Cru status. The Pinot Noir, held in such high regard in Champagne and Burgundy, was excluded, probably because of its limited plantation and the fact that it was not being made into a solid red wine.

Alsace Grands Crus are limited to a maximum yield of 750 gallons per acre (70 hl/ha) – which is over twice the allowable ratio for Grands Crus in the Côte d'Or. As of mid-1980, quite a few of Alsace's well-regarded vineyards had not applied for the Grand Cru designation for various reasons, among them the yield constraint. By 1990, however, 50 Grands Crus had been approved.

In a letter to me in November, 1983, "Johnnie" Hugel of Hugel et Fils suggested that possibly up to that time some good winegrowers were just lax in getting their paperwork done in applying for Grand Cru status. Hugel took a critical position on the concept saying "Personally, we feel that the level of Grand Cru is too low to have any practical merit. It only recognizes the quality *potential* (my emphasis) of a vineyard. Unfortunately, people seem to think, or have been led to think, that the words 'Grand Cru' on a bottle of Alsace wine indicate a wine of very top quality. This is not necessarily true nor untrue. It simply indicates that the vineyard in which the grapes were grown has been judged *capable* (again, my emphasis) of producing fine wines."

He continued, saying "An important point to remember, too, is that all vineyards that could be entitled to the appellation 'Grand Cru' have not been officially classified yet [1983]. The applications were processed strictly in the order received. For this reason, it is wrong to infer that the order in which Grand Cru vineyards were designated has any significance concerning quality. First to be designated has no more intrinsic merit than any others. Personally, I feel it would have been more sensible to have completed the entire classification first, and then declared that the Appellation Grand Cru would come into force on a certain date. It would certainly have caused far less confusion."

The Centre d'Information du Vin d'Alsace in Colmar published an excellent pamphlet, "Le Guide des Grands Crus d'Alsace" showing the 50 terroirs. The format includes a photo view of the vineyard and frequently a topographic map showing its position on the terrain. The text contains information on the soils, exposure, and cépage. Inclusion in an attractive picture-book was a strong incentive for growers who wished to qualify for the Grand Cru classification to complete their applications. Figure 3.4 locates the 50 Grands Crus plus additional terroirs which have achieved renown but are not Grands Crus. If one of your favorite vineyards has been omitted, I apologize.

The terroirs

Vignoble d'Alsace, never more than 2 miles (3 km) wide throughout its 60 miles (96 km), has 35,000 acres (14,000 ha) under vine. Only 4 percent of the vineyard area is at present classified Grand Cru. In time, the number of Grands Crus will increase, but many growers remain uncertain whether there are advantages worth the effort to prepare the application. Nevertheless, the existing Grands Crus are a good basis on which to discuss the terroirs of Alsace. Remember that the Grand Cru classification is based on the *potential* for quality production with emphasis on the geologic nature of the soil and sun exposure.

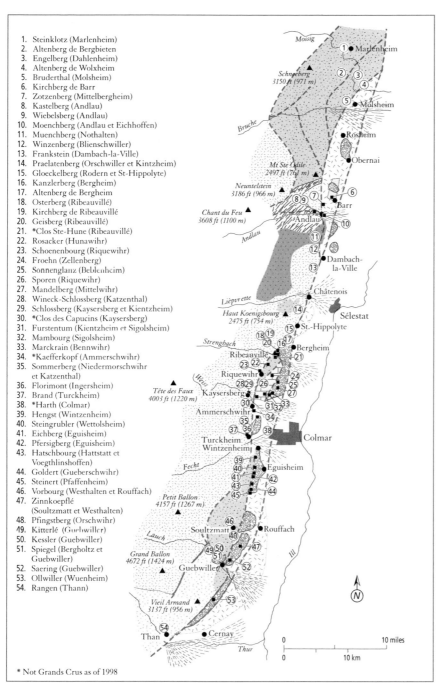

1. Steinklotz (Marlenheim)
2. Altenberg de Bergbieten
3. Engelberg (Dahlenheim)
4. Altenberg de Wolxheim
5. Bruderthal (Molsheim)
6. Kirchberg de Barr
7. Zotzenberg (Mittelbergheim)
8. Kastelberg (Andlau)
9. Wiebelsberg (Andlau)
10. Moenchberg (Andlau et Eichhoffen)
11. Muenchberg (Nothalten)
12. Winzenberg (Blienschwiller)
13. Frankstein (Dambach-la-Ville)
14. Praelatenberg (Orschwiller et Kintzheim)
15. Gloeckelberg (Rodern et St-Hippolyte)
16. Kanzlerberg (Bergheim)
17. Altenberg de Bergheim
18. Osterberg (Ribeauvillé)
19. Kirchberg de Ribeauvillé
20. Geisberg (Ribeauvillé)
21. *Clos Ste-Hune (Ribeauvillé)
22. Rosacker (Hunawihr)
23. Schoenenbourg (Riquewihr)
24. Froehn (Zellenberg)
25. Sonnenglanz (Beblenheim)
26. Sporen (Riquewihr)
27. Mandelberg (Mittelwihr)
28. Wineck-Schlossberg (Katzenthal)
29. Schlossberg (Kaysersberg et Kientzheim)
30. *Clos des Capucins (Kaysersberg)
31. Furstentum (Kientzheim et Sigolsheim)
32. Mambourg (Sigolsheim)
33. Marckrain (Bennwihr)
34. *Kaefferkopf (Ammerschwihr)
35. Sommerberg (Niedermorschwihr
    et Katzenthal)
36. Florimont (Ingersheim)
37. Brand (Turckheim)
38. *Harth (Colmar)
39. Hengst (Wintzenheim)
40. Steingrubler (Wettolsheim)
41. Eichberg (Eguisheim)
42. Pfersigberg (Eguisheim)
43. Hatschbourg (Hattstatt et
    Voegthlinshoffen)
44. Goldert (Gueberschwihr)
45. Steinert (Pfaffenheim)
46. Vorbourg (Westhalten et Rouffach)
47. Zinnkoepflé
    (Soultzmatt et Westhalten)
48. Pfingstberg (Orschwihr)
49. Kitterlé (Guebwiller)
50. Kessler (Guebwiller)
51. Spiegel (Bergholtz et
    Guebwiller)
52. Saering (Guebwiller)
53. Ollwiller (Wuenheim)
54. Rangen (Thann)

* Not Grands Crus as of 1998

Figure 3.4
The Grands Crus of Alsace
and other noted terroirs

Alluvial fans

Slope wash from Crystalline
terrain of Vosges

Oligocene: Lattorfian
conglomerate and marls,
primarily from weathered
Jurassic. (Minor areas of
Pliocene clays and sands.)

Jurassic: Middle and Lower:
Oolitic limestones, marls
and calcareous sands.

Triassic: Upper – marls, thin
limestones, gypsiferous clays
and calcareous sandstones.
Lower – sandstones with some
clay, coarse conglomerates,
"puddingstones" and
sandstones at base.

Permian: coarse, angular
sandstones and conglomerates
with some schists.

Mississippian: coarse, angular
volcanic material derived
from old lavas.

Siluro-Devonian: "Stiege schist"
north of east–west fault at
Andlau, hard and slaty with
micas. South of fault the
"Villé Schist," gray to greenish
with some angular streaks.

Crystalline Vosges: over 14
types of granitic rocks are
identified in the Crystalline
Vosges Massif.

Faults: only the major faults
are shown. It is the numerous
smaller faults which make
significant soil differences
(see Color Plate 12).

Peaks: elevation in feet
(meters).

Vineyards

The Grand Cru vineyards cover 1445 acres (585 ha), with the average size of holding being approximately 29 acres (11.7 ha). The numbered locations shown on Figure 3.4 are referred to in the following sections by numbers in parentheses. Largest of the Grands Crus is the 200-acre (80-ha) Schlossberg (29), which overlooks the Weiss below Kaysersberg. One of the smallest is the 8-acre (3-ha) Kanzlerberg (16) on the slope of the hill at Bergheim. (Ironically, a German military cemetery is located on the crest of the hill at Bergheim in full view of the soldiers' homeland across the Rhine.)

The Grands Crus can be related to the three key geologic terrains I described earlier (*see* pages 85–86). The soils of each of these terrains have particular characteristics, and the exposures are always southerly.

Terroirs of the sub-Vosgian Hills

These are the fault "bundles" with a great variety of soils. The strata involved in this terrain are of the Tertiary Oligocene, Middle Jurassic, the Lower Jurassic (Liassic), and the Upper, Middle, and Lower Triassic.

The Oligocene is represented by a facies called the Lattorfian, composed of marls and limestone conglomerates derived primarily from erosion of the Jurassic. The Middle Jurassic is made up of marls and massive limestones. The Lower Jurassic is composed of fossiliferous marls and limestones with some phosfate nodules.

The Upper and Middle Triassic strata contain dolomites interbedded with anhydrite and gypsiferous clays. The hard dolomites help form the low hills of this terrain. They also contribute to the pebbly texture of the soil. The Lower Triassic is made up of sandstones and shales, with conglomerates and puddingstones in the lower part. Although there are some hard layers in the overall stratigraphic sequence, few classic cap rock and slope landforms develop, rather the typical features are low, rounded hills. In addition to the alluvial fans, there was some Quaternary sheet wash of pebbles and sands from the Vosges mixed with the calcareous, sandy-clay soils.

The Grands Crus and other acknowledged quality vineyard sites are well distributed among the sub-Vosgian Hills, making the fault "bundles" convenient sub-divisions for discussing the individual terroirs. Because of the similarity of the geology of many of these Grand Cru sites, repetition of description will be avoided as much as possible.

The Saverne Fault Bundle, the largest of the fault "bundles," is better suited to hops and fruit, owing to the coolness of the loessic soils and reduced protection of the lower Sandstone Vosges. Nevertheless, the southern part includes sub-Vosgian Hills of the favorable stratigraphic sequence.

The Route du Vin begins (or ends) at Marlenheim with the Steinklotz (1), with Bergbieten (2), Engelberg (3), Altenberg de Wolxheim (4), Bruderthal (5), and Kirchberg (6) nearby in the direction of Barr. All of these terroirs are on well-stirred calcareous, marly, pebbly soils, which are essentially free of loess.

The Ribeauvillé Fault Bundle opens up southward at St.-Hippolyte and continues to the Fecht fan delta at Colmar. The area, viewed in panoramic perspective in Figure 3.3 (page 85), contains a large number – more than a third – of the Grands Crus of Alsace. The detail of the geologic map shown in Color Plate 12 covers the same area as the panoramic drawing, the colors bringing out the patchwork nature of the faulting.

The cross-section of the sub-Vosgian Hills shown in Figure 3.2 illustrates how the step faulting lowers successively younger strata into place toward the Rhine fault. The fault blocks are between 100 and 150 acres (40 to 60 ha) in size. Coming through the vivid patchwork, the dominant orange and yellow (Triassic), blue and lavender (Jurassic), and the pink of the Oligocene "colorize" the sequence of the step faulting.

Along the Route du Vin, several suffixes will appear frequently: "berg" is the Germanic word for hill. "Bourg" or "burg" indicates an ancient walled town. "Heim" is home or the "place of," as Wolxheim was the home or estate of the Wolx family. "Wihr" or "willer" indicates a small, isolated locality, often with difficult access, and occurs in the names of villages in small Vosges valleys, such as Riquewihr and Guebwiller.

Color Plate 6

Well-drained chalk is a measure of fine Champagne. Vineroots penetrate deep into the rock in search of moisture. The photograph on the left shows the Tertiary chalk soil melange over fractured Cretaceous chalk. On the right, Professors Michel Laurain (left) and Hubert Guérin indicate the loess/chalk contact near Cramant in the Côte des Blancs

Color Plate 7

Tertiary lignite (black band) interbedded with sands and marls in an open-pit quarry (cendrière) near the base of the plateau above Verzenay in Champagne

Color Plate 8
Mont Aimé, the "reviewing stand" for Tsar Alexander's imperial guests, looks down on to the "parade ground", the chalk plain below. Vertus is in the mid-distance with the Côte des Blancs beyond

Color Plate 9
Hundreds of miles of tunnels under Epernay contain millions of bottles of champagne. The chalk is soft enough for easy excavation but competent enough not to require shoring

Color Plate 10
Alsace architecture is very different from that of the rest of France: half-timbered houses, oriel turrets, wall paintings, and flower-filled window boxes typify the wine villages in the lee of the Vosges. The mountain range keeps precipitation off the vineyards, making Alsace one of the driest parts of France. Clear skies and hot sun extend the grapes' ripening period well into October, resulting in intense, aromatic white wines

Color Plate 11
Mont Sigolsheim northwest of Colmar was the high ground fought for in the battle of the "Colmar Pocket," December, 1944. On this south-facing slope is the Alsace Grand Cru Mambourg. On the summit is the French military necropolis from which annotated photographs were taken north and southward along the sub-Vosgian hills

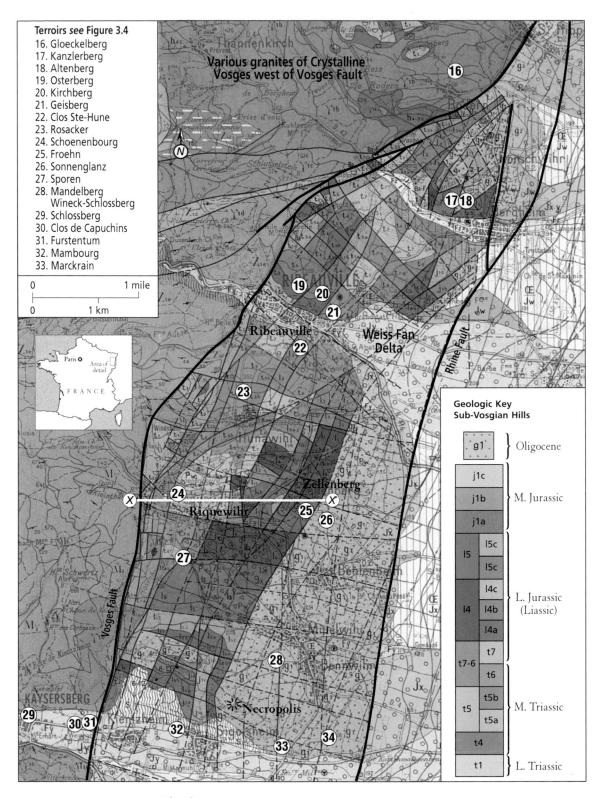

Terroirs *see Figure 3.4*
16. Gloeckelberg
17. Kanzlerberg
18. Altenberg
19. Osterberg
20. Kirchberg
21. Geisberg
22. Clos Ste-Hune
23. Rosacker
24. Schoenenbourg
25. Froehn
26. Sonnenglanz
27. Sporen
28. Mandelberg
    Wineck-Schlossberg
29. Schlossberg
30. Clos de Capuchins
31. Furstentum
32. Mambourg
33. Marckrain

Various granites of Crystalline Vosges west of Vosges Fault

Ribeauvillé

Weiss Fan Delta

Rhine Fault

Vosges Fault

Riquewihr

Zellenberg

Necropolis

KAYSERSBERG

Geologic Key
Sub-Vosgian Hills

g1		} Oligocene
j1c		
j1b		} M. Jurassic
j1a		
l5	l5c	
	l5c	
l4	l4c	} L. Jurassic (Liassic)
	l4b	
	l4a	
t7-6	t7	
	t6	
t5	t5b	} M. Triassic
	t5a	
t4		
t1		} L. Triassic

Color Plate 12
Geology of the Ribeauvillé Fault Bundle
(B.R.G.M. 1:50,000 Colmar-Artolsheim, sheet no. 342, by kind permission of Editions du B.R.G.M., France)

Beginning with the tiny Kanzlerberg terroir (16) at Bergheim, six Grands Crus are located in the orange-yellow Triassic zone: Osterberg (18), Kirchberg (19), Geisberg (20), Rosacker (22), and Schoenenbourg (23). Clos Ste.-Hune (21), although not a Grand Cru, is also on Triassic soils.

In the zone of Lower Jurassic (Liassic) we have the Grands Crus Altenberg de Bergheim (17) (with some Middle Jurassic), Froehn (24), Sporen (26), and Furstentum (31). The Florimont (36), pinpointed in Photograph 3.3, is located on Upper and Middle Jurassic soils.

On the outer zone of the Oligocene Lattorfian conglomerate complex are the substantial terroirs of Sonnenglanz (25), Mandelberg (27), Mambourg (32), Marckrain (33), and the Hengst (39).

Physiographically, the Ribeauvillé Fault Bundle ends with the Fecht alluvial delta fan on which is located the Harth terroir (38) – which is not a Grand Cru. The piedmont structure continues southward into the Rouffach Fault Bundle.

South of Wintzenheim, the Vosges fault makes a wide indentation into the Vosges, leaving a large lens of Triassic strata bordering the narrow avenue of gently undulating sub-Vosgian Hills. The Triassic sandstones of this wedge have been eroded into steep ridges that delimit vineyard development much the same way as the granitic Vosges. Nevertheless, about half of the Grands Crus of the Rouffach Fault Bundle are found along the flanks of this Triassic massif. The marls higher up the steep slopes of the Zinnkoepflé (47) contribute a good clay mix for the sandy soils.

Out from the hill on which stand the three castles of Eguisheim, the gentle slopes support the terroir of Pfersigberg (42), which has produced wines since the 14th century. Pfingstberg (48) is on more gentle slopes of marls and dolomites of the Middle Triassic.

The valley of the Lauch above Guebwiller known as Florival (meaning vale of flowers) leads up to the abbey of Murbach. It was monks of this abbey who introduced vines to the area and constructed the first terraces where the Grands

Crus of Domaines Schlumberger overlook the town. The now extensive terraces are on some of the steepest wine slopes in France – between 32 and 40 degrees. Upkeep of the domaine's 35 miles (56 km) of dry-stone walls requires continuous employment of five masons.

The Schlumbergers' terraces form an arc around the spur of l'Unterlinger, a prominent massif of Triassic sandstones. The large, 64-acre (25-ha) Kitterlé (49) extends around the nose from a southwest to a southeast exposure. Two further Grands Crus, the Kessler (50) and Spiegel (51) are northeastward extensions of the Kitterlé. Texture of the sandy soil is improved by lenses of micaceous clay from higher up the slope. A small fault block of Paleozoic graywacke at the western end of the Kitterlé provides some variety to its soils. The Kitterlé terroir is particularly noteworthy for the floral bouquet in its Gewurztraminer, and for Pinot Gris with a fine nose and discreet aroma.

The lower slope of the southeast flank of l'Unterlinger merges with a lobe of the Oligocene Lattorfian on which Schlumberger's Grand Cru Saering (52) is located. Pebbles of Triassic sandstones from the higher slopes are mixed with the soil which produces Muscats, Gewurztraminers, and Pinot Gris of some renown.

Along the narrow strip of low mounds bordering the Rhine fault substrata of Middle Jurassic, oolitic limestone provides deep, well-drained soils for the large Hatschbourg (43) terroir (117 acres/47 ha). The equally large Goldert (44) and only slightly smaller Steinert (45) are likewise located on the oolitic soils. (The name Goldert suggests the golden color of the rich, white wines of the Côte d'Or which also grow on Jurassic oolitic limestones.)

Further south, just west of the famous Château d'Isenbourg at Rouffach, is Vorbourg (48). Wines of the four Grand Cru grapes from this terroir are noted for aromas of peaches and apricots.

Several areas of Oligocene Lattorfian occur in the lobes of strata along the avenue of sub-Vosgian Hills. Steingrubler (40) and the long, rambling 142 acres (57 ha) of the Eichberg (41) near to Eguisheim are located on soils of this conglomerate of limestone and marls.

Photograph 3.4
View over Guebwiller towards the sub-Vosges showing the Kitterlé terroir. The most renowned vineyards on these sandy slopes are owned by Domaines Schlumberger, the biggest property in Alsace, rightly famous for its luscious Riesling, Pinot Gris, and Gewurztraminer

Between Guebwiller and Thann, a small fault block leaves a wedge of Oligocene on which the Grand Cru terroir of Ollwiller is located. Literally in the shadow of the Vieil-Armand (3137 feet/956 m), the vineyard receives an annual average of little more than 17 inches (43 mm) of precipitation – barely enough for grape growing. The peak is named for a French soldier who heroically occupied the peak as an observation post during the German invasion of World War I. The favorable, sunny exposure and dryness of Ollwiller give the Riesling and Gewurztraminer a particular elegance and *goût de terroir*.

The southernmost terroir on the Route du Vin d'Alsace is the Rangen (54) at Thann which is discussed under the following category.

Terroirs of the crystalline terrain

Eleven of the Grands Crus are on soils derived from crystalline rocks: granites, schists, and Paleozoic volcanic complexes.

At Barr is the small (14-acre/5.6-ha) Kastelberg (8) terroir on the Steige schist of early Paleozoic age. The Steige is a hard, dark rock that was strongly metamorphosed when the granite intruded a sedimentary crust. The Riesling from this terroir has a delicate and distinct bouquet.

Just south of the Barr–Andlau sector is the Muenchberg (11), on a pocket of sedimentary material within the crystalline terrain. Soils are from "old rocks" (Permian) of puddingstones and conglomerates interbedded with old volcanic material. The lean soils are on the slopes of a crescent-shaped valley which produces a favorable microclimate. Cistercian monks of the former abbey of Baumgarten started cultivating vines here in the 12th century. Because the poor soil keeps yields low, the Riesling develops a fullness of all its aromatic qualities.

Northward from St.-Hippolyte toward Dambach-la-Ville, the Vosges and Rhine faults merge, leaving a pediment slope little more than a stone's throw in width. The terroirs of Winzenberg (12), Frankstein (13), and Praelatenberg (14) are located on this narrow slope. However, vines range up the steep granite slope some 400 feet (120 m). The Riesling and Gewurztraminer produce wines of rich floral aroma and great finesse from these east-facing slopes.

Gloeckelberg (15), just west of St.-Hippolyte and overlooking the village of Rodern has granite soils with a mixture of Paleozoic schist and gritstone. In the Middle Ages, the vineyard was the property of convents in Colmar and Sélestat.

The most famous of the terroirs on granite slopes is Wineck-Schlossberg (28) and the adjoining Schlossberg (29) below Kaysersberg. Hill and vineyard take their names from the castle-fortress (*schloss*) that controlled the valley of the Weiss in the Middle Ages. The soils are coarse and sandy, rich in nutrients with enough clay weathered from the feldspars for good binding. Their Rieslings and Gewurztraminers are noted for their richness of aroma and fruitiness.

As viewed in Photograph 3.3, southwest from Mont Sigolsheim, the Vosges Fault branches south of Kaysersberg, leaving a wedge of granite eroded to low relief on which are located the Sommerberg (35), at Niedermorschwihr, and the Brand (37) terroirs. Although the coarse-textured soils have poor water retention, they are very rich in mineral nutrients, having weathered from the "granite with the two micas." The terroirs produce exceptional Rieslings, Pinot Gris, and Gewurztraminers.

At the southern end of the Route du Vin is the Rangen (54) at Thann. Facing the town across the Thur is one of the most unusual vineyard bedrocks in France. A large pocket of volcanic rocks – ash, lava, and graywacke (fragments of granitic material) was caught up in the granite intrusion, producing a very hard, complex mass of rock. The soil is thin and the slope is steep (almost 60 degrees). Who would try to grow wine on such terrain? Monks, of course. Monks from the St.-Thiebaut abbey-cathedral. The wine proved to be exceptional, and fame of the powerful "Rangenwein" was spread far and wide by pilgrims coming to the collegiate church of St.-Thiebaut.

As a result of the phylloxera devastation, the Rangen deteriorated sadly, until some 25 years ago when Léonard Humbrecht led a program of restoration. Terraces were rebuilt, parcels consolidated, eroded soil restored, etc. Completion of the restoration was celebrated with an open house in the Cabane des Bangards in Thann (*see* the facing page for the story of the bangards and the "little hut" where they lived).

Terroirs of the alluvial fans

Alluvial fans constitute a significant area of the viticultural terrain of Alsace, although the Kaefferkopf (34) is at present the only exceptional terroir, but not classified Grand Cru. Some good wines are produced on the fans, but their flavors are short-lived, a characteristic revealed by the Herrenweg Riesling of our impromptu tasting in the cellar of Léonard and Madame Humbrecht. The Kaefferkopf is located on the edge of the Weiss fan, but the alluvium here is thin and the rootings actually derive their sustenance from the underlying Oligocene marly conglomerates.

The soils of the fans are somewhat sandy and typically pebbly but they are deep and generally well-drained. Because there were no carbonate rocks in the granite terrain where the fan material originated, the soils are shy of active calcium carbonate. However, appreciable calcium for plant nutrition is provided by the chemical weathering of the feldspars and micas of granite wash present in the alluvium.

Having been fed by the largest of the mountain glaciers during the Ice Age, the swollen streams of the Fecht and Weiss produced fans that coalesced to form the very large, flat alluvial cone that extends outward under much of the city of Colmar. The experimental vineyards of the Institut Viticole Oberlin, established in 1895 by Chrétien Oberlin, are situated on this fan. The Institut continues its research on the varieties best suited to the various soils of Alsace. Production from the Oberlin vineyards goes primarily to the city of Colmar for municipal banquets and receptions.

Good basic drainage within the alluvial fan and soils with adequate water retention together with long, daily sun exposure account for the high quality of the wines of the Harth (38), the Herrenweg, and other terroirs located on this fan. For the most part, the Riesling and Sylvaner are grown here, the latter used to produce an all-purpose wine.

Gaining a true appreciation of Alsace wines is greatly aided by some knowledge of its poignant history and diversity of cultural development.

Historical sketches of Alsace

It is not possible to date just when the viticultural history of Alsace began, but it was evidently in Gallo-Roman times for there were flourishing vineyards by the Merovingian period beginning in the 6th century. By the 14th century, there were over 60,000 acres (24,000 ha) under vine – about twice the amount today. Much of the early-day planting, however, was on land recognized as more suitable for other crops.

During most of the Middle Ages, wine was one of the major sources of wealth for Alsace. Its position on the Rhine permitted a thriving export trade with the Netherlands, England, and even Scandinavia. In 1138, a Hohenstaufen emperor of the Holy Roman Empire came to power in the part of Germany which at the time included Alsace. The Hohenstaufens liked the pleasant Alsace climate, and in the 12th century, they built the immense castle at Haut-Kœnigsbourg which was patterned after their ancestral castle in Swabia (east of the Black Forest). The Hohenstaufens were in conflict with the papacy. As a consequence, under their sovereignty, bishoprics were allowed to become quite independent and powerful, acquiring extensive vineyard estates for commercial purposes. The ruling nobles themselves acquired vineyards, often in violent conflict with their bishops. Fostered by such an atmosphere, several cities such as Haguenau, Strasbourg, and Colmar became independent city-states. Colmar came to be regarded as the wine capital of Alsace, promoting trade associations which brought about stringent regulations on winegrowing and winemaking.

In the 15th century, the Société des Bourgeois d'Ammerschwihr (the future Confrérie St.-Etienne) was established, bringing together the most competent people of the region to oversee the quality of wines being marketed.

Winegrowing reached a high level in the 16th century, and many of today's venerable wine families of Alsace started business. Dopff 'Au Moulin' started in Riquewihr in 1574, followed by the Léon Beyer family of Eguisheim in 1580. The Humbrecht family, originally of Gueberschwihr, now Zind-Humbrecht of Wintzenheim, began making wine in 1620. F. E. Trimbach started in Ribeauvillé in 1626; A. & O. Muré of Rouffach, 1630, and Hugel et Fils in 1639.

Although the major fighting during the Thirty Years War (1618–1648) took place in Germany, Alsace suffered great privation, depredation, and destruction. Half of the population died or disappeared. The stone bas-relief carved by the bangards in 1648 tells a woeful story of those times.

The Thirty Years War was 17 years along before Cardinal Richelieu finally involved the Catholic Bourbons of France on the side of the Protestant German princes in successfully opposing the hegemony of the Austrian Habsburgs. In the end, a devastated Alsace was ceded to France by the Peace of Westphalia and Treaty of Munster. The relinquishment of Alsace to France was to be a vengeful bone of contention between Germany and France for the next 300 years.

Break-up of the ecclesiastical properties and other large estates following the French Revolution in 1790, brought about many new owners to Alsace vineyards. Regrettably, many of the new growers favored ordinary, low-quality wine which could be sold quickly, albeit cheaply. The time-honored wine-growers named above, plus others, however, were steadfast advocates of quality and have led in recovery programs for quality after each period of occupation.

After France lost the short but decisive Franco-Prussian War of 1870, Alsace and Lorraine were reattached to Germany. Everything possible was done to Germanize Alsace and its population. Unfortunately, winemaking was one of the easy victims. The Germans required the vineyard owners to produce greater quantities of more acid wines from the inferior varieties Chasselas and Auxerrois. Moreover, Alsace wines could only be sold in cask; no identification of origin of the wine was allowed.

Wine could be regulated, but the Alsatian spirit was another matter. Alphonse Daudet's poignant story, "The Last Lesson," set at the time of the 1870 war, well illustrates André Maurois' perception that the German and French nationalities could be distinguished by how men "felt." From a certain date it was decreed that only German would be taught in the schools. In Daudet's story, as the church clock struck twelve on the fateful day, Schoolmaster Hamel, choked with emotion, wrote on the blackboard, "Vive La France" and without turning, dismissed the class with a gesture.

It was somewhat ironical that soon after Alsace was reannexed to Germany, phylloxera arrived. By 1913, the vineyards had become more devastated than by a trampling army. At the conclusion of World War I in 1918, Alsace was returned to France. The phylloxera ravage had also been brought under control by the grafting of European vines on resistant American rootstocks. Freed from foreign coercion and required production of cheap wine, the Alsatian growers, opting for quality rather than quantity, began to replant their vineyards with "noble" vines. But they had to deal with the damaged reputation of Alsace wines, as well as now compete with other French wines. Alsace wines were considered "cheap," and there was simply no market for such wines. Furthermore, the market had collapsed for all French wines. Nevertheless, the proud, older growers were determined to restore the good reputation of Alsace.

The reestablishment of quality vineyards and wines was barely completed when Alsace was once more subjected to German rule by World War II. The occupier was again determined to Germanize Alsace. The vineyard owners were ordered to produce volume rather than quality wine. Liberation eventually came, but the vineyards and villages paid a price. As the Allies in their advance eastward sought to gain crossings of the Rhine, fierce fighting for the "Colmar Pocket" caused more material destruction in Alsace than in any previous war. The Sigolsheim ridge northwest of Colmar, site of some of Alsace's finest wines, was also the high ground for which the fiercest fighting took place. The Germans called the ridge "Blutberg" (Blood Mountain). The French military necropolis on Sigolsheim is mute evidence of the intensity of the fighting. (The American soldiers of the XXI Corps killed in this battle are buried in the U.S. military cemetery at Epinal, west of the Vosges.) The villages and adjacent vineyards of Ammerschwihr, Kientzheim, Sigolsheim, Bennwihr, Mittelwihr, and Katzenthal, were either totally destroyed or severely damaged. When the villages were rebuilt, the ancient wine fraternity, the Confrérie St.-Etienne Alsace, was also resurrected, in 1947, in Ammerschwihr.

Famous people of Alsace

No larger in size than the state of Delaware, Alsace has given to the world more than its share of illustrious people. Pope Leo IX (1002) was a native of Eguisheim. Rouget de Lisle, a poet and musician of Strasbourg, composed a war song for the revolutionary army of the Rhine (1780) which later became "La Marseillaise," the French national anthem. Napoleon's able generals included the Alsatians Ney, Kellerman, and Rapp. Of perhaps more lasting fame were Frédéric-Auguste Bartholdi, a native of Colmar, who designed the Statue of Liberty that stands in New York Harbor, and Albert Schweitzer, theologian, organist, philosopher, and mission doctor, who was born in 1875 in Kaysersberg.

In medieval times, Gottfried von Strassburg (Strasbourg) put into poetic form the Celtic legend of the Rhine, which Richard Wagner later set to words and music as *Tristan und Isolde*. Earlier Wagner had put the Burgundian-Frankish myths of the Rhine into the opera *Das Rheingold*. Johann Gutenberg's printing presses developed for sustained, heavy-duty printing were very likely modeled after the wine presses he observed while living in Strasbourg.

Joseph Dreyer, in his chapter on Alsace in *Le Grand Livre du Vin*, says the Alsatian is his own master despite foreign efforts to make him otherwise. He makes his wine his way, and ensures that it is good enough for himself and his friends. Alsace gastronomy is equal to the interesting variety of Alsace wines, reflecting the renown of the mountains, streams, meadows, and farmyards of this land of enchantment.

4 Burgundy: parade of cap-rock scarps

Figure 4.1
General geology of
Burgundy
(modified from B.R.G.M.
sheets by kind permission of
Editions du B.R.G.M., France)

The wine areas of Burgundy are on hills and slopes for 100 miles (160 km) along the western side of the Saône Valley. For the most part, the relief is modest, the plateaux of the Côte d'Or being only 500 feet (115 m) above the valley, whose elevations average about 725 feet (220 m). Further south, in Beaujolais, vineyards are located up to almost 2000 feet (600 m) on the granite slopes of the Morvan, whose highest ridges are around 3000 feet (900 m). Figure 4.1 shows the general geology of this famous region of fine wines.

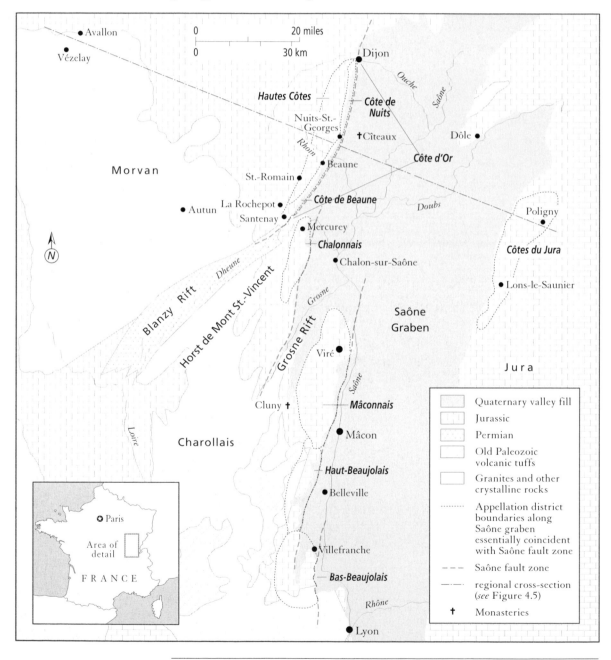

Marvelous, maddening wines

One moment Burgundy's wines are praised as marvelous, in the next breath, they may be faulted for maddening inconsistency. The two principal grapes, the Pinot Noir and Chardonnay, have found a genuine compatibility with the soils of the Côte d'Or with the potential for producing exceptional wines. The inconsistency arises with a number of growers in a single terroir making their own wine in their own way, so there is no one Chambertin, no one Le Montrachet. Neither the praise nor blame lies altogether with nature or man. Important but obscure variations in the geology and soil occur in very short distances. One terroir may produce superb wines while an adjacent one, which on the surface appears quite similar, yields wines of lesser quality. This is one of the confounding fascinations of wine.

On one of my early visits to Burgundy, I was extremely fortunate to have as my guides Professor Noël Leneuf and Dr. Robert Lautel, two of the foremost authorities on the geology, soils, and wines of Burgundy. Leneuf is Emeritus Professor of Geology at the University of Dijon. Dr. Lautel, recently retired Deputy Director of B.R.G.M., the French Geologic Survey, was co-editor of *Terroirs et Vins de France*, a geologic field guide to the French vineyards.

On this September morning, a thick cloud cover was nailed down tightly to the ridges of the Côte d'Or. We had planned a reconnaissance flight in a small plane along the frontal scarps. On learning the cloud cover was not predicted to lift until later in the day, we decided to take our tour by car. Looking back on it, my disappointment was actually good luck, for the secrets of "marvelous, maddening Burgundy" are best learned on the ground, not from the air.

As we departed Dijon, travelling south via route N74, almost immediately the names of famous wine villages began to flash by like a roadside ticker tape – Fixin, Gevrey-Chambertin, Morey-St.-Denis, Chambolle-Musigny. At Vougeot, Leneuf wheeled into the road leading to the château of the Clos de Vougeot (Frenchmen never turn, they wheel). We took the small road along the west side of the famous Grand Cru vineyard enclosed by the dry-stone wall making it a "clos." From a vantage point on the high side of the vineyard, we had a splendid view of the historic château and the long sweep of vines down to the highway. It was an impressive sight – 125 acres (50 ha) of golden grapeland developed by the Cistercians and enclosed by the hand-fitted stone over five centuries ago.

As we stood there, Lautel asked me if I knew the legend of how the monks supposedly reserved wine from the upper slope for the pope, that from the mid-slope for the cardinals, and wine from the lower slope for the bishops. Yes, I had heard such a story, assuming it was part of the local wine lore. At this point I was surprised to hear Leneuf state that he had serious doubts, bishops and history notwithstanding, whether the lower slopes should be classified Grand Cru. He then pointed to where the slope shows a perceptible flattening along a north–south line about 250 yards (230 m) up from the highway. A veneer of slope-wash soil makes it difficult to distinguish, but there is also a faint change in color to a darker soil downslope from this line. He explained that this line across the lower part of the vineyard marks the surface trace of a major fault bordering the west side of the Saône Valley. The valley is a graben, an offset companion to the Rhine

Figure 4.2
The Clos de Vougeot
The defining stone walls of the château help prevent slope wash from the vineyards of Echezeaux. The geology of the Grands Crus is shown in cross section below (geology based on Régis Bertrand's unpublished thesis, "Contribution à l'étude de quelques sols de la Côte de Nuits-Saint-Georges," 1969, University of Dijon)

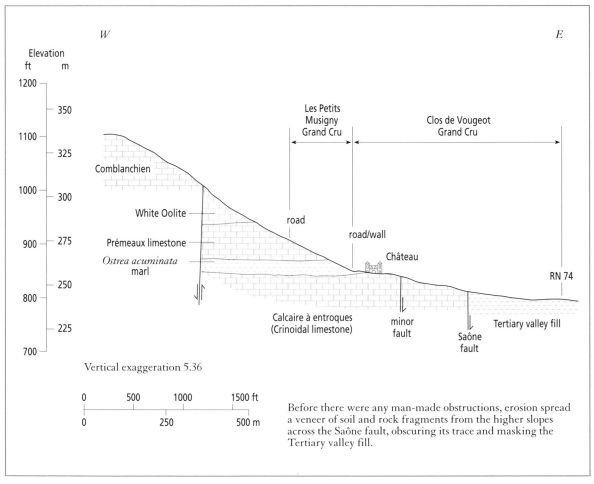

Vertical exaggeration 5.36

Before there were any man-made obstructions, erosion spread a veneer of soil and rock fragments from the higher slopes across the Saône fault, obscuring its trace and masking the Tertiary valley fill.

graben discussed in chapter 3. This geologic feature is a topographic trench created by downfaulting on both sides. The annotated photograph in Figure 4.2 shows the position of the fault line. (It was taken at the time of my first visit in spring before leafing had begun.) The companion cross-section illustrates the geologic relationships that Leneuf was describing.

The Saône fault zone represents a profound break between two quite different geologic worlds: on the upslope are Jurassic limestones and marls, the heart and soul of Burgundy's greatest vinelands. On the downthrown (valley) side of the fault are sands and clays of the Tertiary valley fill. As the water table (zone of saturation) in the valley is typically at a shallow depth, crossing the fault is like stepping off a hard pathway onto soft, damp ground. Consequently, the vines on the downthrown side of the fault – the bishops' wine – soon find their roots uncomfortably damp. Vines, like cats, don't like wet feet. Grapes grown where water is too available tend to yield juice that is less concentrated and produce wines of lesser quality.

The geology at work across this very important fault zone is illustrated in greater detail in Figure 4.3. This is one of a series of shallow-depth seismic profiles that was conducted over several of the famous Côte d'Or vineyards. (The technique is described in the section titled "Seeing through the soil.")

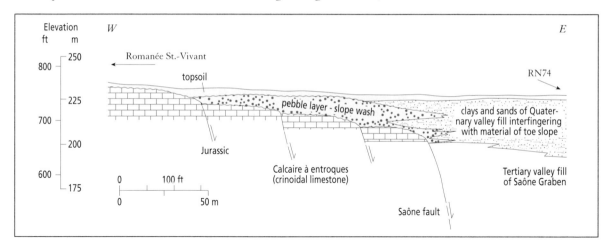

The Saône fault zone extends the entire length of Burgundy and continues southward as the Rhône rift. The landforms typified by this faulting are classic cap rock and slopes modified by the angle and direction of tilt of the fault blocks. The downslope boundaries of the Grands Crus terroirs are generally limited for the most part by the valley's high water table which stimulates excess growth to the vine. The two notable exceptions are Clos de Vougeot and Bâtard Montrachet. Many terroirs of commune quality, however, enjoy this environment.

The scarp-slope of the Côte d'Or is lacerated with faults, all very small compared to the Saône zone, which has a displacement of more than 5000 feet (1500 m). The surface evidence for many of the small faults may be obscured by slope wash, as in the case of the major fault across the Clos de Vougeot. Even small faults, however, can materially affect the sequence of bedrocks and makeup of the soil. Figure 4.4 illustrates how faulting may subtend or extend good soilmaking strata.

Figure 4.3
Seismic profile
Detail of Saône fault zone (seismic/geologic interpretation by Catherine Ponsot-Jacquin)

Figure 4.4
Affect of faulting with
minor displacement on
slope outcrops

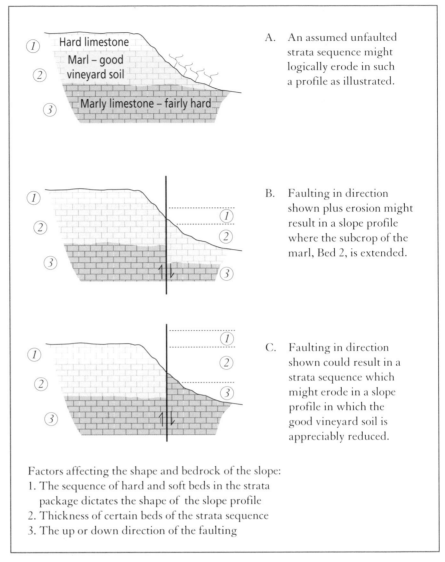

A. An assumed unfaulted strata sequence might logically erode in such a profile as illustrated.

(1) Hard limestone
(2) Marl – good vineyard soil
(3) Marly limestone – fairly hard

B. Faulting in direction shown plus erosion might result in a slope profile where the subcrop of the marl, Bed 2, is extended.

C. Faulting in direction shown could result in a strata sequence which might erode in a slope profile in which the good vineyard soil is appreciably reduced.

Factors affecting the shape and bedrock of the slope:
1. The sequence of hard and soft beds in the strata package dictates the shape of the slope profile
2. Thickness of certain beds of the strata sequence
3. The up or down direction of the faulting

There is nothing fairyland about the château of the Clos de Vougeot. "Severe and monumental, with no extraneous gardens or useless greenery, without artifice or adornment, it rises abruptly in a sea of vines," is the way Gaston Roupnel, a winegrower at Gevrey-Chambertin and former Professor of History at the University of Dijon, saw it. That architectural severity and incongruous massiveness sitting in a vineyard, simply spell Burgundy.

There is a scene in Hugh Johnson's excellent television series, *Vintage*, in which he stands in one of the Côte d'Or Grand Cru vineyards and asks, "Why this one," walks across the road and finishes his sentence with "and not this one?" Some answers may be due to obscured changes in geology such as faulting or depositional changes in the bedrock. Not only can such changes alter the viticultural potential between neighboring vineyards, but also within a single vineyard itself.

When the Cistercian monks cultivated the Clos de Vougeot vines they undoubtedly recognized a difference in the quality of grapes from different parts of the slope. Whether they vinified grapes from different levels separately as the legend would have it is doubtful. Today there are 95 owners in the Clos – the number grows yearly – with properties of various shapes and sizes varying from a few rows to several acres. There is no one wine representing the Clos de Vougeot. Each owner or négociant can make and market his own wine as Grand Cru Clos de Vougeot.

Soils of the pope's and cardinals' slopes are a mixture of weathered slope-wash and limestone fragments over a fractured bedrock of Jurassic limestone. A veneer of this soil obscures the subsoil of valley fill across the Saône fault zone. Quality of grapes of the Clos de Vougeot depends to an appreciable extent on which part of the slope they are grown, but to imply that those from the valley soil are wholly inferior is just not true. However, according to some experts, they are not consistently up to Grand Cru standards. But from whatever part of the slope the grapes are sourced, the final "signature" is that of the winemaker.

It is this multiplicity of "signatures" as well as the geology that contribute to the "maddening" aspect of Burgundy wines. The exponential growth of multiple ownership is not a Burgundy problem exclusively, rather, it is due to the Napoleonic code of heredity. The code, which decrees that each heir shall inherit equal shares of a property, may seem like a fair law, but it is obviously destined slowly but surely to fragment to extinction many vineyards along with other agricultural estates.

In no other wine region of France does the interplay of man and geology result in the dichotomy of marvelous and maddening to the extent that it does in Burgundy. In the following pages I have tried to describe in more detail precisely how this works. The research and observations of Leneuf and Lautel are acknowledged in places, but the impromptu tutorial that September day set me on the right course for understanding and appreciating fascinating Burgundy.

The making of the landscape

The overall landscape and geology of Burgundy is a narrow band of scarps, fault blocks, and hills along the western side of the Saône Valley (graben) extending over 100 miles (160 km) from Dijon southward to Lyon. The rocks involved are Jurassic, Triassic, and basement granites with minor exposures of Paleozoic rocks, schists, and old volcanic intrusions. Variations in the crust resulted in different structural styles and landforms creating four viticultural compartments: the Côte d'Or, Chalonnais, Mâconnais, and Beaujolais. The first three are all scarp slopes and block faults; Beaujolais is a bulge of basement granite. (Chablis, in wine terms, is part of Burgundy, but in geologic terms it is part of the Kimmeridgian Chain, and so is included in chapter 9.)

The Rhône–Saône–Rhine rifts are lasting, visible scars of a major tear in the earth's crust which zig-zagged across western Europe from the Mediterranean to the North Sea. Before the rifting began, a thick blanket of Jurassic limestones and some Triassic strata lay relatively undisturbed over the region from the British Isles to the Middle East. The Saône graben faulting lowered the overlying strata a mile or more into the trough. Formations along the western margin remained high, but were fractured and broken into the scarps and hills of Burgundy. Topographically, the graben never actually got to be a mile deep as an open trough; debris (valley fill) accumulated in the trench about as fast as it sank. The regional cross-section, Figure 4.5, shows the crustal configuration from the Paris Basin across the Morvan and the graben zone to the Jura.

When the Saône rifting began, cracks in the basement from an earlier geologic period came to life. The older trend was more easterly than the new Saône rifting so that, south of the Côte d'Or, competition between the two

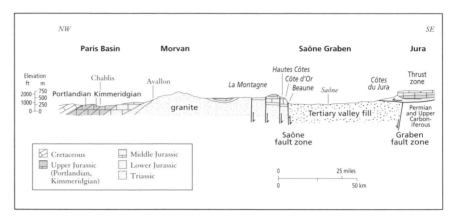

systems compartmentalized the Burgundy sectors (*see* Figure 4.1). The Blanzy Rift of the older trend separates the Côte d'Or from the Chalonnais, and the Grosne Rift Valley divides the Chalonnais and the Mâconnais.

Structurally, the Côte d'Or is one long north–south fault scarp, broken only by combes and a few small river valleys (*see* Figure 4.6). The Côte d'Or strata are either laying flat or slightly dipping westward. Chalonnais, wedged between converging elements of the older trend, is a complex of fault blocks tilted both east and west with some lying flat. In Mâconnais, the series of long north–south blocks are tilted eastward. The direction of tilt may seem inconsequential until the relationship of the sun and scarp faces of east- and west-tilted blocks is considered, as indicated in Figure 4.7. The east-facing scarps continue to be the preferred configuration as they catch the early morning sun, hastening to dispel the evening dew and to warm the soil. It was during the freeze-thaw cycles of the Ice Age that the scarps developed concave slopes and accumulated slope-wash soil in which the vines are now planted.

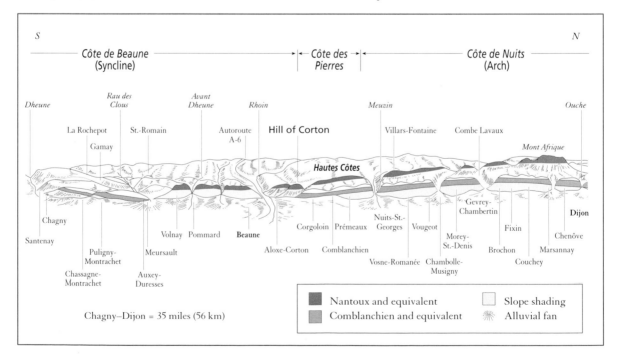

Figure 4.7
Significance of direction of
dip of fault blocks

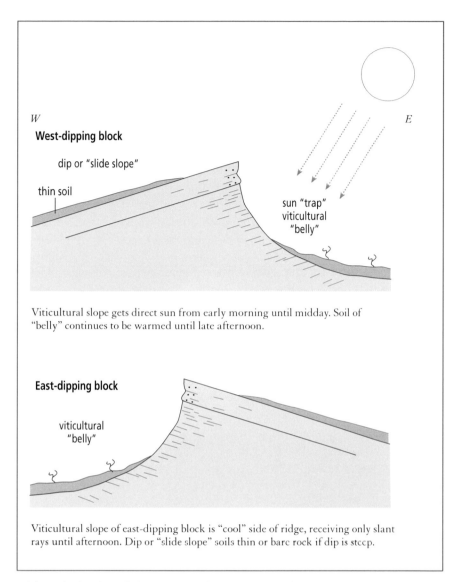

West-dipping block

W

E

dip or "slide slope"

thin soil

sun "trap"
viticultural
"belly"

Viticultural slope gets direct sun from early morning until midday. Soil of "belly" continues to be warmed until late afternoon.

East-dipping block

viticultural
"belly"

Viticultural slope of east-dipping block is "cool" side of ridge, receiving only slant rays until afternoon. Dip or "slide slope" soils thin or bare rock if dip is steep.

Although the dip of the strata in the wine area of Pouilly-Fuissé is essentially eastward, geologic complexities in this part of Mâconnais result in a topographic bowl floored with excellent soil formations, which account for the recognized quality of Pouilly-Fuissé wines.

To the south of Mâconnais a bulge in the basement exposes the granitic and metamorphic rocks of Haut-Beaujolais – home of Beaujolais' best. South of the granites (*see* Figure 4.1), a small sector of east-dipping fault blocks is known as the Bas- or Sedimentary Beaujolais – the spigot of Beaujolais Nouveau.

The rifting and crustal disturbances began to quiet down toward the end of the Tertiary. The Quaternary Ice Age followed, with about two million years to go before the present, during which the landscape got its final "face-lift," and the "bellies" or "kidneys" of the slopes began to be filled with slope wash. The Ice Age tapered off about 10,000 years ago, allowing the climate to moderate, vegetation to return, and weathering of the rocks to begin to produce the vineyard soils of today.

Soil: the soul of Burgundy wine

Every winegrower of Burgundy is born knowing that soil is the soul of his terroir. In *Making Sense of Burgundy*, Matt Kramer says the Burgundians are very nearly Freudian about the influence of soil in shaping the character and quality of their wine. Professor Leneuf's conviction that soil is a critical factor in the difference between ordinary and exceptional wines is more scientific than emotional. His conviction is based on research with associates at the University of Dijon and government soil scientists.

These almost-sacred soils of Burgundy (primarily the Côte d'Or) are the result of weathering from 1000 feet (300 m) of Jurassic limestone and marls, *see* Figure 4.8. Variations in the strata occur both vertically and horizontally. Vertical differences represent changes in depositional environment with time. Horizontal differences within the same time period also represent different depositional environments. Deposits in shallow waters and littoral zones (between high and low tide) are characteristically variable. They may either be transitional or occur quite rapidly. Lateral changes in facies occur particularly in the Côte de Beaune.

In addition to the stratigraphic changes, two other geologic phenomena affecting the vineyard soils and exposures have already been discussed – minor faulting and tilt of fault blocks. A fourth phenomenon also affects the Côte d'Or – an uparching of the Côte de Nuits and a downwarping of the Côte de Beaune.

Figure 4.8
Stratigraphic chart of the Côte d'Or
(modified from sketch by Catherine Ponsot-Jacquin)

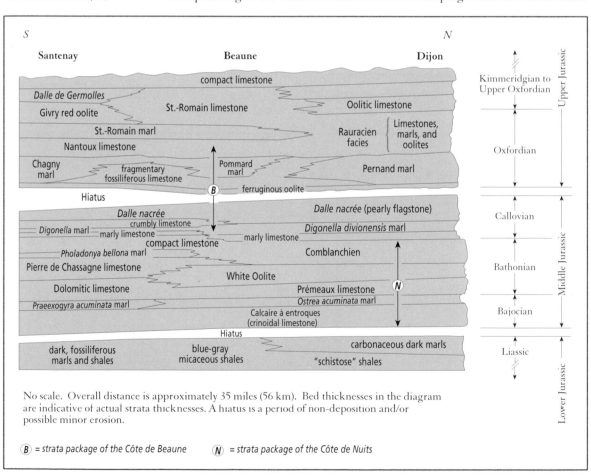

No scale. Overall distance is approximately 35 miles (56 km). Bed thicknesses in the diagram are indicative of actual strata thicknesses. A hiatus is a period of non-deposition and/or possible minor erosion.

Ⓑ = strata package of the Côte de Beaune   Ⓝ = strata package of the Côte de Nuits

The average height of the Côte d'Or frontal scarp is about 500 feet (150 m). The arching of the Côte de Nuits brings into play the stratigraphic section labeled "N" in Figure 4.8 while downwarping of the Côte de Beaune involves the strata sequence labeled "B". Two key layers are shaded in the diagram to trace the shape of the wave whose inversion occurs at Corgoloin-Comblanchien. Both sequences of strata make excellent soils with "B" having more marls and more white wines, and "N," being more limy, having more red wines. The strata of these two packages continue southward through Chalonnais, Mâconnais, and Bas-Beaujolais with only minor changes in thickness and character.

South of the Côte d'Or, the Lower Jurassic (Liassic) and Triassic are more involved in the vineyard slopes – but their soils are poorer than those of the Middle and Upper Jurassic. The Liassic limestones are more carbonaceous than the younger Jurassic, and the shales are typically micaceous and fissile. The Triassic, which lies directly on the crystalline rocks of the Morvan, has shales which tend to be sterile (non-calcareous) and interbedded with sandstones.

As described in Part One, environmental conditions during the Middle and Upper Jurassic were rather inviting, comparable to the present-day Bahamas or southern Florida. Warm, shallow seas and a semi-tropical climate encouraged almost an over-population of sea life, making the Jurassic the most fossiliferous strata in Europe.

The king of the shell-bearing sea creatures of the Jurassic was the ammonite. Resembling a wound-up squid, this ancient cousin of the nautilus ranged more widely than any other non-vertebrates in the Jurassic seas. The ammonite, found not only in Europe but around the world, was a real survivor, managing to evolve and exist throughout all phases of the Triassic and Jurassic time. Differences in ecologic conditions resulted in dwarfs of only a few inches to giants several feet across. Evolution of the ammonite shells and species provides guides correlating the strata and environment of the wine rocks.

At the base of the Middle Jurassic (Figure 4.8), is the *Calcaire à entroques* (crinoidal limestone). It is formed by the accumulation of broken stalks and fragments from extensive underwater gardens of sea lilies (crinoids) that became imbedded in lime mud. Color Plate 13 is a microscope photograph of a thin (translucent) section showing how this garden litter is cemented into a rock. In turn, the fragmentary nature of the rock aids breakdown in weathering to soil.

The limy mud in which beds of oysters grew plump solidified to marls, which in turn now "fatten" (or thicken) soils derived from weathered and shattered limestones to form a well-structured soil. The Burgundy marls are often named for their fossils – such as the *Ostrea acuminata* which overlies the *Calcaire à entroques*. The shells of the *acuminata* are so well preserved that they appear to be discards from last weekend's clambake rather than 150 million years old (*see* Color Plate 14).

In a more marine environment than that in which the oyster beds grew, extensive undersea dunes of oolites (calcium carbonate pellets resembling fish eggs), became the White Oolite formation. Oolites and other fossils not only add their names to such formations, they help create an arable texture to the soil. Bonding between the rock matrix and the oolites and fossils are lines of weakness allowing invasion of freeze-thaw and chemical weathering.

The slabby limestone is known as *Dalle nacrée*, meaning pearly flagstone. It was a fragment of this rock which I picked up on my first visit to Burgundy (*see* page 8). The formation takes its name from the nacreous (pearly) luster of the inside of the shells which compose the rock. The formation represents the burial ground of a great population of oysters and other bivalves which settled into a bottom mush of carbonaceous mud. In quiet, protected waters, a pure calcareous sludge accumulated which hardened into the compact, finely crystalline Comblanchien limestone. Quarried at Comblanchien as a building stone, it rises in the arch of the Côte de Nuits as the cap rock of the scarp.

Similarly in quiet but turbid waters, thick deposits of calcareous clay accumulated, now known as the Pernand and Pommard marls. These marls interfinger with clayey limestones to make the excellent soils on the slopes of the Hill of Corton, Pommard, and Volnay.

The soils have inherited from the calcareous parent materials a "maternal immunity" against acidity giving most of the soils a pH from 7 (neutral) to a mildly basic 8.5. The granitic soils of Beaujolais, however, are on the acidic side as there are no calcareous rocks in the soil makeup. (Most grapevines are at their best in soils on the basic side, the Gamay being one exception.)

Marine sediments at the time of burial retain varying amounts of sea water interstically (within pores). The sea water contains a variety of chemical elements in one form or another which provide a portion of the mineral nutrients required by grapevines. Unfortunately, phosphorus, one of the most critical nutrients, normally occurs as only 5–10 percent of desirable levels, which is why vines require supplemental organo-mineral fertilizers. Jean-Marie Ponsot, a prominent grower in Morey-St.-Denis on the Côte de Nuits, believes (and he says other growers and enologists agree) that it is phosphorus in the soil that has the greatest influence on *le goût du vin*, the taste of wine.

Soil analyses from several sources show that a good supply of the clay mineral, montmorillonite (discussed in Part One, and *see* Color Plate 4), is found in the mid-slopes of the Côte d'Or. Its high cation-exchange capacity helps the mid-slope "belly" to function well.

Madame Lalou Bize-Leroy on terroir

The head of the firm of Maison Leroy and co-owner of Domaine de la Romanée-Conti, Madame Bize-Leroy is acknowledged throughout the wine world as a formidable force in Burgundy. Knowing how passionately she feels about the terroirs of Burgundy, I invited her to express her thoughts on soils. In a personal letter, her reply was typically forthright:

"Suppose that one day we might know the nature of all the elements which compose this nourishing 'new earth' between the pebbly surface [the topsoil] and the Jurassic sub-basement [bedrock], would we then be able to determine exactly the physical and chemical influence of these elements on the intrinsic, fundamental character of the wine issued from them?" Madame Bize-Leroy went on to answer her own question: "Personally, I do not believe so, for all of this is too dynamic – I would say almost alive – to put in an equation. I remain convinced, however, that the fundamental character of each wine depends on the nature of its subsoil."

No matter how passionately, "Freudian," or scientific one may feel about the importance of soils to the wines of Burgundy, climate and its year-to-year weather are also critical to their quality.

The climate

Each spring begins with high hopes for a great year, but, on average, it is only about every third year that weather factors north of the Midi combine favorably to produce a superior vintage. Burgundy's climate is about the median of the wine districts of France – not the warmest nor the coolest, not the driest, nor the wettest (*see* Figure 1.5 in Part One). The median conditions bring out some of the best in both the Pinot Noir and the Chardonnay.

Burgundy lies within the transition zone between the continental and maritime climatic influences (*see* Color Plate 3). Here it experiences the unsettling competition between these two zones. The resulting weather is like the finishing lines of the couplet about the little girl with the curl in the middle of her forehead, "When she was good, she was very, very good, but when she was bad, she was horrid." Those exceptionally good-weather years are times of high excitement – and high prices.

Occasionally, twinges of Mediterranean climate sneak through the Valence Gateway riding the "vent du Midi" to reach Beaujolais. Burgundy weather can be miserable, but it is seldom unduly severe. Hot, dry Augusts are unpleasant for the people, but delightful for the grapes – if it is not too dry.

Cold, wet weather, particularly frost, is feared from April to early June, when budding and flowering take place. The vignerons do not rest easy until after May 17th, the Advent of St.-Boniface, the final observance of the three "ice saints." However, delay in budding due to weather may be compensated by abundant good sunshine during the remainder of the season.

The prevailing Westerlies approaching the 100-mile (160-km) long strip of Burgundy vineyards are variously modified by the Morvan and the Montagne. Beaujolais, being in the lee of the higher mountains, is provided some protection, but the ridges are not really sufficiently high to be an effective rain-shield, as are the Vosges in Alsace. Rather than offer weather protection, the lower Morvan hills seem to breed thunderstorms that move out over Mâconnais, Chalonnais, and the Côte d'Or, all too frequently accompanied by hail, the "white peril" which the vignerons dread.

Hail has always been a lurking even though helpless fear in Burgundy. Shortly after World War II, the firing of explosives into threatening hail clouds was tried, a technique practiced by the Swiss and North Italians. The idea was to explode an artillery shell near the base of the cumulonimbus clouds, dispersing a mixture of fine silver iodide crystals and silica. The particles would provide hundreds of thousands of hailstone nuclei. The number of hailstones were deliberately multiplied, but, hopefully, they would be of much smaller size and either melt on the way down or only pelt the vineyard with little damage. But the gunners were winegrowers, not artillerymen, and their placements were nearly always erratic.

Later, greater accuracy of placement was achieved by rockets fired from a plane flying into the cloud. A pilot, plane, and radar system had to be at the ready all summer long. Many growers refused to share this expense, as they thought the effort might benefit others more than themselves. When hail insurance became more affordable, it provided specific protection for individual growers, and the cloud seeding was stopped.

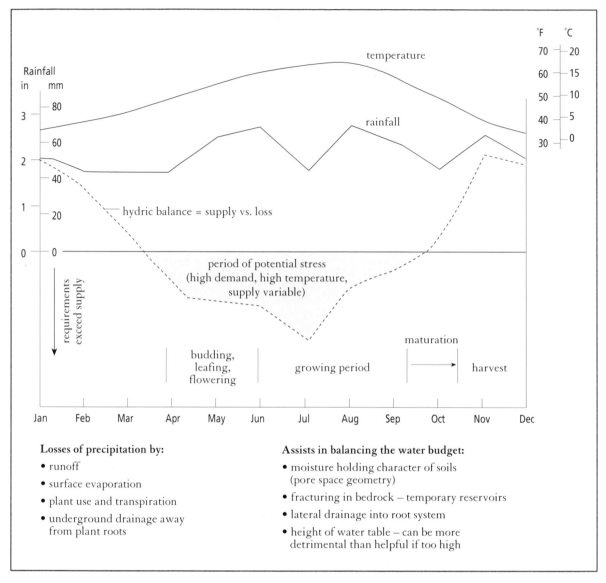

Figure 4.9
Hydric balance of the
Côte d'Or

The average annual rainfall is about 28 inches (700 mm) – near the marginal level for grapevines. Fortunately, fracturing of the bedrock, associated with the faulting along the border of the Saône graben, helps conserve the water supply.

Figure 4.9 shows the hydric balance (water supply vs. loss) for a typical Burgundy year, plotted with rainfall and temperature. Relative humidity and winds have an important bearing on water loss, but records are essentially non-existent. The period of greatest plant stress occurs during July when low rainfall coincides with high temperatures and high water requirements by the plants. (Recall that no irrigation is allowed by the French wine authorities.)

The high amount of rainfall in the spring is helpful in replacing storage water for the growing season, but may also promote plant disease and hamper flowering. Heavy rainfall in June that interferes with flowering is of particular concern, as poor fertilization of the flowers may lead to their abortion, known as *coulure*. No flowers, no grapes, no wine.

As September approaches, the vignerons pray for less rain and lots of sun. The prayerful combination is for sunny, dry weather, but "Dear Lord, not too dry or the grapes *ne grossissent pas* (do not fatten up)." Urban dwellers may complain about the weather, but the vignerons pray about it. To them good weather means fat grapes and fat pocketbooks.

The northward trend of the Burgundy slopes provides exposures which are generally eastward. With a latitude about that of the U.S.–Canadian border, every hour of sunshine, every calorie of reflected heat in Burgundy are important during maturation. It is somewhat controversial whether the tree-covered ridges west of the vineyards create beneficial microclimates. Some feel that the cool, damp air flowing down the combes increases risk of frost and mildew. Others contend that the funneling affect mixes the air – nature's own wind machine.

The grapes of Burgundy

The marvelous part of the marvelous/maddening dichotomy is that the great wines of Burgundy are from one red and one white grape. We can appreciate the nuances of Pinot Noir or Chardonnay from various terroirs. The maddening part comes from what the number of winemakers do with the grapes.

The calcareous soils of Burgundy seem heaven-made for its grapes, with the Chardonnay showing a preference for more clayey conditions, and Pinot Noir for soils that are more limy. These preferences respond respectively to the dominant geology of the Côte de Nuits and the Côte de Beaune.

In addition to the two ruling nobles are the red Gamay of Beaujolais and the white Aligoté whose domaine is the Hautes Côtes. Some Pinot Blanc and Pinot Gris are cultivated by special permission, primarily as experimental planting in areas of less-privileged exposure – although wine from these grapes will not be sold as white burgundy.

With the exception of Beaujolais which has a special classification (*see* page 157), Burgundy has four levels of appellation hierarchy: Grands Crus, Premiers Crus, Village or Commune A.O.C., and Regional or Bourgogne A.O.C.

Rolande Gadille, in her comprehensive research on the wines of Burgundy, concluded that the winegrape was first cultivated in Burgundy as early as the 3rd or possibly even the 2nd century. However, in 1952 came that shocking archeologic evidence detailed in Part One (*see* page 45), indicating that there was something going on with wine in Burgundy long before the Roman era. The discovery, near Châtillon-sur-Seine northwest of Dijon, of the grave of a Celtic princess containing artifacts dating from the 6th century B.C. meant that the Celts were at least trading in wine with the Etruscans or Greeks at that early date. There is no evidence that the Celts themselves were actually growing grapes and making wine.

There is no "grape trail" of either the Pinot Noir or the Chardonnay that can be traced back through either of the gateways to a foreign provenance. It is conceivable that the four grapes of Burgundy were developed from seeds or plants that had reverted to the wild state from the Etruscan era. Possibly the Pinot Noir may have been developed from the *Allobrogica*, cultivated by the Celtic tribe in what is now Haute-Savoie. However or from wherever, the grapes got to Burgundy, they are happily married to her soils.

Wines of monks

Burgundy viticulture was propelled to greatness by monks. In turn, viticulture became an important subvention in the spread of Christianity from Cluny and Cîteaux across western Europe.

Christianity in Gaul got its big impetus in 496, when Clovis agreed to take his wife's religion, if he prayed to her God and was successful in an upcoming desperate battle. His wife was a Burgundian princess and a Christian. Clovis was successful in his battle and let it be known that this Christianity might have its good points. Soon, most of the Burgundians became Christian along with their Frankish neighbors, renouncing the heretical Arianism which they had brought with them. In the 5th century, the Romans resettled the Burgundians in the area north of Lake Geneva and in the Saône Valley. The Burgundians had a well-organized royal house and soon their territory extended from Champagne to the Mediterranean – the "Lost Kingdom."

The Franks came to Gaul about the same time as the Burgundians, the two peoples managing to coexist peacefully for over half a century. The Burgundians were good-natured and tolerant people; the Germanic Franks were noted for their harsh and cruel chauvinism. In the late 6th century, however, through intrigue and murder, the Franks under Clovis took over the Burgundian kingdom.

These were the "Salin Franks" coming from the region of the Salin River (now the Yssel or Ijessel) in central Netherlands. The Frankish ruling house was also well structured, with many tribal customs and laws being adopted later by the French ruling houses – one such law being the Salic Law of Succession which recognized that royal title could only come through the male line. This "law" shaped the course of many events in French history, including the Hundred Years War. It was also responsible for both the beginning and the end of the line of Valois dukes (*see* page 124).

In 587, King Guntram, an early Merovingian (Frankish) king gave lands including vineyards to the Abbey of St.-Bénigne in Dijon. Soon afterwards, Amalgaire, a duke of the early Burgundian kingdom founded the Abbey of Bèze. In 630, vines were planted in the area of Chambertin, now known as the Clos-de-Bèze. But the events that were to have the most far-reaching and lasting affect on wine came with the founding in 910 of the monastery of Cluny in the Grosne Valley, west of Mâcon. The monastic influence was reinforced a century later with the establishment of a new order at Cîteaux in the Saône Valley, south of Dijon.

Under the Benedictines, Cluny became the greatest abbey-church in western Europe until St.-Peter's was completed in Rome in the early 17th century. By the beginning of the 12th century, over 1200 monasteries and 10,000 monks in France, Germany, Spain, Italy, and England were under Cluniac control. The Benedictines, known as the "black monks" for their black habits, were respected for their letters, architecture, and liturgy, but they also had excellent farmers among their numbers. Cluny and its satellite monasteries developed extensive vineyards in Burgundy. Work in the fields and vineyards was organized into cells or groups, which included lay brothers as well as monks. Wherever the Benedictines went, viticulture went along.

By terms of its endowment, Cluny reported directly to the Holy See in Rome. Because of the distance, it enjoyed considerable freedom and grew in power and wealth. It also became more worldly – in fact too much so to suit Robert, Abbot of a satellite monastery at Molesmes on the small Laignes River southwest of Bar-sur-Seine. In 1098, Robert with twenty companions who shared his desire to observe the strict Rule of St.-Benedict left Molesmes to start an independent monastery in the Côte d'Or. The place they selected was 12 miles (20 km) east of Nuits-St.-Georges in the Saône Valley on land donated by Robert's cousin Raynard, Viscount of Beaune.

The "eight journeaux" from the Viscount of Beaune was not a particularly generous gift as much of the ground was swampy and full of reeds. (One *journal* is the amount of land that a man can plow in one day.) The word for reed in Old French was *cistel*; hence this place in the reeds was called *cîteaux*. Members of the fledgling monastery and the new order became known as Cistercians. Dubbed the "white monks" because of their gray-white woolen habit with linen cowl, the Cistercians interpreted the Benedictine rules with severe strictness of fasting, worship, silence, and field labor. Their motto was "Under Cross and Plow."

As their vineyard and farm acreage increased to include better upland areas, the Cistercians adopted a cell and grange system similar to that of the Benedictines. Lay brothers happily worked for them in exchange for food and protection. The combination of the monks of Cîteaux and geology of the Côte d'Or would make its terroirs and wines immortal.

The Cistercians and the Clos de Vougeot

In 1110, a small piece of land on the hillslope west of the village of Vougeot was given to Cîteaux by Guerrie de Chambolle (his name is preserved in the *lieu-dit* of Chambolle-Musigny). The Cistercians planted vines and continued to acquire adjacent land by gift or barter until 1336, when they enclosed their now 125 acres (50 ha) with a stone wall making it a *clos* – the Clos de Vougeot. The monks' dedication and emphasis on good husbandry set the viticultural standard, and showed that the terroir could produce marvelous wines.

First the Cistercians built a press house and storage cellar on the property. Eventually a dormitory was authorized to be added. As the story goes, the original plans drawn by one of the monks who had been an architect were quite elaborate, and the monk became boastful of his grand building-to-be. More than a little annoyed, the authorities at Cîteaux decreed that the plans be changed to a plain structure, and as punishment for his sinful pride, the vain monk was to supervise its construction.

The Romanesque-style building is indeed as plain as the habit of the monks who built it, but it is one of Burgundy's most heavily visited tourist attractions. Viticultural equipment of early times including two ancient, huge, wooden wine presses, are impressive items in its museum. It took some pretty burly monks or lay brothers to operate those monsters. Jacques Chevignard, Director-General of the Confrérie des Chevaliers du Tastevin, notes that the massive oak timbers used to build these 12th-century machines were from trees 400 years old, young saplings at the time of Charlemagne in the 8th century.

Entering the museum section of the château to be confronted by these giant presses is rather like stumbling upon a hall of dinosaurs. Unlike the dinosaurs, however, it was the very size of these monsters that preserved them from extinction – too big to be carried off, and almost indestructible. One story relates that German soldiers who occupied the château during World War II tried to chop off pieces for firewood. Finding the 1000-year-old beams of oak as hard as iron, the great presses were left alone.

Although with much creaking and groaning, the machines still operate perfectly. One of them, known as "Le Têtu," is shown in Color Plate 17. It was used to do a pressing for Hugh Johnson's television documentary, *Vintage – the Story of Wine*.

After several centuries of being the center of the Cistercian wine activities in Burgundy, the château was abandoned when religious orders were abolished at the time of the Revolution. The Cistercians of France dispersed to Germany, Italy, Spain, and other countries tolerant toward monasticism. Then, late in the 19th century, the Cistercians returned to the Côte d'Or, bought back land around the site of the original abbey and resumed a gradual, quiet farming business, but not viticulture.

Basically, life goes on at Cîteaux much the same as it did in the centuries before the Revolution. But today, the monks of Cîteaux tend no vines; dairy farming and producing cheese provide their sustenance. That there is no Clos de Vougeot of their own making on their tables matters not. As the monks work their farm in the Saône Valley, they can see in the hazy distance the low ridges where in the long ago their Cistercian brethren, "Under Cross and Plow," painstakingly converted 125 acres (50 ha) of pasture land into one of Burgundy's most famous vineyards.

Several years ago, it was arranged for a group of us to attend the noon-time prayer service at Cîteaux. Soon after we were seated, monks moving as silently as shadows appeared in ones and twos and quickly took their places in the choir. The monophonic tones of the plainsong of the Gregorian Chant began – unchanged for centuries. The only incongruous thing in this time warp between the 12th and the 20th centuries was the modern building in which the service was held.

As the ecclesiastical dimension gave Burgundy a gentility on the one hand, its political history gave it a robustness on the other.

A goodly heritage

> *"Of a verity, the heritage of the old dukes was a goodly one. To the traveler who goes through this fair and rich province, the wonder is, that, with such wide and fertile valleys to nourish them – such strong, full-bodied drink to nerve them, such rivers at their feet and mountains at their backs, the rulers of Burgundy did not become kings of France."*

So wondered William J. Flagg, the 19th-century American viticulturist, as he bumped along in his buggy outside Beaune. The "old dukes" to which he referred were the four great dukes of Valois who reigned in Burgundy from 1364 to 1477.

Being king of France at that time would have been no great prize for ambitious, young dukes. Most of the western half of the country legally belonged to the English Plantagenets, devised from Henry of Anjou and Eleanor of Aquitaine. The two countries were at war because Edward III of England had challenged the selection of Philip of Valois as king of France, claiming his own kinship was closer in line of succession. (Edward's claim to the throne was through his mother, which ran counter to the French Salic Law of Succession which recognized that royal titles could only be inherited through the male line.)

No, the dukes had their eyes on a brighter if more distant star. While the duchy was indeed a "rich and fair land," it was only a small portion of the original kingdom of Burgundy of the 10th and 11th centuries. Might not the "Lost Kingdom" be re-created and some desirable parts added? This would be a challenge worthy of "the Bold" and "the Fearless," monikers of the first two Valois dukes.

This kingdom that was lost was that of the original Burgundians, a Scandinavian people originally from the island of Burgundarholm, now Bornholm, in the Baltic Sea. After coming to the mainland, they moved to the Rhine–Danube area. The ruling clan were the Nibelungens, sons of Niflis, God of the Northern Mists. Ancient Rhineland legends tell of murders and intrigues. These legends were put to words and music in Richard Wagner's epoch, *Der Ring des Nibelungen*.

Christopher Cope in his book, *The Lost Kingdom of Burgundy, a Phoenix Frustrated*, gives a thorough account of the original kingdom of Burgundy and efforts of the Valois dukes to equal if not exceed its glory.

The Valois era

The Valois dukes made the most lasting impression, but, ironically, it was the Capetian dukes of Burgundy whose 300-year rule is generally known as the "golden age of Burgundy."

The Capetian duchy was a bastion of Christianity: monasticism from Cluny and Cîteaux spread across western Europe. With religion went viticulture. Burgundy was the crossroad of trade and travel, a center for the exchange of ideas. It was indeed a "goodly heritage" left to the Valois when, in 1361, the Capetian line of hereditary dukes ended with the sudden death of the young, unmarried, duke Philip of Rouvres. John II, the Good, now Valois king of France, appointed his son, Philip the Bold, as the first Valois duke of Burgundy at the age of just 24.

The Valois dynasty of Burgundian dukes would number only four, ending for the same reason it began – the line of succession ran out of male heirs. With the last Valois, the duchy would revert to the crown. In the meantime the dukes would have christened French history with Burgundian wine and glamorized it in elegant courts.

Philip had won his nickname "the Bold" (le Hardi) at age 14, fighting beside his father at Poitiers against Edward the Black Prince, son of Edward III of England. This was early in the Hundred Years War; the reign of the Valois dukes would coincide essentially with this war.

The Burgundy which was Philip's appanage at age 24 was rich, rural country, but it was landlocked. Philip visualized that the manufacturing centers and ports of the Low Countries would be a marvelous complement to his Burgundy. This he accomplished by marrying Margaret, daughter and heiress of the Count of Flanders. (Fourteenth-century Flanders included the Netherlands, Belgium, and a portion of northern France.) His marriage to Margaret marked the beginning of Flemish cultural influence in Burgundy, of which the showpiece is the Hospice de Beaune (*see* page 143).

Philip chose to reside at the royal court in Paris and he governed Burgundy through a ducal council and officers in Dijon. During his long reign his patronage of music, art, sculpture, and literature was lavish and would become a hallmark of the Valois dukes.

A little Valois history

Philip the Bold reigned for 40 years before he was succeeded by his son, John the Fearless, who also married a Hollander. John was involved in French politics and spent much time feuding with his cousins. He continued improvement of the administrative system inaugurated by his father. Also like his father, he lived most of the time in Paris, where his court was the most brilliant in western Europe. Burgundy wines may have had rural origins, but they became "Prince Charmings" in the glamorous royal court. John ruled only 15 years before he was murdered by the Dauphin.

John's son, Philip, known also as the Good, was filled with vengeance at the assassination of his father, and allied himself with the English against the French crown. It was his troops who handed over Joan of Arc to the English. When the tide later turned in favor of the French, Philip attempted unsuccessfully to bring about a compromise solution to the extended conflict between the two countries.

To celebrate his marriage to Isabella of Portugal, Philip created the Order of the Golden Fleece, which became the most exclusive international club in Christendom. The duke's extravagant gatherings outdid those of his father and grandfather, rivaling the most outrageous imitation that Hollywood would produce.

Nicolas Rolin, Philip's chancellor, was a native of Autun in the Morvan, west of Beaune. He and his wife, Guigone de Salins (another Hollander), founded the Hôtel-Dieu (the Hospices de Beaune) in 1443 and deeded their vineyards for the upkeep of the hospital. Similar bequests followed, so that today the Hôtel-Dieu is one of the largest vineyard owners in Burgundy (*see* page 143).

Philip reigned for 48 years, so his son Charles was in his forties when he at last succeeded his father. Charles' moniker was "le Téméraire" – Rash or Bold. Burgundy was at its zenith, its territory now including most of Holland, Brabant, Hainaut, Artois, Luxembourg, and the lands between the Loire and Jura. The " Lost Kingdom" of Burgundy, or worthy substitute territory, was almost restored.

Attesting to the wealth and power of Burgundy was its standing army, unbelievably larger and stronger than any in western Europe. To the east, the Austrian (German) Emperor, Frederick III, had been greatly perturbed about the Turks who had taken Constantinople and were threatening his capital, Vienna. In an unprecedented move, Charles and his father took their army to the aid of Frederick of the old eastern Franks. The infidels were stopped. No other dynasty at the time was capable of saving Christendom. Now came payback time. Charles pressed Fredrick to recognize him as heir to the Austrian domain. This would have been "Lost Kingdom, Plus." The two were to meet in Trier in 1473, on which occasion Charles expected formally to receive the recognition he craved. In current slang, it was a "done deal." But something about the eagerness with which Charles reached for a crown not yet proffered, disturbed Fredrick. The night before the big meeting, Fredrick slipped away quietly, taking his crown with him.

Foiled, but living up to being "the Rash," Charles took on Switzerland and Lorraine in an unwise winter campaign. He met an inglorious death in the siege of Nancy. He had no male heirs, so upon his death the duchy legally reverted to the French royal domain. However, Marie, his daughter, was able to retain the Low Countries as her dowry. In one of history's ironies, Marie married Maxmillian Habsburg, son of Fredrick III – so instead of Austria and Savoie coming to Charles, part of Charles's duchy went to the Habsburgs!

The grand lifestyle of the Valois dukes and their courts set the pattern for all of Europe; the Côte d'Or was their wine cellar. The Valois dukes put Burgundy wines on the tables of all Christendom and embroidered the Valois name in the wine history of France.

It was monks who brought Burgundy wines to world-class; the Valois put the province on the glamor marque. During the three centuries from the reign of the Valois to the Revolution, Burgundy suffered along with all of France through disastrous internal wars and foreign conflicts, and saw kings come and go. The Revolution brought about the break-up of large estates and the expulsion of the religious orders. The Côte d'Or vineyards endured many new landowners, but the wines continued to develop as marvelous. The maddening aspect of Burgundy wines began with the multiplicity of vineyard ownerships which was only exacerbated by the Napoleonic Code decreeing that all heirs should share equally in an inheritance.

In the latter part of the 1800s, phylloxera devastated Burgundy along with the other vineyards of France. The proud and traditional Burgundians resisted grafting their vines to recover from this crisis until it was imperatively evident that this was the only solution.

In two World Wars only a generation apart, Burgundy, along with the other wine districts of France, lost vignerons and suffered disruptions. During the unprecedented last half century of relative peace, agronomic and technologic advances have helped to make Burgundy wines potentially ever more marvelous. The following section will not minimize the maddening aspects of Burgundy wines, but it will tell you why and where both the great and lesser wines grow.

The Côte d'Or

The Côte d'Or or simply La Côte – the "golden slope" – may sound regal, but the landscape is simple enough, although classic cap rock and slopes. This simplicity seems to emphasize the straightforwardness of its wines from two separate single grapes.

The wine villages are modest, more businesslike than colorful. There are a few châteaux, but mostly the local people are as unpretentious as their villages and landscapes, but on appropriate occasions they can be as festive as their most robust wines. It is not at all unusual to see a wealthy grower turn out in *bleus de travail*, the typical workman's blue coveralls, and participate "hands-on" in his winemaking.

When communes were being created in the early 18th century, one criterion used was to balance the population to the size of the parish church. In the case of the Côte d'Or, the east–west boundaries were drawn to give each commune a portion of the plateau for woods and grazing land, a portion of the slope for vineyards, and a portion of the valley for other agriculture. With only a few exceptions, commune boundaries follow property lines.

The east–west trending boundaries of the communes were an admirable effort at fair treatment of the economic terrain. However, they were at right angles to the north–south trending geology and "soil bellies," blessing the wine potential in some communes more than others. In time, several villages hyphenated their names with one of their famous vineyards, for example Gevrey-Chambertin and Puligny-Montrachet.

I indicated earlier that irregularities in the depositional patterns gave some Côte d'Or communes more limestones and others more marls. The scarp faulting cuts across these depositional irregularities, adding further to the complexity of the vineyard slopes. These stratigraphic variations are shown in Figure 4.8. Variations are particularly evident in the Upper Jurassic Beaune package, "B," which is characterized by large thicknesses of marl interfingering with marly limestone. The Middle Jurassic is more uniform in thickness, and lithology with limestones and oolites dominates. It seems almost uncanny that nature devised the up and down arching as a devise to get the Upper and Middle Jurassic strata packages into the Côte d'Or vineyards.

Apparently, the vignerons of long ago recognized the Chardonnay's preference for calcareous, clayey soils, giving a plausible explanation why the Côte de Beaune has so many excellent white wines. Similarly, the Pinot Noir with its preference for limy soils has responded marvelously to the predominantly limestone soils of the Côte de Nuits. The "belly soils" form an avenue of Grands and Premiers Crus throughout the Côte d'Or.

The foot and toe slopes interfinger with strata of the valley fill whose soils are typically damp. The deep, rich soils of the lowermost slope produce luxuriant vines, but the grapes tend to be too "flabby" for quality wine. These lower slope and valley vineyards are either classified -Villages or simply take the regional Bourgogne appellation.

In the upslope direction toward the cap rock, the gradient increases rapidly, sometimes reaching 20 percent (12 degrees) before the soil "feathers" out to bare rock. (A gradient of one percent is an ascent or descent of one unit (foot or meter) in a horizontal distance of one hundred units. For a comparison of high slope angles, the steepest part of the Powell Street cable car route in San Francisco is 17 percent.) The "high-angle" vineyards are also classified -Villages or Bourgogne. Most of the great wines are found in the lower "belly" where the slopes have tapered out to 3–6 percent.

Even though the mid-slope "belly" is a catchment for slope wash, the soils of the Côte d'Or are surprisingly thin; 80 percent of the Grands and Premiers Crus have rootings of less than 4 feet (little over a meter). Vineroots, however, often venture deeper into the fractured bedrock. Only rarely does the soil thickness reach as much as 6 feet (up to 2 m), usually toward the foot slope. Shallow rooting means the vines are quite vulnerable to droughts. Fortunately, the bedrock along this zone of faulting is well fractured, providing important water storage for the maturation period.

"Seeing through the soil"

The thickness and nature of the soil and type of bedrock were questions of constant interest during my study of the vineyards of Burgundy and the other wine areas of France.

In petroleum exploration, the secret of success – in addition to an ample helping of luck – is understanding the "habitat of oil," that is, having a "picture" of conditions down where oil or gas may accumulate. Similarly, I felt that "seeing" the habitat down where the vineroots live might help answer why fine wines grow where they do.

A backhoe (mechanical digger) would do the job, but one can imagine how overjoyed a vineyard owner would be to see a geologist coming with equipment of this type, bent on finding out why his vineyard was so good. (Thierry Matrot of Meursault, concerned to demonstrate to tasting experts from around the world the affect of soil and bedrock on the character of his wines, may prove to be the exception – *see* page 147.)

I had discussed my wish to "see through the soil" with Catherine Ponsot, a geologist and former student of Professor Noël Leneuf at the University of Dijon, who was undertaking some geologic field checking for me in Burgundy. (Catherine is also the daughter of the prominent winegrower, Jean-Marie Ponsot of Morey-St.-Denis.)

One Sunday morning Catherine telephoned from France to tell me that a company in the area which was undertaking shallow-depth seismic work for a hydrographic survey would loan us their equipment on weekends. Also members of the field crew would be interested in "moonlighting" to operate the equipment. Here was a chance not to be missed.

This particular seismic method is akin to what the medical profession would term "non-invasive" investigation. In the seismic technique, sound waves are sent into the ground by heavy thumping rather than by setting off an explosive charge in a borehole as was done in earlier days. The "picture" of the subsurface habitat is obtained by recording the echoes (reflectors and refractors) of the sound waves from the underground layers. Depending on the nature of the material, the sound waves travel at different speeds and develop distinctive echo signatures.

These were the physical characteristics that translated into the geologic habitat down where the vineroots live. In oil exploration, the "thumper" is a 2-ton (2000-kg) weight; the "thumper" for our survey was a 10-lb (4.5-kg) sledge hammer. Our interest was in the bedrock a few feet below the surface, not oil reserves at greater depths.

Catherine Ponsot supervised the fieldwork, plotting the shape of the subsurface layers from their echoes. These data were integrated with other geologic information to give a "picture" of the habitat – to see through the mask of topsoil, determine the thickness of the pebbly subsoil, and identify the nature of the bedrock.

Our seismic profiles were single lines along one side of a vineyard. The pebbly layer is composed of nappes of slope wash deposited on eroded bedrock. In characterizing a vineyard from a seismic profile, we are extrapolating a two-dimensional picture across a wide area that undoubtedly may have important variations. Moreover, the subcrop of the bedrock strata would be irregular across the vineyard.

This was the first time such an investigative technique had been applied to vineyards. Although the seismic method gave only an incomplete "bone-scan" of the slope anatomy, it revealed important clues as to why some are quality vineyards and others are not. These interpretations are discussed in the following areas where profiles were run: Chambertin, Vosne-Romanée, Morey-St.-Denis on the Côte de Nuits and, separated by only a short stretch where grapevines give way to quarrying of Comblanchien limestone: Pommard and Puligny-Montrachet on the Côte de Beaune.

It should be pointed out, that the ratio of the vertical to horizontal scale in these vineyard cross-sections is often very much exaggerated, which can give a distorted impression as to the steepness of the slope. The annotated photographs throughout the chapter, however, give a more realistic view of the lie of the land.

The Côte de Nuits

This strip could well be called Burgundy's "Red Côte" – its 15-mile (24-km) stretch of vineyards is jam-packed with world-renowned wines almost all of which are red (*see* Figure 4.10). Why red and why so good? Tradition and geology have much to do with why red.

**Figure 4.10
Sketch map of the Côte
de Nuits**

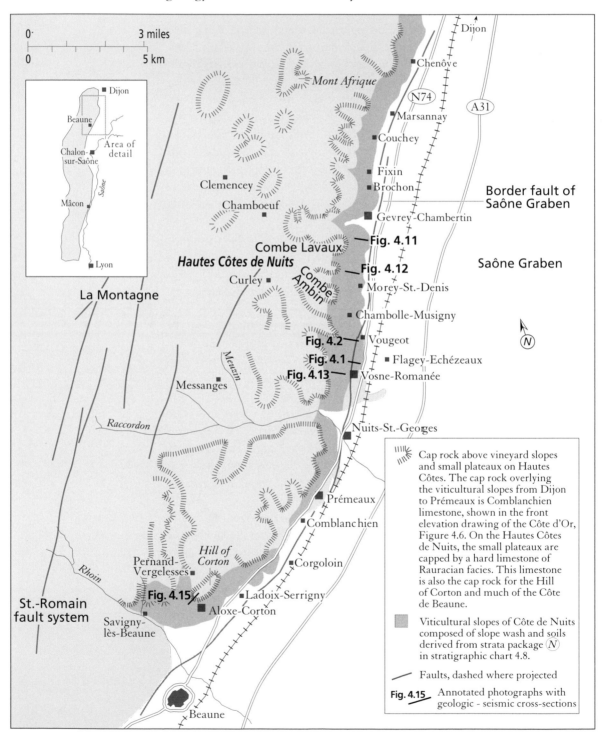

Cap rock above vineyard slopes and small plateaux on Hautes Côtes. The cap rock overlying the viticultural slopes from Dijon to Prémeaux is Comblanchien limestone, shown in the front elevation drawing of the Côte d'Or, Figure 4.6. On the Hautes Côtes de Nuits, the small plateaux are capped by a hard limestone of Rauracian facies. This limestone is also the cap rock for the Hill of Corton and much of the Côte de Beaune.

Viticultural slopes of Côte de Nuits composed of slope wash and soils derived from strata package (N) in stratigraphic chart 4.8.

Faults, dashed where projected

Fig. 4.15 Annotated photographs with geologic - seismic cross-sections

As to tradition, red wines were monks' wines, and from earliest times, this was monks' country: Clos-de-Bèze, Clos St.-Denis and Clos de Tart, Clos de Vougeot, Romanée-Conti, La Tâche and Romanée-St.-Vivant, and Les St.-Georges – these were the terroirs where monks brought viticulture to a high agronomic level. As to geology, it helps answer why red and why so good, aided, of course, by good husbandry and favorable exposures.

The "N" strata package shown on Figure 4.8 is predominantly limestones whose soils the Pinot Noir find greatly to its liking. Throughout the length of the Côte de Nuits the strata package remains essentially uniform in thickness and character. The fossiliferous and crumbly limestones and White Oolite weather easily into soils which the *Ostrea acuminata* marl thickens to the right consistency and structure. This once lowly mud of ancient oyster beds contains an abundance of the clay mineral montmorillonite. You will recall that this clay mineral has an amazing cation-exchange capacity. In early days, the absorptive ability of this marl was the *terre à foulon* (fuller's earth) used for degreasing raw wool from the sheep of the region and also "fulling" the woolen cloth. In soil making, the *acuminata* performs a similar function in "fulling" ("fattening") the crumbly White Oolite and the pebbly limestones. This combination of limestones and marl weathers into some of the finest soils found in wineland anywhere.

Almost throughout the Nuits, the bedrock is the *Calcaire à entroques* (crinoidal limestone). This limestone "floor" is cracked by numerous small faults that "shuffle the cards" of strata, but generally are not large enough to "cut the deck" to introduce markedly new strata. The well-fractured bedrock provides a water storage system for the relatively thin soils. These geologic factors, together with good easterly exposures, combine to make the terroirs of the Côte de Nuits some of the best in Burgundy.

Communes of the Côtes de Nuits

The traveler leaving Dijon for the Côte de Nuits by the N74 doesn't feel he has gotten "out into wine country" until Fixin or beyond. Perhaps without realizing it, he has passed the very old wine communes of Chenôve, Marsannay, and Couchey hidden in the suburbs of Dijon. Located in the northwestern outskirts of Marsannay is the government center for experimental viticulture and enology. Long before man and his vines came to Burgundy, the viticultural quality of the lower slopes of these communes was unfortunately adulterated by flood-time alluvium from the Ouche. In more recent times, vineyards began to lose out when urban growth of Dijon made the land more valuable for commercial or housing development than for wine. The three communes are struggling to keep alive their few remaining vineyards as well as memories of former greatness. The Clos du Roy and Le Chapitre of Chenôve like to remember that their wines once sold at higher prices than those of Gevrey (they are now sold as Marsannay La Côte); while Marsannay itself has been producing wine since the 7th century. Uniquely, Marsannay has appellations for red, rosé, and white wines.

Fixin is upstaged by the fame of the Chambertins on one side, and threatened by Dijon's urban sprawl on the other. Time forgets that Fixin's history dates from the Romans, and that it had an important viticultural tradition throughout the Middle Ages, especially with the dukes of Burgundy.

La Perrière, Le Clos du Chapitre, and four other Premiers Crus grow on the same strata package as Chambertin. However, the slopes of Fixin are considerably shorter than Chambertin, and the soil contains more of the river alluvium. Nevertheless, Fixin's very sound wines will ensure it survives the smothering affects of Dijon's urban sprawl.

The Nuits arch reaches its apex at Brochon, where shales of the Lower Jurassic (Liassic) are involved in the soil mixture. These shales are sterile compared to marls of the Middle Jurassic and the soils are likewise poor. The better slopes of Brochon are adjacent to Gevrey-Chambertin and produce wines under the Gevrey appellation. However, the remainder of Brochon wines only have the commune classification of Côte de Nuits-Villages or Bourgogne.

The eight Grands Crus of the famed commune of Gevrey-Chambertin receive varied reviews by the tasting experts. One reason for this is the large number of growers who make and market their own wines. Geology also plays a significant part. In spite of the fame of its name, Chambertin is a contributor to this "maddening Burgundy."

It is apparent from the annotated photograph and accompanying cross-section in Figure 4.11 that there is no typical "belly." The slope is like a shelf tilted with a gradient of about 6 percent. The wooded welt is the Comblanchien, but faulting has eliminated the typical cap rock and slope profile. Our seismic profile shows only a thin cover of slope wash on this shelf. It does, however, show erosional pockets in the bedrock in which thicker soils accumulate. Over the width of the vineyard an erosional "pockety" surface and faulting could result in considerable variation in the soils.

Catherine Ponsot tells me that while assisting her father in removing older vines for replanting in Griotte-Chambertin, she noted some abrupt changes in the vineyard subsoil which appeared to be faulting hidden by slope wash. Our seismic profile did reveal several small faults that disleveled the bedrock. (The survey only extended the width of the Chambertin–Clos-de-Bèze and did not reach the Griotte.)

Several of the hyphenated names of Grands Crus reflect soil conditions as they were observed in the early days: "Latricières" means shallow soil covering a very hard substratum; "Griotte" may have meant pebbly terrain, but some think it refers to the wild cherry; "Charmes" may stem from "chaume," meaning fallow land, or it may be just what it sounds like; "Ruchottes" may be derived from "roichot," an area where there are rocks. Even today, the topsoil of Ruchottes is thin and the subsoil shallow and pebbly. For those who hold that thin, stony soils make good vineyards, Chambertin is your perfect model.

Whereas the Grands Crus of Chambertin come in for some criticism, the Premiers Crus clustered around the base of the large knoll northwest of the village of Gevrey are well-regarded. The outcrop pattern appears to be undisturbed around this topographic shoulder. On the south-facing slope of a branch of the spectacular, steep-walled Combe Lavaux is the fine Premier Cru Lavaut-St.-Jacques.

A large alluvial fan from Combe Lavaux extends across the N74 and onto the valley side of the Saône border fault where a large number of commune-classed vineyards are found. Here the soils are deep, somewhat leached, and tend

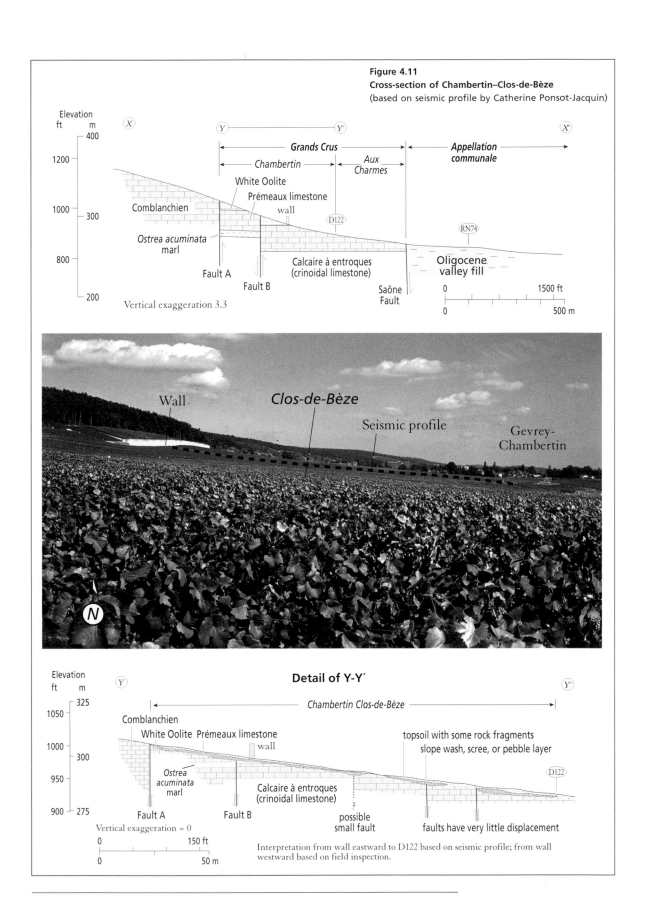

Figure 4.11
Cross-section of Chambertin–Clos-de-Bèze
(based on seismic profile by Catherine Ponsot-Jacquin)

BURGUNDY: PARADE OF CAP-ROCK SCARPS   133

Monts Luisants

Premier Cru

Grand Cru

Seismic profile

N

Clos de la Roche

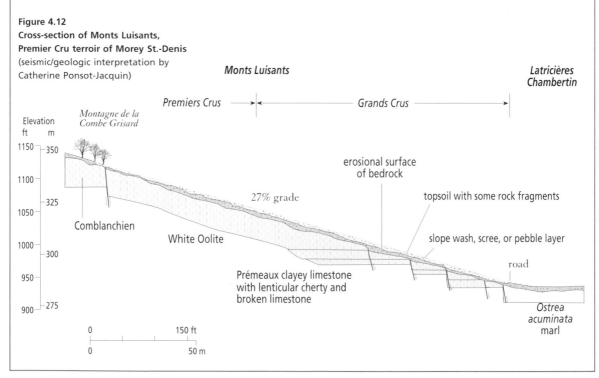

Figure 4.12
Cross-section of Monts Luisants,
Premier Cru terroir of Morey St.-Denis
(seismic/geologic interpretation by
Catherine Ponsot-Jacquin)

Monts Luisants

Latricières
Chambertin

← Premiers Crus → ←——— Grands Crus ———→

Montagne de la
Combe Grisard

Elevation
ft   m

1150 ┬ 350

1100 ┤

       ├ 325
1050 ┤

1000 ┤ ├ 300

950 ┤

900 ┴ ├ 275

27% grade

erosional surface
of bedrock

topsoil with some rock fragments

slope wash, scree, or pebble layer

road

Comblanchien

White Oolite

Prémeaux clayey limestone
with lenticular cherty and
broken limestone

Ostrea
acuminata
marl

0   150 ft
├────┬────┬────┤
0   50 m

to be damp. Geologically, this explains the observation that the commune-level wines of Gevrey-Chambertin are quite unreliable. Nevertheless, this large volume of wines carries the magical name of Gevrey-Chambertin, even if they are only commune in classification.

Morey-St.-Denis, unfortunately, has an identity problem in spite of the fact that all its Grands Crus and several of its Premiers Crus are widely known and highly respected. Morey's history goes back to Gallo-Roman times – Roman coins are still frequently turned up by the plow, but its appellation designation is relatively new. Its wines were previously sold either under the name of Chambertin or Musigny. The upper part of Morey is a steep shed-like slope of 27 percent (15 degrees), one of the steepest in the Côte d'Or, *see* Figure 4.12.

The Nuits strata package outcrops well up on the slope where the upper part of the Grand Cru Clos de la Roche is situated. Higher still on the rocky slope, Jean-Marie Ponsot grows Monts-Luisants, one of the few white wines of the Côte de Nuits – grown as much for its novelty as its quality. The adjacent red wines are less rich and intense in color than the Grands Crus on the middle slope just below.

The *Ostrea acuminata* marl mixes with the crumbly White Oolite to form shallow, well-drained soils for Morey's belt of Grands Crus. The Premiers Crus, slightly lower on the slope, have the happy privilege of living in slope wash from the Grand Cru belt.

The terroirs of Morey, in addition to having excellent geologic pedigrees, also led a good religious life in early days. A large part of the commune was owned by Cîteaux, the properties having been a gift from Savarie de Vergy. Clos St.-Denis belonged to the collegiate church of St.-Denis de Vergy which was founded in 1023. Records show that the abbey of La Bussière also owned vineyards in Morey, as did the abbey of St.-Germain-des-Prés of Paris.

Clos de Tart is one of the few monopoles (meaning a vineyard in single ownership) in Burgundy, and makes consistently fine wine. This small vineyard, originally assembled by the Sisters of Notre Dame du Tart of Genlis near Dijon, has not changed in size since 1250. The Morey-Monge family who bought it at the time of the Revolution held it until 1939 when it was sold to the current owners, the Mommessin family. A tiny portion of a fifth Grand Cru, Bonnes Mares, lies in Morey-St.-Denis, the major part in Chambolle-Musigny – a case of a commune boundary cutting across a terroir. Identity problem or not, Matt Kramer says Morey-St.-Denis is one of the safest blind bets you can place on Burgundy wine, as it has a cadre of unusually high-minded growers.

Chambolle-Musigny village sits daringly in the mouth of the deeply incised Combe Ambin. Nature sometimes takes the dare, sending a "gully-washer" through town, as evidenced by the large outwash fan and the town history records. Pierre Forgeot, a deep-dyed Burgundian and historian, says the name of Chambolle is derived from *campus ebulliens*, meaning "boiling field," perhaps describing the surging floodwaters as the Romans saw them. An alternative derivation of the name Chambolle is that it is from Guerrie de Chambolle who gave the piece of land that was the nucleus of the Clos de Vougeot. Did Guerrie take his name from Chambolle? You have your choice about the origin of the name Chambolle, but it is the Musigny part that is associated with fine wine.

The neck of the Ambin fan extending well up in the combe, separates the Grands Crus of Bonnes Mares on the north from les Musigny and les Petits Musigny on the south. The name, Bonnes Mares, is thought to derive from "Bonnes Mères," referring to the female religious order which originally owned the vineyard. A large number of small Premiers Crus are found on the fan itself, two of notable reputation: les Amoureuses and les Charmes. Les Petits Musigny, high on the slope, overlooks the Clos de Vougeot, shown in the foreground of the annotated photograph in Figure 4.2.

The 125-acres (50-ha) of the Clos de Vougeot takes up almost the entire commune. In this large terroir, there are some 90 owners of vines – the list grows yearly. Holdings vary from a few rows to several acres. In order to make use of the legend about quality related to location on the slope, one would need a cadastre (map of ownership) to identify winemakers from the "pope's" and "cardinal's" part of the terroir.

There may be some question about the wines of the Clos de Vougeot but there is none about the old château being the centerpiece of viticultural Burgundy. From wherever the visitor may hail, there is an instinctive respect for this simple, massive structure incongruously dominating the vineyards.

The château was abandoned and deteriorated badly after the time of the Revolution. The Confrérie des Chevaliers du Tastevin, who acquired it soon after France was liberated in World War II, have accomplished extensive authentic restorations. The Confrérie holds spectacular dinners in the great cellar for 500 "Knights of the Tasting Cup" and guests from around the world. Excellence of the food, wine, and service for this number of people is phenomenal. Officials dressed in robes copied from the wardrobe of Rabelais, with pomp and ceremony, knight distinguished personages from around the world with a vine stock rather than a sword. An ebullient chorus of local talent entertains the guests with lusty drinking songs, a repertoire which now includes the "Yellow Rose of Texas," taught them by a confrérie from Texas. A writer some years ago, called the dinners at the Clos "the greatest meal on earth, served with laughter, flooded with wine, and eaten in an uproar."

South of Vougeot is Flagey-Echezeaux. The village itself is on the river plain, but its two Grand Cru vineyards, Echezeaux and Grands-Echezeaux, are on excellent soils on the upper part of the slopes of the avenue of Grands Crus.

If Cripple Creek, Colorado, was early-day mining's "richest square mile on earth," then the Grands Crus of Vosne-Romanée are wine's counterpart – and the six vineyards total less than half a square mile (1.3 square km). Wine may not have the irresistible allure of gold, but gold mines deplete, wine is a renewable resource. Given a choice of an interest in a gold mine or, say, a share in a Vosne-Romanée Grand Cru, the world's most costly wine, grab the vineyard quickly.

Out of 30 miles (48 km) of vineyards along the Côte de Nuits why would this one small area (see Color Plate 15) be so outstanding? Some contend that the Grands Crus such as Romanée-Conti are not all that superior compared to the better parts of several other communes. That is something for the tasting experts to debate and the market to decide. Let's look at the geologic conditions, shown on the page opposite in the profile of Figure 4.13, where the "dream team" of the Grands Crus of Vosne-Romanée grow.

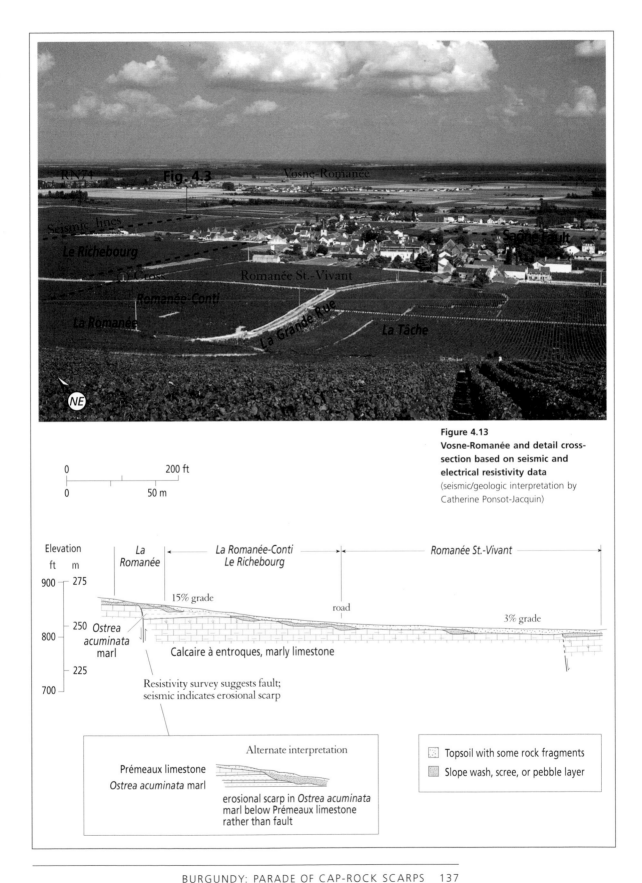

Figure 4.13
Vosne-Romanée and detail cross-section based on seismic and electrical resistivity data
(seismic/geologic interpretation by Catherine Ponsot-Jacquin)

Topsoil with some rock fragments

Slope wash, scree, or pebble layer

The annotated photograph in Figure 4.13 gives a good view of the Vosne-Romanée Grands Crus, the location of the shallow-depth seismic profile and the Saône Valley beyond. (The famous stone cross of Romanée-Conti, circled, is just apparent.) Each of the six Grands Crus: le Richebourg, Romanée St.-Vivant, la Romanée, Romanée-Conti, la Tâche, and la Grande Rue (the most recently approved) is an individual appellation within the commune.

As to the "why" of the high quality of this small area of Grands Crus, the seismic geologic profile illustrates its "potential for greatness." First, we have a near-perfect soil, blended from a blue-ribbon recipe of White Oolite, Prémeaux marly limestone, *Calcaire à entroques*, and thickened by the *Ostrea acuminata* marl. Second, the topsoil and pebble layer are spread at an average thickness of about 4 feet (over a meter) on a gently sloping bedrock disleveled by only very minor faulting. Centuries ago, vignerons knew nothing about soil science or geology, but the plants told them that they liked this place very much.

As the same geology is projected to underlie each of the Grands Crus, it is the art of the individual winemaker which has the last say. Although Domaine de la Romanée-Conti dominates the marketing scene (owning or managing most of the Grands Crus), there are a dozen winemakers of the other Grands Crus, with their own ideas of vinification. The result is at least that many distinctive wine "signatures," subjects for interesting debate among tasters.

"Nuits" in the name Nuits-St.-Georges has nothing to do with "nighttime." According to Pierre Forgeot, these slopes in ancient times were noted for their walnut trees. The Latin for walnuts, *Nutium* or *Nuettium*, apparently evolved to "Nuits." In time, vines replaced the walnuts. The "St.-Georges," by then an outstanding vineyard, was added in 1892.

No Grands Crus are produced in the Nuits-St.-Georges commune, but in the opinion of several experts, the Premiers Crus are of Grand Cru quality. The Nuits strata package is still contributing to the soil, but the slopes narrow rapidly as the Comblanchien cap rock dips closer to valley level at this end of the arch of the Côte de Nuits. The Meuzin River divides the Premiers Crus into north and south sectors. Those north of the river are said to resemble Vosne-Romanée – well-balanced and complex – which is perfectly logical since the area is contiguous and the geology similar.

Ironically, the vineyards south of the river, farthest from Vosne-Romanée, are generally acknowledged to have the better wines; certainly they are better known. The very steep scarp back of the narrow vineyards serves as a stone wall, providing a protective microclimate. Les St.-Georges, conceded to be the number one terroir of the commune, dates from the year 1000. The adjacent Les Vaucrains and Les Cailles are close runners-up to Les St.-Georges.

Prémeaux-Prissey is the last of the communes of the Côte de Nuits on the south. Its Premiers Crus, being of small volume, are entitled to be marketed as Nuits-St.-Georges. The cliffs of Comblanchien continue to act as a garden wall for a constrained band of vineyards little more than 100 yards (90 m) wide. Of these, the long, narrow Clos de la Maréchale (24 acres/10 ha), leased to Maison Joseph Faiveley, is perhaps the better known. At this point the strata-package of the Côte de Nuits has already gone underground in its inversion into the Beaune syncline (*see* Figure 4.8).

The *Dalle nacrée*, the fossiliferous, pearly flagstone which was introduced in my Contemplation in a Vineyard (*see* Prologue), appears for the first time in our slope geology. Mixed with scree from the "back wall" of Comblanchien, this flagstone makes a respectable, though very stony soil in the Prémeaux vineyards.

The Côte des Pierres

The rockiest part of the wine road of the Côte d'Or occurs between Ladoix (La Doix on some maps), and Prémeaux where stone quarries rather than vineyards dominate the landscape. Along the "Rocky Côte," only an intermittent, narrow line of brave vineyards, a "stone's throw" in width, lies between the N74 and the sheer face of the Comblanchien. The small vineyards of this Côte are classified only Côtes-de-Nuits-Villages.

The Comblanchien formation, which is about 30 feet (9 m) thick, takes its name from the village. This compact, lightly tinted, very fine-grained limestone resembles marble in taking a high polish. Its attractive, pinkish colorations are due to the presence of iron oxide which precipitated in the rock before it was "marbleized." The stone has been quarried for centuries, but became commercial only with invention of the wire band saw and opening of the Paris–Lyon railroad in the 19th century.

The Côte de Beaune

If we dubbed the Côte de Nuits the "Red Côte," perhaps the Côte de Beaune should be called the "Red and White Côte," for it produces some of the world's greatest white wines and some very respectable reds. Strata package "B" which comes into play in the downwarp of the Côte de Beaune should not be considered the second team for it produces some "hall of fame" wines.

The Hill of Corton just north of Beaune produces Grands Crus of white Corton-Charlemagne and red Corton. At the southern end of the Côte are the white Montrachet Grands Crus. Linking these two superlative Grand Cru areas is an almost continuous belt of famous Premiers Crus: Beaune, Pommard, Volnay, Meursault, Puligny-, and Chassagne-Montrachet (*see* Figure 4.14).

Some feel that several of the Premiers Crus of the Côte d'Or should be Grands Crus. I understand that growers and négociants of most of these Premiers Crus prefer to retain that classification rather than apply for Grand Cru status. This seemingly strange attitude is a marketing decision influenced by labeling rules. For Premiers Crus, the commune name must be in bold letters on the label along with the terroir name, e.g., VOLNAY-CHAMPANS. In Grand Cru labeling, the Volnay would be dropped and the terroir name Champans appears alone. While many of the terroirs, as in this example, are highly regarded, not many shoppers would identify the name Champans alone as a Volnay. The rationale is that the names of Pommard, Volnay, Meursault, and the two Montrachets have a significant product recognition that would be lost or at least minimized in changing to Grand Cru labeling.

Important stratigraphic changes of facies occur along the Côte de Beaune. This is in contrast to the Côte de Nuits where the stratigraphic layers remained fairly uniform. These facies variations, primarily limestones to marls, are indicated by the jagged lines in the stratigraphic chart (Figure 4.8).

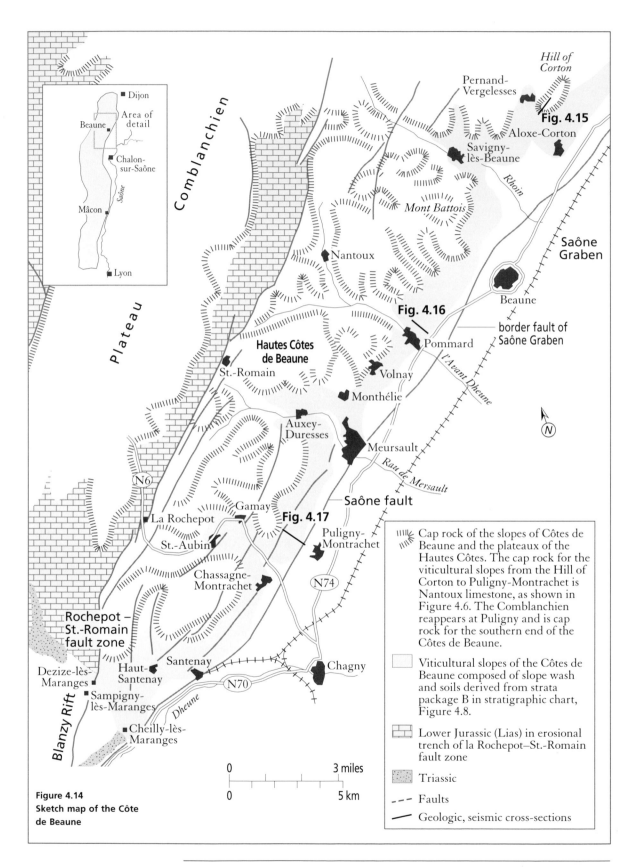

Figure 4.14
Sketch map of the Côte
de Beaune

Cap rock of the slopes of Côtes de
Beaune and the plateaux of the
Hautes Côtes. The cap rock for the
viticultural slopes from the Hill of
Corton to Puligny-Montrachet is
Nantoux limestone, as shown in
Figure 4.6. The Comblanchien
reappears at Puligny and is cap
rock for the southern end of the
Côtes de Beaune.

Viticultural slopes of the Côtes de
Beaune composed of slope wash
and soils derived from strata
package B in stratigraphic chart,
Figure 4.8.

Lower Jurassic (Lias) in erosional
trench of la Rochepot–St.-Romain
fault zone

Triassic

--- Faults

— Geologic, seismic cross-sections

Another difference in the two Côtes is that several large faults in the Côte de Beaune materially affect the geology of the terroirs. This is discussed in the Montrachet and Meursault sections. Relating geology to the vineyards on the geologic map of the Côte de Beaune is greatly aided by a key bed which the cartographers have helpfully colored red on 1:50,000 scale maps. The layer is a thin ferruginous oolite, stained red due to weathering of iron minerals. The ferruginous bed occurs about mid-section of the stratigraphic group, but it frequently outcrops high enough upslope to provide some iron to the soils.

The Hill of Corton, a symmetrical butte with pert wooded cap, conveys a sense of importance. Indeed, there is. Its commodious slopes are covered from cap rock to valley with terroirs of distinction. Of unusual interest is that both red and white Grands Crus grow on the same band around the hill, *see* Figure 4.15. The communes of Aloxe-Corton, Ladoix-Serrigny, and Pernand-Vergelesses all have a slice of this rich hill-side pie, with Aloxe claiming the largest share.

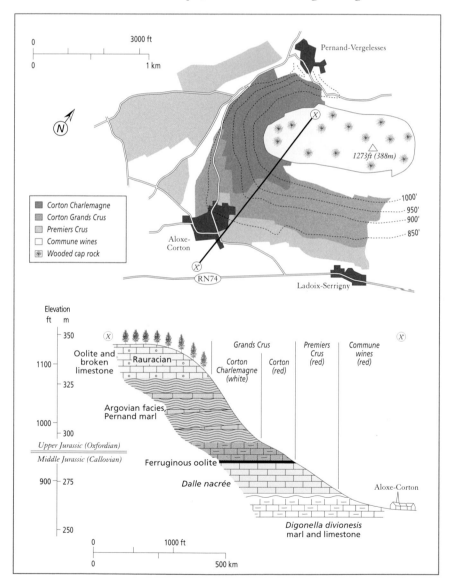

Figure 4.15
The Hill of Corton
Slopes of red and white
Grands Crus

Tasting experts sagaciously point out that Corton's robust, red wines are quite unlike the opulent La Tâche or elegant Romanée-Conti just a few miles up the road. They should be different. The geology is different. This is the very *essence* of terroir – each doing its own thing with its inherent attributes. Comparing the Grands Crus of Vosne-Romanée and Corton is fine, if one remembers it is like comparing the performance of the same play by two different casts of actors.

Professor Leneuf and other Burgundian geologists enjoy taking visitors to the west side of Corton below the village of Pernand-Vergelesses to point out the interesting relationship of Corton-Charlemagne with its white Chardonnay sharing the same bed as it were with the Pinot Noir's group of red Cortons.

The phenomenon – if one wishes to call it that – may possibly be a relic of the time when Charlemagne owned vineyards on Corton. According to legend, Charlemagne's wife did not like to see red-wine stains on his white beard. His vignerons found the area where white grapes did best in his Corton vineyard and that is where we find the Corton-Charlemagne. According to Pierre Forgeot, the great Emperor in 775 gave his vineyard on Corton to the Abbey of Saulieu (north of Autun) for caretaking – including the white grapes.

Serena Sutcliffe, who edited the second edition of André Simon's *Wines of the World*, says it was the great-grandfather of the négociant Louis Latour–currently the most celebrated Corton grower – who first planted white grapes on Corton. Whoever started the Chardonnay on Corton, for whatever reason, did white wine and its lovers a great favor.

Two factors of habitat may abet the "white grape anomaly." First, the Corton-Charlemagne occupies a portion on the cooler west-southwest face of the hill, extending into the valley notch above Pernand-Vergelesses. The Chardonnay tolerates cooler conditions more so than the Pinot Noir. Second, apparently the Pernand marl develops a particularly clayey facies on the slope which the Corton-Charlemagne occupies (*see* Color Plate 16). This may be the reason underlying the success of the "white grape anomaly."

One day back in 1982, with Professor Leneuf and Dr. Lautel, I was tasting a '78 Corton-Charlemagne from the barrel in the cellar of Domaine Pierre Dubreuil-Fontaine in Pernand-Vergelesses. As Bernard Dubreuil, in working-man's coveralls, served us generous "tastings" of his fruity, well-textured golden wine with a pleasant *goût de terroir,* I couldn't help but wonder if one day a formally dressed sommelier might present for my inspection a bottle of this very wine and I would gasp cross-eyed at the price. (This occasion has yet to occur, but I have enjoyed as many bottles of Corton-Charlemagne as I could afford.)

Communes of the Côte de Beaune

On the edge of the plateau above la Côte, the "aire de repos" (rest stop) on the Autoroute du Soleil has a panoramic view of the Saône Valley and the Hill of Corton. Across the narrow Rhoin Valley below is Savigny-lès-Beaune.

One is looking full in the face of slopes that are of the same geologic section as Corton, but the vineyards are Premiers Crus, not Grands Crus. Corton's Grand Cru strata "vee" into the Pernand-Vergelesses valley like a layer cake minus a wedge. When the outcropping strata come back around the hill at Savigny, thin limestones have begun to appear which are well developed at Beaune.

Savigny-lès-Beaune, not on the road to anywhere in particular, is bypassed by all but the most curious wanderers. It is a very old town, where the adventurer is rewarded by discovering some amusing oddities such as the inscription on a doorway lintel that alleges, "The wines of Savigny are nourishing, theological, and banish depression." With such promises of emancipation, it is a wonder that the town is not overrun with pilgrims.

The slope of the Beaune commune has the same stratigraphic equivalent as on Corton, but at Beaune the upper section contains more limestones. This stony, upper part of the slope is dotted with hillside homes overlooking the city of Beaune. The lower slope, however, is a "universe of vines" where the growers have opted for the best quality possible rather than volume.

The *Dalle nacrée* occupying the lower part of the slope is underlain by the *Digonella* marl. When water, seeping through the fractured and porous limestone reaches the less pervious marl, it issues as springs. In medieval times, these waters were channeled into the moat which surrounded the old fortress town of Beaune. Parts of the ramparts and moat can still be seen in the southeast sector of the town.

Beaune is viticultural capital of Burgundy. Among the must-see sights in the town along with the Hôtel-Dieu (Hospices de Beaune) is the Musée du Vin de Bourgogne. Of particular interest in the wine museum is the relief model of the Côte d'Or constructed by Dr. Lautel. It provides an excellent high-level view of the physiography and geology of the Côte d'Or.

The Hospices de Beaune

Showpiece of the Flemish-Dutch influence brought to Burgundy by the Valois dukes is the Hospices de Beaune. The former hospital is now a museum with its charitable work conducted elsewhere in modern facilities. In addition to 15th-century medical and hospital equipment, the Hospice museum contains among other art works the remarkable polyptych by the Dutch painter, Roger Van der Weyden, "The Last Judgment."

When the Chancellor to the Duke of Burgundy, Nicolas Rolin, founded the Hospices de Beaune in 1443, he and his wife, Guigone de Salins, also endowed them (plural, as they serve charities other than medical) with wine properties. Emulating this charitable spirit and hoping for eternal life, bequests of vineyard properties by others have continued over the years, making the former hospital one of the largest vineyard owners in Burgundy. The Hospices now own over 30 vineyard properties in the Côte d'Or, almost half of which are on the slopes of Beaune. Wines of the Hospices, each one named after an important benefactor, are sold at auction, traditionally the third Sunday in November as part of "Les Trois Glorieuses" – the three glorious days of celebration after the grape harvest. The wine auction (now a fashionable social occasion in America) was the first and still the greatest charity event in the world. It is also something of a price bellwether for Burgundy wines.

Of the 1300 acres (525 ha) under vine in the Beaune commune, 34 terroirs are classified Premiers Crus. It is difficult to find agreement on the ranking of the terroirs, but the consensus seems to be that Les Fèves, Les Grèves, Le Clos des Mouches, and Les Marconnets would be in a top group. (Unfortunately, part of Les Marconnets was sliced off by the Autoroute du Soleil.) Les Grèves, a large (80-acre/32 ha) terroir, lies in the lower part of the slope and extends down over the underlying *Dalle nacrée* to the base of the slope.

Pommard is easy to pronounce in most languages (never mind whether to sound the "d" or not. It is silent). And like Chablis, the adaptability of its name to the Anglo-American tongue has surely helped its popularity in both the

Figure 4.16
**Seismic-geologic section
of Pommard vineyards**
(seismic/geologic
interpretation by
Catherine Ponsot-Jacquin)

British Isles and North America. It has been alleged that there is more Pommard drunk in the United States than is produced in Pommard. This does not imply that the high reputation of a true Pommard is not otherwise well-deserved.

Pommard has some of the longest, gentlest slopes in the Côte d'Or. The seismic-geologic cross-section, Figure 4.16, is located between Les Petits Epenots

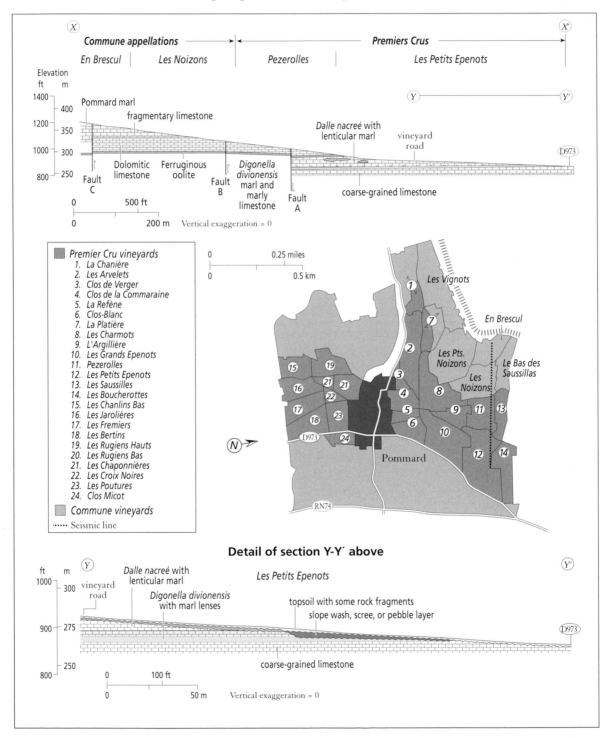

and En Brescul, near where I stood during my "contemplation" mentioned at the beginning of this book. The seismic and electrical resistivity profiling indicate that several small faults exist and apparently affect the sequence of bedrock. This "shuffling" of strata may account for subtle differences in flavors of Pommard Premiers Crus (as in Beaune, there are no Grands Crus) noted by growers and wine tasters alike – but the Pommard character is never lost.

S. T. Harris of Dallas, Texas, owns Les Jarolières which adjoins Volnay. Bud Harris is an enthusiastic American-Burgundian who taught the Cadets de Bourgogne of Clos de Vougeot the "Yellow Rose of Texas." He says there appears to be little difference in the surface soils from one end of Pommard to the other, but quickly adds that there are indeed real differences in the wine flavors.

Known in Gallo-Roman times as Polmareum, Pommard may have been named originally for Pomona, Roman goddess of tree fruit. A myth says Pomona spurned all woodland suitors until Vertumnus, who had tried various other guises, dressed as a pruner of vines and wooed her successfully. *In vino veritas!*

Pommard village straddles the Avant Dheune. Most of the time it is a small, gentle, "mouse-leap" stream. But in times past, its floods have brought dismay and disaster to Pommard. Flash floods born of thunderstorms out of sight in the Hautes Côtes would arrive unannounced. Before the stream was bridged, travelers were duly warned that the ford at Pommard was a treacherous crossing.

Vineyards around Pommard have had some important historical owners such as the dukes of Burgundy, the abbots of Cîteaux, and Nicolas Rolin, a native of the Morvan, west of Beaune. The Château de la Commaraine, dating from 1180, is the most impressive of several châteaux in the village, and Clos de la Commaraine ranks among the top terroirs of Pommard. Other excellent Premiers Crus are Les Rugiens (Hauts and Bas) on the slopes southwest of the village, and Les Jarolières and Les Frémiers which adjoin the commune of Volnay. The Rugiens name comes from the reddish color of the soil derived from iron in the red oolite. It was the red soils of Pommard which reminded me in my "contemplation" of the soils of the Weches formation in Texas, whose red color is also due to weathering of an iron mineral.

Volnay is sometimes incorrectly hyphenated with Pommard. Only a mile apart, center to center, their wines are indeed similar in style, but they are separate communes, each with its own history and legends.

It has been suggested that the name Volnay evolved from the Celtic Belen to Velen or Volen, to Volnay. Belen, or Bel, was an important Celtic god, and the prominent hill back of Volnay may have been a place of pagan worship. The hill offers one of the finest, most accessible panoramas in the Côte d'Or (*see* Color Plate 18). On clear mornings, Mont-Blanc, bathed in early morning pink, can be seen on the horizon 90 miles (145 km) to the southeast.

The Volnay slope below the hill does a roller-coaster drop then a long glide out to route D973. Most of the Volnay slopes are composed of Pernand-Pommard marl with several lenticular beds of broken limestone providing interesting variations in the character of wines grown on them. For example, the limestone lens at the level of the village may be responsible for giving the Clos-des-Ducs an unusual finesse and perfume. Matt Kramer suggests that this limestone might also be responsible for the particular character of Les Fremiers.

In January 1990, when he was working on *Making Sense of Burgundy*, Kramer telephoned from Portland to ask if an isolated outcrop of limestone shown on the geologic map under the Fremiers vineyard might account for this wine being lighter and fruitier than its neighbors. It was a delightful surprise to find a wine writer who studies geologic maps. I verified that the limestone bedrock was a lens in the Pernand-Pommard marl, but that he would have to vouch for its possible influence on the characteristics of the wine. Caillerets and Champans are two of Volnay's acclaimed wines. They each border the east side of route D973 where the slope has become very gentle. Champans, said to have a noticeable *goût de terroir* with an ironlike tinge, apparently derives this characteristic from the key bed of red, ferruginous oolite which outcrops just up slope.

The name Caillerets is supposedly derived from the Château Caille (quail) de Roi owned by the first Valois king, Philip VI. In 1328, the wines of Volnay were drunk at his coronation in Reims. A portion of Caillerets was also held by the order of Malta up to the time of the Revolution. The names of the outstanding Premiers Crus of Volnay may have not changed in 700 years.

Philip the Bold, the first Valois duke, built a château above the present village site. The château enjoyed the purity of air and proximity to excellent wines as well as the panoramic view. (Unfortunately, the château was completely destroyed in 1749.)

When the Edict of Nantes, granting religious freedom in France, was revoked in 1685, Volnay's large Protestant population dispersed to Germany, Holland, and Belgium. These expatriates, longing for their native wine, started an import trade that spread the name of Volnay to international fame.

From Pommard to the Montrachet area, the red, ferruginous oolite marker bed is very helpful in identifying the position of the strata package "B" on the slopes of Monthélie, Auxey-Duresses, and Meursault. The key bed varies higher and lower on the slope through the area with the Premiers Crus following the package outcrop rather than always the "belly" of the slope.

In recent years, Monthélie was perhaps as well known for its venerable grande dame winegrower, Armande Douhairet, as for its 11 Premiers Crus. Of these the best, Les Champs-Fulliot and Sur la Velle, are adjacent to Volnay. The terroirs wrap around the nose of the hill and between the face of la Côte, the oversize valley of the small Ruisseau de Cloux. The Cloux was the legendary *muris saltus*, the "mouse-leap" stream so named by the Roman soldiers. Their camp site on the hill opposite Auxey-Duresses is still visible. It was from *muris saltus* that the name Meursault was supposedly derived.

Auxey-Duresses is only a short distance back from the frontal scarp into the valley of the Cloux. Its half-dozen Premiers Crus on the north side of the valley and along the Combe Danay are on Pommard marl lightly covered with slope wash. The original name of the village, Auxey-le-Grand, was changed in 1924, to incorporate the name of its best-known terroir, les Duresses. Within this terroir, the best-known label is Cuvée Boillot of the Hospices de Beaune, marketed by Domaine Leroy.

The spire of Meursault's 15th-century church is the highest in Burgundy (187 feet/57 m). It could symbolize the universal high esteem with which Meursault's white wines are held. Its red wines are good, but less highly prized.

The front elevation drawing, Figure 4.6, shows the beds in the vicinity of Meursault perceptibly rising to the south. This upturn at the end of the Beaune downwarp brings up the Nuits strata-package from its submergence and back into the slope geology. But, a large fault (call it the Meursault fault), downthrown toward the valley, maintains the Beaune strata package at "belly" level. This is where Meursault's red wines grow (about 5 percent of commune production).

South of the village, the Beaune strata package provides home for the highly acclaimed white wines of Meursault. These terroirs lie in a narrow belt just below ancient quarries of the Nantoux limestone. When the soil overburden was removed for the quarry operation, it was cast downhill enriching the avenue where we now find the Premiers Crus of Les Perrières, Charmes, Genevrières, Le Porusot, Les Bouchères, and Les Gouttes d'Or.

A "slope tasting" of Meursault

In 1990, Chardonnay experts from California, France, and Italy gathered in Burgundy to explore the secrets of this great white grape. During the meeting, discussion arose concerning the affect of soil and bedrock on wine character. To prove a point that it did, Thierry Matrot of Joseph, Thierry et Pascale Matrot in Meursault, had a backhoe (mechanical digger) excavate two holes in his prized Premiers Crus, Les Perrières and Charmes. In Les Perrières, which happens to be on the upthrown side of the Meursault fault, the machine had dug little more than a foot before striking solid limestone. In Charmes, downslope across the Meursault fault, it was over 6 feet (nearly 2 m) to solid bedrock. Les Perrières, although very good wine, has a mineral, stony taste. The Charmes is less flinty, more mellow and rounded than its neighbor across the fault. Call the Burgundians Freudian about soil, if you wish, Thierry Matrot gave a dramatic demonstration of how subsurface geology influences the character of wine.

In another instance, Hubrecht Duijker in his *Great Wines of Burgundy* relates what might also be described as a "slope tasting" of four 1975 Meursaults. The first wine on this stony soil of the upper slope above the Premiers Crus was described as rather light. Two very good Premiers Crus from the mid-slope were evidently on soils in the "belly" similar to Mr. Matrot's Charmes. Duijker says that wine from the lower slope was difficult to distinguish from a Premier Cru, but its flavor faded quickly. This wine evidently grew in rich, damp soil where grapes are often "flabby."

The Matrot experiment is recounted by Per-Henrik Nansson, "Exploring the secrets of great Chardonay," *Wine Spectator,* Oct. 25, 1990.

The vineyards of Blagny have followed the strata package to almost 300 feet (90 m) above the slopes of Meursault proper. Blagny's reds can only be sold under the *appellation communale* Blagny, but its whites go to market as Meursault-Blagny, Meursault, and Puligny-Montrachet as it has holdings in both of these two last communes.

The communal boundary between Puligny-Montrachet and Chassagne-Montrachet cuts right across the Grands Crus Le Montrachet and Bâtard-Montrachet, giving about half to each commune. Each of the communes is justifiably proud of its share of the Grands Crus, but when it comes to geology, logic says forget the commune identity and treat the Montrachets as a "family."

The first time I visited Puligny-Montrachet, I had a difficult time convincing myself that such prosaic landscape could produce the world's greatest white wines. The annotated photograph in Figure 4.17 is the view I had as I approached the slopes from the village of Puligny. Clearly, it emphasizes that it isn't what one sees on the surface, but what lies below that makes the wine.

What is it that makes this Montrachet family of Grands Crus so special? In a seeming contradiction, the family is great because it has a fault – a geologic fault that is responsible for bringing together some of the best of both the Beaune

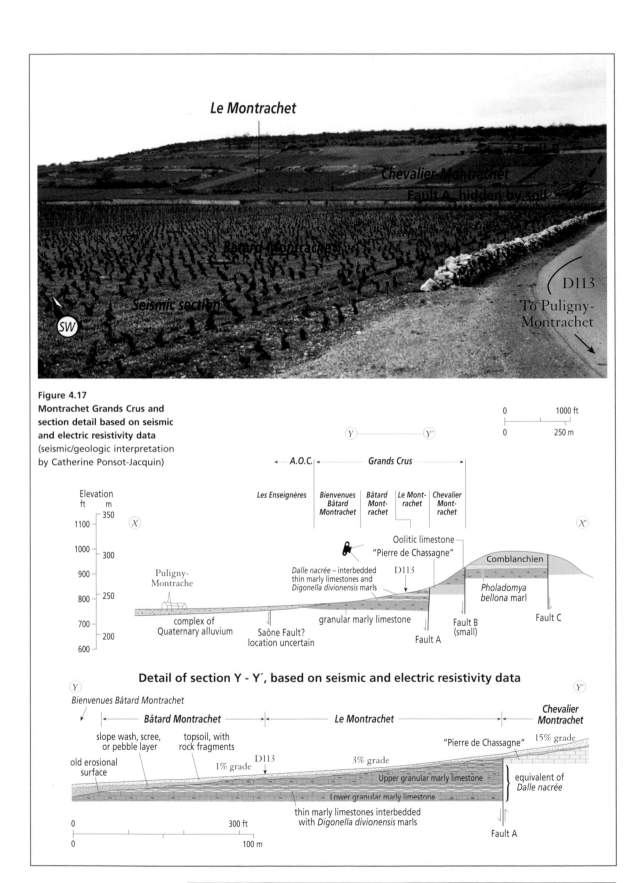

Figure 4.17
Montrachet Grands Crus and section detail based on seismic and electric resistivity data (seismic/geologic interpretation by Catherine Ponsot-Jacquin)

Le Montrachet

Chevalier-Montrachet
Fault A hidden by soil

Bâtard-Montrachet

Seismic section

SW

D113
To Puligny-Montrachet

0 — 1000 ft
0 — 250 m

Y ——— Y′

A.O.C. ← → Grands Crus

Les Enseignères | Bienvenues Bâtard Montrachet | Bâtard Mont-rachet | Le Mont-rachet | Chevalier Mont-rachet

X

Elevation
ft m

Oolitic limestone "Pierre de Chassagne"

Comblanchien

Dalle nacrée – interbedded thin marly limestones and *Digonella divionensis* marls

D113

Pholadomya bellona marl

X′

1100 350
1000 300
900
800 250
700 200
600

Puligny-Montrache

complex of Quaternary alluvium

Saône Fault? location uncertain

granular marly limestone

Fault A

Fault B (small)

Fault C

Detail of section Y - Y′, based on seismic and electric resistivity data

Y

Bienvenues Bâtard Montrachet

← Bâtard Montrachet → ← Le Montrachet → Chevalier Montrachet

Y′

slope wash, scree, or pebble layer

topsoil, with rock fragments

old erosional surface

D113

1% grade

3% grade

"Pierre de Chassagne"

15% grade

equivalent of *Dalle nacrée*

Upper granular marly limestone

Lower granular marly limestone

thin marly limestones interbedded with *Digonella divionensis* marls

Fault A

0 ——— 300 ft
0 ——— 100 m

and Nuits strata packages. That fault is labeled "A" in the cross-section of Figure 4.17, with the Nuits strata on the right of the line and the Beaune strata to the left. Faults "B" and "C" are small and do not materially affect the geology of the vineyards. All three of the faults are related to the Saône system and are more or less parallel with it.

As the Nuits package reappears from underground in the Côte de Beaune downwarp, we find that the Comblanchien limestone has become thinner and less marble-like. The White Oolite has begun to interfinger with a new limestone, the Pierre de Chassagne, and a new marl bed, the *Pholadomya bellona* has appeared. These are the strata that outcrop in Chevalier-Montrachet, a stony, fairly steep slope of over 15 percent (between 8 and 9 degrees).

The break in the slope between the Chevalier-Montrachet and Le Montrachet was a logical property boundary. That break is also the surface trace of geologic Fault "A."

The seismic profile, Y–Y' in Figure 4.17, reveals the marvelous geologic heritage of Le Montrachet – thin, marly limestones interbedded with marls on an extremely gentle slope. There is without a doubt some Chevalier slope wash of the Nuits strata in the bloodstream of Le Montrachet, but it is all royal plasma. It is interesting that tasting experts note that Chevalier-Montrachet is somewhat "stonier" than Le Montrachet. Geology says it should be. All of the Bâtards – Montrachet, Bienvenues, and Criots – are within the fault block of Le Montrachet.

Our seismic line did not extend far enough toward the valley to pick up the Saône fault, but a rapid thickening of the soil in the lower part of Bâtard-Montrachet suggests that the slope may be approaching the major fault zone. Borings in the lower slope of Bâtard found the soils to be somewhat damp, also suggesting that the lower part of the Bâtard soils may be interfingering with valley fill, which typically has a high water table. Experts note a lessening of vitality of wines from the lower slope of Bâtard, presumably due to the damp soil which produces leafy plants and watery grapes.

Fault "A" continues northward from the area of the Grands Crus, extending beneath the Premiers Crus Le Cailleret, with the same geology of Le Montrachet, and beneath Les Pucelles and Clavoillon, with that of Bâtard-Montrachet.

Vincent Leflaive of Domaine Leflaive, a grower in the Premiers Crus, observes that although two of his properties have similar slope and sun exposures, roots of his Le Cailleret (Le Montrachet extension) do not go as deep as those of Les Pucelles (the Bâtard extension). Mr. Leflaive says the wines of Le Cailleret (the same geology as Le Montrachet) are fruitier, more delicate, and mature sooner than the deeper-rooted Les Pucelles of the Bâtard geology. He suggests that the difference between the wines of the two terroirs may be due to uneven water feeding below the surface. Mr. Laflaive's interpretation is probably correct. Lateral and downslope migration of soil water in the slope-wash nappes will be different in the relatively shallow pebbly layer under Le Cailleret and Le Montrachet than under Les Pucelles where the nappes are thicker, the soil more clayey with permeability more restricted. What is more, the mineral nutrients are probably more concentrated in the shallow soils, but leached to some extent in the deeper soils of Les Pucelles.

Fault "A" extends southward from beneath the village of Chassagne-Montrachet toward Santenay. The Beaune strata package lies to the west of D113 on the downthrown side of Fault "A" where it supports a belt of Premiers Crus of Chassagne-Montrachet. Further displacement of Fault "A" puts the Nuits strata outcrop well up on the hillside out of the vineyard picture, but contributes to the Premier Cru soils by slope wash. Whether or not they are aware of the soil mix, almost every grower has planted the vineyards to both red and white grapes.

St.-Aubin and Gamay could logically belong to the Hautes Côtes, but they are included in La Côte because they are on the Beaune strata package which "vees" into the large dry valley of highway N6. This was the main route from Paris to the south coast before the autoroute was built. The red wines are described as somewhat rustic – very much like the two villages. The climate of Gamay and the two dozen Premiers Crus of St.-Aubin is drier and cooler than the main Côte, therefore their grapes mature a little later.

Any wine journey that begins or ends at Santenay is bound to have a rocky time. Rock fragments are to be found in all Côte d'Or vineyards, but this southern extremity has rocks to spare. The Dheune has washed out the bone-deep gash of the Blanzy Rift, exposing the fault-splintered end of La Côte and the Hautes Côtes. The geology here is confusion corner. Nevertheless, patient vignerons in centuries past identified the areas of better soils, removed the larger stones and improved the patches to Premier Cru quality. Today's growers seem rather uncertain whether to concentrate on red wines or to try some whites. The commune's reputation was made on the reds, but after all, the famous Montrachets live just around the corner. Les Gravières, La Comme, and Le Clos de Tavannes along with Beaurepaire and La Maladière are Santenay's better known vineyards.

The thermal springs of Santenay-le-Haut (-lès-Bains) have been utilized as public baths since Roman times. The waters come up along deep-seated faults carrying unusual minerals such as lithium. In times past, Santenay was better known for its baths and gambling casino than for its wines.

The wine villages of Lès Maranges with prefixes of Dezize, Cheilly, and Sampigny are just west of Santenay. The southerly exposures are on Liassic marls, Triassic dolomites, and shales – all second-class soilmakers compared to the Middle and Upper Jurassic. Nevertheless, through the perseverance of village mayors and emphasis on quality by the growers, a substantial number of Lès Maranges terroirs have been accorded Premier Cru status.

The Hautes Côtes

The Hautes Côtes, or Arrières Côtes (high or back hillslopes), refers to the plateau above the Côte d'Or on the west, *see* Figures 4.1 and 4.5. The plateau, generally about 300 feet (90 m) higher than the valley, is divided into the Hautes Côtes de Beaune and the Hautes Côtes de Nuits, corresponding to the respective sectors of the Côte d'Or itself.

The St.-Romain fault paralleling La Côte strikes northward from the Blanzy Rift through La Rochepot and St.-Romain. The western side is up-thrown several hundred feet higher, exposing Triassic and Liassic formations in

Gamay seems to fret not that the grape that bears its name is forbidden fruit in its "home commune." Banned from the Côte d'Or in 1395 by Philip the Bold, it eventually found a new home and respected status in the stingy, granitic soils of Beaujolais.

east-facing slopes. The soils from these formations along this incision are fair, but not nearly so good as those of the Upper and Middle Jurassic of the Côte de Beaune. Lateral valleys of the St.-Romain and other erosional features back of Pommard provide good vineyard sites.

Northward, about opposite Nuits-St.-Georges, the St.-Romain fault splinters into numerous faults of lesser displacement, thus diminishing the opportunity for vineyard slopes. However, the dendritic (tree-like) drainage system of the Meuzin River which flows through Nuits-St.-Georges does create some growing slopes. As the Hautes Côtes de Nuits become less dissected northward, the elevations become higher and the hills heavily wooded, and commercial vineyards disappear.

In the Hautes Côtes generally, the vineyards are small and found only on the sunny, eastern-facing slopes. Due to the higher elevation, the climate is somewhat cooler, causing grapes to ripen later than on the Côte d'Or.

The Hautes Côtes is the province of the white grape Aligoté which makes a sharp wine which can be good when young, or drunk mixed with the local blackcurrant liqueur as a Kir. Some Chardonnay is grown too, and there is experimentation with the Pinot Gris. The red grape of the Hautes Côtes is mostly Pinot Noir, but also Gamay is allowed. The Pinot makes a fairly light, red wine while the Gamay is usually made into a rosé.

Before the phylloxera, the land under vine in the Hautes Côtes was six times the scant 1200 acres (485 ha) of the mid-1950s when a pioneering effort of replanting was begun. In 1961, *appellations contrôlées* were awarded for both the Beaune and the Nuits Hautes Côtes. Development continues, but opportunities for suitable vineyard sites are limited due to the sparsity of protected east-facing slopes. Despite these limitations, the great demand for A.O.C. Burgundy wines is a strong incentive for development even of marginal areas in both of the Hautes Côtes.

Chalonnais

Chalonnais or the Côte Chalonnaise is sometimes known as the Région de Mercurey, referring to the largest of its five parishes. This designation ignores the old and important areas of Montagny-Buxy, Givry, and Rully. True, the red wines of Mercurey are the better known, but Rully and Montagny-Buxy produce white wines of Premier Cru classification.

Geologically, Chalonnais is a broken-up continuation of the Côte d'Or crustal fault blocks wedged between the Saône graben and the Horst de Mont St.-Vincent. The horst is part of the Blanzy Rift system, *see* Figure 4.1. Fault blocks within the wedge are tilted both east and west with some flat-lying. Soils of Mercurey, Rully, and Givry, located in the northern sector, are from the Côte de Beaune strata package. Cap rock of the ridges is the Nantoux limestone, the approximate stratigraphic equivalent of the Comblanchien. The vineyards of Montagny-Buxy in the south of Chalonnais are on Liassic and Triassic soils.

Slopes of the Côte d'Or face generally eastward, the most efficient for sun-trapping. In Chalonnais (and, further south, in Mâconnais), we find fault blocks tilted east, with the sun-trapping concavity facing west. The importance of east or west tilt for best sun exposure is illustrated in Figure 4.7.

The Région de Mercurey carries the name of the winged messenger of the Roman gods. Like the terrain of the Eternal City, Mercurey's vineyards are distributed around seven (or more) hills. The characteristic knobby terrain is the result of a patchwork of faulting. The slopes are mostly Chagny interbedded with thin, marly limestones. The Chagny is the stratigraphic equivalent to the Pommard marl.

There are 111 tiny terroirs clustered around the village, but, oddly, only five are classified Premiers Crus. I say oddly, for geologically, there is nothing that distinguishes the first-growth terroirs from those classified only A.O.C. As a matter of fact, experts point out that some of the commune vineyards often produce better wines than the Premiers Crus. It is the magic name of Mercurey that counts more in marketing than the classification. Mercurey's Pinot Noir red wines dominate production over white wines by twenty to one.

Rully's wine history goes back to Roman times, but it has had its ups and downs. Mostly downs since 1791, when départements replaced the historical provinces, separating Rully from its previous association with the Côte d'Or. Abetting the down-turn of Rully was the havoc played by phylloxera, followed by the serious loss of vignerons in the two World Wars. However, under the leadership of several determined growers, among them Henri Jacquesson, Xavier Noël-Bouton, and Aubert de Villaine, there has been a rebuilding of Rully's former fine reputation. L'Hermitage and la Fortune are two showcase terroirs of the restoration work.

Rully's red wines are often cautiously compared to those of the Montrachets. Why not? Rully's geology is essentially the same as the Montrachet slopes, less than 5 miles (8 km) across the valley of the Dheune. Of the 50 small vineyards between the villages of Rully and Bouzeron, 19 are Premiers Crus. Red and white wines are produced in about equal proportions. Unfortunately for the grower, but happily for the consumer, Rully wines suffer something of an identity problem by being in the Chalonnais. (I hesitate to bring this up, for I am enjoying some excellent Rully at reasonable prices.)

Givry's wine history is of long duration: the labels of its red Premiers Crus make much of the report that their wines were the preferred drink of Henry of Anjou. The vineyards' pebbly, yellowish to pink, sticky soil is developed from a combination of Givry marl and "red oolite" (not the key-bed red oolite of the Côte de Beaune). These strata are from higher in the Jurassic geologic section than any others involved in the Côte d'Or. The soil is good, but not exceptional, yielding a wine somewhat lighter than those of Mercurey.

Montagny-Buxy's vineyards have good exposures, but are on Liassic strata which just doesn't produce soils of the quality to compare with the strata packages of the Côte d'Or. The appellation granted under the name Montagny is reserved for white wines produced from the Chardonnay grape. Any of the 64 named vineyards has the right to Premier Cru status, provided its wine has the required minimum alcohol strength of 11.5 percent. (That quality status was awarded on the basis of alcoholic strength is scarcely justifiable, a fact tacitly acknowledged by the wine authorities. A fairer classification, which should be complete by 2000, is underway.) The villages in the area do produce red wines, but they are not entitled to the Premier Cru classification.

Mâconnais

Mâconnais, the region around the town of Mâcon, occupies a 30-mile (48-km) long peninsula formed by the Saône graben and the Grosne Rift Valley, as shown in Figure 4.1 at the beginning of this chapter. On a reduced scale, the physiography resembles the valley and ridge provinces of the Appalachians of the United States. As illustrated in the cross-section of the block diagram (Figure 4.18), this terrain is the result of eastward- tilted fault blocks. Several of the valleys are filled with heavily forested pods of flinty-clays. These pods accumulated when normal drainage was interrupted by the damming of the Saône by the Rhône glacier.

The adversity of the geology makes the vineyard areas so patchy that 9000 winegrowers in the region average less than 2 acres (0.8 ha) each; in only a few cases does viticulture provide sole support for a family. Before phylloxera, vines occupied three times the current acreage. Now most of the farmers have orchards of fruits and nuts as well as vines, with small herds of cattle and goats grazing the picturesque *bocage*.

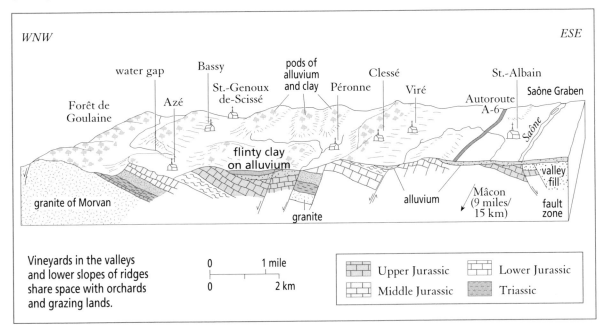

The entire -Villages appellation is restricted to white (Chardonnay) wines, with 43 villages being allowed to hyphenate their name with Mâcon itself. Among those worthy of note are: La Roche Vineuse, Verzé, Igé, Azé, Clessé, Viré, and Chardonnay. Documents from 989 link that last village name to the eponymous noble grape, but whether the grape derived its name from or gave it to the village is uncertain. Growers are beginning to plant more Aligoté as it requires appreciably less care than the Chardonnay. Nevertheless, over 60 percent of the terroirs, especially in the north, is now given to the Chardonnay.

The Pinot Noir does well in the more limy parts of Mâconnais, but because this grape requires extra care it occupies only about 10 percent of the total acreage under vine. It may be blended with Gamay, but the latter never achieves the softness of good Beaujolais. Red Mâcon wine cannot be labeled -Villages.

Figure 4.18
East-tilted fault blocks, portion of Mâcon-Villages
(reproduced with minor modification by kind permission of Editions du B.R.G.M., France et de Total Edition-Presse, originally published as Figure 17 in *Terroirs et Vins de France*, 1984)

Little vineyard extension is taking place because of the labor shortage in this sparsely populated area. In a season, a 2-acre vineyard requires about 400 man-hours to tend the vines and gather the grapes. The only thing that keeps viticulture in this area above the marginal economic level is the cooperatives.

The panorama in the annotated photograph above, looking south from the Mâcon–Cluny highway, shows a flotilla of prow-shaped rocks facing into the Westerlies. Inside this cordon is Pouilly-Fuissé, the flagship of Mâconnais. The area of this popular wine is composed of the communes of Fuissé, Solutré-Pouilly, Vergisson, and Chaintré, all flying Premiers Crus pennants.

The "prows" of Solutré, Vergisson, and Mont de Pouilly are reef-like build-ups in the *Calcaire à entroques* called "bioherms." In the later structural phase when the strata were tilted eastward, these bioherm masses were raised like the prows of ships. The most famous and often-photographed of these "ship-rocks" is the Rock of Solutré which overlooks the village of Solutré-Pouilly. Viewed from directly in front, the Rock of Solutré rears up like a panicked horse (*see* Color Plate 19). The metaphor is not without meaning, for at the base of the cliff is a Stone Age archeologic site containing the skeletons of an unbelievable number of over 100,000 horses. This amazing ossuary gives name to the archeologic era of the Solutrian.

The heartland of the Pouilly-Fuissé appellation, in a topographic bowl between the Rock of Solutré and Mont de Pouilly on the west and the horst of Bois de St.-Léger on the east, is comprised of the communes of Solutré-Pouilly and Fuissé, *see* Figure 4.20. The bowl is floored with some of the best soil-forming strata on which the Chardonnay grows in the Côte d'Or, as indicated in Figure 4.21. The formations outcrop in the basin in a "reverse-shingle" affect. That is, they dip eastward at a low angle so that rather than scarps and dip

Figure 4.19
Panoramic view of the heart of Pouilly-Fuissé, flagship of Mâconnais
(Catherine Ponsot-Jacquin)

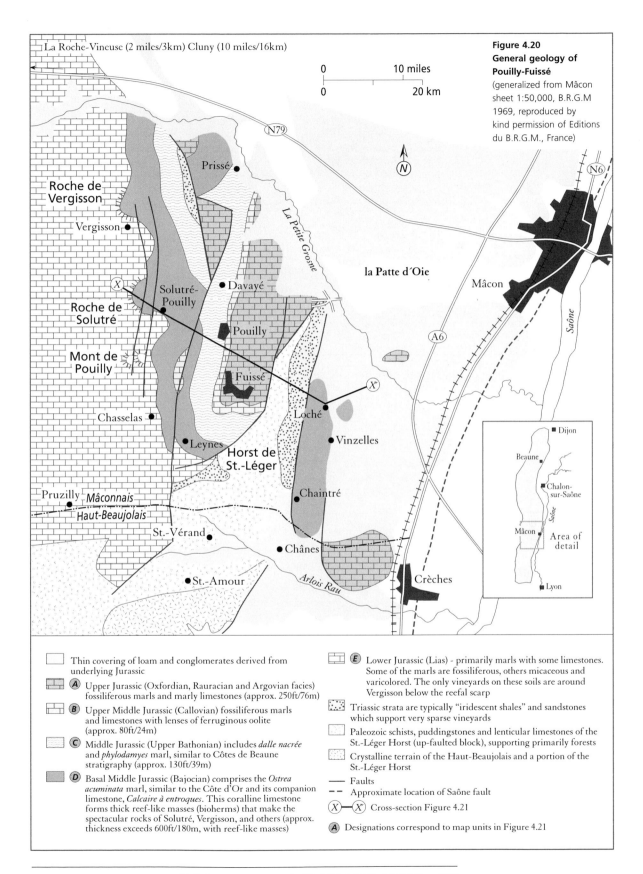

Figure 4.20
General geology of Pouilly-Fuissé
(generalized from Mâcon sheet 1:50,000, B.R.G.M 1969, reproduced by kind permission of Editions du B.R.G.M., France)

La Roche-Vineuse (2 miles/3km) Cluny (10 miles/16km)

0 — 10 miles
0 — 20 km

N79

N6

Prissé

Roche de Vergisson

Vergisson

La Petite Grosne

la Patte d'Oie

Mâcon

X

Solutré-Pouilly

Davayé

Roche de Solutré

Pouilly

Saône

Mont de Pouilly

Fuissé

A6

X'

Chasselas

Loché

Leynes

Vinzelles

Horst de St.-Léger

Dijon

Beaune

Pruzilly Mâconnais

Chaintré

Chalon-sur-Saône

Haut-Beaujolais

Saône

St.-Vérand

Mâcon

Area of detail

Chânes

St.-Amour

Arlois Rau

Crèches

Lyon

Thin covering of loam and conglomerates derived from underlying Jurassic

A Upper Jurassic (Oxfordian, Rauracian and Argovian facies) fossiliferous marls and marly limestones (approx. 250ft/76m)

B Upper Middle Jurassic (Callovian) fossiliferous marls and limestones with lenses of ferruginous oolite (approx. 80ft/24m)

C Middle Jurassic (Upper Bathonian) includes *dalle nacrée* and *phylodamyes* marl, similar to Côtes de Beaune stratigraphy (approx. 130ft/39m)

D Basal Middle Jurassic (Bajocian) comprises the *Ostrea acuminata* marl, similar to the Côte d'Or and its companion limestone, *Calcaire à entroques*. This coralline limestone forms thick reef-like masses (bioherms) that make the spectacular rocks of Solutré, Vergisson, and others (approx. thickness exceeds 600ft/180m, with reef-like masses)

E Lower Jurassic (Lias) - primarily marls with some limestones. Some of the marls are fossiliferous, others micaceous and varicolored. The only vineyards on these soils are around Vergisson below the reefal scarp

Triassic strata are typically "iridescent shales" and sandstones which support very sparse vineyards

Paleozoic schists, puddingstones and lenticular limestones of the St.-Léger Horst (up-faulted block), supporting primarily forests

Crystalline terrain of the Haut-Beaujolais and a portion of the St.-Léger Horst

— Faults

- - - Approximate location of Saône fault

X — X' Cross-section Figure 4.21

A Designations correspond to map units in Figure 4.21

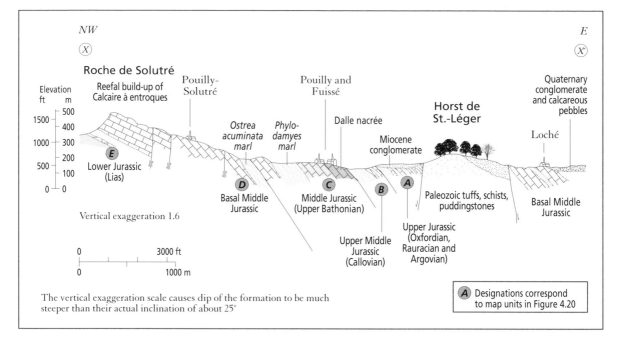

NW   E

The vertical exaggeration scale causes dip of the formation to be much steeper than their actual inclination of about 25°

A Designations correspond to map units in Figure 4.20

Figure 4.21
Cross-section of the "vineyard bowl" of Pouilly-Fuissé

slopes the formations have weathered as an undulating surface. (Because of the vertical scale exaggeration in the cross-section, the dips appear at a high angle.) It is this particular geologic situation, emphasized in the cross-section above, which accounts for the quality of the Pouilly-Fuissé vineyards.

Within the "bowl" are a number of exceptional individual terroirs such as Château Fuissé, Clos du Bourg, Château de Beauregard, and others, which can produce rich and succulent wines. But all marketers play up the Pouilly-Fuissé name for all it is worth – which is sometimes questionably high.

The Vergisson vineyards lie along the west-facing slopes below the Roc de Vergisson. Soils from the dark marls and limestones of the Liassic are reasonable, but not approaching the excellence of the Côte de Nuits strata package within the Pouilly-Fuissé "bowl." The smaller, lesser known, communes of Chaintré, Vinzelles, and Loché along the eastern side of the St.-Léger horst lie in part on coralline limestone and part on river terrace deposits from the Petite Grosne.

Surrounding the Pouilly-Fuissé "bowl," but ranking below it in quality are the communes of the St.-Véran appellation: Prissé, Davayé, Leynes, Chânes, Pruzilly, St.-Vérand, St.-Amour, and Chasselas. The last name is the same as the grape variety, but there is no Chasselas grown in the area. It is not known whether the village name and the grape are related in any way.

Highly faulted Jurassic strata with adjacent old alluvial terraces of the Petite Grosne make the geology of these communes as complicated and confusing as the road-net. Worry not, it is a delightful area in which to be lost.

One afternoon past normal lunch hours, my family and I stopped in Davayé at Françoise Barthelemy's small, but convenient bar-restaurant. She agreed to provide a late lunch of cold cuts and, of course, a Davayé wine. Cold cuts one can get anywhere, but in true small-town, wine-country hospitality, Françoise prepared a heaping platter of *sauté de champignons*, gathered just that morning. Davayé ranks high in my wine-trip memories.

Beaujolais

Turn west off the N6 anywhere a few miles south of Mâcon, and it is immediately apparent that things are unlike the Burgundy we have been visiting. The landscape is different; the soil is different; the architecture is different. This is Beaujolais. This is granite country (*see* Figure 4.22) with some of the most pleasing scenery of the winelands of France. The landscape is almost seductive – symmetrical hills meet in deep cleavages. Nestling in the valleys are neat, attractive villages. The houses with flattish, red-tiled roofs and balconies resemble Mediterranean-style architecture.

The wines and history of Beaujolais are also different. This is the land of the Gamay, the grape which was banished from the Côte d'Or by Philip the Bold. It found refuge here on these thin, sandy soils. The sin for which it was expelled was that its vines grew too profusely on the rich, limestone soils, yielding thin, fast-fading wines. The Gamay found a home in the granite terrain of the Beaujolais. These thin, sandy soils were the right challenge for the voracious growth of these vines. Granite, being more or less homogenous and massive, weathers more uniformly as rounded hills and knobs. The Gamay exhibits no hard feelings; here it produces a hospitable wine in an equally hospitable land.

Beaujolais was only a neighborly, regional wine until a group of enterprising growers took some wine that had just completed fermentation to Paris. For some perverse reason, it was a hit. This was the start of the Beaujolais Nouveau fad. A California importer says that the excitement of downing a newborn wine that has barely left the grape must be the most inspired invention in the history of wine. A fad, yes, but an enjoyable one which has brought more fame and fortune to Beaujolais than any amount of advertising of its quality wines.

Beaujolais has only two principal categories of quality: regular Beaujolais and Cru Beaujolais, with cru being reserved for the ten highest ranked appellations in Haut-Beaujolais. Each cru is an appellation comprising portions of several communes. The name of the cru is that of the most prominent village, similar to the labeling of Grands Crus of the Côte d'Or. As the Gamay is not a "noble" grape, the term Grand Cru is not permitted here. Beaujolais, the second category, is for the general wine of both Haut- and Bas-Beaujolais. If the alcohol strength of regular Beaujolais is up to 10 degrees, it may be upgraded to the seldom used term of Beaujolais Supérieur.

Haut- or Crystalline Beaujolais

As evident in the cross-sectional drawing of the granite knob, Figure 4.22, these convex hills of Beaujolais have no "belly" in which to accumulate slope wash; consequently, soils are typically thin. A handful of the reddish, sandy soils of Haut-Beaujolais is seen to be mostly crumbly pieces of granite. The sparse clay to bind the sandy particles comes only from the weathering of feldspars and micas in the granite. These sandy soils are known locally as "arène", from the Latin *arena*, meaning sand. An accumulation of the weathered earthy mass is also known as "gore" or "gorrhe." Arène or gore are composed primarily of partially weathered feldspars, quartz, and other hard "minerals." While soils are for the most part very thin, arène accumulates in shallow depressions or sometimes in "streams," as seen in the Régnié appellation.

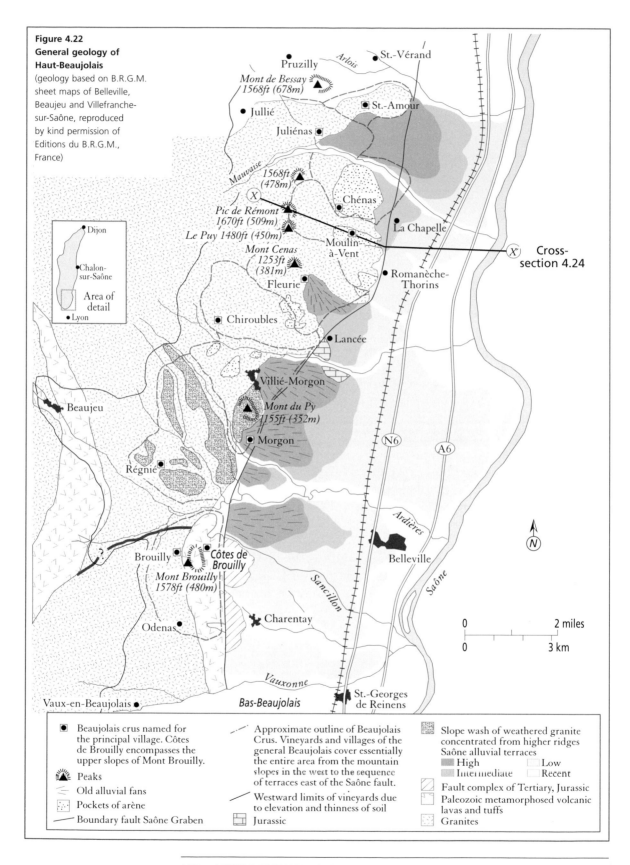

Figure 4.22
General geology of Haut-Beaujolais
(geology based on B.R.G.M. sheet maps of Belleville, Beaujeu and Villefranche-sur-Saône, reproduced by kind permission of Editions du B.R.G.M., France)

Pruzilly
Arlois
St.-Vérand
Mont de Bessay 1568ft (678m)
Jullié
St.-Amour
Juliénas
Mauvaise
1568ft (478m)
Chénas
X
Pic de Rémont 1670ft (509m)
La Chapelle
Le Puy 1480ft (450m)
Moulin-à-Vent
Mont Cenas 1253ft (381m)
X'
Cross-section 4.24
Fleurie
Romanèche-Thorins
Chiroubles
Lancée
Villié-Morgon
Mont du Py 1155ft (352m)
N6
A6
Beaujeu
Morgon
Régnié
Ardières
Belleville
Sancillon
N
Brouilly
Côtes de Brouilly
Mont Brouilly 1578ft (480m)
Saône
0 ____ 2 miles
0 ____ 3 km
Odenas
Charentay
Vauxonne
Bas-Beaujolais
St.-Georges de Reinens
Vaux-en-Beaujolais

Area of detail
Dijon
Chalon-sur-Saône
Lyon

Beaujolais crus named for the principal village. Côtes de Brouilly encompasses the upper slopes of Mont Brouilly.

▲ Peaks

Old alluvial fans

Pockets of arène

Boundary fault Saône Graben

Approximate outline of Beaujolais Crus. Vineyards and villages of the general Beaujolais cover essentially the entire area from the mountain slopes in the west to the sequence of terraces east of the Saône fault.

Westward limits of vineyards due to elevation and thinness of soil

Jurassic

Slope wash of weathered granite concentrated from higher ridges Saône alluvial terraces

High   Low

Intermediate   Recent

Fault complex of Tertiary, Jurassic

Paleozoic metamorphosed volcanic lavas and tuffs

Granites

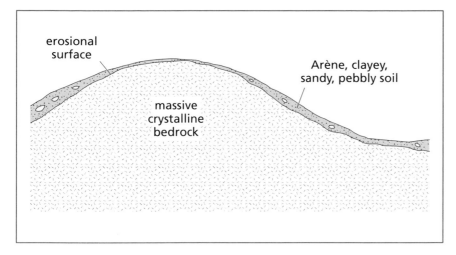

Figure 4.23 Granitic terrain typical of Haut-Beaujolais
Granites and other massive rocks of uniform character tend to weather in rounded knobs rather than in sharp relief terrain

The granites of Haut-Beaujolais were born at great depths some 300 million years ago, and brought to the surface in the mid-Tertiary by uplift of the Massif Central and its thumb-like projection, the Morvan. The deep-seated molten masses were intruded into an overlying crust of ancient lavas and volcanic ash (tuff). Heat and pressure of the intrusions cooked and squeezed (that is, metamorphosed) the lavas and ash into the foliated rock called schist. The uplift brought large masses of the schist along with the granites.

One of these schist masses at Villié-Morgon weathers to soils with a smoky-gray "moldered" color. They are called "morgon" after the village name. These soils are also referred to as *roches pourries*, literally "rotted rocks."

The principal vineyards of the Haut- or Crystalline Beaujolais are on a large massif known as the Odenas granite. It is a pink rock, containing abundant biotite or black mica, which weathers readily to clay minerals. Although the physical nature of the granite is reasonably uniform throughout, the actual mineral concentrations vary considerably. Dr. Robert Lautel tells me that differences in the character of the wines can be related to variations in the granite where they grow, especially when there is some schist in the soil.

Thinness of the soil is compensated to an extent by the arène being high in mineral nutrients such as potassium, phosphorus, and magnesium. Unfortunately, it is shy of nitrogen – as are most soils everywhere. The soils are on the acid side, as the only carbonates available are from the weathered feldspars and micas.

Professor Noël Leneuf reports that a white, clay-like material found in fissures in the granite in the area of Brouilly and Chiroubles is smectite (montmorillonite) of high purity. Smectite greatly enhances the cation exchange of the soils and hence enhances the wines of Brouilly and Chiroubles, two of the best wines in Beaujolais.

Beaujolais wines are not "investment" wines, but are for drinking young. Some, however, do age reasonably well for a few years. All the wines within an appellation will be blends from many growers, for the size of individual vineyards averages only between 8 and 15 acres (3–6 ha). The appellations too vary in size, from small Chénas, with 457 acres (185 ha), to Brouilly which is more than four times that size.

St.-Amour, a postcard-pretty village dating back to Roman times, leads a parade of hamlets along a ridge immediately south of the contact between the sedimentary strata of Pouilly-Fuissé in Mâconnais and the crystalline rocks of Beaujolais. St.-Amour was awarded appellation status in 1946 after which its wines became better known. The wines are somewhat lighter than neighboring Juliénas, perhaps because the soils of its "ridgy" terrain are unusually thin.

Juliénas, reputed to be the oldest of the crus in Beaujolais, presumably pays homage to Julius Caesar. Its vineyards are spread on a wide south-facing ridge below Mont de Bessay. Outwash from sedimentary strata of the adjacent Pouilly-Fuissé area is mixed with schists and thin arène, giving the wines of Juliénas a certain depth and complexity.

Chénas, smallest of the appellations, occupies a narrow width of slope between Juliénas and Moulin-à-Vent. In times past, the region is said to have been covered with oak trees (*chênes*) from which the village takes its name. The only remaining evidence of the oaks is a magnificent wood carving in the Caveau des Deschamps in the village. Although smallest of the ten crus, Chénas wines are considered to be as big and generous as its neighbors.

Moulin-à-Vent is generally conceded to be the "King of the Beaujolais." Its wines possess a fullness and richness which invite comparison with the good red burgundies of the Côte d'Or. The cross-section, Figure 4.23, shows the thin arène weathered from the crumbly granite on the slope below the Pic de Rémont. Color Plate 20 emphasizes the nature of this pinkish soil. Dr. Lautel and Professor Leneuf are of the opinion that the unusual robustness and special character of Moulin-à-Vent wines may be due to seams of manganese found in the granite bedrock.

The windmill at Moulin-à-Vent is as famed as the one at Verzenay in Champagne. The 300-year-old *moulin* with its one remaining sail has not operated in many years and is now a classified national monument. In times past, farmers brought their grain to be ground. They still come, but now to tilt a glass of Beaujolais in the little bistro within the mill house. A friendly, curious, but reserved reception greeted my wife and me when we visited there one cold, rainy Sunday afternoon. A glass of Moulin-à-Vent improved the disposition of my wife, who had seen all the vineyards she cared to for that day. Our interest in their vineyard soils (conveyed in my wife's limited but enthusiastic French) thawed the native reserve of the gathered vignerons – a little.

The large cru of Fleurie spreads out on granite slopes southwestward from Moulin-à-Vent. Good sun exposures are indicated by the names of Fleurie's leading terroirs, Grille-Midi and Côte Rôtie (not to be confused with the Côte-Rôtie of the Rhône, but probably named for the same reason). As the name of Fleurie implies, its wines are notable for their flowery bouquet.

The vineyards of Chiroubles are Beaujolais' highest, reaching elevations of 1300 feet (400 m) with lovely panoramas looking eastward toward the Saône Valley. The wines of Chiroubles are fragrant but light and must be drunk young – perhaps a characteristic imparted by the high elevation.

Chiroubles was the birthplace and home of Victor Puillat, a pioneer in grafting French scions on phylloxera-resistant American rootstock. Puillat, a self-taught plant scientist, had an enormous collection of 2000 varieties of

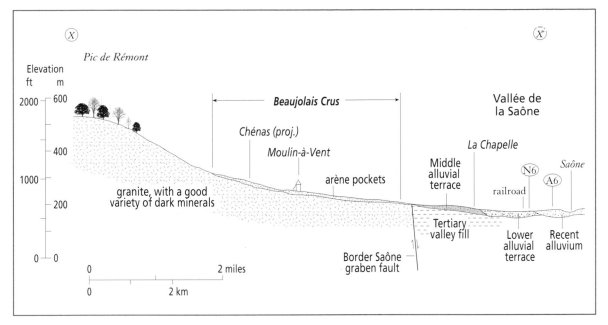

Figure 4.24
Cross-section of
Moulin-à-Vent

grapevines, which greatly assisted in matching French scions with American phylloxera-resistant species. Friends erected a bust of Puillat in Chiroubles in appreciation of his contribution to the restoration of viticulture in France.

Mont Brouilly, a conical landmark hill, rises 1000 feet (300 m) above a gently rolling countryside. The suggested name derives from the French *brûlé*, meaning burned, as the bluish-black rock appears as if it had been in a fire. Indeed, Mont Brouilly was at one time a "hot rock" – a volcanic plug that was intruded into the lava and ash that composed the crust over the granite. The fresh rock is exceedingly hard and has been quarried in the past for road metal. The crystals of this very fine-grained rock are microscopic, but when exposed to weathering, the plagioclase, biotite, and other dark minerals produce an excellent soil with a bluish cast. Because of this greenish-blue color it is sometimes called *cornes vertes*, "green horns."

On the summit of the Mont is the tiny chapel of Notre Dame de Brouilly, built in 1857. On September 8th, vignerons of the surrounding area make a pilgrimage to the chapel chanting hymns to their patron saint for a good harvest.

Vineyards surrounding the upper part of the conical hill are the Côte de Brouilly, while those around the broader apron of the hill are Brouilly. Parts of some Brouilly vineyards extend out over granite bedrock, imparting marked differences in the flavor of wines grown on the two different terrains.

Just north of Mont Brouilly, we find the vineyards of Morgon/Villié Morgon situated primarily on the *morgon* or "rotted rocks" of schist. Their wines are notable for their unusual, and delightful, cherry-like flavor. The local vignerons will tell you that the flavor, unique in all of Burgundy, is due to the particular nature of the soils. In all probability, it is true.

Régnié, the newest cru, is a narrow strip between Morgon and Brouilly with soils partly on morgon and partly on granite. The arène and broken schist are gathered in streaks and streams washed from the higher slopes. The character of its wines reflect whether they are grown on soils of arène, or on schist.

Bas- or Sedimentary Beaujolais

The growers of the region feel that "Bas" has a demeaning implication, and have joined together to promote the name, Les Pierres Dorées – the Golden Stones. The name recalls a yellowish-brown Lower Jurassic limestone quarried in the area as a building stone. The proposed name might satisfy local vanity, but the "Bas" does not seem to have been commercially damaging, as the area produces the bulk of Beaujolais Nouveau. The current problem is not identity but being able to produce enough to meet market demand.

It seems agreed among those who might know, that the locale for Gabriel Chevalier's humorous *Clochemerle* was Vaux-en-Beaujolais, southwest of Mont Brouilly. (The name of the fictitious village is the song of the blackbird.) The somewhat bawdy story is supposed to be a caricature of rural Beaujolais, the core of the story being a controversy about where to locate a new *vespasienne* (public convenience). The local curé, frustrated with the arguments, restores his composure with ample Beaujolais, *Bonum vinum lactifizat*." (Good wine gladdens the heart.)

Bas-Beaujolais is residual between the two granitic massifs of Beaujolais and Lyon. Geologically it is a continuation of Mâconnais, although somewhat reduced in overall thickness. The geology and structural style of the area is illustrated in the cross-section Figure 4.25.

Thick soils have developed in the Tertiary terraces and in "pods" of alluvium in the valleys, residual from the time of the damming of the Saône by glacial moraines. Unfortunately, these are poor vineyard soils as they are deeply leached. Nevertheless, the variable soil conditions of Bas-Beaujolais are offset to a large extent by the vigor of the Gamay. Popularity of the Beaujolais Nouveau has the vignerons using all suitable terrain and looking for more. A little white Beaujolais is also produced in the north of the Bas-Beaujolais, though it is rarely seen outside the region.

**Figure 4.25
Fault-block terrain,
Bas-Beaujolais**

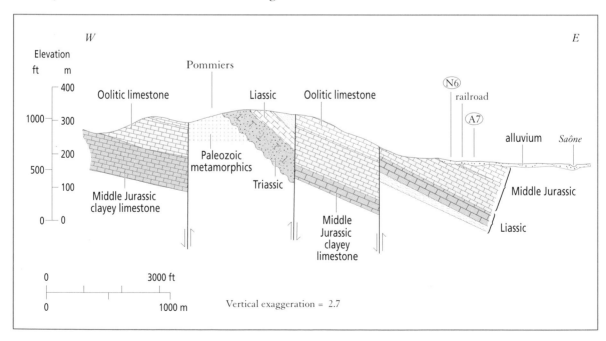

Epilogue

Burgundy was the land of "Genesis" for this book. It was the contemplation in the Pommard vineyard where the concept of the elements of the vineyard habitat came together. The variations in geology from the classic cap-rock slopes of the Côte d'Or to the granite hills of Beaujolais – along with the influence of rock type on the soils, and the importance of faulting and exposure – became guidelines for evaluating terroirs of the other wine areas of France. The marvelous, maddening wines of Burgundy pre-eminently illustrate the individuality in style and characteristics of diverse ownership.

My tutorial with Professor Leneuf and Dr. Lautel at the "vantage point" at the Clos de Vougeot on one of my early visits to the Côte d'Or began an absorbing but difficult study of the geology and wines of Burgundy. Difficult, because of all the wine areas of France, Burgundy literally demands answers to the question "Why do fine wines grow where they do?" It could be an absorbing and delightful geologic study to last a lifetime if one had a backhoe (mechanical digger) and a willing seismic crew – but most of all, time enough to spend leisurely with the countless, hospitable, and generous winegrowers in their wine rooms and kitchens.

Who would want to be king of France with such a "goodly heritage?"

5 Aquitaine: a basin filled with rivers, geology, and history

This chapter will prepare the reader for a better understanding and appreciation of the landscape, geology, and history of the wines of this great basin of France. The beating heart of the Aquitaine wineland is the Bordeaux region, but around the basin, satellite areas add a strong pulse to the flow of wine, *see* Figure 5.1.

Unlike the scrambled, vivid colors of the geologic map of Southeast France and Languedoc, which represent a complex deformation of the earth's crust, the surface of Aquitaine is relatively simple. From the Massif Central-Limousin southward across the Basin to the foothills of the Pyrenees, the blues, greens and pastel colors are distributed in a more coherent pattern, *see* Color Plate 1. The

**Figure. 5.1
General geology of
the Aquitaine Basin**

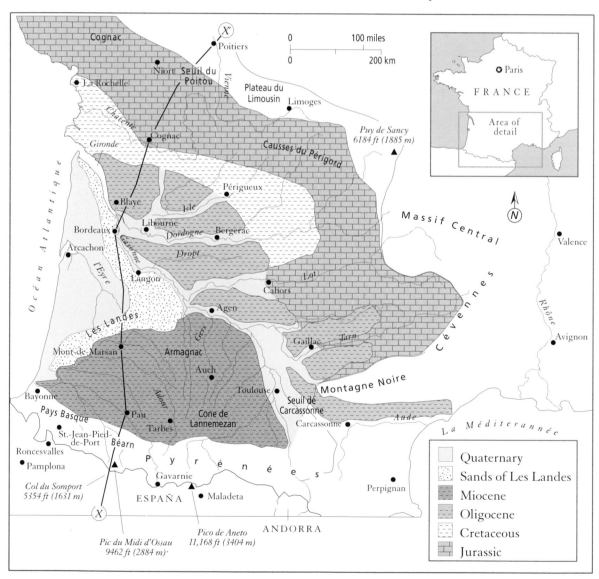

blue Jurassic and green Cretaceous were involved in the early part of the basin downwarp. The pastel colors represent Tertiary and Quaternary formations deposited during the closing phases of filling of Aquitaine. Molasse was shed into the Basin from the Pyrenees and the Massif Central, while streams laced the central basin, and limestones were precipitated in freshwater lakes. These continental deposits interfingered with marine incursions from the Atlantic.

The Quaternary Ice Age saw periods of flooding which lined the rivers with steps of gravel terraces. Sands from wide beaches were spread over low expanses along the shoreline and into lines of dunes. The migrating sands would eventually threaten vineyards before being stabilized by special plantings. Except for an area or two in the Basque country along the flank of the Pyrenees, the wine landscape of the Aquitaine Basin is one of deposition and erosion, not one of deformation as occurs in Southeast France.

Aquitaine is a well-defined topographic basin with the River Garonne as the master stream. The Romans named it *Aquitaine*, a "well-watered place." Transalpine Gaul extended into the eastern part of the basin, including the head-waters of the Garonne and the Gallo-Roman towns of Toulouse and Gaillac.

The geologic history of Aquitaine presents two important phases – the deep phase relating to oil and gas and the shallow phase which created the wine landscape. Figure 5.2 helps tell the story. The cross-sectional view shows a deep, asymmetric basin quite in contrast to the relatively shallow bowl of the Paris

**Figure 5.2
Cross-section of Aquitaine,
Pyrenees to the Paris Basin**

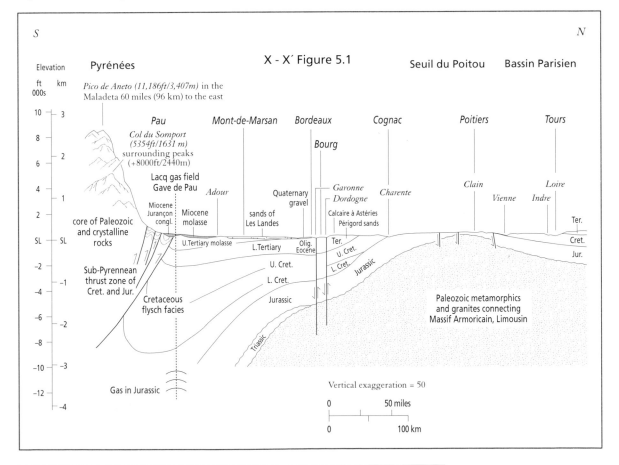

Basin. The stratigraphic sequence in Aquitaine starts with the Triassic – during which red desert sands, mud flats, and salt basins were laid down. During the Jurassic, seas extended from the British Isles across France to the Middle East, depositing variable thicknesses of limestone which now outcrop along the north flank of the Aquitaine Basin.

In the Cretaceous, a welt appeared along a zone that would become the Pyrenees. As the mountains rose, a downwarping developed along the north side. During the late Cretaceous, and into the Tertiary, sinking continued at about the same rate as the Pyrenees rose. In mid-Tertiary, the rate of mountain growth increased with the Pyrenees "blossoming" into high, rugged peaks. Sheet-like detachments (nappes) of the overbuilt mountains slid down the side, later to become the wine terrain of Béarn and the Basque country.

Deep in the basin, heat and pressure plastified the vast layers of Triassic salt. Lighter than its confining strata, the salt tended to bubble toward the surface, doming overlying formations. Gas accumulated in the domed strata as the giant Lacq gas field. Discovery of this gas field in the 1950s saw the economic fortunes of the Aquitaine Basin soar. Today, well-heads of this gas field stand among the vines of the Jurançon wine field.

Paleozoic, Triassic, and Jurassic rocks at elevations of up to 10,000 feet (3000 m) in the mountains have counterparts at depths of twice those numbers in the bottom of the trough. While we speak of a deep trough, the water was never very deep as detritus from the rising mountains kept the basin filled, often to overflowing. From mid-Tertiary through the Quaternary represented the final phase that created the wine landscape.

The erosional materials of the early stages of mountain building were fine-grained sands, silts, and clays named "flysch" by the European geologists. As uplifting intensified, the debris became coarser – sands and gravel interbedded with marls called "molasse." These detrital clastic (molassic) deposits constitute the principal soils of the south half of the basin, from the Basque region to Gaillac. Interfingering with these molassic beds are river deposits and freshwater limestones precipitated in the lakes.

A continental environment dominated the eastern portion of the basin. Roaming among the lakes, rivers, and gravel plains were mastodons, wild boars, cat-like creatures, and the three-toed ancestor of the horse.

But the retreating seas did not give up easily. During the Eocene and continuing until the Pliocene-Quaternary, they launched at least five major invasions from the Atlantic. None got very far inland nor stayed very long. The retreat of each marine invasion was followed by an extension of the continental environment. This see-sawing of deposition resulted in a vertical interfingering shown in Figure 5.3. The interfingering of these beds upward through time from the Lower Eocene to the Pliocene-Quaternary constitutes a section several thousands of feet thick.

One particular marine embayment supported a literal firmament of starfish. Fragments of these fragile sea-creatures became imbedded in the calcareous precipitation, now hardened into what is known as the *Calcaire à astéries*, or the "starfish limestone". This thick limestone is the bedrock below gravel terraces of the southern Médoc and Graves, the location of so many crus, or classed growths.

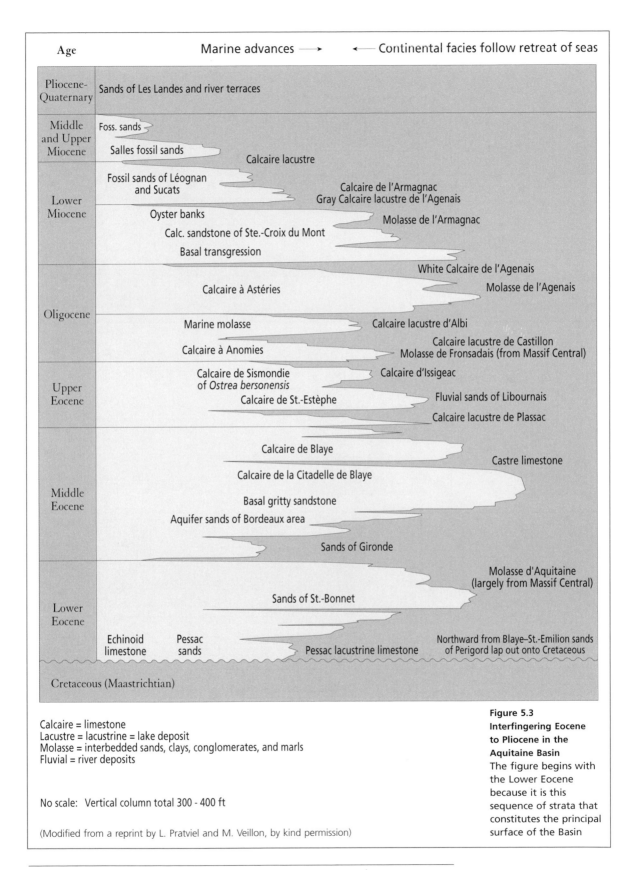

Age	Marine advances ⟶	⟵ Continental facies follow retreat of seas

Pliocene-Quaternary
Sands of Les Landes and river terraces

Middle and Upper Miocene
Foss. sands
Salles fossil sands
Calcaire lacustre

Lower Miocene
Fossil sands of Léognan and Sucats
Oyster banks
Calc. sandstone of Ste.-Croix du Mont
Basal transgression
Calcaire de l'Armagnac
Gray Calcaire lacustre de l'Agenais
Molasse de l'Armagnac

Oligocene
Calcaire à Astéries
Marine molasse
Calcaire à Anomies
White Calcaire de l'Agenais
Molasse de l'Agenais
Calcaire lacustre d'Albi
Calcaire lacustre de Castillon
Molasse de Fronsadais (from Massif Central)

Upper Eocene
Calcaire de Sismondie of *Ostrea bersonensis*
Calcaire de St.-Estèphe
Calcaire d'Issigeac
Fluvial sands of Libournais
Calcaire lacustre de Plassac

Middle Eocene
Calcaire de Blaye
Calcaire de la Citadelle de Blaye
Basal gritty sandstone
Aquifer sands of Bordeaux area
Sands of Gironde
Castre limestone

Lower Eocene
Molasse d'Aquitaine (largely from Massif Central)
Sands of St.-Bonnet
Echinoid limestone
Pessac sands
Pessac lacustrine limestone
Northward from Blaye–St.-Emilion sands of Perigord lap out onto Cretaceous

Cretaceous (Maastrichtian)

Calcaire = limestone
Lacustre = lacustrine = lake deposit
Molasse = interbedded sands, clays, conglomerates, and marls
Fluvial = river deposits

No scale: Vertical column total 300 - 400 ft

(Modified from a reprint by L. Pratviel and M. Veillon, by kind permission)

**Figure 5.3
Interfingering Eocene to Pliocene in the Aquitaine Basin**
The figure begins with the Lower Eocene because it is this sequence of strata that constitutes the principal surface of the Basin

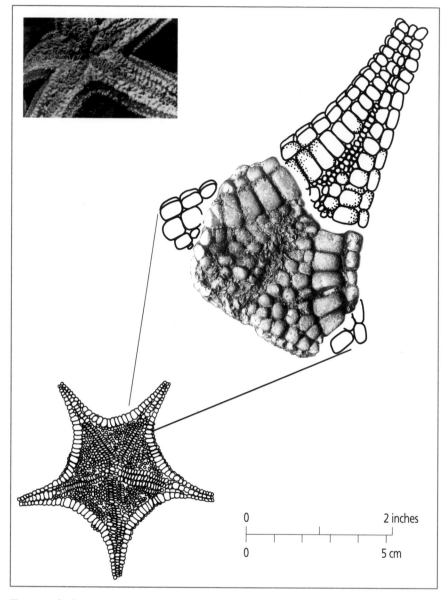

Eastward, the *Calcaire à astéries* is the cap rock of the plateaux of Bourg-Blaye, St.-Emilion, and the Entre-Deux-Mers. The limestone scarp provides abundant wine storage tunnels, building stone, and the basis of cave-homes for early man. In Figure 5.4 is an artist's reconstruction of the fossil starfish.

As upthrusting of the Pyrenees began to taper off, it was the turn of the Massif Central to put on a show. It began quietly with a broad, turtle-back uplift which continued intermittently through the remaining 25 million years of the Tertiary. Although the uplift itself was unspectacular, it was accompanied by fireworks. Effusive volcanoes (not the explosive type) built the impressive peaks, cinder cones, the Chaîne des Puys (chain of volcanic peaks), Mont Dore, and the crowning Puy de Sancy. Some of the lava flows spilled into the Limagne Valley around Clermont-Ferrand, forming plateaux and excellent soils for vineyards of the Auvergne – yet their wines remain mediocre.

Toward the end of the Tertiary, the sea gave up trying to invade the land and retreated to near its present shoreline. The western part of Aquitaine was a flattish landscape over which the River Garonne flowed in rambling pursuit of the retreating sea. The shifting stream spread a vast delta-like sheet of sandy gravel over the land during the Pliocene. Later faulting created the plateaux of Bourg-Blaye and Entre-Deux-Mers, confining the Garonne and its estuary the Gironde to its present valley.

As the Tertiary closed down, it turned the landscape work over to the Quaternary which opened with the Great Ice Age lasting almost two million years. In spite of its name, the Ice Age period was not one long freeze-up, rather a sequence of periods of intense cold alternating with four major "interglacials" or warm periods. Age-dates of the glacial stages and their correlation with historical events and archeologic cultures are summarized overleaf in Table 5.1. As the Ice Age progressed, trapped in the growing continental ice cap were incredible quantities of water, which resulted in a progressive lowering of sea level. With lowering of their base levels, streams cut progressively deeper and deeper channels during flood times of the warm periods. This continued downcutting left successive levels of overflow terraces, of which at least one is of great viticultural significance in Bordeaux.

As you were warned in the first part of this book, geologists like to name, classify, and correlate the rocks and strata with which they deal. No less is accorded the homely gravel deposits of the Garonne-Gironde. The Médoc-Graves terraces have been correlated with the classical stages of the Pleistocene Ice Age, studied and named for small tributaries of the Upper Danube on the north side of the Alps, east of Munich. The different levels of terraces are related to the lowering of sea level during the Ice Age. As the Garonne dug its channel deeper, terraces of the previous stage were left high and dry.

The earliest (uppermost) recognizable terrace in Bordeaux is the Pliocene Donau (Danube) which was spread by the rambling Garonne at the very end of the Tertiary. The four successive stages of the Pleistocene terraces are the Günz, Mindel, Riss, and the Würm.

As the sea level lowered and the shoreline receded, wide, sandy beaches developed along the Atlantic coast. Winds whipped up clouds of sand and dust, spreading them over the triangular-shaped gravel plain and piling up waves of dunes. This desert-like expanse is Les Landes. Arrayed like panzers for attack, the dunes were driven inland by the prevailing Westerlies. Migration of the dunes continued into historical time, burying villages and threatening to overwhelm the vineyards of the Médoc and Graves. In 1788, "sand fences" were constructed to interrupt the flow of sand while special grass and maritime pines from Provence were planted to stabilize the restless sand, halting them within yards of many prime vineyards. Les Landes is now Europe's biggest manmade forest, at 2.47 million acres (a million hectares)

About 10,000 years ago, as the Great Ice Age drew to a close, sea level began to return to its previous position. Return of sea level to normal drowned the over-deepened Gironde, creating an estuary similar to the Chesapeake Bay and the Hudson River at New York. The Würm and the Riss terraces of the lower Médoc were inundated by waters of the estuary, leaving the Günz as the main

Time/date	Geology System	Geology Epoch	Glacial-Interglacial Stages	Historical Events and Archeological Cultures	Ages	Morphologic and Other Affects on Vineyards
1866 1815 1789	Quaternary	Recent (Holocene)		Phylloxera appeared in Bordeaux Waterloo Beginning of the French Revolution		• 1867 work completed in planting pine trees to stabilize sand dunes of Les Landes. • 1855 hierarchical list for the exhibition in Paris. • Large estates broken up. • Colbert, Louis XIV's Minister of Finance and engineer by training, ordered draining of Médoc marshes. • Development of large estates in Médoc.
1564-98			Little Ice Age (cooling period)	Wars of Religion		
1492			Sub-Atlantic (milder and wetter) continues to today with some minor variations	Columbus discovers America		• Carthusian monks built Chartreuse in marshy land near Bordeaux.
1337-1453 1152				Hundred Years War Eleanor of Aquitaine marries Henry Plantagenet		• Land grants near Bordeaux on condition land reclaimed and vines planted.
732				Saracen invasion defeated at battle of Poitiers		
511				Clovis conquers Aquitaine		
A.D.				Jesus Christ		• First vineyards in Bordeaux - circa A.D.50
B.C. (000's years before)			Sub-Boreal (cooler and dryer)	Caeser conquers Gaul	Iron La Terne Halstatt	• Sea level returned to near present stage.
					Bronze	
5			Atlantic (warm and wet)	Stonehenge - England First pyramids - Egypt Domestication of plants and animals	Copper Neolithic	• Sea level rose some nearly 230 feet by melting of continental glacier. Straits of Dover opened by end of Boreal and reached present level about 2,000 B.C. Flandrian incursion silted up low-lying areas along Gironde estuary creating "palus" marshland.
			Boreal (warm and dry)	Tardenoisian (Fére-en-Tardenois, Aisne) Azilian (Mas d'Azil in Pyrenees)	Meso-lithic	
10			Pre-Boreal			• Sand dunes of Les Landes strongly active.
		Pleistocene (Great Ice Age)	Würm IV	Magdelenian (La Madeleine, Dordogne) Solutrean (Solutré, Burgundy)	Upper Paleolithic	• Solifluction "dressed" slopes and periglacial erosion softened typography of Aquitaine landscape.
20			Würm III-IV	*Cro-Magnon Man		• The Würm was the coldest and the longest of Pleistocene glacial periods.
			Würm III	Perigordian (Périgord region) developed parallel with Aurignacian (Aurignac, upper Garonne Valley)		
			Würm II-III Würm II		Middle Paleolithic	• Sea level reached maximum low stage. Gironde channel became common outlet for Garonne and Dordogne and was at least 200 feet lower than at present at its outlet
			Würm I-II	Mousterian (Le Moustier, Dordogne)		
50			Würm I Würm I-IV = N. Am. Wisconsin	Micoquian (La Micoque-aux-Eyzies, Dordogne)		• Rissian gravel of Nappes almost totally destroyed.
				*Homo Sapiens *Neanderthal Man		• Erosion on Dordogne less violent than Garonne. Rissian gravels are preserved on lower slopes at St.-Emilion.
100			Riss-Würm			
200			Riss	Acheulian (St. Acheul, Amiens) and Levalloisian (Levallois-Perret, near Paris)		• Eolian sands threatened to obliterate gravel sites of Médoc and Graves.
			Mindel-Riss	*Homo Erectus *Heidelberg Man *Peking Man	Early Paleolithic (Stone Age)	
500			Mindel	Abbevillian-Chellean Clactonian (Abbeville, Somme; Chelles near Meaux and Clacton-on-Sea, Essex, England)		
			Günz-Mindel			
1,000			Günz	Use of fire Pebble culture		• Detritus from Périgord deposited by the Isle and Dronne in Pomerol and Haut-Médoc.
			Günz-Donau			
2,000			Donau			• Broad crustal plate and upthrust of Pyrenees.
	Tertiary	Pliocene	Biber			• Pyrenean conglomerates deposited widespread in north and east Aquitaine Basin.
5,000			Climate of Aquitaine Basin was primarily warm and damp			• End of Miocene, final retreat of seas to Atlantic Ocean.
10,000		Mio.				• Uplifting of Pyrenees mid-Eocene to mid-Miocene shed conglomerates of Jurançon, Orignac and Lannemezan which interfingered with molasse of Armagnac and Agen.

Table 5.1

Geologic and historical setting of the Aquitaine Basin

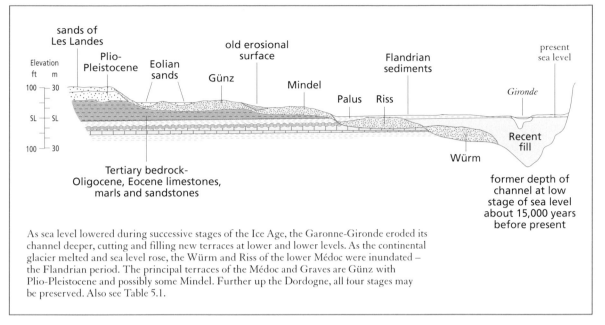

As sea level lowered during successive stages of the Ice Age, the Garonne-Gironde eroded its channel deeper, cutting and filling new terraces at lower and lower levels. As the continental glacier melted and sea level rose, the Würm and Riss of the lower Médoc were inundated – the Flandrian period. The principal terraces of the Médoc and Graves are Günz with Plio-Pleistocene and possibly some Mindel. Further up the Dordogne, all four stages may be preserved. Also see Table 5.1.

viticultural terrace for the Médoc and Graves. Figure 5.5 is a model illustrating the successive terraces of classical glacial stages of the Garonne–Gironde channel. Although geologists are not in complete agreement as to the exact identity of these terraces, we will go with the Günz as the uppermost (that is earliest) of the four downcutting terraces and as the most widespread principal vineyard terrace.

The final phase of the return of sea level European geologists call the "Flandrian," named for the inundation of the low lands of Flanders and the Rhine delta of the Netherlands. Tidal action in the Gironde estuary created mud flats or "palus" along the shoreline. During the reign of the Sun King, Louis XIV (1643–1715), draining of these marshy palus by Dutch engineers lowered the water table of the adjacent gravel terraces, making them significantly more habitable for people – and for vines.

These gravel terrace-mounds became home for the world-famous wines of Médoc, Graves, Sauternes, and Pomerol. The walnut-size gravel and pebbles of the terrace-mounds are not particularly colorful, but they are an interesting assortment of rocks. Geologists knowledgeable of Aquitaine recognize what they call *galets directeurs*, "director pebbles," meaning identity of the particular mountain areas whence the gravel came: white and pinkish quartz and agates from the Massif Central, black Lydian stone from the Pyrenees, and flintstones from Périgord-Limousin.

Of the mountains surrounding Aquitaine, the most spectacular are the Pyrenees. The Garonne originates in the Maladeta Massif (the name translates as accursed mountain) on the Spanish side of the Pyrenees and flows for 30 miles (48 km) as the Rio Garona before it becomes the French Garonne. But tributaries down the Lannemezan Cone (a giant depositional fan which spreads north from the base of the Pyrenees at Torbes) contribute only modest volumes of water. The important tributaries of the Garonne come out of the Massif Central-Limousin – the Dordogne, Tarn, and Lot.

Figure 5.5
Model of terraces of classical glacial stages in Médoc–Graves

The Dordogne is more a partner to the Garonne than a tributary, as it has a system of its own. Its tributaries, the Isle, Dronne, and Vézère, cut steep-walled, scenic gorges in the limestone plateau flanking the Limousin. Numerous caves and rock shelters eroded from Cretaceous limestone are veritable museums of prehistoric man. World famous are the wall paintings by Paleolithic artists in the caves of Les Eyzies, Lascaux, and Pech Merle.

In the southwest sector of Aquitaine, the Adour and its tributaries form a separate, well-watered arcuate basin. Slopes and terraces of this river system support the wine areas of Béarn, Bas-Armagnac, and other ancient vineyards. Originating in the Pyrenees above Tarbes, the Adour makes a sweeping turn of 90 degrees to enter the Atlantic at Bayonne.

History and wine in Aquitaine

As the Ice Age released its grip, the earth began to warm. Advanced stages of human cultures replaced those of the early Paleolithic (Stone) Age. History and geology began to approach the same timescale. The logarithmic scale in Table 5.1 is a convenient device by which ten million years of geologic time and events of this history – pre-history – are shrunk into eye-reach. History is an integral part of winegrowing in Aquitaine.

The frequently found "-ac" ending in Aquitaine placenames is the abstraction of an Old Latin suffix meaning the place or estate of a person.

Wine was growing in the Gaillac region several centuries before Caesar came to Gaul. Emigrants from the Mediterranean coast had ventured across the Carcassonne Gateway into Aquitaine as far as Toulouse, Gaillac, and the headwaters of the Garonne, but not much further. This was part of the Roman province of Transalpine Gaul. During Caesar's campaign for northern Gaul, tribes of Aquitaine remained relatively quiet. When the conquest appeared about complete, an uprising occurred at the oppidum (native fortress) of Uxellodunum. This historical site is some 60 miles (100 km) up the Dordogne from Bergerac. Caesar took personal command of the siege of the oppidum which was perched on a steep promontory. It is probable that this was the first time Caesar was ever in Aquitaine. With this final rebellion put to rest, viticulture spread westward down the valley of the Garonne where it met new geology and new grape varieties from Spain.

The Benedictines, Cistercians, Carthusians, and Knights of Malta quickly followed Romanization of Aquitaine, setting up abbeys and monasteries. But, as Desmond Seward observes in *Monks and Wine*, none of the orders exercised as strong or as lasting an influence on viticulture here as in Burgundy, Alsace, and other parts of France, due to the general hostility of the Basques to Christianity.

In the 5th century the Basques descended from the Pyrenees, overrunning the country as far as the Garonne. The Romans called these people Vascones. Vascone became Gascon – Gascony. The boundary of Gascony was where Eskura, the very different language of the Basques, was spoken. The Basque country of today extends along the piedmont and mountains from Pau to the Atlantic, which includes the old Pyrenean states of Navarre and Béarn.

The Basques have maintained a cultural individualism since pre-history. Strangely, the modern Basque bears little resemblance to the archetypal Gascon – volatile and spoiling-for-a-fight musketeer portrayed by d'Artagnan and Cyrano de Bergerac in novels by Alexandre Dumas and Edmond Rostand.

In the 6th century, the sword and crescent of Islam spread rapidly from the Middle East along the coast of North Africa, crossed the Straits of Gibraltar and subjugated the Iberian peninsula. Gaul, rich and Christian, lay irresistibly just across the Pyrenees. Soon the "Saracens" skirted the western end of the mountains and swept northward toward Tours, the religious capital of Gaul.

Charles Martel of the northern Franks with a rag-tag army attacked and defeated the plunder-laden invaders in 732, near Poitiers. Western historians accord this battle as having saved western Europe from the mortifying hand of Islam. However, the Saracens, and the Moors, the black Islamics of North Africa, remained in Spain for another 400 years.

The 10th century brought boom times for Aquitaine wine. A pilgrimage to Santiago de Compostella in the northwest corner of the Iberian peninsula was considered almost as blessed as a journey to Rome or Jerusalem. The route from the interior of western Europe to Santiago was through Aquitaine, either to cross the Pyrenees or by ship from the Gironde.

As many as two million pilgrims a year converged on St.-Jean-Pied-de-Port in preparation for crossing the Pyrenees. As the name indicates, the town is at the foot of a pass, Col de Roncevaux, the most accessible in the western Pyrenees. Pilgrims in those days were in no hurry and made many side trips. "Tourism" and wine became big business along the pilgrim route. A recent visitor to the region reports that there are still numerous pilgrims travelling the route by foot.

Eleanor of Aquitaine's marriage to Henry Plantagenet, count of Anjou, in the 12th century was to have a profound affect on wine and European history. Henry's inheritance of Normandy and the Loire region together with Eleanor's dowry of most of Aquitaine, meant this young French couple controled the western half of France – as much land and wealth as the royal house.

The stunning part of this marriage came when Henry became king of England. Even so, by feudal law, Henry remained a vassal to the king of France. Title to their French properties remained valid so long as Henry or his successors paid homage in person to the French crown. Aquitaine became, in effect, an English colony. In the feudal requirement of personal homage were the seeds of the Hundred Years War.

It would take two centuries for the seeds to germinate. For English kings to have to pay personal homage to French kings became increasingly demeaning to the English. Having English kings owning lands in France irked the French, especially since they received no taxes from this English "colony." This homage business was the sticking point that led to the open break that came in the mid-14th century. A proud, young King Edward III refused to pay homage to the French king, Philip of Valois, as he considered he had a more valid claim to the crown. The French considered Edward's claim to be invalid. Such claim was questionable under the Salic Law as his inheritance was through his mother. Eventually Edward renounced his fealty as a vassal of the king of France. The Hundred Years War was on.

The end of that long series of conflicts also ended 300 years of English occupation of Aquitaine when the final battle took place at Castillon, just east of St.-Emilion. To commemorate the 500th anniversary of the event, in 1953 Castillon was allowed to add la-Bataille to its village name.

European Christians refused to recognize Islam as a rival religion and referred to the Muslims by ethnic names such as Saracen. The Saracens were the Arabs of the Banu Sara Bedouin tribe of the Sinai.

The Bordeaux Privileges

Even though the end of the Hundred Years War meant the English were finally militarily expelled from France, their fondness for "claret" had become an institution.

The first 200 years of English control had seen Aquitaine wine trade flourish with England and the North Atlantic countries. Shipping was controlled through the port of Bordeaux with merchants and wine syndicates becoming rich and powerful.

Leading the wine trade with England was "claret," (a corruption of French "clairet," blended to the English taste as a light, red wine). It was a cozy business; the vineyards were very near the port, and shipping was controlled by the English.

Wines from both sides of the Garonne upstream began to participate in the trade. The Bordeaux merchants were determined to protect local sources of wine in which they had financial interests. At the behest of the merchants, in 1325, the English king granted full jurisdiction to Bordeaux to control shipping through that port. Shipping constraints known as the "Bordeaux Privileges" effectively eliminated competition of upriver wines from Cahors, Gaillac, Armagnac, and other areas.

The Bordeaux prohibition stated that no "vin de pays" above St.-Macaire could enter the port of Bordeaux from the 8th of September until the feast of St.-Martin, November 11th. By the latter date, the numerous ships loaded with new wine would have sailed for England and ports on the North Sea in order to arrive before Christmas. But don't underestimate the ingenuity of country boys.

The Dordogne enters the Gironde waterway below the Bordeaux jurisdiction. Here was an opening that could be exploited. Bergerac on the Dordogne was also a possession of the king of England. For good political and economic reasons, he wished to keep the loyalty of the people of both Bergerac and the "Haut-Pays." Accordingly, the king decreed that the constraint of "above St.-Macaire" did not apply to wines coming down the Dordogne to the seaway. So, Garonne upriver wines were carried overland from St.-Macaire to Bergerac, thence by barge down the Dordogne to the ocean-going ships in the Gironde. The end-run put country wines on North Atlantic Christmas tables but a bitter taste in the mouths of Bordeaux merchants, a taste which lasted for centuries.

In spite of circumvention of the Bordeaux Privileges, the constraint had a serious negative affect on winegrowers of the "Haut-Pays," many of them turning to fruit farming and other crops. Growers in the Armagnac region, however, increased the production of wines that were distilled into brandy, primarily for the Dutch trade.

The Hundred Years War had seriously disordered all France, but there were problems about religion even more disturbing and emotional that would affect Aquitaine and its wine. The Catholics and Protestants were soon at war, the Wars of Religion — there were to be 8 in 31 years. Important pockets of Huguenots (Protestants) existed in Aquitaine; otherwise, the region remained either Roman Catholic or indifferent to Catholic traditions. As Bordeaux and the regions upstream of the Garonne were primarily Catholic, the Protestant countries of Holland and England did not care to purchase wine from those who persecuted the Huguenots. As it turned out, the towns of Cognac and Jarnac in the Charente and the port of La Rochelle were Protestant strongholds. Trade in cognac boomed.

The two centuries following the Wars of Religion up to the French Revolution saw important progress in winegrowing in Aquitaine, particularly during the rule of Louis XIV. It was the Sun King's innovative Minister of Finance, Jean-Baptiste Colbert, who had hired the Dutch engineers to drain the tidal marshes and mud flats along the Gironde. As mentioned earlier, drainage of the marshes lowered the water table, tremendously improving the habitability of the Médoc for people as well as allowing the deep rooting of vines in the gravel mounds.

Huguenots were named for the Protestant leader Hugues combined with the German word, *Eidgenossen*, meaning confederate. The combination was Latinized to Huguenot.

The 17th century also witnessed the rise of many new families of importance in the Bordeaux region. This new aristocracy, the so-called "noblesse de robe," was created for those who had served in the Bordeaux parliament. The status symbol for these "nouveaux nobles" was ownership of a château and vineyard estate. The fashionable areas for new estates were the former hunting moors of the Médoc, and before long a parade of châteaux was competing for prestige and unique architecture.

Completion in 1755 of the 300-mile (480-km) long Canal du Midi along the Garonne and over the Carcassonne Gateway to the Mediterranean gave important impetus to trade between the two coasts.

During the American War of Independence, the British navy blockaded the Gironde because the French were supporting the Americans. All the same, enough claret managed to "slip through" the Bordeaux blockade to satisfy British thirst. Less than a generation later came France's own revolution. Initially the affects of the violent changes taking place in Paris were little felt in Aquitaine. However, as vicious reprisals spread to include citizens of means, many estates in the Bordeaux region were abandoned by their owners who emigrated to avoid the guillotine. These properties were confiscated by the State and sold to new owners.

The post-revolutionary years also witnessed many new winegrowers and businessmen come to Bordeaux from Switzerland, England, and Germany, as well as other parts of France. They were entrepreneurial by nature and usually had important trade connections with their former countries. It was a period of strong development in the Médoc and the surrounding region.

The Napoleonic era was a particularly difficult one for Aquitaine, as the important overseas markets were again at the mercy of the British navy. Wine trade with England ceased. After Waterloo, and Napoleon's second banishment, trade was normalized, but owing to distressed economic conditions, many properties in the region changed hands. The wine business deteriorated seriously in all of France.

In the latter part of the 19th century, the Bordeaux region was one of the two centers from which phylloxera spread. When the pest put in its devastating appearance in 1866, it made no distinctions between blue-ribbon and ordinary vines. The Bordelais were as reluctant as any in France to accept the heresy of grafting prized French vines on ordinary American rootstocks. Only after it became abundantly clear that this was the sole real solution to the crisis was grafting adopted in the area.

The growers in the Charentes, the cognac region, maintained that their chalky soils presented a special problem of rootstock adaptation. They were able to persuade the French government to send a special mission to America to discover which of that country's phylloxera-resistant vines were most adaptable to the calcareous soils of the Charentes. Thomas Volney Munson, the plant scientist in Texas (*see* page 47), led the French mission to the area west of Austin, Texas, where wild, phylloxera-resistant, vines were growing on chalky formations. In 1892, the Station Viticole de Cognac was established, designed primarily to relate soils with grape variety. It was the first research laboratory of its kind in the country.

In the Great War of 1914–18, Champagne and Alsace were the only wine regions under enemy control, but from all of France many vignerons lost their lives in battle. The vintage years during and after that war were generally good, but labor shortages, increasing costs, and lessening demand due to economic conditions made recovery extremely slow.

In 1939, there was no labor shortage in Aquitaine as half a million refugees from the Civil War in Spain crowded in. Then, when Germany invaded France, the refugees reversed direction and returned to Spain, which officially remained neutral during World War II. The Pyrenees became the "promised land" by which downed Allied airmen and other military escapees might reach Spain. Within those mountains were the Basques who were master smugglers, with a code of silence as impenetrable as the granites among which they lived.

Shortly after World War II, a new kind of excitement and activity gripped Aquitaine – geophysical exploration for oil and gas. Efforts were handsomely rewarded in 1951 with the discovery of the giant Lacq gas field. A few years later oil was found in the Parentis area southwest of Bordeaux. The focus and interest has continued with the completion of additional arterial autoroutes, and increasing numbers of travelers are discovering the Aquitaine Basin with its many vacation attractions – some of them world-famous: the curative waters of the Lourdes grottos and the prehistoric cave paintings of Lascaux, for instance – as well as the colorful Basque country, the sandy beaches at Arcachon, the once fashionable resort of Biarritz, and the gorges of the Dordogne, Lot, and Tarn. And, of course, its food, wines, and spirits. Chapter 6 is devoted to Bordeaux, plus Cognac, since these two large regions have a geologic relationship as well as a common boundary. Bergerac, Cahors, Gaillac, Béarn, Jurançon, Armagnac, and other wine areas of the Southwest form the subject of chapter 7.

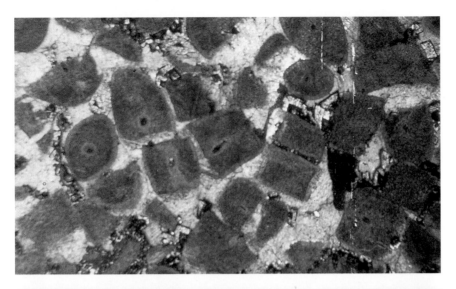

Color Plate 13
A chip of *Calcaire a entroques* (crinoidal limestone) has been ground to a thin section of near-transparency. Viewed under a microscope, with light projected from below and with little magnification, reveals fossilized plant fragments cemented into a rock. A chemical dye colors the crinoid fragments brown while the calcium-magnesium cement is gray. The small holes in some fragments are canals through the joints of the crinoid stalks

Color Plate 14
Ostrea acuminata marl. The tiny oysters (5 cm = approx. 2 in) thrived in the calcareous mud of shallow, Middle Jurassic seas. The calcareous clay, now marl, is a "thickening" constituent in the vineyard soils of the northern Côte d'Or, and contributes to some of finest wineland terroirs in France

Color Plate 15
The terroir of La Romanée-Conti in Burgundy produces the most costly red wines on earth

Color Plate 16
The hill of Corton with its distinct wooded crown dominates the winelands of the Côte de Beaune. The hill is home to two Grands Crus: Corton-Charlemagne (white) and Corton (red)

Color Plate 17
The giant Clos de Vougeot winepress, its oak beams 1000 years old, still operates. It is known as Le Têtu (the "stubborn one"), presumably referring to the creaking and groaning as the monster is put to work

Color Plate 18
Marls and clayey limestones combine to produce the excellent soils on the rollercoaster slope
of Premier Cru Volnay

Color Plate 19
View from the St.-Léger horst to the Roche de Solutré. The rocky outcrop is often likened
to a rearing horse, frozen as it pawed the air. Below it is the topographic bowl containing the
vineyards of Pouilly-Fuissé, the flagship region of the Mâconnais

Color Plate 20
The famous Moulin à Vent (windmill) with part of its one remaining sail. It no longer grinds corn but is now a national monument. The pink arène soils of this Beaujolais cru are rich in iron and manganese but thin and easily eroded

Color Plate 21
A gravel mound pit in the Médoc. Why these seemingly sterile gravel terrace mounds should produce some of the world-class wines of the Médoc, Graves, and Sauternes is one of the most intriguing aspects of the wine geology of Bordeaux

Color Plate 22
Professor Louis Pratviel points out oyster beds in the marine Miocene strata 60 feet (20 m) above the *Calcaire à astéries* near Ste.-Croix across the Garonne from the Sauternes

Color Plate 23
Côtes de Bourg vineyards bordering the Gironde, the estuary of the Dordogne and Garonne which dominate the winelands of Bordeaux. In the distance is the suspension bridge spanning the Dordogne at St.-André de Cubzac. The river system has been crucial to the history and development of the wines of Bordeaux and the Southwest. It also divides the geology of the cuestas, slopes, and plateaux of Bourg and Blaye on the northwest and the low hills and gravel terrace mounds of the Médoc, Graves, and Sauternes on the southeast

Color Plate 24
The first-growth Château Margaux certainly looks the part: its setting, buildings, even its *chais* are palatial. Its vineyards are atypical in being on bedrock with only a veneer of gravel, rather than wholly on a classic terrace mound, but in great years it can produce one of the most perfect of all clarets

Color Plate 25
Château Haut-Brion is the first growth of the Graves (meaning gravel), a unique terroir within the confines of the city of Bordeaux. It has survived urban pressure because its coarse gravel soils yield truly superlative wine. The centimeter marks on the knife give scale to the size of the gravel

Color Plate 26
Château Ausone has one of the best locations in all Bordeaux. Its vineyards are on the Côtes
St.-Emilion, in deep loamy *Calcaire à astéries* soils, overlooking the Dordogne Valley

Color Plate 27
Château d'Yquem is the
crown jewel of Sauternes,
perfectly located to benefit
from the valley mists of
the River Ciron which
promote noble rot. Its best
parcels of vines are on a
low dome of calcareous
clay overlain by a thin
covering of sandy gravel

Color Plate 28
Vineyards near Condom occupy part of the Lannemezan Cone. The east-facing slopes, being long and gentle, favor vines and other crops. The grape here is principally the Ugni Blanc, either to be distilled into Armagnac or vinified as dry white Côtes des Gascogne

Color Plate 29
The Pyrenees form the sharply etched backdrop of any panorama in Jurançon. South of Gan, vines vie with pastures and woodland

6 Bordeaux: gravel mounds, limestone plateaux

The beautiful city of Bordeaux is the unofficial wine capital of the world. Its principal building stones are of *Calcaire à astéries*, the cap rock of the plateaux across the river. Enormous volumes of the some of the world's finest wines are produced within an hour's trucking time of Bordeaux's deep water harbor. Moreover, a surprising amount of France's wines made in other regions is exported through Bordeaux.

The Gironde is the deep estuary (Color Plate 23) combining the waters of the Garonne and the Dordogne. The Garonne–Gironde divides the wine region into two different geologic landscapes: conventional cuestas, slopes, and plateaux to the northwest, gravel terrace-mounds to the southeast, *see* Figure 6.1. How the gravel mounds of Médoc and Graves-Sauternes operate to produce world-class wines is one of the most intriguing aspects of the natural history of Bordeaux.

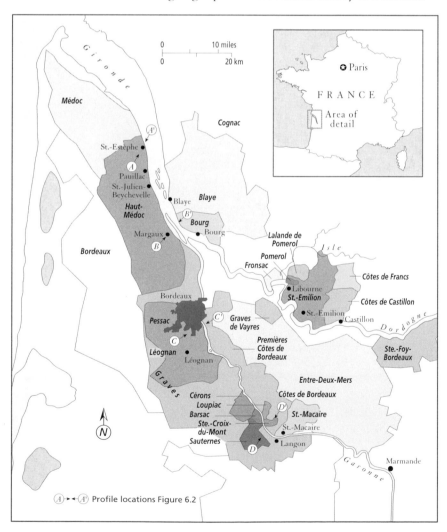

Figure 6.1
The appellations of Bordeaux

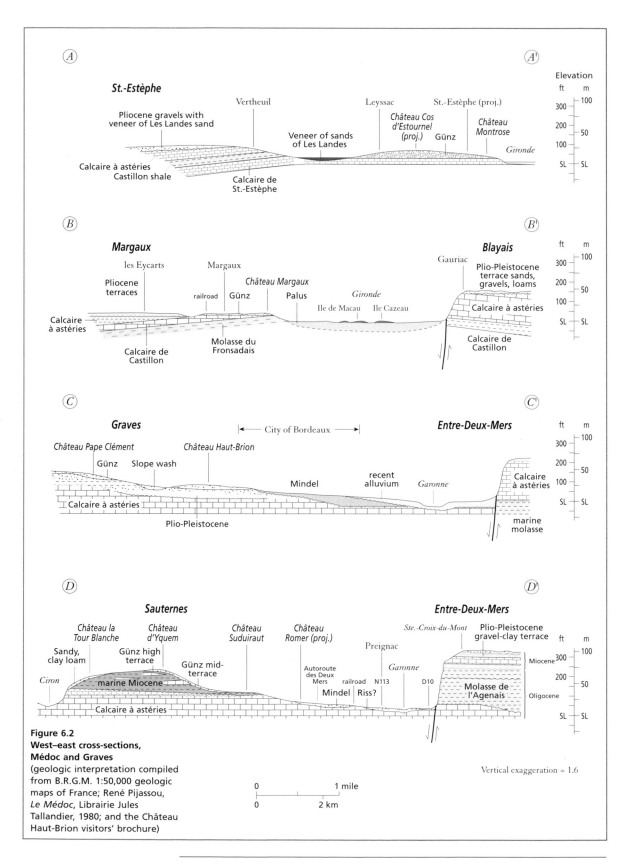

Figure 6.2
West–east cross-sections,
Médoc and Graves
(geologic interpretation compiled
from B.R.G.M. 1:50,000 geologic
maps of France; René Pijassou,
Le Médoc, Librairie Jules
Tallandier, 1980; and the Château
Haut-Brion visitors' brochure)

Vertical exaggeration = 1.6

0   1 mile

0   2 km

The low hills and gentle terrain on the southwest side of the river are in contrast to the abrupt wall of a plateau on the northeast. The Dordogne further divides the northeast plateau into two sectors: Bourg-Blaye, St.-Emilion, Pomerol, and Fronsac on the northwest, and the Entre-Deux-Mers and associated appellations on the southeast. The panel of cross-sections in Figure 6.2 dramatically illustrates the geologic relationships across the Gironde–Garonne.

The Médoc–Graves sector

The vineyards of the Médoc and Graves-Sauternes occupy a strip, 5 miles (8 km) wide at most, for 75 miles (120 km) from the mouth of the Gironde to Langon, upriver from Bordeaux. Over 300 châteaux, including 61 classed growths (crus classés) in the Médoc and 39 in Graves-Sauternes, are found in this narrow zone.

The Médoc comprises the Northern Médoc (formerly Bas-Médoc) which has no classed growths, and Haut-Médoc which has well-known communal appellations such as St.-Julien, Pauillac, and Margaux. (A communal appellation covers all or parts of several communes, the name being that of the principal wine village.) The Graves, including metropolitan Bordeaux, extends over 30 miles (48 km) upstream to Langon. The Haut-Graves region now has its own appellation: Pessac-Léognan. Like the Médoc, its classed wines are mostly reds but a tiny amount of sometimes superlative white is also made. Sauternes is an enclave in Graves, on occasion hyphenated with that name, but Sauternes carries its own appellation for its famous sweet white wines.

Geology of the Médoc–Graves gravel terrace-mounds

Admiring the slender, graceful turrets of Château Pichon-Longueville in Pauillac, William Flagg wondered how ground too poor even to grow mullen could yield profits from wine to build such fine châteaux. (Mullen, or mullein, is a wooly-leafed herbaceous plant that seems to thrive in barren soil. William Flagg was an American viticulturist who visited the Médoc in the mid-19th century.) The geology of the Médoc–Graves is indeed the most unlikely and therefore perhaps the most unusual in the world.

The secret of the quality of vineyards of the Médoc is found in the internal composition and functioning of the gravel mounds. That is where the roots find their livelihood. The poor, gravelly ground that any casual observer sees on the surface is only skin-deep. If there is anywhere in France the vineplant has to work hard for a living, it is here in the gravel mounds of Médoc and Graves. (Graves is French for gravel.) To understand how this erstwhile "mullenland" can be good wineland and how the life-sustaining hydric regime (water feeding) functions, we must examine the anatomy of the gravel mounds.

Seeing gravel on the surface and in thick banks in quarries, one might logically assume the mounds to be gravel throughout (*see* Color Plate 21). This is not the case. If it were, it would be a sterile sieve; there would be no vines – only mullen. Closer examination of the gravel, however, reveals interbedded lenses of clay, silt, and dirty sand. These are the "vital organs" of gravel viticulture. It is in these fine-grained sediments that roots find moisture and mineral nutrients. Such lenses within the mounds are the deep secrets of the vineyards.

To understand Bordeaux it is well to define certain terms of its wine vocabulary which are described more fully in the Glossary.

Château in strict wine usage means a vineyard with associated dwelling and active winemaking apparatus. If it meets these criteria, a tumble-down farmhouse has as much right to be called a château as does a castle. Vineyard properties of some châteaux are scattered, but collectively they take the name and most generally the classification of the château.

Growth in Bordeaux means specifically the vineyard of a château. It is also synonymous with cru. Edward Féret's *Bordeaux and Its Wines*, the 1800-page "Bible of Bordeaux" discusses the efforts of several experts to define the term growth. We are told that the late Baron Le Roy, winegrower and jurist of the Bordeaux region, concluded that growth conjures up the notion of a wine property of superior quality. Others agree that in Bordeaux the term is almost inevitably tied to classification, for example, First Growth, classed growth etc. *See* the section headed Classification, page 193.

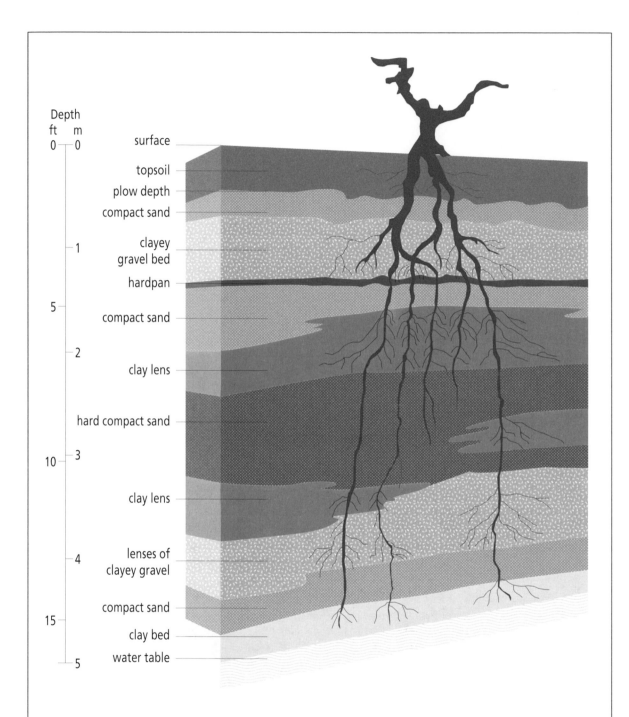

Depth
ft   m

0 — 0 ——— surface

—— topsoil
—— plow depth
—— compact sand

— 1 ——— clayey
         gravel bed

—— hardpan

5 —
—— compact sand

— 2 ——— clay lens

         hard compact sand

10 — 3 ——— clay lens

— 4 ——— lenses of
         clayey gravel

—— compact sand

15 —
—— clay bed

— 5 ——— water table

Figure 6.3
Theoretical soil profile
and rooting system in
Médoc gravel mound
(interpreted from
G. Seguin, *Influence des*
Facteurs Naturels sur
les Caractères des Vins)

This is an interpretation based on the soil profile developed by the research of
Professor Gérard Seguin in St.-Julien of the Médoc.

It illustrates the lenticularity and heterogeneity of river terrace deposits which make
up the Médoc gravel mounds. Roots find and exploit beds of clayey material and clay
lenses for moisture and mineral nourishment, passing through the sterile zones without
branching. The drawing also illustrates the geologic axiom – the greater the thickness
of strata above the water table, the greater the opportunity for nourishing lenses of clay
and fine grained sediments.

The only published autopsy of one of these Médoc gravel mounds was by Gérard Seguin of the University of Bordeaux in 1978. Figure 6.3 is based on a dissection made by Professor Seguin at St.-Julien-Beychevelle. This soil-vineroot profile is representative of the life-sustaining anatomy of the gravel mounds.

The most striking thing in the soil profile is the heterogeneity or lenticularity of the strata. Vineroots are predatory in their search for these lenses of fine-grained material and pounce on them ravenously. Roots are almost human in their perseverance to penetrate the barren layers and hardpan (alios), passing through them without branching, in search of nourishing lenses. Alios are surfaces of former water tables or percolation levels where cementation and mineralization occurred. They offer little by way of life support to the vine. Iron and other minerals in the zone exist but as insoluble, hence unavailable, compounds. Fortunately, in the Médoc, these hardpans are not very thick nor continuous over very wide areas.

Many of the Médoc vineyards, including some of the best, have patches of "sour ground" where vineplants are sickly. Fertilizer, chemical treatment, or even replanting are to no avail. These sour patches are the result of "perched" water tables, where an impermeable layer beneath the surface "ponds" water. Remember, "wet feet" are anathema to grapevines. These impermeable layers are clay plugs ("pingos" of the arctic permafrost) which were formed when the Médoc region was subjected to freeze–thaw of the periglacial zone during the Great Ice Age.

The lenticularity or heterogenous occurrence of the "vital organs" of these gravel mounds, as well as the impermeable clay plugs, explains how the quality of vines may vary row to row, and vineyard to vineyard. A closer look at the sedimentary processes that formed these terrace-mounds will help us understand how the lenticularity came about.

If you have ever been along the banks of a river that had recently overflowed, you would have seen long lenses of sand and mud, and possibly gravel. Stack up several layers of such lenticular deposits, especially where there is much gravel, and you have the composition of the Garonne–Gironde river terraces built during the Ice Age floods.

Soil and sands eroded from the countryside formed a muddy slurry which could transport heavier material such as gravel more easily. Depending on the velocity of flow at flood time, a stream may carry loads 5–25 times its normal capacity. As stream velocity slows, the flood water begins to "drop its load," heaviest baggage first. The "load" of gravel, sand, silt, and mud settle out, typically in linear streaks on the terraces paralleling the stream course. The next flood may destroy some of the earlier deposits, possibly to mix and redeposit them along with new material. River (fluviatile) deposits are notoriously heterogenous. That characteristic is both the good and bad of the Médoc and Graves vineyards. Location of the life-supporting strata below the surface determined the "who's in, who's out," classification.

Short, lateral streams at right angles to the river, called *jalles*, cut the linear terraces into segments. Freeze–thaw action and weathering rounded the surfaces of these segments into the mounds, lobes, or "gravel islands" of the communal appellations of the Médoc.

The previous, introductory, chapter on the Aquitaine Basin and its Figure 5.5 described how the nondescript, homely gravel deposits of the Garonne–Gironde have been correlated with the classical stages of the Pleistocene Ice Age, which are related to the changing sea level during the Ice Age.

As the continental ice cap grew, more and more water was captured, lowering the sea level. With reduction in sea level, rivers such as the Danube in Germany and the Garonne dug their channels deeper, leaving terraces of the previous stage high and dry. The earliest (uppermost) recognizable terrace in Bordeaux is the Pliocene Donau (Danube) which came at the very end of the Tertiary. The four succeeding stages of the Pleistocene terraces are the Günz, Mindel, Riss, and the Würm, as illustrated in Figure 5.5 (*see* page 171). Age-dates of the glacial stages and their correlation with historical events and archeologic cultures were also given in the previous chapter, *see* page 170. Return of sea level to normal drowned the over-deepened Gironde, inundating the lower terraces of Riss and Würm. The Günz, with possibly some Mindel, remained as the principal viticultural terrace for the Médoc and Graves. Geologists do not fully agree on the exact identity of these terraces, but the latest interpretation is that the Günz is the principal vineyard terrace.

The hydric regime

What makes the "vital organs" function is the life-sustaining water system or hydric regime in the gravel mounds. Professor Gérard Seguin and his colleagues recognize that there are numerous factors which influence the character of wine, but they conclude that quality of the wines of the Médoc is determined by their hydric regime. The term character is more easily defined in the negative – a wine without character is lackluster and unexciting. Professor Seguin defines quality as the pleasure one gets in tasting and drinking a wine. That attribute, he says, comes from vines of low productivity which is dependent upon its water supply or hydric regime. As the regulations governing appellation vineyards do not permit irrigation, the hydric regime is dependent upon adequate rainfall, drainage, and water-retention characteristics of the soil. How the water supply is made available to the roots depends on the internal geology of the mounds, surface conditions, and farming practices.

Figure 6.4 is a cross-section of the hydric system of a terrace complex deposited on an erosional bench. The prime mover of the system is, of course, an adequate supply of rain during the growing season. Critical factors are also how the downward percolating water is conserved (soils with good water retention), and where the water table or zone of saturation is positioned (it should be at such a depth to provide a deep growing zone). Not shown in the cycle are surface evaporation and plant transpiration which are an important part of the hydric equation. Although relatively high temperatures prevail in Bordeaux, gentle winds and the generally high humidity of the region slow transpiration.

Water percolates rapidly through gravel and coarse sand, but the lenticular strata within the mound act as baffles, slowing and dispersing the downward movement, allowing the finer-grained material to store water in pores for later use. Size and shape of the pores of the layers and the type of clay mineral govern the water-holding characteristics of these sediments (*see* Color Plate 4).

There is a popular saying that for a quality vineyard in the Médoc, the "vines must see the river." This has nothing to do with the view and little if anything to do with the microclimate due to the water body. What the adage implies is that if the vines can "see the river," both the surface and the water table slope toward the Gironde. This means a well-drained surface, and the drop-off of the water table results in a deep growing zone. Most of the crus classés do in fact "see the river" as they lie along the slope overlooking the Gironde or along the *jalles*.

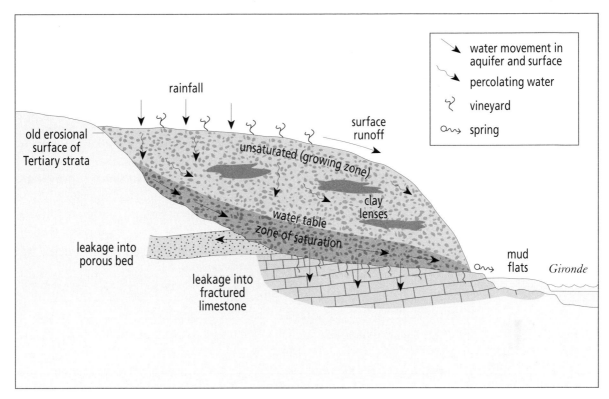

	water movement in aquifer and surface
	percolating water
	vineyard
	spring

rainfall

old erosional surface of Tertiary strata

surface runoff

unsaturated (growing zone)

clay lenses

water table zone of saturation

leakage into porous bed

leakage into fractured limestone

mud flats

Gironde

**Figure 6.4
Hydric cycle of a gravel mound**

The water table, the surface of the zone of saturation, is not a plane or horizontal surface as the name suggests, but mirrors to an appreciable extent the topography of the mound itself. Seasonally, the water table is lowest during the summer when rainfall is lowest. This is also when evaporation and plant use are at their highest. If the hydric regime does not function well, the vineplants may suffer stress. As the water table falls, feeder roots follow the "fall away" zone to catch that last bit of moisture. The internal workings of a gravel mound cannot be observed, but we can be assured that the quality vineyards are where the hydric regime functions well.

The climate

The gaping mouth of the Gironde estuary gulps in a maritime climate that is moderated by an eddy off the warm Gulf Stream. The oceanic influence places Bordeaux in a very privileged position with few unwelcome extremes of temperature. But remember, the 45° north parallel runs just north of the city of Bordeaux. Sometimes the normally mild region is rudely reminded of its northern latitude, such as one particularly hard frost that occurred in February, 1956. Many of the Bordeaux vineyards were devastated when temperatures dropped below zero Fahrenheit (–18°C).

During the "rust-colored moon of May" there is always the lingering concern that the Saints de Glace (ice saints) may visit the budding vines. The year 1982 turned out to be a fine vintage, but most of the first week in May that year was cold, rainy, and miserable. The vineplants evidently did not suffer, but my wife did. There was only enough heating oil in the hotel where we were staying for one hour each day.

The name Gironde comes from the French word "hirondelle," meaning swallow (the bird). In map view, the gaping mouth of the estuary is indeed like a swallow in pursuit of flying insects – the Garonne and Dordogne form the bird's scissor-tail.

The record keepers have observed that in any ten-year span, the grape harvest will average three great years, three poor years, and four that are good to mediocre. Winegrowing requires great patience and real staying power as well as hard work.

Fogs and heavy mists of the maritime climate give the appearance of a rainy country, but those conditions add little to the measurable precipitation. The rainfall graph in Figure 1.5 (*see* page 36), however, shows that Bordeaux's average of 33 inches (830 mm) of precipitation is indeed the heaviest of the major wine regions. Much to the concern of the vignerons, harvest time and the rainy season arrive about the same time. But in the sweet-wine areas of Sauternes, Barsac, and, across the River Garonne, Ste.-Croix-du-Mont, it is the fall-time dampness which promotes growth of the all-important mold *Botrytis cinerea*, the "noble rot" which attacks and shrivels the grapes, sapping their water content, concentrating the sugars and flavoring elements in the juice – the secret of these exceptionally intense, sweet white wines.

While the overall Bordeaux climate is moderate, the sun angle and hours of sunshine at 45° latitude are critical. From mid-May through August the sun shines almost all day every day, but its rays are filtered by the maritime haze. The heat summation (degree-days) of 2400–2500 is comparable to the cooler parts of the Napa and Sonoma Valleys of California. You will recall from Part One that degree-days are the total hours from mid-May through mid-October when the temperature is above 50°F (10°C).

The grape varieties

Invariably, wine connoisseurs want to compare the great red wines of Bordeaux with those of Burgundy. This may be done with a pleasant and interesting exercise, but it should be remembered that Bordeaux reds are blends of several grapes while those of the Côte d'Or are from a single grape, the Pinot Noir. Also a Bordeaux wine, say a Château Montrose, is the product of a single winemaker, whereas in Burgundy, there is no one wine representing, say, Chambertin, but a number of growers making and marketing their own wine, each with their own "wine signature" or style of vinification.

Bordeaux traditionally cultivates five red and three white grape varieties. Merlot and the two Cabernets make up 90 percent of the entire Bordeaux red-wine vineyard area. Others are the Cot (Malbec) and the Petit Verdot, the latter currently enjoying a revival of interest. Particular varieties are planted in soils and exposures where the vignerons have found each does best. Merlot, for instance, is predominant in Pomerol, the Cabernet Sauvignon in the Médoc, although the Cabernet Franc does better in St.-Emilion. Planting ratios are designed to achieve the balance in style of the winemaker's formula. The principal white varieties are the Sémillon, Sauvignon Blanc, and Muscadelle, the latter used sparingly as it yields a heady wine and tends to impart a Muscat flavor (strong odor of ripe grapes). The Sémillon is the predominant grape in the blending of sweet wines, the Sauvignon in the dry blends. Other white varieties are the Colombard and Ugni Blanc – these are "Cognac grapes," found mainly north of the Gironde (*see* page 211). The Folle Blanche and Merlot Blanc are also found in minor plantings.

Classification

The oldest, most famous — some regard as infamous — wine classification in France is that of 1855 in Bordeaux. For purposes of discussion, this is the classification I shall use. (St.-Emilion subsequently installed its own classification system and sectors of the Graves were recognized as appellations in their own right. These will be elaborated upon in the respective sections.)

The 1855 Classification of Bordeaux

In reality it was the deep-plunging roots of the grapevines on the gravel mounds that established the basis for the classification of Bordeaux wines. The roots located the "sweet spots" under whichever property the most favorable underground conditions happened to occur. Fame and fortune came to the lucky châteaux with that favorable sub-surface geology. True, it took good husbandry to develop the privileged properties, and a cellarmaster who could craft a consistent wine. By the middle of the 18th century, most, if not all, the well-blessed vineyards had been identified by the marketplace. But no formal classification scheme was developed until 1855. The impetus came from preparations for the grand exhibition which was to take place in Paris.

As Queen Victoria of England was to come to the exhibition, the organizers wanted to display the best of "claret," which had been crafted for the English palate several centuries before. In response to the request from the exhibition's organizers, the Bordeaux Chamber of Commerce proposed to place the wines of Bordeaux hors concours, that is, in a class by themselves, without further identification. The Chamber contended that such a presentation was justified as the Bordeaux wines (Médoc and Graves) were derived from soils not like any other, that is, the gravel mounds.

Organizers of the exhibition, however, were insistent there be an order of ranking. The Chamber sought help from the négociants, the syndicate of brokers, who had kept price records for over a century. Based on the historical pricing data, lists were submitted for red and white wines. For reds, five categories termed "growths" were provided, with the admonition that wines within each category (growth) were considered of equal merit. (Féret's "Bible" gives a good account of the development of the classification, with prints of some of the original documents.) From the point of view of today and that time, rationale for this approach seems logical enough – a classification based on historical market price should remove or at least minimize any political bias. At the same time, price should reflect the consumer's recognition of quality. Indeed, the 1855 Classification has stood for almost 150 years without serious questioning. Questioning, that is, as to the chateaux that were listed. One or two châteaux have gone out of business, a few have been divided. One château, Château Mouton, was upgraded from Second to First Growth in 1973, when it also changed its name to Mouton-Rothschild (more under discussion of the First Growths).

The question arises from time to time as to why the wines of St.-Emilion were excluded. Several theories have been advanced, but the question will probably never be fully answered. Both St.-Emilion and Graves have in more recent years developed their own classifications.

Roots of the vines did the underground exploration for the classification, helping the vigneron decide on the most suitable varieties; history and commerce determined the château's place in the quality scale. Occasionally, there are differences in the soils, but generally, apart from farming practices, the gravelly surface of a Fifth Growth looks very much the same as a First Growth. There are, however, other meaningful criteria such as elevation, slope, and drainage. From the general geology of the local area, the nature of the formation base on which the terrace-mound was deposited may be known. These criteria will be used in interpreting the geologic reasons for the châteaux classification. I feel that elevation is a particularly important criterion for estimating thickness of the growing zone in the all-important hydric regime as illustrated in Figure 6.4.

I will discuss the First Growths on an individual basis, then the Haut-Médoc by communal appellations.

Habitat of the Médoc–Graves First Growths

Although the Bordeaux Chamber of Commerce admonished Paris that all growths within a category of the 1855 Classification were of equal merit, there is endless debate as to which is really first of the First Growths. The order in the following list is not a ranking, but rather to simplify geologic discussion.

First Growths (Premiers Crus)

Commune	Name in 1855	Present-day name
Pessac (Graves)	Ch. Haut-Brion	Ch. Haut-Brion
Pauillac	Ch. Lafite	Ch. Lafite-Rothschild
Pauillac	Ch. Latour	Ch. Latour
Pauillac	Ch. Mouton	Ch. Mouton-Rothschild (from Second to First, 1973)
Margaux	Ch. Margaux	Ch. Margaux

The story of how the Baron Philippe de Rothschild brought Mouton from Second Growth in the 1855 Classification to First Growth is one of 50 years of innovative winemaking and passionate efforts for reclassification. Baron Philippe's lifetime efforts were finally rewarded with the decree in 1973 raising Mouton to First Growth status.

Various authors offer reasons why Mouton was not originally classed First Growth, such as not having a habitable building, and the question of nationality of the new owner, a Rothschild from England. Cyril Ray says these questions had nothing to do with the classification decision in 1855. He quotes Edmund Penning-Rowsell who maintains that the placement was based on hard commercial facts of the historical price of Mouton wine. These authors point out that Mouton held a singular place in its original Second Growth category, with an appreciable gap between Mouton price at the top and the next four of the ten Second Growths.

First and Second Growths are identified on Figure 6.5 by triangles and squares respectively. The base is a geologic sketch map of the Médoc and upper part of Graves modified from Professor Pijassou's splendid study *Le Médoc*.

Château Haut-Brion in Graves is generally held to be the prototype of gravel mound terroirs (*see* Color Plate 25), even though it may rankle the Médociens a bit. Whether or not Haut-Brion is placed first among the First Growths, it has all the right geologic credentials. Its First Growth attributes, illustrated in panel C of Figure 6.2, are 30 feet (9 m) of Günz gravel overlying a bed of coarse Pliocene gravel, which in turn rests on an erosional surface of *Calcaire à astéries*. The anatomy of the mound plus a gentle topographic slope toward the river are elements for an excellent hydric system. From the château's long history of producing quality red wines, it can be assured that the deep vineroots found and fully exploited ideal sub-surface conditions.

Recognized early in the 16th century as an exceptional vineyard, Château Haut-Brion has been privileged to have had wealthy owners who have given the land great care. Its well-heeled owners in the 18th-century, through research and experimentation, developed the blend of wine known as "Bordeaux style" – Cabernet Sauvignon with a good proportion of Cabernet Franc and Malbec. The Merlot grape did not enter the picture until the 19th century. The individuality of Bordeaux wines was enhanced by preferential additions of the Petit Verdot and Carmenère. (The latter grape is scarcely seen today but was widely planted in the early 18th century; some maintain that the Carmenère, along with the Cabernet Franc, did much to establish the reputation of many of the best Médoc properties.)

Château Haut-Brion is completely surrounded by urban development. However, rather than blighting the vineyards with atmospheric pollution, the "city heat" of Bordeaux apparently provides a beneficial microclimate. The companion châteaux to Haut-Brion have the same geology as this 1855 First Growth. They carry the top rank of the Graves classification and will be discussed under that appellation heading.

Châteaux Lafite-Rothschild and Mouton-Rothschild are adjacent properties on the large gravel lobe north of the village of Pauillac, *see* Figure 6.5. At elevations of 80 feet (24 m), the vineyards occupy some of the highest crests in

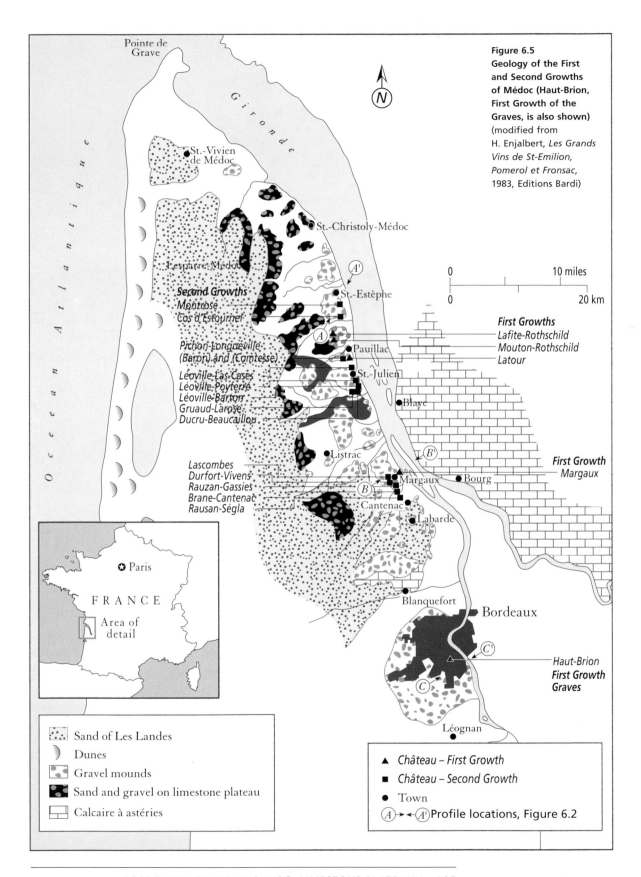

Pointe de Grave

Gironde

Océan Atlantique

St.-Vivien de Médoc

St.-Christoly-Médoc

Lesparre-Médoc

Second Growths
Montrose
Cos d'Estournel

Pichon-Longueville
(Baron) and (Comtesse)

Léoville-Las-Cases
Léoville-Poyferré
Léoville-Barton
Gruaud-Larose
Ducru-Beaucaillou

Lascombes
Durfort-Vivens
Rauzan-Gassies
Brane-Cantenac
Rausan-Ségla

St.-Estèphe

Pauillac

St.-Julien

Blaye

Listrac

Margaux

Bourg

Cantenac

Labarde

Blanquefort

Bordeaux

Léognan

Figure 6.5
**Geology of the First
and Second Growths
of Médoc (Haut-Brion,
First Growth of the
Graves, is also shown)**
(modified from
H. Enjalbert, *Les Grands
Vins de St-Emilion,
Pomerol et Fronsac,*
1983, Editions Bardi)

0   10 miles

0   20 km

First Growths
Lafite-Rothschild
Mouton-Rothschild
Latour

First Growth
Margaux

Haut-Brion
**First Growth
Graves**

Paris

F R A N C E

Area of detail

- ⬚ Sand of Les Landes
- ◗ Dunes
- ⬚ Gravel mounds
- ⬛ Sand and gravel on limestone plateau
- ⬚ Calcaire à astéries

- ▲ *Château – First Growth*
- ■ *Château – Second Growth*
- ● Town
- Ⓐ→ ←Ⓐ' Profile locations, Figure 6.2

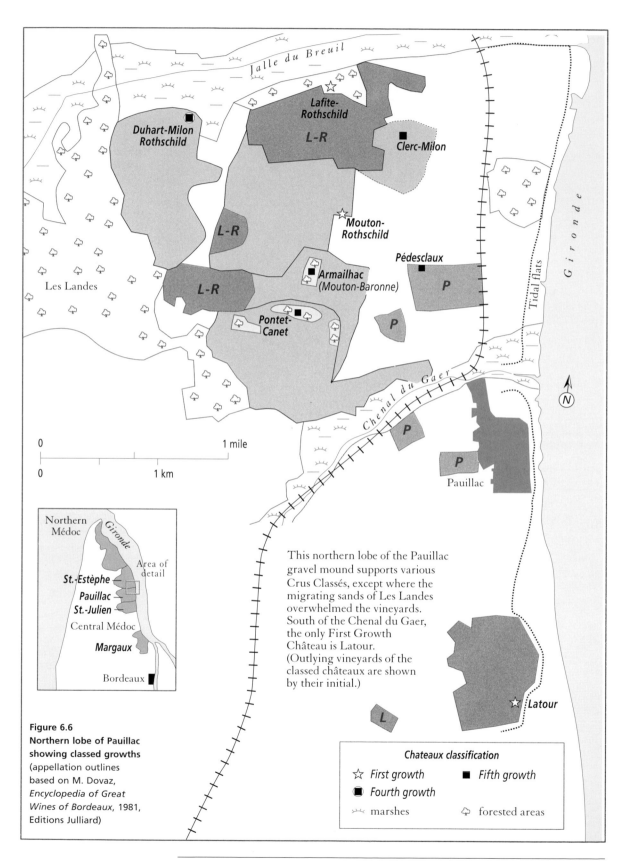

Jalle du Breuil

Duhart-Milon
Rothschild

Lafite-
Rothschild

L-R

Clerc-Milon

L-R

Gironde

Les Landes

L-R

Mouton-
Rothschild

Armailhac
(Mouton-Baronne)

Pédesclaux

P

Pontet-
Canet

P

Tidal flats

0   1 mile

0   1 km

Chenal du Gaer

P

N

P

Pauillac

Northern
Médoc

Gironde

Area of
detail

St.-Estèphe

Pauillac

St.-Julien

Central Médoc

Margaux

Bordeaux

This northern lobe of the Pauillac
gravel mound supports various
Crus Classés, except where the
migrating sands of Les Landes
overwhelmed the vineyards.
South of the Chenal du Gaer,
the only First Growth
Château is Latour.
(Outlying vineyards of the
classed châteaux are shown
by their initial.)

L

Latour

Figure 6.6
Northern lobe of Pauillac
showing classed growths
(appellation outlines
based on M. Dovaz,
*Encyclopedia of Great
Wines of Bordeaux*, 1981,
Editions Julliard)

Chateaux classification

☆ *First growth*   ■ *Fifth growth*

▣ *Fourth growth*

⌣ marshes   ♧ forested areas

the Médoc. On the hypothesis that high elevations mean a thick growing zone above the water table, the two châteaux should have growing zones of some 30 feet (9 m). A terrace base of fossiliferous, sandy marl, and St.-Estèphe limestone aid the underground drainage. Figure 6.6 shows the cluster of classed growths on the northern lobe of the Pauillac gravel mound.

The major plot of Lafite "sees the river" on a broad topographic nose sloping toward the Gironde. The north side falls off steeply to the Jalle du Breuil. The surface of Mouton, however, is more an undulating plateau. The water table should mirror closely the topography. Thick gravel and good drainage are hallmarks of these two First Growths. Except for slight topographic differences, geologically, Mouton and Lafite are essentially the same. The water table may be a little higher under Mouton, but the growing zone is still adequately deep.

The Fifth Growths Mouton-Baronne (now named Armailhac), Pontet Canet, and Clerc Milon are adjacent to Châteaux Lafite and Mouton, but were evidently not as well blessed with subsurface conditions.

Château Latour, one of the oldest of the Médoc vineyards, owes its First Growth status to a relatively thick growing zone and good bottom drainage. The Latour vines not only "see the river," but almost fall into it. Latour is on the corner of the gravel lobe south of the village of Pauillac. The main 125-acre (50-ha) tract is on a level plateau at an elevation of 50 feet (15 m), overlooking both the mud flats along the Gironde and the Ruisseau de Juillac. The gravel terrace, estimated to be at least 30 feet (9 m) thick, contains some beds of very large stones. The bedrock is an Upper Eocene sandy oyster-shell marl underlain by the St.-Estèphe limestone.

Companion to Latour, immediately west overlooking the Juillac, are the Second Growth châteaux admired by Mr. Flagg, Pichon-Longueville (now divided into two, Baron and Comtesse-de-Lalande, *see* Figure 6.5).

Château Margaux is considered by many experts to be first of the First Growths of the 1855 Classification. Ironically, by my geologic interpretation, this esteemed château is less than a whole-hearted gravel mound vineyard (*see* Color Plate 24). This does not mean that Château Margaux is less than great, only that its geology is a bit unusual. For example, just northwest of the château, a low knob called the Cap de Haut was pointed out to me by the château manager, Philippe Barre, and consultant enologist, Professor Emile Peynaud, as the choice tract of the château's properties, yielding wines of unique flavor. This part of Margaux is essentially a "bedrock" vineyard, not a typical gravel-mound growth.

Apparently, underlying the commune is an erosional ridge of bedrock with local "highs" and pockets of thick gravel. There is only a thin covering of gravel over the deeply weathered Lacustre de Plaisac, a freshwater limestone at Cap de Haut. The mixture of weathered limestone, Fronsadais marl, and terrace deposits makes a soil locally known as *la terre blanche* (the same name as the white, chalky soils of Sancerre).

Further evidence of the "Margaux high" was revealed at the time of my visit in an excavation being made for additional cellar storage. Only a thin veneer of gravel overlies the blue-gray marl of the Molasse du Fronsadais. This impermeable, clay-like bedrock undoubtedly required installation of special drainage for the cellar.

Across the road from the Cap de Haut is a plot called "Puch Sem Peyre," which the writer Nicholas Faith reports to be Gascon patois for the French "puits sans pierre," a hand-dug well that does not require walling up. Apparently strata to the depth of the water table are well consolidated and require no shoring.

The half-dozen scattered tracts comprising Château Margaux overlie a diversity of geology. The vignerons know which grape variety prefers which soil. Blending of the spectrum of flavors undoubtedly contributes to the uniqueness of the wines of this First Growth. Had the geology underlying all the tracts of Château Margaux been the same, it certainly would have been a great wine, but it would not have been "Margaux."

The remaining classed growths of the Médoc

In the four communal appellations of Haut-Médoc there are 53 crus classés. From north to south, the communal appellations are St.-Estèphe, Pauillac, St.-Julien, and Margaux, *see* Figure 6.5. Central Médoc has no crus classés.

The uneven distribution of the classed growths emphasizes the erratic nature of river terrace deposits and lack of symmetry of the "vital organs." From the very beginning it was a royal "crap shoot" as to what the roots would tell the owner about his potential wealth. Emphasizing the erratic nature of the "who's in, who's out" habitat of the terrace-mounds, there is no "halo affect" surrounding the First and Second Growths, except possibly Margaux.

As shown in the following tabulation of Second Growths, the numbers in Pauillac and St.-Julien were increased from the 1855 Classification by sub-divisions of châteaux:

Second Growths (Deuxièmes Crus)		
Commune	**Name in 1855**	**Present-day name**
St.-Estèphe	Ch. Cos d'Estournel	Ch. Cos d'Estournel
St.-Estèphe	Ch. Montrose	Ch. Montrose
Pauillac	Ch. Pichon-Longueville	Ch. Pichon-Longueville-Baron
		Ch. Pichon-Longueville-Comtesse-de-Lalande
St.-Julien	Ch. Ducru-Beaucaillou	Ch. Ducru-Beaucaillou
St.-Julien	Ch. Gruaud-Larose	Ch. Gruaud-Larose
St.-Julien	Ch. Léoville	Ch. Léoville-Las Cases
		Ch. Léoville-Poyferré
		Ch. Léoville-Barton
Margaux	Ch. Vivens-Durfort	Ch. Durfort Vivens
Margaux	Ch. Lascombe	Ch. Lascombes
Margaux	Ch. Rauzan Ségla	Ch. Rausan-Ségla
Marguax	Ch. Rauzan Gassies	Ch. Rauzan-Gassies
Cantenac	Ch. Brane	Ch. Brane-Cantenac

Like hundreds of thousands of probes of the Médoc, vineroots have given the gravel a fair three-dimensional evaluation of conditions of the "vital organs." The "print out" of this investigation is the chateaux classification.

Apart from the unique geology of the Margaux appellation, about the only direct evidence by which to explain the occurrence and distribution of the crus classés is the surface elevation, slope, and nature of the bedrock strata on which the gravel terraces were deposited. Statistically, distribution of the crus classés in the communal appellations emphasizes the erratic nature of river deposits.

Significance of the surface elevation is indirect evidence, but a reasonable hypothesis is that the higher the elevation, the thicker the growing zone. The bedrocks on which the Günz terraces were deposited slope gradually from approximately 100 feet (30 m) in the Graves area to where the gravel islands are submerged beyond St.-Estèphe.

St.-Estèphe is northernmost of the appellations, and one of the smaller gravel islands, but it supports five crus classés. The reason is the relatively high elevation of the island. The Second Growth Château Cos d'Estournel is on a knoll 60 feet (18 m) above the surrounding marshy lowland. ("Cos" is regional patois for "hill.") The knoll is shared with Château Lafon-Rochet, a Fourth Growth and Château Cos Labory, a Fifth Growth. The gravel lies on fractured bedrock of St.-Estèphe limestone, giving good underground drainage, while the surface slopes steeply to the Chenal du Lazaret. Château Montrose, overlooking the Gironde, has considerable iron in its gravel which contributes to good tannin in this Second Growth wine. Third Growth Château Calon-Ségur occupies high ground with the village of St.-Estèphe overlying the limestone of the same name.

The Pauillac gravel mound separated from St.-Estèphe by the Jalle du Breuil is divided into two lobes by the Chenal du Gaer on the north side of the village of Pauillac, *see* Figure 6.6. The geology of this northern lobe was discussed for First Growths Châteaux Lafite and Mouton. Terrain of the southern lobe is more diverse with the best vineyards along the outer slopes of the lobe. The geology was also discussed for First Growth Château Latour.

St.-Julien is a continuation of the gravel lobe of Pauillac across the Ruisseau de Juillac which has barely eroded to bedrock. The comparison of terrain and distribution of its 11 classed growths emphasize the tremendous importance of the theorem: the higher the elevation, the thicker the growing zones.

A ridge of thick gravel overlooks the Gironde supporting the three Second Growths of the Léoville group – Las Cases, Poyferré, and Barton. Originally the three châteaux were one property composed of 500 acres (200 ha). The numerous separate tracts of the Léoville group are mixed with those of Third Growth Château Langoa-Barton, which illustrates how scattered tracts may take the classification of the basic property of the château.

In the southeast corner of the gravel mound, the Second Growth Ducru-Beaucaillou is located on a dominating elevation of 45 feet (14 m) overlooking the Gironde. However, the calcareous bedrock is also high, restricting the gravel thickness to about 15 feet (nearly 5 m). This suggests that the internal geology must be unusually favorable. Also in this corner are the Fourth Growth châteaux Branaire-Ducru, St.-Pierre, and Beychevelle. The gravel deposits of these châteaux lying on a base of clay and limestone are relatively thin and coarse.

Ducru-Beaucaillou was the birthplace of "Bordeaux Mixture," a simple but effective antidote to vine mildew. The château manager customarily sprayed the vineyard perimeter with a mixture of copper sulfate whose tell-tale blue color would rub off on vandals stealing grapes. One year it dawned on him that the mildew had not attacked those vines which had been sprayed with the copper sulfate. After study by Alexis Millardet, Professor of Botany at the University of Bordeaux and Ulysse Gayon, Professor of Chemistry, they developed an effective cure for mildew – copper sulfate and sulfur slaked with lime (chalk).

Westward along the ridge overlooking the Jalle du Nord is the Second Growth Château Gruaud-Larose with excellent surface drainage. A thick section of gravel is underlain by calcareous marl.

Château Talbot, near the gravel mound center, comprises 300 contiguous acres (120 ha) at an elevation of 60 feet (18 m). Good drainage for this interior location is aided by sandstone bedrock below a thick section of gravel.

The two oldest vineyards in the region are Fourth Growth Château La Tour Camet (or Carnet), and Third Growth Château Lagrange. Camet and its Fifth Growth companion, Château Belgrave, lie where the gravel is thin and its permeability reduced by an admixture of sands from Les Landes. It was in this area that the migrating sands of Les Landes almost broke through to overwhelm the vineyard belt. The fine sand and windblown dust clog the porous gravel, forming an impermeable surface layer and creating a sodden soil which supports only shallow-rooted plants such as pine trees and grasses.

Wines from the four villages of Central Médoc can only use the Haut-Médoc appellation. The 6-mile (10-km) gap between St.-Julien and Margaux is without classed vineyards, for geologic reasons. A low-relief domal uplift at Listrac extending under the gravel terrace belt caused either non-deposition or subsequent erosion of much of the Günz gravel here. An outwash of mud from weathered marl on the eastern side of the dome clogged the gravel. Eocene strata are exposed in the center of the dome inside a rimrock of Oligocene *Calcaire à astéries*. One point on the rimrock reaches an elevation of 140 feet (43 m), the highest in the Médoc. Although there are no crus classés, there are a number of very respectable châteaux (including Chasse-Spleen, Maucaillou, and Citran) in the communes of Moulis, Lamarque, and Poujeaux. Around the village of Listrac, the vineyard soils are developed from the bedrock limestones and marls exposed by the doming. The two châteaux named Fourcas and Château Clarke can be outstanding.

First Growth Margaux has already been discussed. The gravel island itself, under 3 square miles (7 square km), is crowded with 20 crus classés. Cantenac, the southeast portion of the commune, is often hyphenated with Margaux. Five Second Growths are sited along the backbone of the island in line with the better tracts of Château Margaux. The geology of this central ridge is similar to that of Château Margaux – pockets of thick gravel and thinner beds covering Tertiary substrata. Properties of the several châteaux form a patchwork of small tracts – those of Château Lascombes might be aptly described as shattered. The tracts of the classed châteaux interlock in almost solid coverage of the gravel island, but none appears to have the lucky combination of geology of Château Margaux. Nevertheless, the summation of the sub-surface geology is sufficiently favorable for all five classed growths to be identified within the Margaux appellation.

Southern Médoc, the 8-mile (12-km) stretch from Margaux to the outskirts of Bordeaux city, is mainly marshlands and sandy tongues of Les Landes with only a few low, gravelly islands. This is not a communal appellation but contains one Third and one Fifth Growth. The southernmost mound has Third Growth Château La Lagune (the lagoon). On a nearby mound to the north is Fifth Growth Château Cantemerle (song of the blackbird). Blackbirds are a common sight in the Médoc as they like the seeds and berries of marsh plants.

Graves

Bordeaux is the hub of the biggest fine-wine growing region in the world – as well as its unofficial capital. Not many years ago, no fewer than 53 vineyards clustered close around the city. Gradually, urban development reduced the number to the present half a dozen. Those early-day châteaux, many of them pre-dating the Médoc development, established the fame of Bordeaux wines. Survivors are the First Growth Château Haut-Brion and its close neighbors Chateaux Pape Clément, La Mission Haut-Brion, La Tour Haut-Brion, and (for white wine) Laville Haut-Brion.

Bordeaux city and its vineyards are situated on a large gravel mound. In recognition of the significance of gravel in the vineyard soils, the area was named Graves, the French for gravel.

The Jalle de Blanquefort north of the city officially separates the Médoc and Graves. In a band somewhat wider than the Médoc, Graves extends south along the Garonne 35 miles (56 km) to Langon. The geology of Graves is substantially the same as the Médoc, but the terraces have remained more intact as landforms than the gravel islands in marshes. A comparison of the geologic framework of the Médoc and Graves can be made in the panels of cross-sections, Figure 6.2.

In 1987, the large Graves appellation was divided into north and south sectors. The northern sector in turn was divided into two: Pessac-Léognan, recognized as an appellation in its own right, includes metropolitan Bordeaux with its red Grands Crus Classés; and the area around Léognan, which is known mainly for dry, white wine – although deep, fruity reds are also being produced. The southern sector is composed of the sub-appellations of Sauternes, Cérons, and the enclave of Barsac, all famous for producing sweet white wines.

The reason for the preference of red grapes in the north and white grapes in the south is a combination of geology, climate, and happenstance. The red grapes like the clay and silt lenses in the northern terraces; the white grapes like the limy soils of the southern vineyards.

Geology of the châteaux in the environs of Bordeaux is typified by Château Haut-Brion: thick Günz gravel on the *Calcaire à astéries*. From metropolitan Bordeaux to Sauternes the change in geology is transitional, with a number of châteaux producing both red and white wines. Southward from Bordeaux, the bedrock *Calcaire à astéries* gives way to Miocene marine marl and limestones (*see* Color Plate 22) Although pockets of deep gravel occur, much of the rooting in the Sauternes is in a mixture of calcareous clay with gravel and sand.

Pessac, the recently recognized appellation for the southern environs of the city of Bordeaux, contains the Haut-Brion group of châteaux and Pape Clément. The reds of Château Haut-Brion rejoice in intense color, balance between fruity and earthy flavors, and delightful finish and aftertaste. It was the 17th-century owner of Château Haut-Brion who first established the concept of truly great red Bordeaux wine.

Château Pape Clément is a mile west of Haut-Brion, further out of town, and somewhat higher. Here the gravel size is much smaller, but otherwise its soils and drainage are similar to Haut-Brion. This vineyard was started in 1300 by Bertrand de Goth, archbishop of Bordeaux, who, six years later, was elected pope and took the name Clément V.

Château Pape Clément is not the sole viticultural legacy of Clément V. It was he who moved the papacy from Rome to Avignon on the lower Rhône. The famous vineyards of Châteauneuf-du-Pape north of Avignon are a lasting monument to Clément's encouragement of viticulture in the Rhône Valley.

The three companion châteaux, La Mission Haut-Brion, La Tour Haut-Brion, and Laville Haut-Brion, do not have quite as good surface drainage and also slightly less gravel than Haut-Brion. These are all adjacent properties which the Clarence Dillon family operates with the same manager and cellarmaster as Haut-Brion. The wine from each château is distinct, which may reflect deliberate differences in vinification as well as subtle variations in the geology and microclimate.

In Léognan, small streams have cut the terraces into mounds in much the same way as the *jalles* in the Médoc. The erosional bedrock surface is quite irregular, producing pockets of thick gravel as well as "bedrock highs" with a thin covering of sandy gravel. Some châteaux produce either red or white wines, while others produce both.

The Ruisseau de l'Eau Blanche running through the town of Léognan in the south of the newly recognized appellation, has nine classified châteaux clustered on its ridges and slopes. Vineyards are for the most part single tracts, sharing the landscape with small pastures, woods, and other crops. (Pine trees have always been the Graves' main crop. The vineyards are mostly isolated clearings in the great forest of Les Landes which extends south and east as far as the foothills of the Pyrenees.) Châteaux Malartic-Lagravière, Olivier, La Tour Martillac, Bouscaut, Carbonnieux, and Domaine de Chevalier (the last the commune's most outstanding property) all produce white as well as red wines. Châteaux Smith Haut-Lafitte, Fieuzal, and Haut-Bailly produce only red classed wines, while Couhins-Lurton produces whites only. There are, furthermore, numerous other reputable but unclassified châteaux in the 6-mile (10-km) stretch between Léognan and Cérons-Sauternes.

According to Féret in his "Bible of Bordeaux," Cérons is as much a tradition as a defined appellation, having existed for over a hundred years without official delimitation. Producing red wines and whites that are either dry or sweet, it represents a transition between Graves and Sauternes-Barsac. Geologically, about the only difference from Graves is that Cérons gravel is poorly sorted, containing some large cobbles. The vineyards are on gravelly hillocks at elevations averaging about 60 feet (20 m) above the Garonne. The bedrock is limestone and marl with some "alios" or ironpan. Although old and famous, none of the Cérons châteaux is classified.

Sauternes

Originally a part of the Graves district, Sauternes was given its own appellation in 1936. Unquestionably, Sauternes produces the greatest sweet white wine in the world. (The final "s" is part of the name, but is not sounded.)

Château d'Yquem, owned by the Lur Saluces family for two centuries, is the crown jewel of Sauternes. It was awarded the title of "Premier Cru Supérieur" in the 1855 Classification for sweet white wines. Today, it bothers little with classification as the château name is famous enough in its own right.

In 1936, five communes producing sweet wine in this small area of 15 square miles (38 square km) on the right bank of the Ciron, a tributary of the Garonne, got together, established strict criteria for quality, applied for and were granted the Sauternes appellation.

Topographically, Sauternes is a broad north-plunging nose with natural terraces stepping down to the Garonne (*see* the Sauternes section in panel D, Figure 6.2). The Sauternes ridge is bounded on the west by the deeply incised Ciron. Erosion hollowed out concavities in soft bedrock in which thick pockets of gravel were deposited, some as thick as 20 feet (6 m). Freeze–thaw during the Ice Age stirred the erosional "highs," producing an agglomeration of gravel, limestone, marl, and sandstone. Wines from the gravel pockets and those from the "churned" soils show different nuances.

The best parcels of Château d'Yquem are located on a low-relief dome of calcareous clay under a thin cover of sandy gravel (*see* Color Plate 27). The clay base creates a shallow water table requiring over 6 miles (10 km) of drainage tiles which were installed in the 19th century. Drainage is aided by a slope gradient of 8 percent (1:12). It is the asymmetry of the valley – a steep north bank and the slope on the Sauternes side – that promotes the river mists which encourage the development of botrytis which is essential to make the speciality sweet wine.

Nine First Growths, and six Second Growths by the Sauternes classification are located on the hummocky ridge extending through four communes. The soils are similar to d'Yquem, sandy gravel mixed with calcareous clay.

On one of the rounded knobs west of Château d'Yquem is Château La Tour Blanche, operated by the Ministry of Agriculture as a viticultural school. It was in this area that in the 19th century, experimentation with late harvesting discovered the beneficial affects of the fungus, *Botrytis cinerea*. The fungus grows on the skin of the grape, literally sucking the water out of the pulp, thus concentrating the sugars. The botrytis is called the "noble rot," as its affects are welcome in contrast to other fungi such as penicillium which has an unpleasant affect on the taste of wine.

The small enclave of Barsac is something of a geologic oddity for this region, being on flat terrain with almost no gravel. In the late Tertiary/early Quaternary erosion by wind and water hollowed out a large depression in the *Calcaire à astéries*. (It is amazing how effectively wind-blown sand can erode solid rock.) The bedrock became deeply weathered and fissured resulting in a red, sandy, limy soil onto which a veneer of coarse river sands was plastered. This unusual soil is only about a foot (30 cm) deep which means the vineplants may suffer in times of drought.

In spite of what appear to be geologic limitations, the Classification of 1855 gives Châteaux Climens and Coutet First Growth status for white wines; with seven other Barsac châteaux classified as Second Growths. White wines from this appellation may be labelled either Sauternes or Barsac.

Château Climens is sited on perfectly flat terrain of fissured limestone, but at an elevation of 65 feet (20 m), it is one of the highest in Barsac. Coutet is considerably lower. It is puzzling how this terroir, its topsoil varying from river silt and coarse alluvium to wind-blown sand and fine gravel, was recognized as a First Growth. Nevertheless, it produces exceptionally fine wines.

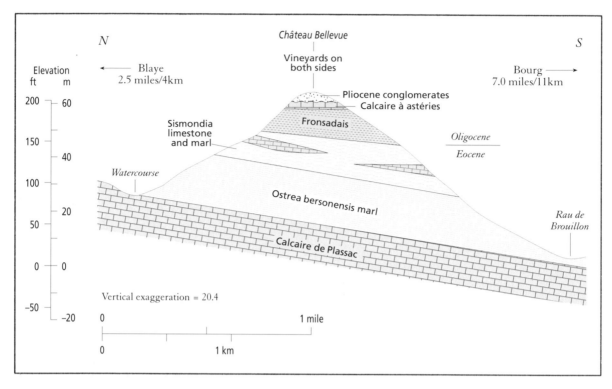

Figure 6.7
Cross-section, Bourg–Blaye

The Bourg–Blaye to St.-Emilion sector

Across the Garonne-Gironde from the Médoc-Graves, the plateau of Bourg-Blaye–Entre-Deux-Mers rises like a wall, best seen in Figure 6.2. The Dordogne separates the Bourg-Blaye–St.-Emilion portion of the plateau from the trapezoidal plateau of Entre-Deux-Mers. Except for Pomerol and Graves de Vayres, soils of these plateau appellations are weathered *Calcaire à astéries* limestone admixed with a thin layer of Pliocene gravely sand. In a few places, Miocene limestones and marls contribute to the soils.

Bourg and Blaye

These two towns, less than 10 miles (16 km) apart, literally hang on the edge of the plateau overlooking the Gironde-Dordogne. Sands and dust of Les Landes, blowing from across the river, were deflected upward by the plateau wall and spread over the upland surface to mix with soils of weathered limestone and the veneer of gravel. The soil is a complex of sand, dust, loam, gravel, and decalcified clay low in humus. Below the leached zone, nutrient minerals increase, carried there by downward percolation. The dominant clay mineral is kaolinite, which has a low cation-exchange capacity, but the soils have good water retention.

Widespread over the plateau surface is an ironstone called "sidérolithique," formed by the weathering of iron minerals concentrated in a clay matrix. These deposits are found around the north side of the Aquitaine Basin from Bourg-Blaye eastward to Cahors. In early times, concentrations were sufficiently rich for an iron smelter. Iron in the soils contributes to the full-bodied, well-structured red wines. The grapes are the Bordeaux standard: Merlot, Cabernet Sauvignon, Cabernet Franc, and Cot (or Malbec).

The geology and terrain shown in Figure 6.7 is typical of the Côtes de Bourg-Blaye. The terrain is gentle, so please note that the vertical scale has been greatly exaggerated in order to show details of the strata.

The Blaye appellation, about 20 miles (30 km) long, is several times larger than that of Bourg. Although the two appellations both produce red and white wines from similar soils, Blaye is generally more noted for its white wines and Bourg for its reds.

The Romans, always with an eye for commanding terrain, occupied the area around Blaye in 25 B.C. It was part of the shield to protect Bordeaux from invasion by sea. Seventeen centuries later, in 1689, for the same reason, Sébastien Vauban, Louis XIV's innovative military engineer, built Blaye's impressive citadel. Vauban's system included Fort Médoc on the shore opposite Blaye and Fort Pâte on an island in the estuary. The citadel, in perfect state of repair, is now a classified national monument.

Although Blaye does not have a protected harbor, it overlooks a crowded deep-water anchorage, which centuries ago was a staging area for pilgrims traveling by ship to Santiago de Compostella on the northwest coast of Spain. It was also one of the embarkation ports for the Crusades. Today, the principal function of its small harbor is for fishing boats and the ferry crossing to Lamarque in the Médoc.

Blaye whites are said to be ideal accompaniments to the oysters of Marennes harvested from the extensive *parcs à huîtres* (oyster farms) in the tidal estuary of the River Seudre just north of the mouth of the Gironde. The Marenne oysters are the famous *huîtres vertes*, whose greenish tint is due to microscopic algae which abound in the waters where the molluscs feed.

The smaller Bourg appellation is typified by rounded hills and ridges topped with villages, churches, and châteaux. Among Bourg's tourist attractions are its caves and rock shelters at Pair-non-Pair, which contain artifacts dating from the Early Stone Age – some 400,000 years ago. The caves are eroded from the massive *Calcaire à astéries* which continues around the perimeter of the plateau facing the Dordogne. The *Calcaire* is the cap rock for the vineyard slopes of Fronsac and St.-Emilion. Building stones for the city of Bordeaux were taken from underground quarries, and these excavations were later utilized for growing mushrooms.

About 15 miles (25 km) up the Dordogne at Libourne, the Isle River cuts the *Calcaire* scarp, with Fronsac on the west, the terraces of Pomerol on the east, and St.-Emilion beyond. The French name for this region is the Libournais, after its principal town on the Dordogne. Figure 6.8 shows the general geology.

Fronsac

This corner of the *Calcaire* is typically a dimpled scarp with hillocks (*tertres*) overlooking the two rivers. Le Tertre de Fronsac, on the point of the angle, is 240 feet (70 m) above the river. A château on the *tertre* built by the Duc de Richelieu, grandnephew of the famous cardinal, was the scene of elegant parties for international guests who spread the fame of the solid, fruity Fronsac wines. The Fronsadais molasse is named for the marls and sands in this area underlying the *Calcaire à astéries*.

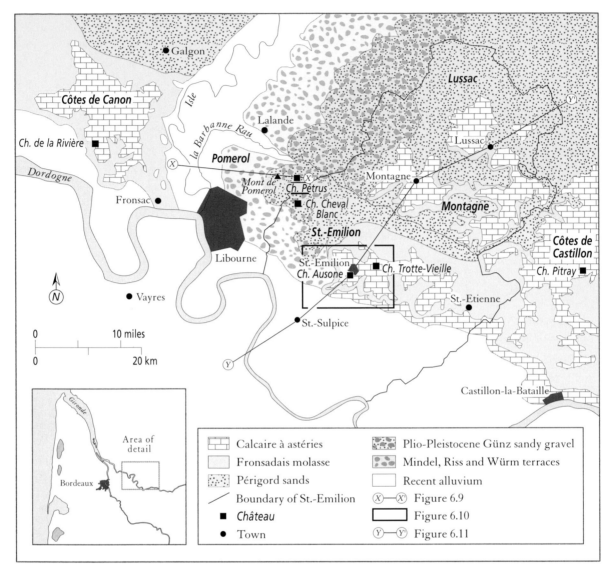

Figure 6.8
General geology of Fronsac, Pomerol and St.-Emilion

(geology reproduced by kind permission of Editions du B.R.G.M., France; wine detail after Figure 20, H. Enjalbert, *Les Grands Vins de St-Emilion, Pomerol et Fronsac*, 1983, Editions Bardi)

The 13th-century Château de la Rivière, commanding a splendid view over the Dordogne Valley, has a beautiful park as well as ancient vineyards, producing very good wines. Jacques Santier, cellarmaster of La Rivière, told me that during World War II the château was occupied by the Germans. When the soldiers inquired what was in the caves dug far back into the limestone scarp, they were told some people had been murdered there long ago and that the place was haunted. The soldiers never ventured into the tunnels to discover the vast stores of wine hidden there.

The hilly countryside on the Fronsac plateau known as the Côtes de Canon or Canon-Fronsac produces the best of Fronsac wines. Fronsac's clayey limestone soils with sandy variations produce quality reds, of which the best are competitive with many crus classés of Bordeaux. The Malbec does especially well on the limestone soils here. The great potential of this small appellation has been recognized, not least by the house of Libourne négociant J. P. Moueix whose three châteaux make excellent Fronsac.

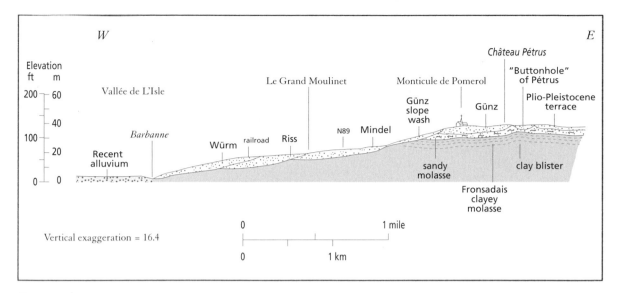

```
W                                                                                    E
                                                              Château Pétrus
Elevation
ft   m                                                                   "Buttonhole"
200 ─ 60                    Le Grand Moulinet    Monticule de Pomerol    of Pétrus
          Vallée de L'Isle                              Günz                Plio-Pleistocene
     ─ 40                                               slope        Günz   terrace
                                                        wash
100 ─                                    N89  Mindel
     ─ 20        Barbanne        railroad  Riss
            Recent         Würm
            alluvium                                         sandy          clay blister
  0 ─ 0                                                      molasse
                                                         Fronsadais
                                                         clayey
                                                         molasse
         Vertical exaggeration = 16.4
                                      0                   1 mile
                                      0        1 km
```

Pomerol

Don't look for the town of Pomerol. There isn't one. However, about a mile northeast of Libourne and west of Pétrus, a small chapel with an impressive steeple sits on a low mound. This mound is the Monticule de Pomerol, the namesake landmark of this small, highly regarded appellation. A vast number of small yet highly regarded properties are scattered around the little chapel, representing an impressive concentration of some of the richest, most perfumed of all clarets.

The geology of Pomerol is similar to the gravel terraces of Graves, except that the Pomerol terrace deposits are from the crystalline Limousin and Jurassic limestone plateaux brought by the Isle and its tributaries. Some geologists are of the opinion that all four of the glacial stages of the Ice Age are represented in the Pomerol terraces, *see* Figure 6.9. This is possible, since the returning sea level which submerged the lower terraces of the Gironde did not extend this far up the Dordogne. The question, however, is largely academic since the principal vineyards of Pomerol are on the uppermost (Günz) terraces and the widespread Plio-Pleistocene gravels.

Some of the famous châteaux of Pomerol: Pétrus, which is unquestionably the outstanding vineyard of the region, Trotanoy, Bourgneuf-Vayron, Latour à Pomerol, and Vieux Château Certan, are all situated on this upper terrace of thin, sandy gravel underlain by Fronsadais marl. An excellent soil resulted from the long period of freeze–thaw, heaving action, and mixing of molasse with sandy gravel. The famous *boutonnière* (buttonhole) of Pétrus shown in Figure 6.9 is a "blister" of the underlying clay that during the heaving action bulged through the thin gravel cover.

It is ferruginous sand in the soil that apparently imparts a particular vigor to the Merlot and Cabernet Franc in the wines of Pomerol, giving them a plummy nose, velvet texture, and the ability to age superbly. Pétrus is almost pure Merlot.

North of the Barbanne, are the vineyards of the Lalande-de-Pomerol. The vineyards, sited on post-Ice Age alluvial terraces of the Isle, have no important châteaux, but the wines are reasonably good.

Figure 6.9
The terraces of Pomerol

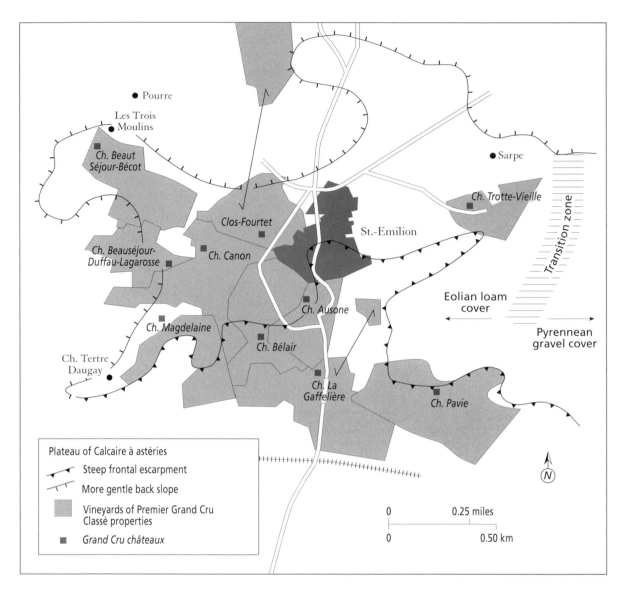

Map labels:
Pourre
Les Trois Moulins
Ch. Beaut Séjour-Bécot
Sarpe
Ch. Trotte-Vieille
Clos-Fourtet
St.-Emilion
Transition zone
Ch. Beauséjour-Duffau-Lagarosse
Ch. Canon
Eolian loam cover
Ch. Magdelaine
Ch. Ausone
Pyrennean gravel cover
Ch. Bélair
Ch. Tertre Daugay
Ch. La Gaffelière
Ch. Pavie

Legend:
Plateau of Calcaire à astéries
Steep frontal escarpment
More gentle back slope
Vineyards of Premier Grand Cru Classé properties
Grand Cru châteaux

| 0 | 0.25 miles |
| 0 | 0.50 km |

N

Figure 6.10
St.-Emilion plateau
(modified from H. Enjalbert,
Les Grands Vins de St-Emilion, Pomerol et Fronsac,
1983, Editions Bardi)

St.-Emilion

St.-Emilion is on, in, and below the plateau of *Calcaire à astéries*. One may dine in a restaurant on the plateau above a church excavated into the *Calcaire*. The scarp is pock-marked with wine storage and mushroom-growing tunnels. Famous châteaux are located around the slope and base of the plateau. The village itself cascades down the notch in the escarpment.

St.-Emilion was omitted from the Bordeaux Classification of 1855 and later developed its own system which became official in 1954. The nomenclature utilizes an excess of adjectives: Premier Grand Cru Classé; Grand Cru Classé; and St.-Emilion, for the general appellation. Unlike the "inviolate" 1855 Classification, the St.-Emilion system requires that the classed châteaux must be reviewed every ten years, most recently in 1996. Ten of the Premier Grand Cru Classé châteaux are located either on the plateau near the town of St.-Emilion itself or on the slopes around the plateau, *see* Figure 6.10.

Soils of the plateau are deep, loamy residues of weathered *Calcaire à astéries*. It has been estimated that during the several million years of exposure on the plateau, the original thickness of the *Calcaire* has been reduced by as much as 15 feet (5 m). Insoluble residues (impurities) of the limestone – clay, silt, and sand – settle in place as the basic loamy soil. In the weathering process, calcium and other soluble mineral nutrients were leached. Fortunately, during the latter part of the Quaternary, silt and "rock flour" from the wide flats of the confluence of the Isle and Dordogne were whipped up and spread onto the upland. The "rock flour," ground from Cretaceous and Jurassic limestones, replaced many of the leached minerals and gave a high pH to the decalcified soils.

The late Professor Enjalbert, author of *Les Grands Vins de St.-Emilion, Pomerol, and Fronsac*, expressed the opinion that this "seasoning" is the key to the high quality of the St.-Emilion and Fronsac vineyards. Mineral composition, texture, and structure of the plateau soils vary considerably. A study by Guilloux, Duteau, and Seguin at the University of Bordeaux, identifies 17 variations in the soils of the major terrain features, that is, plateau, slopes, and alluvium.

The early vignerons learned the best fit of their grapes to the major soil conditions. St.-Emilion uses the same suite of red grapes as the Médoc – Merlot and Cabernet Franc, with Cabernet Sauvignon and Cot/Malbec in decreasing combinations. The predominance of Merlot and Cabernet Franc particularly influences the solid, full-bodied character of St.-Emilion wines.

The top two châteaux, Cheval Blanc and Ausone, are in a special "A" class of the Premiers Grands Crus. Geology of these two terroirs is quite different. Ausone's vineyards start on the plateau and spill down the slope (*see* Color Plate 26). Cheval Blanc is on the Quaternary terrace with Pomerol's best. Château Figeac, a Premier Grand Cru Classé, is also on the Pomerol terrace illustrated in Figure 6.9. The cross-section, Figure 6.11, shows the clustering of other Premiers Grands Crus Classés situated partially on the *Calcaire* plateau and partially on slopes of the Fronsadais molasse. They include Châteaux Beauséjour (Duffau), Belair, Canon, Magdelaine, and Pavie. Fourtet and Trottevieille lie wholly upon the plateau, while La Gaffelière is on the foot-slope. (Château l'Angélus, which was upgraded in 1996, lies on the slope just below Beauséjour-Bécot.)

Figure 6.11
Cross-section, St.-Emilion
(geology suggested by Figure 10 of H. Enjalbert's *Les Grands Vins de St-Emilion, Pomerol et Fronsac*, 1983, Editions Bardi. Remainder of section interpreted from Bergerac sheet, 1:80,000, B.R.G.M. 1970)

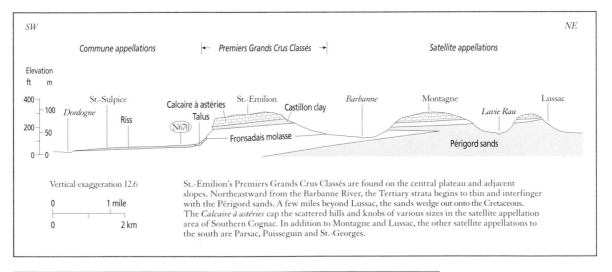

St.-Emilion's Premiers Grands Crus Classés are found on the central plateau and adjacent slopes. Northeastward from the Barbanne River, the Tertiary strata begins to thin and interfinger with the Périgord sands. A few miles beyond Lussac, the sands wedge out onto the Cretaceous. The *Calcaire à astéries* cap the scattered hills and knobs of various sizes in the satellite appellation area of Southern Cognac. In addition to Montagne and Lussac, the other satellite appellations to the south are Parsac, Puisseguin and St.-Georges.

The surprising number of 54 Grands Crus Classés are on the St.-Emilion plateau as it extends west toward Pomerol. Interspersed with these châteaux are other properties, ranked simply as St.-Emilion. Northeastward, the *Calcaire à astéries* and the Fronsadais molasse finger out, giving way to non-marine Périgord sands, *see* Figure 6.11. Wines of this area are also St.-Emilion appellation. The several buttes capped by *Calcaire à astéries* north of the Barbanne are the "satellite" communes of St.-Emilion: Lussac, Parsac, Puisseguin, and St.-Georges. Although of only commune classification, many of their wines are of exceptionally good quality. Vineyards also thrive on the low terraces of Recent deposits along the Dordogne. ("Recent" in geologic terminology began about 10,000 years ago.)

The marine *Calcaire à astéries* undergoes a change in facies eastward as well as northward being replaced by a lake-bed limestone. The lacustrine limestone is the cap rock for the Côtes de Castillon plateau along the north side of the Dordogne. The zone of Périgord sand north of Castillon is known as the Côtes de Franc. Côtes de Castillon and Franc are both appellations in their own right. The wines are similar, but lighter and without the ability to age of St.-Emilion.

Upriver from Castillon, the Périgord sands come down to the Dordogne in the Bergerac area which is outside the Bordeaux appellation.

Entre-Deux-Mers and perimeter appellations

To the Romans, crossing at the confluence of the Garonne and Dordogne, the wedge of land must indeed have appeared to be "between two seas."

The Bec (beak) d'Ambès expands as a triangular plateau for 40 miles (over 60 km) along the fronts of both rivers. The base of the triangle is the political boundary of the Gironde département and of the Bordeaux appellation.

The principal cap rock of the Entre-Deux-Mers plateau is the Oligocene *Calcaire à astéries*, which wedges out a short way eastward. Over 100 feet (30 m) of Miocene strata overlie the *Calcaire,* forming the major uplands of Entre-Deux-Mers. The backbone of the plateau is a watershed with short rivulets draining to the Garonne and Dordogne. These lateral streams cut through the cap rock into softer underlying marls providing good vineyard slopes.

The principal vineyards, however, are on the undulating upland of the plateau. The soils are similar to the St.-Emilion plateau with a veneer of Plio-Pleistocene gravel mixed with residues of the deeply weathered limestones. The soils are seasoned here and there with loess, wind-blown fine sand and silt, which translates into pockets of very good wine.

In the 1920s, the several communes around the perimeter of Entre-Deux-Mers obtained court rulings allowing them to "secede" from Entre-Deux-Mers and set up their own appellations. All that remains of the original Entre-Deux-Mers appellation is the interior and a small sector along the Dordogne. Nevertheless, Entre-Deux-Mers is now well-noted for its lively dry, white wines with a definite style.

At the base of the scarp along the Garonne, sand bars and alluvial flats of Recent river gravel and silty clay-loam produce fairly respectable wines. The A.O.C. Premières Côtes de Bordeaux is a narrow band of communes along the Garonne side of the plateau, *see* Figure 6.1. Someone has observed that, viewed from the opposite side of the Garonne, the church steeples of the 37 communes along the plateau margin appear as pickets of a giant fence. The appellation is for both red and white wines, with reds predominating in the north.

Continuing along the plateau southeastward, the enclaves of Cadillac, Loupiac, and Ste.-Croix-du-Mont produce sweet white wines after the fashion of Sauternes. The grape varieties, method of harvesting, and vinification are the same as in Sauternes. However, the soils are somewhat different, so it is no surprise that experts detect a difference in the wines from opposite sides of the river. The wines on the right bank are allowed higher yields. Although the Ste.-Croix growers cannot match the greater sweet wines, they market at a fraction of the price. The plateau soils are on slopes and ridges of Miocene marls and limestones, *Calcaire à astéries*, and Fronsadais molasse with a sparsity of gravel.

The Côtes de Bordeaux-St.-Macaire, leap-frogging the sweet-wine areas, is a continuation of the same geology and terrain as the Premières Côtes. Its white wines are less sweet, but not bone dry. You will recall that it was the port of St.-Macaire where the Haut-Pays wines started their overland journey to Bergerac to circumvent the Bordeaux Privileges (*see* page 172).

The Graves de Vayres, as the name implies, is a gravel province but with an admixture of loess and silty clay-loam. Lying just across the Dordogne from the mouth of the Isle, the Vayres deposits are a combination of gravel from both rivers. Vines occupy terrace slopes from the top of the plateau down to the bars of Recent alluvium. Although a relatively small appellation, the growers syndicate of Vayres in cooperation with the Bordeaux wine trade is very aggressive in marketing its reds and dry whites along with its white *moëlleux* (slightly sweet).

Ste.-Foy-Bordeaux is an appellation of political creation where the boundary of the Gironde département arbitrarily separates Ste.-Foy from the Monbazillac area of Bergerac, both making sweet wines. A more complete discussion of the geology is detailed under Bergerac (*see* page 215).

The *Calcaire de l'Agenais*, a fresh-water limestone, has replaced the *Calcaire à astéries* as cap rock for a series of buttes not plateaus. Vineyards occupy the calcareous slopes below this cap rock in the hilly terrain of Ste.-Foy. One hill at an elevation of 377 feet (115 m) is the highest in Bordeaux.

Cognac

Although Cognac is a spirit, it is a wine before it is distilled to brandy. Discussion of Cognac logically follows Bordeaux as the two major appellations have a common boundary. They also have a geologic relationship as the Périgord sands wedge out onto the Cretaceous of southern Cognac, *see* Figure 6.12. In its own right, Cognac is a showcase example of the relationship of geology and wine.

In the mid-19th century a French geologist by the name of H. Coquand was sent to the Charente to map the geology of the region along the river by that name. Coquand took along a friend who was an expert taster of wines and brandies. As Coquand went about outlining on his map the distribution of different chalky formations of the Cretaceous, his companion visited growers and wineries in the region. When they compared tasting notes with geology, a striking relationship was discovered – the chalkier the soil the better the brandy.

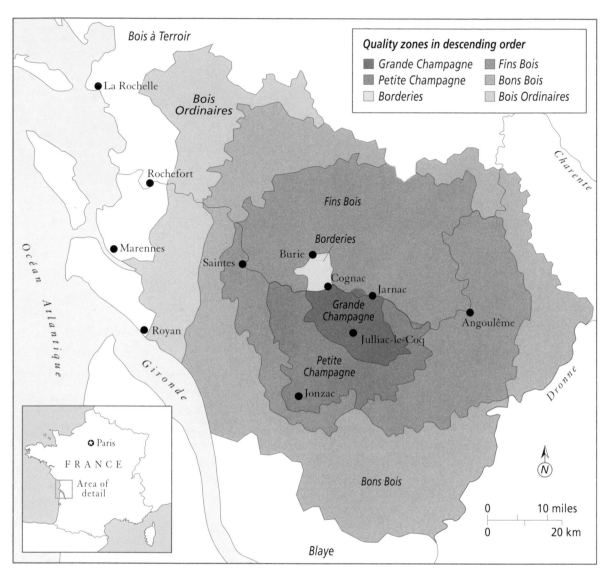

Quality zones in descending order
- Grande Champagne
- Petite Champagne
- Borderies
- Fins Bois
- Bons Bois
- Bois Ordinaires

Figure 6.12
The appellations of Cognac
(compiled from various sources)

The six quality zones of Cognac shown on Figure 6.12 correspond in large measure to the lithology of the geologic formations defined by Coquand. He chose names for the formations he mapped, based on where they typically outcropped (type-localities): Coniacian for the strata around the town of Cognac; Santonian for those around Saintes. Coquand's stratigraphic units became the standard nomenclature for a portion of the Upper Cretaceous in western Europe.

Grande and Petite Champagne, Cognac's top grades, occupy the "bull's eye" of the area, which is also the chalkiest of the formations. Coquand named this very chalky band the Campanian for the same reason the Romans named Champagne after Campania, the "open country" north of Naples. The terms "Grande" and "Petite" Champagne were later introduced by the local growers to exalt those viticultural zones.

Concentric bands of lessening quality encircle the "bull's eye" of Grande Champagne like the zones of a target. The Cognac "target" is bisected approximately east–west by the Cretaceous–Jurassic boundary which essentially follows the Charente River. The Bois Ordinaires and vineyards to the north are on the limestone soils of the Jurassic. By and large, the Cretaceous is the chalkiest and supports the better vineyards.

Across the Charente River northwest of the town of Cognac is an enclave about 8 miles (12 km) in diameter called the Borderies. This is a geologic anomaly within the limestone terrain which produces a cognac much in demand for blending. A thin layer of Tertiary sand covers a bedrock of soft, marly Cretaceous limestones that was weathered to a friable, decalcified, chalky soil. Combined with this soil of sand-on-limestone is a microclimate that swirls the sea breezes in a special way to produce grapes that yield a sweet, full-bodied and full-flavored brandy.

The three "bois": Fins Bois, Bons Bois, and Bois Ordinaires, take their names from the quality of the wood of the trees, which at one time grew extensively in the region. This difference in wood quality was most likely reflecting the nature of the soil which now translates into brandy-wine zones. The zones are quite large, and the vineyards are well dispersed among woodlands and other crops.

You will recall from Part One that it was the growers of the Charente who, at the time of the phylloxera crisis, requested the French government to send a mission to the United States to discover which American plants thrived on chalky soils and might therefore be good graft stock for their region. It was during this period that a viticultural research station was established in Cognac headed by a very young professor, Louis Ravaz. Although only 26, Ravaz was a pioneer in scientific viticulture, advocating grafted vines and emphasizing the importance of the physical and chemical composition of the soil as relating to the quality of brandy.

Even the very best of wines produced in the Charente do not make suitable table wines. A popular tenet holds that the worse the wine, the better the brandy. Except for blending the wines of the Borderies, too much flavor in the wine is not desirable. The cognac-makers prefer to concentrate subtle flavors by their distillation process.

The grape that produces 95 percent of the wine for cognac is the white Ugni Blanc, also known locally for some strange reason as St.-Emilion, even though the grape has no relationship with the red-wine district of St.-Emilion. It is interesting that ampelographers identify the Ugni as the Trebbiano of Italy which is quite partial to the volcanic soils of the Campania. In addition to its high yield, what makes the Ugni Blanc a favorite in Cognac, is the fact that its acid level remains quite high right up to late harvest.

Terroir has little application to the vineyards of Cognac where individual vineyards have no status other than the classification zones. Where the terrain permits, many growers have turned to mechanized, large-scale farming. This is mass production, not tender, loving care as lavished on a Côte d'Or terroir or Médoc château. The zones based initially on soil characteristics translate into price. Over the years the zone boundaries have become politicized, especially in the outer zones. The large buyers and blenders, however, know the territory well, and their purchasing practices follow their own knowledge of where the best brandy grapes grow.

The "champagne" of the brandy region bears no relation whatsoever to the sparkling wine of the Reims-Epernay region. The names may be confusing, but the products are not. To confuse further, a blend of Grande and Petite Champagne may be called "Fine Champagne," if half the blend is Grande Champagne. "Fine" is a colloquial expression for any very good brandy. It is a shame that such unique products could not be given more original names.

7 The Southwest: river terraces, sheets of molasse

Figure 7.1
Wine areas of the
Southwest

Bordeaux, heartland of Aquitaine, justified an entire chapter to itself. But on the north and south rims of the huge basin there are a number of ancient and interesting wine areas on a varied geology. Grape varieties and wine styles reflect geology, history, and tradition.

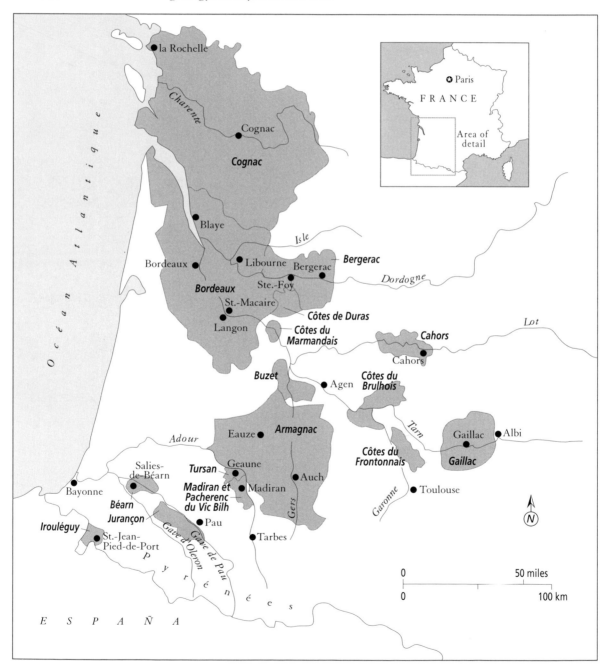

Bergerac

The wines of Bergerac owe their survival of the Wars of Religion to tobacco. Cyrano de Bergerac was a Parisian, briefly a musketeer, but mainly a prophetic philosopher and satirist. It is doubtful if he ever set foot in the town of Bergerac.

Bergerac and Ste.-Foy were Huguenot towns which were all but destroyed during the Wars of Religion. Much of the population fled and with it went winegrowing. Tobacco, a quick "cash crop" requiring less labor to grow and prepare for market than wine, saved the local economy. Many of the vineyards were eventually restored, but now share the land with tobacco farms.

Although the area was Protestant, ironically, it was the Catholic church which had important early-day influence on viticulture. Upstream from Bergerac, the Abbey Beaulieu-sur-Dordogne, abandoned during the Wars of Religion, was reactivated by the Benedictines in 1663. Just downstream from Bergerac was the Abbey St.-Sylvain de la Mongie. The importance of winegrowing in those days is verified by Jacques Beauroy whose studies of church records show that most growers paid their tithes in wine. Many of the vineyards today belong to descendants of those 17th-century growers.

In the deeply incised streams within the terrain of the Périgord sands, the Cretaceous chalk is exposed. Within the general Bergerac appellation are several specific appellations. Tradition and geology have had much to do with the grape varieties grown and the range of wine-styles produced in each sub-district.

On the northeast outskirts of Bergerac town the small area of Pécharmant produces a quality red wine from the traditional Bordeaux cépages: Merlot, Cabernet Sauvignon, and Malbec. The sandy uplands and ridges of Pécharmant are covered with vineyards extending down to the deeply weathered, marly limestone of the Cretaceous. An 1890 geologic map of the area shows the name as two words, "Pech Charmant," which, allowing for cartographic errors, could be translated "charming or sweet peach." Was it describing the wine or the fruit?

The vineyards of Rosette, close by Bergerac on the northwest, once all but forgotten, now thrive again. They produce small amounts of a straw-colored, semi-sweet white wine from the Sémillon with a strong flavoring of Muscadelle.

West from the outskirts of Bergerac to the boundary of the St.-Emilion appellation are three sister appellations: Côtes de Montravel, Haut-Montravel, and Montravel (for whites). The first two are characterized by outlying buttes and knolls capped by *Calcaire à astéries* overlying Fronsadais molasse. The wines of these two sub-districts range from dry to sweet. The Montravel portion is an area of polyculture on terraces and slopes along the Dordogne. Tobacco farms and orchards are actually more plentiful than vineyards.

The geology of Monbazillac across the river is completely different, being lenticular freshwater limestones interbedded with molassic sands and marls, *see* Figure 7.2. The soils of the layer-cake molasse of Monbazillac produce the most famous of Bergerac's white wines, both dry and sweet. Like Sauternes, Monbazillac wines are from the Sémillon, Sauvignon Blanc, and Muscadelle grapes, employing "noble rot" and late, selective picking of the grapes. The lenticular molassic strata on which Monbazillac wines grow are marls and clayey sands interbedded with limestones. The limestones form benches and caps of buttes as illustrated by the cross-section in Figure 7.2.

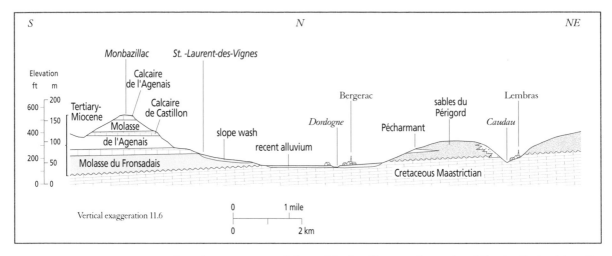

Saussignac, westward from Monbazillac, produces dry fuller-bodied whites. Its vineyards lie on limestone benches where clay soils and scree have accumulated. The frost-fractured limestones provide good water reservoirs for deep rooting.

The Côtes de Duras and Cotes du Marmandais

Geologically the Côtes de Duras is a southwestward continuation of the sandy-clays and limestone benches of Monbazillac and Saussignac. In the Dropt Valley, a tributary of the Garonne, the terrain becomes steeper, and the soils are deeply weathered. Roughly equal amounts of red and white wines are made, the reds compare in style to those of Bordeaux, the whites to Entre-Deux-Mers.

The Côtes du Marmandais, a 1956 appellation, is essentially an extension of the Duras geology down to and across the Garonne. Terraces on the right bank are eroded out of molasse composed of soft, calcareous sandstones, shale, and thin limestones. Across the river on the left bank, the terrain is typical of the lower levels of Sauternes – terraces with gravel and coarse sand. The time-honored local grapes, Fer Servadou, Cot (Malbec), and others are being replaced with the Gamay, Syrah, the Cabernets, and Merlot in response to market tastes. The appellation is A.O.C. for both red and white wines. Whites now favor the Sauvignon over the Sémillon in the blend, plus Muscadelle and Ugni Blanc.

Cahors

The signature of Cahors is the graceful, script-like meanders of the Lot. The best vineyards are on gravel lobes of inside loops of the meanders, *see* Figure 7.3. Two-thirds of the vines grow here, the remainder on the bordering limestone plateau. To continue the metaphor, the signature of Cahors is actually engraved as the meanders are entrenched in the Quercy plateau. The plateau is the gently dipping limestone of the Upper Jurassic (Kimmeridgian) off the southeast flank of the Massif Central. The name Quercy derives from *Quercus*, Latin for oak, which grow in the creases between hills where moisture collects.

The rugged Gramat Causse, part of the Périgord plateau northeast of Cahors, reaches elevations of over 1000 feet (300 m). *Causse* is a regional dialectic term for an arid limestone plateau. The Gramat Causse is sparsely populated and the limited vineyards, situated only on the lower slopes, produce average wines.

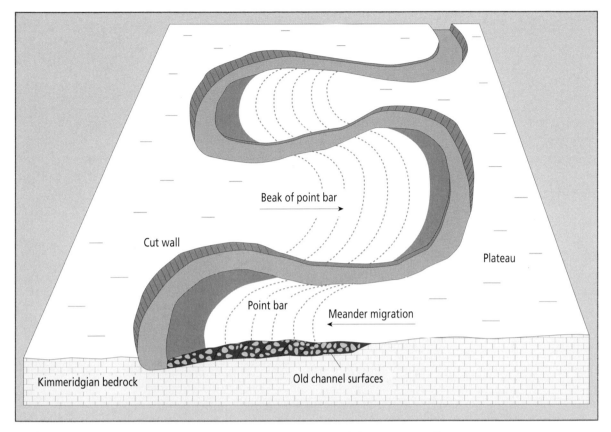

Beak of point bar

Cut wall

Plateau

Point bar

Meander migration

Kimmeridgian bedrock   Old channel surfaces

South of the Lot, the Limogne Causse is extensively cultivated for wine as well as other crops. The Limogne forms part of the Périgord sidérolithique – the concentration of the weathering of iron minerals in broken masses of clay.

As with the gravel terrace-mounds of Médoc, the anatomy and formation of the Lot meander lobes help in understanding how they function to produce some of the best vineyard sites of Cahors. This unique vineyard landform is illustrated in Figure 7.3 and shown overleaf in the extract from the topographic map of Parnac in Figure 7.4.

As the limestone shelf was gradually tilted off the Massif Central, the Lot squirmed out a meandering course to the Garonne. With continued uplift, the river began to entrench its meanders. Hydraulic action of the confined stream undercut the outside bends. As the meander was enlarged, the channel "slipped off" the inside of the loop, eroding a deeper channel. The rebounding current cut into the neck of the meander often forming narrow "goosenecks" such as the one on which the town of Cahors is located.

The "slip off" phenomenon built a cone of alluvial sand, silt, and gravel deposits known as "point bars." The "beak" of these point bars are in places up to 60 feet (20 m) above normal level of the river. The mix of granitic and limestone gravel in the point bars provides excellent mineral nutrition. The depositional origin of Médoc mounds and Cahors point bars is different, but the internal structures are similar and the all-important hydric cycle operates in much the same manner. Some gravel in the Médoc mounds would find many "country cousins" in the gravel bars of Cahors.

Figure 7.3
Development of point bars on the Lot at Cahors
As the channel deepens, swinging of the current cuts into the outer wall, causing the meander to widen. As the meander migrates, the "slip off" on the inside loop leaves arcuate alluvial terraces of gravel, sand, and silt which form the best vineyard sites of Cahors

Figure. 7.4
Parnac loop of the Lot
The cooperative at
Caunezil, started in 1947,
was instrumental in the
post-war rejuvenation of
Cahors, taking musts from
the surrounding *causses*
as well as the vineyards
from the horseshoe loops
of the Lot
(extract from 1:25,000 Map
no. 2139 0, ©IGN Paris 1986,
Authorisation no. 90-8024
by kind permission.)

Vineyards

Bushwood and oaks

0   1 mile

0   1 km

As with the *Calcaire à astéries* on the St.-Emilion plateau, the Kimmeridgian of
the Cahors plateau has been subjected to deep weathering for a very long time,
resulting in the leaching of much of the calcium carbonate. The residual
impurities became concentrated as a deep, red clay along with limestone
fragments. Numerous sinkholes created by underground solution of the
limestone has resulted in a hummocky "karstic" terrain. The term "karst" comes
from the Kars province on the Adriatic coast in former Yugoslavia.

Sands and clays in many of these "sinks" became cemented with iron oxides precipitated from circulating ground waters. Rich pockets of these red sidérolithique deposits were mined in the early days and smelted at a foundry at Fumel, downstream from Cahors.

South of the Lot, vineyards are scattered in patches of native vegetation known locally as *cloups*, which often contain "sinks" of sidérolithique. These plots are in swales with generally good soils and favorable groundwater supply. The Cahors appellation boundary is drawn quite generously to incorporate the many isolated *cloups*.

Cahors made its wine reputation on the Cot, another name for the red grape Malbec, which has the puzzling local synonym of Auxerrois. (The town of Auxerre is 250 miles (400 km) on the other side of the Massif Central.) Iron from the sidérolithique gives wines made from Auxerrois a rich color and strong tannin, but they are soft, low in acid, but less aromatic than the Cabernets.

In the period between the two World Wars, attempts were made to obtain an appellation for Cahors. But, as Pierre Bréjoux, former chief engineer of the I.N.A.O. points out, it was not possible to obtain such a designation on a past reputation when there were only three or four active growers in the area, and fine Cahors was a rarity. It was not until after World War II that a determined and successful effort for improvement resulted in V.D.Q.S. recognition being granted in 1951, upgraded to A.O.C. status in 1971.

The principal climatic influence is from the Atlantic, but occasionally the warm, dry converted *marin* from the Mediterranean slips over the Carcassonne Gateway reaching as far as Cahors. Killing frosts of 1956 and 1957 almost put an end to the few quality vineyards. However, some growers turned devastation to advantage by replacing the dead vines with quality rootstocks.

The Merlot was introduced in the 1960s to add a fruitiness to the Auxerrois. The local Tannat grape provides structure to the wine as well as adding a raspberry-like perfume. Experiments have been conducted with rootstocks to determine the best hybrids for the gravel soils of the valley and also for the arid, calcareous plateau.

Historical sketch of Cahors

For the Romans, Cahors was Divona Cadureorum, chief town of the Quercy. The Roman name recognized the Celtic tribe of Cardurques who originally occupied the region. That name was shortened to Cadurca, and eventually to Cahors.

In the 13th century, Cahors was one of the great cities of Europe, deriving wealth from commerce, banking, and additional renown from its university. Out of that cultural atmosphere came Clément Marot (1496–1544), one of the great medieval French poets, particularly noted for his translations of the Psalms. As the principal crossing point of the Lot, Cahors was for long an important post on one of the pilgrim routes to Santiago de Compostella in northwest Spain. With a steady flow of visitors, tourism and the winetrade boomed.

Cahors red wines are so deeply red they were at one time almost opaque. In the 18th century when the English perversely decided they wanted their light clarets strengthened, the logical wine would have been the "black wines" of Cahors. But the Bordeaux Privileges (see page 174) prohibited wines of the Haut-Pays from competing with local Bordeaux wines. The strengthening had to be found elsewhere.

The coming of the railroads and completion of the lateral canal along the Garonne shifted the axis of commerce between the Atlantic and the Mediterranean from the "high road" through Cahors to the Garonne Valley. Loss of prominence as a communication link, followed by the devastation of phylloxera, all but extinguished Cahors as a wine-producing area.

Gaillac

Vines were cultivated in Gaillac at least two centuries before Caesar undertook the conquest of northern Gaul. Gaillac was a part of the Roman province of Transalpine Gaul with easy passage from the Mediterranean through the low Carcassonne Gateway. The odd assortment of grape varieties currently found in Gaillac may be mutants descended from the plants of those early emigrants.

With Gaillac as the hub, the appellation is approximately 30 miles (50 km) across, bisected by the Tarn. The wines grow on three geologic terrains, each favoring a particular suite of grapes.

The Causse de Cordes north of the Tarn is underlain by the Cordes limestone which weathers to a red, pebbly, calcareous soil. This is the province of the Mauzac, a white grape which varies in color from green to yellow to russet, depending on the particular soil and exposure. When crispy-green, this grape is perfectly suited to be made as *vins mousseux* (sparkling).

The Ondenc, also known as the "Blanc de Gaillac" is being replaced by the more familiar white trio, Sémillon, Sauvignon, and Muscadelle. The Ondenc lacks vigor and has a tendency to drop its fruit early. The new varieties are noted for their dependability in growth and predictable wines.

By some historical quirk, Cordes was named for Cordova, Spain, and is admiringly referred to by the locals as "Cordes of Heaven." Southward toward the Tarn, the Cordes limestone wedges out into molassic puddingstones of the Premières Côtes. This second geologic province of sandy, pebbly soils is planted with several red grape varieties. Of particular note is the renewed interest in the white l'En de l'El or Len-de-lel. This odd name is local patois for "loin de l'oeil," meaning "far from sight." The Len-de-lel is a vigorous vine and has a perfume of some finesse, but Pierre Bréjoux says it makes an "incomplete wine" and needs to be blended with the tart Mauzac.

The third province is a series of terraces on the south side of the Tarn. The local geologists are of the opinion that the terraces represent four sub-stages of the Würm, the last Ice Age glacial period. (The Würm in the Médoc area is deeply buried beneath the Gironde estuary.) The Würm terraces along the Tarn contain considerable clay mixed with pebbles of limestone and crystalline rocks. The terraces are "ribbed" by numerous short, right-angle tributaries to the Tarn, but none has cut deep enough to make "islands."

The Fer Servadou, Valdiguié (or Brocol), and the Duras are red grapes of the terrace region and the Premières Côtes. Found only in Gaillac, these grapes could be relics of Greco-Roman varieties from the Mediterranean. Although adapted long ago to the Gaillac soils, these grapes produce rather ordinary wines and are being replaced by Gamay, Merlot, and Syrah.

Gaillac was long overshadowed in history by Albi, a few miles up the Tarn. Established by the Romans, Albi became a major city of the Visigoths. In the 7th century, Gaillac gained importance when the Benedictines founded an abbey there, giving assurance of the success of its viticulture.

Red kaolinite clays of the region were used extensively by the Romans for making amphorae and other earthenware such as the highly glazed *terra sigillate*. In an area shy of good building stone, the clays were used for making bricks for the great cathedral of Ste.-Cécile in Albi and the Abbey of St.-Michel in Gaillac.

Like Cahors, the wines of Gaillac were among those of the Haut-Pays of the Garonne affected by the Bordeaux Privileges (*see* page 174). These river wines circumvented the prohibition by making an end-run overland from St.-Macaire through Bergerac to overseas shipping.

The variety of soils, sitings, and indigenous grapes make Gaillac wines of great interest to the wine lover, but the lack of a consistent style works against a significant export trade today. The traditional sweet wines of the region made with the Mauzac grape are increasingly being replaced by wines that are lighter and drier to court the current popular taste. As the search for "honest" wines that can be drunk young increases, Gaillac may well be rediscovered.

Côtes du Frontonnais

The vineyards of the Côtes du Frontonnais have the geologic distinction of being on terraces identified as representing a full set of Ice Age glacial stages. Effects of the glacial stages and sea-level changes reached upstream as far as the Tarn, but the stream hydraulics were appreciably different from those which deposited the Médoc gravel terraces. Stream velocity and volume were both considerably less than those of the Garonne. The Côtes du Frontonnais terraces have graded deposits of clay, silt, and sand as well as small gravel. Here the soils, also of interbedded silts, clays, and pebble layers, have been exposed to long weathering.

The local grape is the Negrette which flourishes in the Toulouse climate which is generally hot and dry throughout the growing season. The grape is thought to have been brought back from Cyprus by the Knights Templar at the time of the Crusades. The knights owned much of the Frontonnais area now covered by vineyards. The Negrette yields soft, fruity red and rosé wines from the slopes surrounding Fronton and Villaudric, 20 miles (32 km) west of Gaillac and 15 miles (24 km) north of Toulouse. Generally the wines are quite good: until appellation status was awarded in 1975 they were largely unknown outside the Toulouse area, but only 2500 acres (1000 ha) of vines means a limited supply.

The Lannemezan Cone

This dominant physiographic feature on the south flank of the Aquitaine Basin can only be appreciated from a regional map or the geologic map of France, *see* Color Plate 1. It is not itself a wine district, but the site of several appellations, large and small. The pattern of radiating streams down the cone resemble the ribs of an open ladies' fan.

The Lannemezan is a composite of a number of overlapping Miocene molasse fans emanating from a narrow source in the Pyrenees. There were periods in which still-stands (lakes) developed, in which thin layers of limestone were deposited.

In the Pliocene, a veneer of sandy, pebbly alluvium was spread over the Lannemezan Cone. In the late Tertiary, with a tilting of this flank of Aquitaine to the north, these streams found courses along seams between or within the composite of fans.

The great heart-shaped Armagnac district, together with Buzet, Tursan, and Madiran, occupy select portions of the Lannemezan feature (see Color Plate 28). Of particular preference are the east-facing slopes of the stream valleys which are longer and gentler than those facing west. This asymmetry developed under periglacial conditions when the east-facing slopes caught first sun which commenced thawing and erosion, lasting much of the day. The west-facing slopes remained shaded until past midday and experienced much less day-time thawing. The cross-section in Figure 7.5 shows this asymmetry. Relief from the top of the ridges to the shallow valleys averages about 275 feet (80 m). The ridges are a tan-colored sand with remnants of a loamy clay that binds the underlying sand into a good soil. Limestone outcrops at the base of the sandy slopes. Vines and other crops are found on the east-facing slopes, woods and pastures on the steep west-facing slopes.

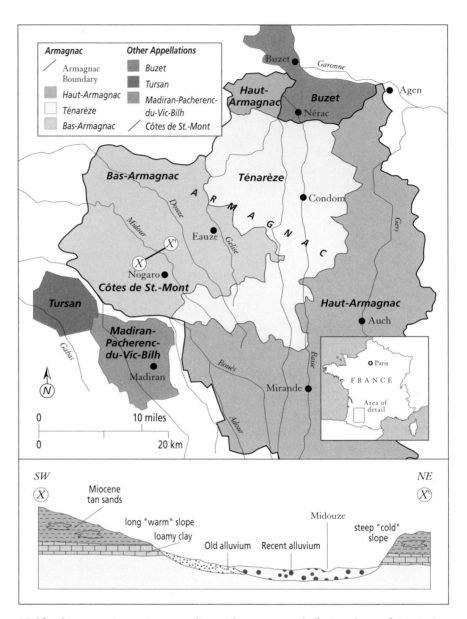

The word brandy has its origin in the Armagnac, according to Jean and Georges Samalens. The Dutch with their powerful merchant fleet were the most important 17th-century customers. They encouraged the Armagnacs to distill their wine to an eau-de-vie, yielding one-fifth the volume of wine with twice the "kick." A quick "jolt" was what the customers of the North Sea climate sought. The Dutch called the eau-de-vie, Brandewijn, or "burnt wine." The term was easily shortened to brandy.

Half a dozen ancient wine areas lie on the great north-facing slope of Aquitaine with the jagged wall of the Pyrenees as a backdrop: Irouléguy, Béarn, Jurançon, Madiran-Pacherenc du Vic-Bilh, Tursan, and the immense Armagnac vineyards.

Armagnac

The heart-shaped area of Armagnac covers some 1800 square miles (4600 km^2) of the Lannemezan Cone. Figure 7.5 shows the three Armagnac zones and adjacent districts which are related to the geology and soils of the Lannemezan complex of Miocene molasse. In general, Haut-Armagnac has most limestone and marl; Ténarèze soils are more clayey; and Bas-Armagnac is sandy. Although Haut-Armagnac, which arcs around the eastern and southern part of the wine region, has most limestone and marl, its soils tend to be waterlogged in winter and dry and cracked in summer. For these reasons it produces the smallest amount of brandy, despite being the largest of the three zones. Ironically, Haut-Armagnac's white wines are more suitable as table wine than for distillation.

Ténarèze, the central zone's heavy, clay soil, is tempered with enough chalky sandstone to produce an acidic wine ideal for distillation. Its wines are reputed to produce flavors distinct from either Haut- or Bas-Armagnac.

Bas-Armagnac is also known as "Armagnac noir," so nicknamed because the oaks which grow there have very dark leaves. The sandy, acidic soil of this zone makes it the premier area for producing brandy grapes. Iron minerals in the sand give the wine a touch of color and contribute to its pleasant flavoring. Variations in the geology and clay of the sandy soil make natural subdivisions of Bas-Armagnac – the westernmost part being the best, the central part next best and a smaller eastern sector the least favored.

Buzet

The brilliant red wines of Buzet have been appreciated from the 13th century, but the area was only granted A.O.C. status in 1973. The principal vineyards are on slopes of molassic hills of the toe of the Lannemezan Cone. The northwest lobe of Buzet is a complex of fossiliferous sands and sandy limestones and marls, and produces the better wines. Southeastward, the appellation overlaps the lower portion of Haut-Armagnac where the molasse contains more marl and clay. Buzet's red wines are made from the Bordeaux trio of Merlot, Cabernet Sauvignon, and Cabernet Franc. A small amount of white wine is produced from the Sauvignon Blanc, Sémillon and Muscadelle.

Tursan

Wines of Tursan avoided the Bordeaux Privileges in the 17th century by being shipped down the Adour through the port of Bayonne to Holland and other North Sea customers. The vineyard slopes of Tursan form an elliptic band around the elongate hills of a gentle, domal uplift of Upper Cretaceous flysch composed of marls, sandstones, and limestones.

The red, rosé, and white wines ranked V.D.Q.S. are produced by many small growers. This small appellation was recognized in 1958. White wine is Tursan's best known, a strong, flavorful wine made from the Baroque, described as a "rural" grape, sometimes leavened with a little Sauvignon. The red and rosé are produced from the Tannat and Cabernet Franc with some Cabernet Sauvignon. All the commercial wine is made at the coopérative.

Tursan was one of three small semi-independent fiefs, along with Chalosse and Pays d'Or. The political boundaries of these fiefs were vague and they were eventually absorbed by the dukes of Aquitaine.

Madiran–Pacherenc du Vic-Bilh

These two appellations cover essentially the same territory: Madiran for red wines, Vic-Bilh for whites. They lie adjacent to Tursan along the Adour, but the geology is that of the Lannemezan ridges. The Adour starts out on a northward course like the other streams of the Lannemezan until downstream from the town of Madiran it makes a curving left turn cutting across the northwest-trending ridges. The hills inside the bend of the river are the Vic-Bilh. The name

During the Hundred Years War, the Armagnacs became a powerful political party supporting the crown and opposing the Burgundians who were often aligned with the English. Their influence, however, suffered a setback after the humiliating defeat of the French at Agincourt in 1415, an engagement which the Armagnacs had encouraged.

Transhumance refers to the seasonal transfer of stock from one grazing area to another.

Vic-Bilh (pronounced *veek-beel*) is the Basque patois for the Latin, *Vic Vieux*, meaning old hill-villages. These are the winter grazing areas for the transhumance flocks of sheep brought down from summer pastures in the Pyrenees. The derivation of Pacherenc is uncertain, but in the local dialect, *pachet-en-renc*, means "pickets in rank," which may refer to the appearance of the individual stakes on which the vines are trained. A supporting interpretation is that "pacherenc" means *raisin d'échalas*, "grape of the vine stake."

Wine has been grown in Madiran since Gallo-Roman times, but the real impetus came when Benedictines from Cluny established an abbey at Madiran in the 11th century.

The long, north-northwest trending ridges are capped with pebbly clay, underlain by marls and thin limestones. Freeze-thaw action developed ample slope wash and good soils for pasturage and vineyards on the long, "warm" slope of the asymmetric valleys, as illustrated in the cross-section of Figure 7.5.

Madiran is considered one of the best reds of southwest Aquitaine. The Tannat is traditionally blended at about 60 percent with the Cabernet Franc (here called Bouchy), resulting in a wine high in tannin, full-bodied, with a good bouquet. The white Pacherenc du Vic-Bilh is made in sweet as well as dry, aromatic styles from the local Ruffiat (or Ruffiac), Manseng, and Courbu. The Sauvignon and Sémillon may also appear in the blend.

Côtes de St.-Mont

This is a fairly recent (1981) V.D.Q.S. appellation north across the Adour from Madiran, overlapping parts of Haut- and Bas-Armagnac. The appellation was created to differentiate between grapes produced for red, rosé, and white table wines from those grown for brandy. Geology of the western portion is the same sandy ridges as Bas-Armagnac illustrated in Figure 7.5. Eastward the appellation extends into the limestone terrain of Ténarèze.

Winegrowing is not new here, grapes having been grown since Roman times. With the establishment of an abbey at St.-Mont in 1050, the monks added their expertise to the local viticulture, but these good wines just did not have a specific identity until the 1981 appellation.

The red wines are produced from the Tannat and the two Cabernets as in Madiran. The whites are from the same grapes which the Armagnac neighbors distill into brandy, but the geology, soils, and exposures in Côtes de St.-Mont are conducive to growing grapes for table wines. Vinified dry, mainly from the Colombard, these wines are marketed as Vins de Pays Côtes de Gascogne, and have attracted much popular interest.

Béarn

This ancient mountain slope principality derives its name from the Celtic tribe Beneharni who occupied the region. In the 9th century, it was a fief of Louis the Débonnaire which included Jurançon and Madiran. The hilly areas bordering the lush valleys support vineyards as well as pastures. In early days, Béarn wines, like those of Tursan, had a special advantage as they were shipped down the Gave de Pau and Adour to Bayonne and foreign markets. (Gave is the local name for streams originating in the mountains.)

The Romans were attracted to the area by the salt springs at Salies-de-Béarn. Brine is leached from Triassic salt beds by circulating groundwater, which issues as springs along faults. (Salies brines are used to cure the Jambon de Bayonne.)

The Salies-de-Béarn vineyards are on leached soils around the margins of Cretaceous nappes which slipped down the mountainside after they broke away from over-balanced upthrusts in the Pyrenees. Soils of the south- and east-facing slopes are limy clays derived from the Cretaceous flysch of the nappe and from the underlying Tertiary. The principal grapes for reds and rosés are the Tannat and the Cabernet Franc (Bouchy). Minor amounts of Cabernet Sauvignon and Fer Servadou, locally called the Pinenc, are also planted. For white wines, both the Petit and Gros Manseng are used, along with the Courbu, Lauzet, and other lesser grapes. It is reputed that the rosés are the best of the three.

Jurançon

Pau, capital of Béarn, is the cultural, historical, and business center here. Just to its south, across the Gave de Pau, Jurançon is for wine – white wine.

A ridge of Tertiary molasse shaped like a loaf of French bread lies between the Gave de Pau and Gave d'Oloron. The ridge is even lanced by diagonal small streams completing the analogy. The crust of the loaf (ridge) is the Poudingue de Jurançon, a clay studded with marble-sized pebbles of various colors. Ironstone over much of the surface adds to the "crustiness," making cultivation difficult. Most of the vineyards are small, hidden away on slopes of the diagonal streams where freshwater limestones, marls, and sandy clays are exposed. The protected valleys aid in late ripening. Iron in the slope wash from the crustal cap adds a distinctive flavor to the wine as do variations in the lithology of different parts of the "loaf" itself. Jurançon's better (sweet) wines, however, are found south of the town on gravelly, clay soils on slopes of the Nez, a tributary of the Gave de Pau.

Jurançon wine was involved in the oft-told legend of how the lips of the infant prince of Navarre who became King Henry IV of France were rubbed with garlic and moistened with the finest of Jurançon wine. Navarre was one of the independent Pyrennean states, partly in Spain, partly in France. The young prince was something of a free spirit, running barefoot with peasant children. This freedom built a toughness of body and mind needed as king, to carry him through the ordeals in trying to heal the enmities of the Wars of Religion.

Jurançon wines are less well known than the legend outside the region, but highly prized in the U.S. The best are strong in alcohol and sweet, but rather than being luscious, they have a refreshing "nut sweet" tang of a *moëlleux*. The concentration of sugars is achieved by the late picking of overripe grapes, sometimes into November, even into the first snows in December. The pleasant autumns are due to the south winds from Spain, warmed as they descend from the Pyrenees (*see* Color Plate 29). Hot days but often freezing nights are ideal for shriveling the grapes and concentrating their juice. The spring frosts, however, can be severe. Accordingly, the vines are individually staked and brought to a height of 5 feet (1.5 m) before the shoots are trained to the cross piece. The dull-painted wellheads of the Lacq gas field are spaced among these staked vines.

The grapes (white only) used are the Petit Manseng and the Courbu, with about 90 percent Petit Manseng. A *demi-sec* is made from the Gros Manseng.

Irouléguy

This is real mountain wine. In the heart of the Basque country, the land is rugged with changes in relief of 2000 feet (600 m) in half a mile (less than a kilometer) from the ridges to the valley. Vineyards are scattered among the jumble of rocks wherever exposures are good, the slope not too steep, and there is enough clay to bind the sands of the weathered sandstone into soil. The appellation is the vestiges of a once great Basque vineyard, dating back to at least the 11th century and the time of the monks of Roncevaux. The name is not as much of a tongue-twister as might appear; it is pronounced *Ee-roo-lay-ghee*, typically Eskura.

Basque wines may not be the country's greatest, but the Basques' colorful culture extends far beyond this corner of France. The Basques are world-famous as shepherds, and their red and rosé Irouléguy goes well with their simple "shepherd's fare" of spicy sausage and charcuterie. A mountain-air vigor in their wine comes from abundant iron in the soil. The reds are often compared with Madiran, and indeed the same grapes are used in the blend. White Irouléguy is based on the Jurançon varieties.

The Basques are more than shepherds; they were in times past ship builders and seafarers. Among other things, the seashore Basques gave us "bisque," a thick soup from shellfish and crustaceans. They invented the bayonet when in a battle at Bayonne they ran out of ammunition. They tied their long "belt knives" on the end of their rifles and charged – to victory. They did not invent smuggling, but perfected that form of trade when Spain and France put a border through their land.

Although the Basques have grown wine since who knows when, the Irouléguy appellation was only awarded in 1952. Most of the wine is vinified by the cooperative at St.-Etienne-de-Baïgorry in the valley just west of St.-Jean-Pied-de-Port. You will recall that St.-Jean is just below the Col de Roncevaux , the pass, through which countless pilgrims in the Middle Ages crossed on the way to Santiago de Compostella. Irouléguy wines must have been at a high premium in those days.

Irouléguy enjoys a marvelous combination of maritime and mountain-slope climate, with abundant rains in the winter and spring and long periods of sunshine in the summer and fall. Warm, dry winds come over the Pyrenees from Spain, while transverse ridges help shelter the valleys from harsh Atlantic Westerlies. Nevertheless, the vines are trained well above the ground in tree-like fashion to guard against spring frosts.

The red wines are deep purple, traditionally half Tannat and half Cabernet Franc. The latter grape is known locally as the Acheria, Basque for fox (not referring to a "foxy" flavor). These grapes seem to have a particular compatibility with the red, pebbly, sandy soils of the Triassic. Although the appellation is for white wine too, not much is produced. Just as well, the names would scare off a potential buyer – Ixiprota Xuri is the local name for the Petit Manseng.

8 The Loire: converging rivers, chalk hills, ancient rocks

The valley of the lower reaches of the mighty Loire, below Blois, is a veritable garden of wines. There are reds, whites, and rosés, in all styles, from dry to sweet; from still to sparkling. There are picnic wines for shady banks of lazy rivers. There are wines for formal dinners. There are wines for remembering history. There are wines for the modern mood. The personality and character of the wines change with the geology.

The river runs through chalk hills of the Paris Basin and "old rocks" of the Massif Armoricain, *see* Color Plate 1. The wine areas of the lower Loire are arranged along the slopes and plateaux of these geologic provinces, as shown below in Figure 8.1.

Figure 8.1
General geology and wine regions of the lower Loire

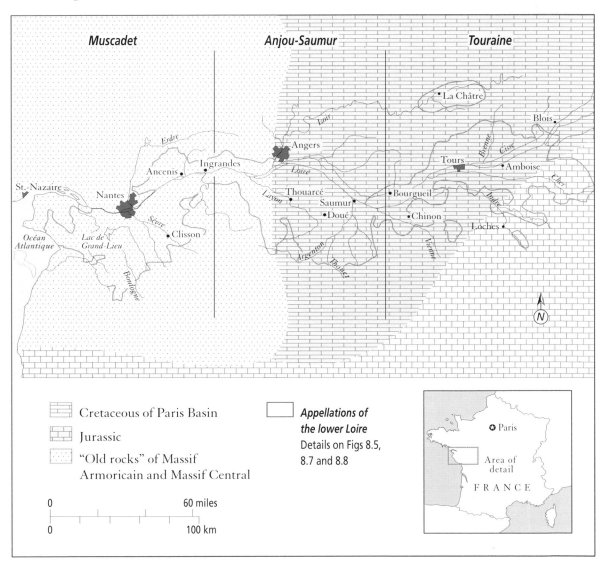

Muscadet   Anjou-Saumur   Touraine

▦ Cretaceous of Paris Basin

▦ Jurassic

▦ "Old rocks" of Massif Armoricain and Massif Central

☐ *Appellations of the lower Loire*
Details on Figs 8.5, 8.7 and 8.8

⊕ Paris
Area of detail
FRANCE

0 ——— 60 miles
0 ——— 100 km

Figure 8.2
Upper Cretaceous
stratigraphy:
Touraine–Saumur

The Turonian is named for
strata typically exposed in
Touraine; the Sénonian for
strata around Sens in the
Paris Basin. The typical
strata around Le Mans,
southwest of Paris give
the Cénomanian its name

Landscape

The Loire portion of the Paris Basin is a valley of valleys. The rivers Cher, Indre,
and Vienne converge like a rooster's tail, as if they are eager to join the Loire
before it enters the Massif Armoricain, but then they approach the actual
confluence with hesitation.

The Cretaceous is made up of soft rocks. There are no limestones to form
cuestas and plateaux. The hills are rounded, but slopes vary from gentle to steep
– there are valley walls that are near vertical. Some Tertiary gravel has become
cemented to form wooded cap rocks of low hills and plateaux, *see* Figure 8.2.

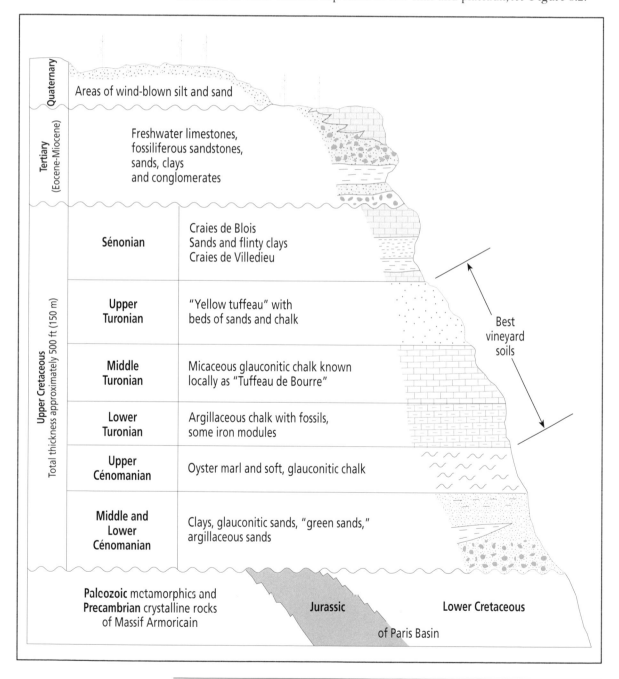

Quaternary	Areas of wind-blown silt and sand	
Tertiary (Eocene–Miocene)	Freshwater limestones, fossiliferous sandstones, sands, clays and conglomerates	
Sénonian	Craies de Blois Sands and flinty clays Craies de Villedieu	
Upper Turonian	"Yellow tuffeau" with beds of sands and chalk	
Middle Turonian	Micaceous glauconitic chalk known locally as "Tuffeau de Bourre"	Best vineyard soils
Lower Turonian	Argillaceous chalk with fossils, some iron modules	
Upper Cénomanian	Oyster marl and soft, glauconitic chalk	
Middle and Lower Cénomanian	Clays, glauconitic sands, "green sands," argillaceous sands	

Upper Cretaceous — Total thickness approximately 500 ft (150 m)

Palœozoic metamorphics and **Precambrian** crystalline rocks of Massif Armoricain — **Jurassic** — **Lower Cretaceous** of Paris Basin

Figure 8.3

Mesozoic	Upper Cretaceous	Seas of Paris Basin advanced over southern portion of Massif Armoricain
	Lower Cretaceous	Massif Armoricain exposed to weathering and erosion. Southern portion reduced to a plain over which the Upper Cretaceous advanced
	Jurassic	
	Triassic	
	Hercynian (Variscan) Orogeny built a high mountain chain - Massif Armoricain.	
Paleozoic	Carboniferous	Schists, graywackes, limestones, beds of hard coal
	Devonian	Red and green schists, limestones
	Silurian	Vari-colored schists, eruptive volcanics, lavas and tuffs (ash), and granite intrusives
	Ordivician	Schists and arkoses (coarse sand with feldspars, similar to graywacke), slates (quaried for roofing)
	Cambrian	Red and black schists, quartzites (silica-cemented sandstones), puddingstones
	Tightly folded Precambrian beds were eroded to plain on which the Cambrian was deposited.	
	Caledonian Orogeny	
	Precambrian	Granite, schists, graywackes (angular grains of quartz and feldspars), puddingstones (cemented rounded pebbles) and limestone lenses

Figure 8.3
Geologic composition of the Massif Armoricain – the "old rocks" terrain of Anjou and Muscadet
The geologic structures are so complex and the rock types so varied that there is considerable disagreement on the interpretation among geologists who have studied the Massif Armoricain. Fortunately, for our purposes, except for a few narrow bands, soils of the deeply weathered bedrock are similar irrespective of their geologic age. Nevertheless, this table summarizes the general rock types by geologic age.

Schists, metamorphosed from immense thickness of shale over several ages, dominate the surface and soils of the Muscadet and Western Anjou.

The ridges and valleys of the Massif Armoricain are only a skeleton of the once-mighty Hercynian range. (The Hercynian was one of the extensive mountain chains that involved the Paleozoic and older rocks which came under long erosion at the end of the Permian.) Long, low ridges are only the roots of great folds. Between the ridges, plains, low plateaux of schists, old volcanic rocks, and granites were the interior of the original folds and the downwarps between. The sequence of these "old rocks" of the Paleozoic and Precambrian is represented schematically in Figure 8.3.

The Hercynian folds were exposed to weathering and erosion for the tens of millions of years from the Triassic through the Jurassic and early Cretaceous, so it is no surprise that these metamorphic rocks are deeply weathered.

The Loire is the longest river in France. It is also said to be the most useless because of its many islands, bars, and shifting channels. It is France's longest river because it stole another river. During a flood time of the Great Ice Age, a low area southeast of Orléans became a large lake. At that time, the area was the headwaters of what is now the lower Loire. The lake also extended into another river which originated in the Massif Central. When the lake began to drain, in the watery confusion, the north-flowing river followed the Loire, abandoning its former course to the Seine. It was this "river piracy" that created France's longest river. This chapter covers the wine areas of the lower reaches; the wines of the upper Loire are considered in the following chapter, the Kimmeridgian Chain.

The geologist in me would like to report that the grapes of the chalky soils of the Paris Basin are quite different from those of the "old rocks" of the Massif Armoricain. Such is not the case. The Chenin Blanc and Cabernet Franc are equally happy on both terrains. There is, however, no mistaking the personality and character of the wines grown on the different rock types.

The boundary between the Cretaceous rocks of the Paris Basin and the "old rocks" of the Massif Armoricain, shown schematically in Figure 8.1 is in fact a ragged erosional contact with some faulting. Southeast of Angers, the boundary is identified as the "Black Anjou" and "White Anjou" – dark slates and stones from the "old rocks" for the "Black Anjou," and white, chalky limestones of the Cretaceous for the "White Anjou." (Anjou refers to the area around the town of Angers as well as its wines; Touraine is the region around Tours.)

By the time the seas during the late Cretaceous advanced from the Paris Basin, the Massif Armoricain had been reduced to a low plain – the outcome of 250 million years of weathering. The sea probably did not advance as far as the Atlantic, and the waters were relatively shallow. The environment of deposition was quite unlike the deep waters of the eastern part of the Paris Basin where globigerina, minute shell-bearing marine organisms, were forming the chalks of Champagne. The succession of Cretaceous and lower Tertiary strata is illustrated in Figure 8.2.

Toward the end of the Cretaceous, the seas became shallow as they began to retreat, leaving deposits of sand and flinty clays. This geologic stage, known as the Sénonian, did not produce the best of vineyard soils, but the sandy slope wash helps aerate the underlying chalks.

During the Eocene of the early Tertiary, rivers deposited sandy gravel which became cemented into *perrons*, "flights of steps." Forests on these *perrons* later became the hunting preserves of kings and nobles. In the mid-Miocene, a narrow arm of the Atlantic occupied the lower part of the Loire, extending almost to Orléans in the Pliocene. Splotches of thick, fossiliferous sands and pebbles from this period are found in the Muscadet region where they now support a vigorous growth of vines – so vigorous in fact that in some parts there is scarcely an acre not planted with grapes.

There are several reasons for there being no Quaternary gravel terrace-mounds along the lower Loire, unlike in the Médoc. Downcutting at successive stages of sea level by the Loire across the hard rocks of the Armoricain was not as easy as into the Tertiary bedrocks by the Garonne–Gironde. Therefore, there was no sequence of terraces. Gradient, stream load, and length of travel of the Loire were quite different from the Garonne. The only significant viticultural terrace on the Loire is the old meander bend at Bourgueil. Most of the islands in the river are in pasture. During the summer, when the water is low, farmers can walk their cows across the river bed to graze on the islands.

The ridges of "old rocks" in Muscadet and Anjou form a muted bas-relief of the toothless Hercynian folds. The sequence of these "old rocks" – Paleozoic to Precambrian – exposed in the Armoricain is indicated in Figure 8.3. The thick shales of the original deposits were metamorphosed by intense heat and pressure of deformation into schists and slates. Sandstones were converted to hard quartzites, and limestones were compacted or marbleized, while granite and old volcanic rocks in the cores of the Hercynian folds were also subjected to the metamorphism.

Only the hardest of the "old rocks" survived the extremely long, deep weathering. These survivors are the ridge-formers, the other rocks rotted down to produce excellent soils.

Climate

The year-round mild climate was the principal reason kings and nobles came to the Loire Valley and built magnificent châteaux. The area is the market garden for fruits and vegetables for metropolitan Paris and also produces a wide variety of wines for a world market. The climate of Muscadet is definitely maritime, but upstream, above Angers, it becomes transitional to a mild continental influence.

With no mountains nearby to create turbulence, thunderstorms and hail are less frequent in the lower Loire than, say, in Burgundy. Nor are there extremes of temperature. This is not to say that devastating freezes do not occur – one in 1907 wiped out the Muscadet vineyards; an April frost in 1991 caused a serious set-back to budding in numerous vineyards lying in low areas.

Rainfall is surprisingly scant for such nearness to the sea, averaging hardly 30 inches (760 mm) per year. With relatively high temperatures from mid-June to mid-August coinciding with low rainfall, the vineplants are frequently in stress. Although summer temperatures are fairly high, it is surprising that total sunshine averages only 1900 hours per year, about that of Champagne.

The weather for any particular year largely influences the dominant style of wine for that vintage – sweet in sunny, warm years; sparkling in cool years when the grapes are rather tart. Overall, the climate of Touraine is about as right for vines, vegetables, and people as can be found in France.

The grapes

It is amazing that the extensive variety of quality wines in Touraine, Saumur, and Anjou derives from only two grapes, the white Chenin Blanc and the red Cabernet Franc. The Chenin Blanc is known also as the Pineau de la Loire, sometimes as Pineau d'Anjou. These synonyms are misleading according to authorities as the Chenin is not a Pinot or even related to that variety. The Pineau names probably come from the period after Gallo-Roman times.

Jean-Jacques Macaire has suggested that this grape was possibly domesticated by St. Martin from local wild vines. This proposition is based on pollen of the genus *Vitis* found in peat of Recent (Holocene) age on the shores of Lac de Grand-Lieu in the Muscadet. While the Chenin Blanc may indeed have developed from native vines, the pollen evidence is not altogether conclusive as the peat deposit also includes material of historical time. The pollen could be from vines of early settlers along the coastal zone bordering the trade route.

The earliest historical record identifying the Chenin Blanc as a grape variety in the Loire was in the 9th century, cultivated at the Abbey of Glanfeuil in Anjou. It was in the 15th century that the grape was officially named Chenin Blanc from Mont Chenin in southern Touraine.

The Cabernet Franc almost surely came from the Bordeaux region. How it acquired the synonym of Breton is a matter of some dispute. One logical theory is that it was brought to the Loire by Abbot Breton, an administrator of Cardinal Richelieu. The good abbot inherited property in St.-Nicolas-de-Bourgueil and, being familiar with the success of the Cabernet Franc in Bordeaux, may have brought it to his Loire vineyard. However it got to the Loire, this sturdy, fruity, red grape found a home on the chalky slopes of Chinon, Bourgueil, Saumur-Champigny, and in the schistose soils of Anjou.

The Muscadet is the grape of the Pays Nantais, the region around Nantes. The name Muscadet was apparently derived from the faint trace of Muscat flavor developed in the grape in these soils and climate. Muscadet is addressed formally as the Melon de Bourgogne. Although that name suggests that it came from Burgundy, the variety is practically unknown in that area.

Until the 17th century, Pays Nantais wines were red. This changed when the Dutch urged introduction of white grapes to be distilled to brandy. The conversion was hastened in the early 18th century when the unbelievably cold winter of 1709 froze all the vines. This was one of the cold periods of the Little Ice Age (*see* Figure 1.4, page 32). Replanting favored the Melon which adapted admirably to the schistose and granitic soils and climate of the Pays Nantais.

The Gros Plant, regional name for the Folle Blanche, is a "carafe wine grape" grown everywhere in the Nantais, usually in the same vineyards with the Melon. Large quantities of this thin, acidic wine were once distilled to brandy.

The Grolleau, or Groslot, is a prolific producer (hence a good money spinner) and widely grown, but its wines, mostly "café rosés," are ordinary. It is rapidly being replaced in quality vineyards by the Gamay and Cabernet Franc.

In recent times, other grapes have been introduced which are used primarily for blending: Chardonnay, Pinot Gris (locally called Pinot Beurot), Malbec (or Cot), and others. The Cabernet Sauvignon is creeping into several areas for blending with the Cabernet Franc. There is no "Loire wine," per se, rather a baffling array of delightful wines.

Rocks of the wine areas

The Loire provides an excellent demonstration of the influence of rocks and soils on the personality and character of wines. Its principal grapes, the white Chenin Blanc and red Cabernet Franc, grow as happily on Paleozoic and Precambrian "old rocks" of the Armorican as they do on the Cretaceous chalks of Touraine and Saumur. Yet a Roche-aux-Moines Chenin Blanc from the Paleozoics will never be mistaken for a Vouvray Chenin Blanc from the Cretaceous chalk. The supple Roche-aux-Moines exhibits a pleasant blend of honey and vanilla, while the lively Vouvray has flavors suggesting ripe fruit. There is no difference in the climate between the two geologic provinces. Apparently, the roots find something in the soils that makes a difference. Just what is that something, is what makes "wine on the rocks" a fascinating study.

The strata sequence preferred by grapevines is shown in Figure 8.2. This includes particularly the "yellow tuffeau" of the Turonian (see Color Plate 30). The wine literature often refers to this formation by the erroneous term of "tufa" or "tuff." "Tufa" is travertine, a deposit formed by evaporation of calcium carbonate waters. "Tuff" is the term for consolidated volcanic ash. The "tuffeau" of the Turonian is neither of these rocks, but a porous, chalky limestone composed chiefly of fragments of bryozoa – marine organisms which live in mass-like, floating colonies. Agitation of near-shore waters breaks up the masses which settle into tabular deposits containing fragments of mica and grains of sand. From time to time, the zone of deposition was exposed to the air, producing hard zones cemented by iron and magnesium oxides. Tuffeau adds valuable chemical and physical properties to the soil profiles.

The sequence of rocks of the Armoricain is indicated in Figure 8.3 by geologic age and descriptive terms such as granites, schists, quartzites, limestones, and arkoses are used. These have frequently been referred to as "old rocks." Generally, for our purposes, this is sufficient identification. What is important for grapes is that these old rocks contain abundant biotite mica, serpentine, and other dark minerals which have weathered to clay, releasing valuable mineral nutrients. Except for the hard-rock ridge-formers, vineplants show no great preference for the "old rocks."

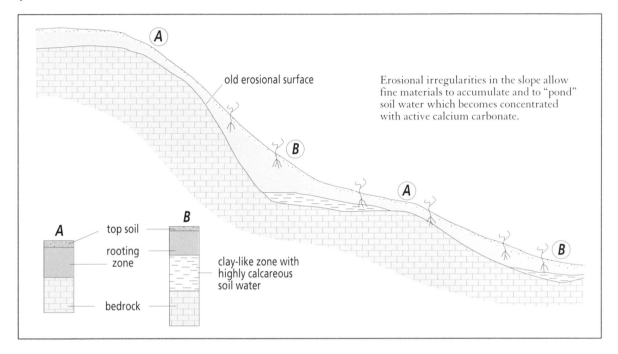

Figure 8.4
Perched soil waterzone on viticultural slope

Chalk: a potentially toxic substance

Chalk, the shells of micro-organisms, is nearly pure calcium carbonate, insuring a favorable basic pH. Its texture provides moisture-holding characteristics. Impurities in the chalk or mixtures with other strata create excellent growing soils.

The chapter on Champagne emphasized that the region's chalks need the Tertiary sands, clays, and lignite to make its soils. The Turonian chalks of the Loire contain micas and the iron-rich mineral glauconite which weather with the calcium carbonate to produce excellent soils. Glauconite is a greenish, pellet-shaped, sand-size mineral of the mica family that is high in iron. But the seemingly innocuous calcium carbonate is a potentially toxic substance, as revealed in the study in 1978 of the Chinon vineyards by Jacky Dupont at the University of Poitiers in preparation for his thesis.

Variations in the chalk slope create shallow benches as sketched in Figure 8.4. The benches tend to "pond" water as well as accumulate soil (Zone B). The vineroots quite naturally seek this source of moisture, which, unfortunately, proves to be a near-fatal attraction. Typically, the water in these "ponds" contain concentrations of about 50 percent active calcium carbonate. These "ponds" are potentially "poisoned springs," as such concentrations are toxic, causing chlorosis – a yellowing of the leaves. The counter agent is iron, but the carbonate solution reacts aggressively with iron weathered from the glauconite. There is a constant battle between the iron compounds and a superior source of calcium carbonate. (This chemical "lock-out" was discussed in Part One, see Figure 1.2 and page 29.)

Chlorosis is widespread in the chalk terrain. Scientists at the Institut National de la Recherche Agronomique at Angers conduct ongoing research regarding chlorosis, soils, plants, and drainage. The results of this research are available to the growers.

Historical sketches of the wine provinces of the Loire

The early political history of the lower Loire was dominated by the competition between the powerful dukes of Touraine and Anjou.

Touraine was named for the Celtic tribe of Turones who occupied the area. The Celt's chief town became the Roman city of Caserodunum and later Tours. Probably the first establishment of Christianity in Gaul was in the 4th century when St. Gatien set up a monastery near Poitiers, south of Saumur. Soon afterwards, in 372, St. Martin founded his monastery at Marmoutier just outside Tours. Tours quickly became the center of Christianity in early Gaul.

St. Martin, the legendary patron of the vine, was originally a Roman soldier. In an abrupt change in faith, he was converted to Christianity. As a monk, then bishop of Tours, and eventually saint, he was revered for his exemplary leadership in faith and charity.

In the 6th century, Gregory of Tours was appointed Benedictine bishop for the region, emphasizing Tours as the religious center of France. Later, the city was the objective of the Moslem invasion from Spain, which Charles Martel, with a rag-tag army, turned back at Poitiers in 732. Safe from this anti-Christian and anti-wine threat, the monks had a glorious time choosing good vineyard sites in the delightful countryside of Touraine; many of these sites are the outstanding terroirs of today.

Peaceful, but only for a while. Early in the 9th century, the Vikings in their longboats came up the Loire plundering and sacking everything Christian. By one of those great ironies of history, the Vikings (later known as the Normans) ended up converted to the very Christianity they had sought to destroy.

After the Vikings, powerful lay lords of Touraine took over the religious administration and appointed laymen as abbots. Hugh Capet, one of the lay abbots, was elected king of France, commencing the Capetian dynasty. His surname was derived from the scarlet cape which he wore as abbot.

Anjou, named for the Celtic tribe of Andes, was created as a county in the 9th century as part of the effort to counter the Viking invasions. The siting of Juliomagnus of the Romans, today Angers, was selected for its commanding high ground on the Maine River, a short distance from the Loire.

The powerful Foulques family became the counts of Anjou. As a young duke of 14, Geoffrey, was married to the 29-year-old granddaughter of the Norman William the Conqueror. A son, Henry, took his father's nickname of Plantagenet as his surname.

Henry inherited Normandy, Anjou, Maine, and Touraine, more than two-thirds of the Capetian realm. With his marriage to Eleanor of Aquitaine, the young couple owned all of western France. The crown was reduced to a few undependable and not very rich duchies and counties. When Henry became king of England, the Plantagenets were to shape three centuries of French history and the fortunes of its wine. Aquitaine became, in effect, an English colony and the seeds were sown for the Hundred Years War. These relationships were developed in the chapters on the Aquitaine Basin and Bordeaux.

Unlike most of the English monarchy Henry and Eleanor, as well as their son, Richard the Lionheart are buried not at Westminster Abbey in London but, by their own request, at Fontevraud-L'Abbaye, southeast of Saumur.

Muscadet's history and an accident of climate account for its grapes being different from those of Touraine and Anjou. This "country of the sea," from the Celtic Ar-Mor, Armoricain was overrun in the 6th century with Briton-Celts expelled from Britain by the Anglo-Saxons. The area became known as Bretagne, Britannia, or Brittany. The stronghold today of these long-ago forced emigrants is the rugged Brittany peninsula.

In the 9th century, Brittany revolted against French influence and was for over 600 years an independent duchy. Rejoined to France in 1491 when Anne of Brittany married Charles VIII, the Pays Nantais region retained many Breton customs, architecture, and winemaking traditions. The Bretons also retained a strong attitude toward independence.

Soon after the French Revolution, the central government announced strict controls over the clergy and invoked universal conscription. The ensuing revolts were bloodily suppressed, a reaction which led to violent uprisings in the Vendée region, south of Nantes, and which to this day causes the people of the Pays Nantais, indeed all of the Brittany peninsula, to view Paris with considerable suspicion.

The wine districts

Touraine, Saumur, and Muscadet, the three principal wine areas of the lower Loire indicated on Figure 8.1, are also shown on the following pages as maps of their appellations. The first two are chalk provinces – part chalk, part "old rocks;" the last is wholly within the Massif Armoricain.

Touraine

The Cher and Indre hesitantly approach the Loire at tangents. This collection of valleys and divides gives Touraine an unusually large number of excellent vineyard sites. Of these eleven are special appellations: Vouvray, Montlouis (which are outstanding for white wines), Chinon, Bourgueil, and St.-Nicolas-de-Bourgueil (particularly for their red wines); Amboise, Azay-le-Rideau, Mesland, Jasnières, Coteaux du Loir (*note*, not Loire) and Cheverny.

Figure 8.5
The appellations of Touraine

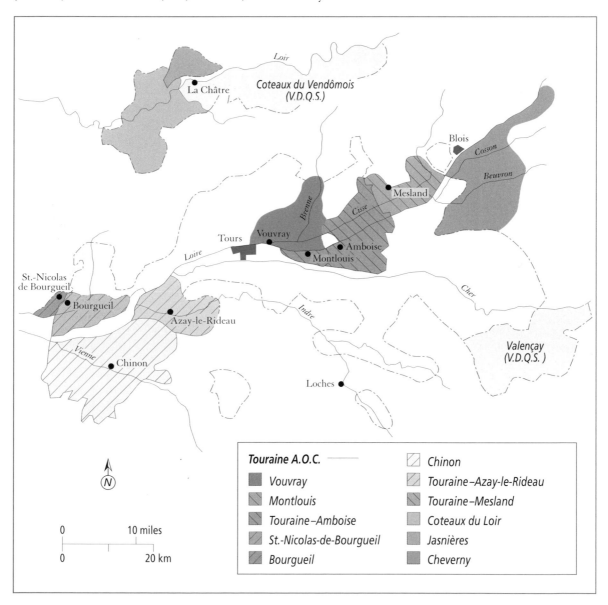

In the following sections the specific Touraine appellations have been grouped on the basis of geology and not according to their reputation.

Vouvray, Montlouis, and Amboise

These three adjacent appellations are geologic prototypes of Touraine chalk vineyards, *see* Figure 8.6. The preferred vineyard slopes (Figure 8.2 refers) are on yellow tuffeau and micaceous, argillaceous chalks. Erosional slopes of the soft but competent chalks vary from vertical cliffs to gentle, workable slopes. Many sheer faces along the valleys of the Cher and Indre form the facades of homes and wine cellars dug deep within the chalk. Temperature in these excavations is a constant 50°F (10°C), summer and winter – a little cool for comfort, but controlable.

Vouvray and Montlouis are cross-river neighbors, the Amboise vineyards are upsteam, on both sides of the Loire. The Brenne and other small lateral streams give Vouvray a large number of good slopes (*see* Color Plate 30). Tangential approach of the Cher toward the Loire gives Montlouis gentle slopes facing both rivers (*see* Figure 8.6). Splotches of wind-blown sand mix with the chalky soil improving the texture of the terroirs of the uplands. Vouvray and Montlouis each cultivate the Chenin Blanc and vinify their wines in the same way, yet experts note that the best of Vouvray are more full-bodied and vigorous than those of Montlouis. (The Montlouis vineyards are on less-favored slopes.) Vouvray has about 1000 growers with terroirs of less than 4 acres (1.5 ha). This means, of course, considerable variations in Vouvray wines.

Pierre Bréjoux makes an interesting observation that, despite precautions to avoid effervescence, Vouvray seems to have a predisposition to re-ferment in bottle. Although stored in a cool, deep cellar, at the first temperature rise in the spring, the wines have an uncanny tendency to develop bubbles. Is there something about wines born of chalky soils that have an innate tendency to fizz? Mr. Bréjoux also remarks that champagnes, being blends, do not recall their vineyards of birth, but the sparkling Vouvray proudly displays its Vouvray label.

Although the geology and terrain of all three appellations are similar, the exposures of Amboise are slightly less favorable and its white wines less well regarded than those of Vouvray and Montlouis. Amboise also produces red and rosé wines from the Cot (or Malbec), the Gamay, and some Cabernet Franc.

Figure 8.6
Cross-section of Loire Valley, Vouvray to Azay-sur-Cher
The nature of the Turonian formation serves wine in two important respects: on gentle slopes and plateaux its soils sustain excellent terroirs. Excavations in the soft rock of near-vertical faces are marvelous storage rooms and living quarters for modern "cave-dwellers"

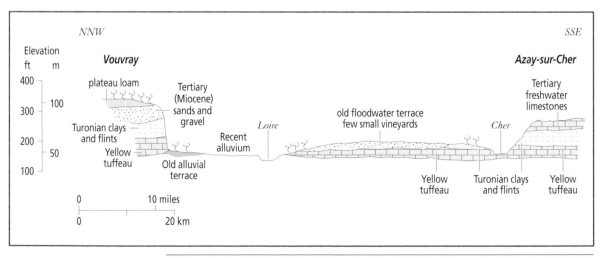

At an earlier time, Amboise wines were sold under the Vouvray name, but now growers like to associate their wines with the name of its famous château. Nearly all of the vineyards are in sight of the turrets and gables of Château d'Amboise. Commissioned by Charles VIII in the 15th century, this splendid château covers only about a tenth the size of the original property.

Chinon and Azay-le-Rideau

Although they emphasize different types of wines, the geology and terrain of these two appellations are similar. This time it is the Indre and Vienne that come to the Loire at a tangent with long, low divides and gentle slopes.

Chinon's red wines are fresh and light, said to resemble those of Bourgueil across the Loire. The comparison has some soil validity, although the geology is quite different. The chalky soils of Chinon are seasoned with sands of the overlying Sénonian (*see* Color Plate 31). This silicaceous component gives the red wines the distinctive character similar to the sandy, chalky terrace of Bourgueil. The Cabernet Franc is most at home here, producing light, claret-like wines the color of fresh raspberries which can age for 7–8 years.

Jacques Puisais, a research enologist in Tours, makes a most revealing observation. He says that wines of this area from the three different soils – chalky, gravel, and sandy terrains – do not taste as if they came from the same grape. A similar observation is made by Raymond Raifault of Domaine Raifault who says that wines from his properties in three different communes vary according to the soil on which they grow – the more full-bodied wines coming from sandy chalk soils.

Chinon is a picturesque medieval town, but unfortunately, its historic château is largely in ruins. It was here that Joan of Arc met the Dauphin and whence she started her epochal campaign to lift the siege of Orléans.

Chinon is also known for being the country of François Rabelais, physician, chemist, author, and paragon of wine to whom wine lovers everywhere pay homage. His identification with wine came naturally, as his birthplace, La Devinière, across the Vienne from Chinon, was surrounded by vineyards. Rabelais' appreciation of wine developed with his career. After first studying law, he became a Franciscan novice then priest, later to join the Benedictines. His tutors were masters of wine; his novels ever in praise of wine. A little of what Rabelais knew as *vin de taffetas* – white Chinon (from the Chenin Blanc) – is still made, and production is on the increase.

Azay-le-Rideau is a fragmented appellation of 125 acres (50 ha) in eight communes. The white wines are from the Chenin Blanc and rosés from the Grolleau. Azay-le-Rideau's fruity, dry to semi-dry whites are described as being akin to lesser Vouvrays.

The gravelly plateau between the Indre and Loire is covered by the forest of Villandry, former hunting preserve for the nobles of Château de Villandry. Around the perimeter of the plateau, the Sénonian–Turonian strata yield a variety of sandy and chalky soils.

South of the Indre, the chalky soils of Saché produce white wines of exceptional quality. Similarly, the yellow tuffeau soils near the famous fairy-tale château of Ussé produce excellent rosés.

It was in the village of Saché that Balzac wrote his classic, *Lily of the Valley* – inspired, no doubt, by the delightful Saché wines.

Bourgueil and St.-Nicolas-de-Bourgueil

During one of the Ice Age floods, the Loire etched out a crescent into the bank opposite Chinon and built a multi-level terrace. A wide terrace of Recent alluvium borders the river. A higher terrace of Quaternary sandy gravel contains lenses of sandy clay and glauconitic sand. Limestone pebbles and fragments make for well-drained soil. A goodly portion of the Bourgueil appellation occupies this terrain. Rising back of the Quaternary terrace is a chalk slope and a wooded scarp.

The village of St.-Nicolas-de-Bourgueil is on a spur, the original site of a Benedictine abbey founded in 999. The wooded plateau gives this crescent cove protection from the north winds and a beneficial microclimate to Bourgueil.

The vineyards of both Bourgueil and St.-Nicolas are about half and half on the chalk slopes and the Quaternary terrace. Experienced tasters can readily distinguish the "gravières wines" of the terrace from the "tuffeau wines" of the chalky slopes (*see* Color Plate 32). According to Pierre Bréjoux, wines from the Quaternary terrace develop their bouquet rapidly, while those from the tuffeau take about a year to develop their fruitiness. A blend of grapes from the two terrains is said to be superior to using either alone.

When appellations were being delimited in the mid-20th century, the story goes that the mayor of St.-Nicolas-de-Bourgueil, himself a large winegrower, persuaded the authorities to designate his commune as a separate appellation. Red wines of the Bourgueil appellations using the Cabernet Franc are often compared to those of Médoc, St.-Emilion, and Pomerol. Production of reds and rosés from these two terroirs is by a large number of small growers using traditional methods of vinification.

The remaining Touraine appellations

Mesland is one of Touraine's lesser appellations with sandy slopes and flinty clays of the Senonian. The uplands are covered with a thick mantle of Eocene sands and gravel with extensive woodlands and only scattered vineyards. The Gamay is the most successful grape for these soils and makes an excellent rosé.

Jasnières and Côteaux du Loir are about 25 miles (40 km) north of and parallel to the Loire and its vineyards. Their geology is the same. Vineyards are distributed along the slopes and hills bordering the River Loir (no final "e"). The Jasnières appellation is for white wines only; in Coteaux du Loir red and white wines are produced, with reds predominating. The nearby forest of Berce was the favorite hunting ground of Henry IV. The mellow Chenin Blanc of Jasnières was his favorite after-the-hunt beverage, and rightly so – the best may be compared to a Vouvray.

Three large V.D.Q.S. appellations complete the Touraine wine areas. Coteaux du Vendômois, adjacent to the Coteaux du Loir has little of the Turonian section exposed, and the soils are quite sandy. They produce mainly reds and rosés from the Pineau d'Aunis, and whites from Chenin Blanc, sometimes with a little Chardonnay in the blend.

On the southeast side of the Loire across from Blois and extending several miles eastward is the V.D.Q.S. sub-district of Cheverny, an appellation for both red and white wines. The reds use the Gamay, Pinot Noir, Cot, or Cabernet

Another monarch, René le Bon, often came through this area on his way to Provence so that he could enjoy the local hunting and wines. Of particular interest to him was a venerated relic of the "True Cross" in the chapel of the Abbey of la Baissière. The relic was a piece of oak, presumably from the crucifixion cross, that had been fashioned by Byzantine artisans into an upright with two cross pieces. A device resembling that cross, now known as the Lorraine Cross, became the heraldic symbol of the dukes of Anjou and the counts of Lorraine.

Sauvignon; the whites are made of Sauvignon and, uniquely in the Loire, Romorantin. The vineyards are on sparse outcrops of the Sénonian sandstones interspersed with Tertiary Miocene sands, clays, and freshwater limestones.

Sprawled across the rolling countryside from Cheverny south to the valley of the Cher are numerous vineyards of the general Touraine appellation. Further southeastward where several tributaries converge on the Cher is the Valençay appellation. The sandy, chalky, and flinty-clay soils of the Sénonian support quite acceptable red (Gamay) and white wines (Chenin Blanc and Sauvignon).

Saumur

Geologically, Saumur is a continuation of Touraine with two special appellations: Coteaux de Saumur, for sweet or more usually semi-sweet white wine, and Saumur-Champigny, for red wine. Historically, it was part of Anjou. In 1025, Foulques Nerra (Foulques the Black), the count of Anjou, "stole" Saumur from the count of Blois. Over the centuries, Saumur has had its own colorful history.

**Figure 8.7
The appellations
of Anjou–Saumur**

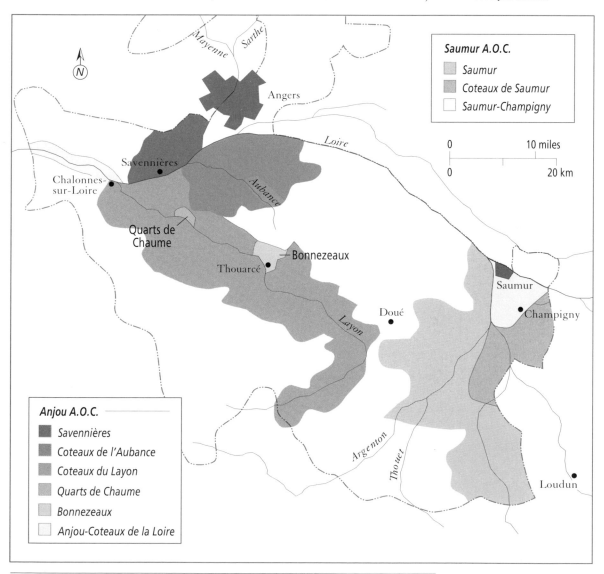

The Coteaux wines are made exclusively from the Chenin Blanc. Champigny produces the best of Saumur's red wines, grown on the chalk hills overlooking the Loire southeast of Saumur. The wines of the general appellation are simply Saumur Rouge and Saumur Blanc.

Saumur has long been noted for its sparkling wines, dating from very early in the 19th century. Sold at one time as a type of champagne, it is now labeled Saumur-Mousseux. White and rosé versions are made from several varieties of red and white grapes.

Slopes of the sandy chalk develop an unusual amount of active calcium carbonate "ponds" which, as in Chinon (*see* page 233), bedevil the Saumur vineyards with chlorosis. Sometimes, when there is excess acidity in the Chenin Blanc wine, some Chardonnay or Sauvignon is blended for added fruitiness. Sandy patches on the chalk, particularly in the Champigny area, make for a "hotter" soil which is preeminently favorable for the red Cabernet Franc.

The great château at Saumur is made doubly imposing by its location on the high cliff above the Loire. The château houses two excellent museums: one for decorative art containing medieval and Renaissance works; the other, the Riding Museum, has displays tracing the history of horseback riding. The latter was inspired by the legendary Cadre Noir, the cavalry school founded in 1814. Naturally, there is a Cadre Noir wine which is made by the *méthode traditionnelle* at Chacé in the south environs of Saumur. It is stored in immense chalk caves where it ages to perfection.

Saumur has its Veuve Amiot, with a history similar to that of Champagne's Veuve-Clicquot-Ponsardin – another young widow taking over a wine business and making a success of it.

Anjou

Anjou plays a crossover role in viticulture by having the same grapes on the chalk terrains of the Paris Basin and on the "old rocks" of the Massif Armoricain. However, the six special appellations are all on the "old rocks." The general appellation vineyards centering around Doué are on Cretaceous chalks and the Quaternary terrace at Bourgueil.

However it came about, the traditional grapes of Touraine and Saumur leaped the geologic boundary to the "old rocks" of the Massif Armoricain where they found the schistose soils of Anjou as much to their liking as the chalks. As I remarked earlier, however, the character of the wines from Anjou and Touraine-Saumur is decidedly different. In particular, the clayey, schistose soils develop a significant amount of tannin in the red wines. For the white wines, there is a verve given by the chalk soils of Touraine-Saumur.

The best of red wines come from Cabernet Franc with rosés being made from the Cabernet Sauvignon, Grolleau, Gamay, and Cot. Although the climate is mild, due to the increased absorption of heat by the dark soils of the "old rocks," the grapes prefer south or southwest exposures.

The special appellations of Anjou are: Savennières, Coteaux de l'Aubance, Coteaux du Layon, Bonnezeaux, Quarts de Chaume, and Coteaux de la Loire. In 1985, a new appellation, Anjou-Villages, was added – for red wines only. So far, 18 communes have been authorized for this new designation.

Savennières, a narrow appellation along the high, north bank of the Loire below Angers, produces excellent, fruity wines from the Chenin Blanc. Vines have been grown in the area for hundreds of years. Moreover, several domains and terroirs have been cultivated by the same family for many generations. Soils of the Savennières terroirs are weathered from a Paleozoic (Silurian) slatey schist with fragments of hard sandstone.

The tiny (17-acre/7-ha) La Coulée de Serrant is one of the most renowned terroirs of the Loire. A dry swale, the Coulée, separates Serrant from the larger Roche-aux-Moines (*see* Color Plate 33). Both of these Grands Crus were planted in the 11th century by the monks of St.-Nicolas-d'Angers.

Coteaux de l'Aubance is a continuation of the slate-like schist across the Loire from Savennières, but its wines are of far less renown. The Aubance winds its way through subdued, hilly terrain with vineyards planted on gentle slopes. Being off any main road, the wines of the area suffer from popular identity as well as by comparison in quality with those of the adjacent, better-known Coteaux du Layon.

This is a large appellation on an undulating plateau on both sides of the Layon. The river meanders back and forth along a major fault which originates far back in the Massif Armoricain. On the south side, Precambrian schists and coarse angular sandstones are faulted against Paleozoic Carboniferous schists and limestones on the north.

The Chenin Blanc vines prefer the southeast exposures on the north side of the Precambrian schists. A few vineyards are found on the plateau above the slopes on soils of the *faluns*, thick Miocene fossiliferous sands, but the better vineyards occur from the mid-course of the Layon near Thouarcé downstream to the Loire confluence. Lesser wines are found on the upper reaches of the Layon on ferruginous sands and marls of the Cretaceous.

In the early 19th century, a half-dozen communes along the Layon were informally recognized by name for the high quality of their wines. In the 1950s two of these, Bonnezeaux and Quarts de Chaume, were officially given special appellation status.

Bonnezeaux is a narrow zone along the Layon with several small lateral streams increasing the slope exposures. Soils of the multi-colored schists produce sweet wines exclusively from the Chenin Blanc. Quarts de Chaume is also exclusively from Chenin Blanc. This small appellation is in a horseshoe cove in the protection of low hills on the north and the Paleozoic limestone and schistose soils here are quite shallow. Mr. Michel Doucet of Château de la Guimonière told me he has to use a small charge of dynamite to loosen the bedrock before he is able to drive in stakes for training wires. The Cabernet Franc wines of Chaume have been praised over the years for their rich, fruity perfume and velvety, full-bodied texture, although only Chenin Blanc wines have Grand Cru status (*see* Color Plate 34). The vineyard gets its name from the early days when the lord rented the land on a quarter of the production, deciding which quarter of the vineyard he would take when he saw which was best at harvest time.

Coteaux de la Loire vineyards are found on both sides of the Loire downstream from Savennières where the steep slopes become workable. The soils are from "old rocks" of schist and limestones.

Just east of Angers is the slate quarry of Trélazé, in the Silurian schist. The quarry has been producing roofing slates since the 12th century, and still supplies nearly half of France's slate production.

Muscadet

Just below Ingrandes on the Loire, the Chenin Blanc and Cabernet Franc abruptly disappear, to be replaced by the Muscadet and other grapes. The reason is history, not geology. The abrupt change is the boundary between Anjou and the old province of Brittany, a land of different wine traditions.

During the 17th century Dutch traders persuaded the Bretons to begin growing the white Melon de Bourgogne or Muscadet to be distilled to brandy. Today the sprawling Muscadet appellation resembles a butterfly with spread wings, the city of Nantes being the head. Two "swallow tails" extend southward along the rivers Maine and Boulogne.

**Figure 8.8
The appellations
of Muscadet**

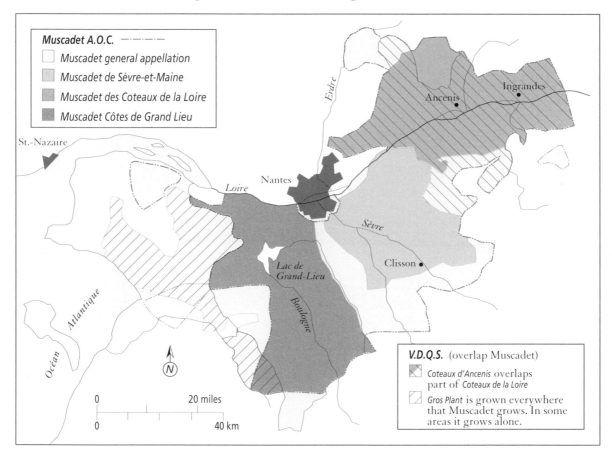

The district is a hodge-podge of appellations, many overlapping. There are, however, three special appellations: Muscadet de Sèvre et Maine, Muscadet des Coteaux de la Loire, and, most recent, Muscadet Côtes de Grand Lieu. Two V.D.Q.S. appellations, Coteaux d'Ancenis and Gros Plant du Pays Nantais, overlap all or parts of the general appellation around Ancenis, *see* Figure 8.8. A third V.D.Q.S. region, away near the Atlantic coast, is the Fiefs-Vendéens, centered on the town of Mareuil-sur-Lay. A surprising range of grapes is used in this small area to produce reds, whites, and rosés.

The "swallow tail" that is the region of Muscadet de Sèvre et Maine is situated on hilly terrain of granite where 90 percent of the Muscadet production is grown – including some of its best wines. Elevations of the hilly plateau range

By chance, the Marquis Robert de Goulaine of Château de Goulaine collects and breeds tropical butterflies as well as producing some of Muscadet's best wines.

from 250 to 300 feet (80–100 m). The soils are deep loams and clays developed from fine-grained granite (*see* Color Plate 35). The excellent soils of the uplands of Le Pallet near Clisson in the northeast of the region are weathered from gabbros, an ancient, dark volcanic rock, and produce a weightier style which contrasts the more delicate ones from the southwest of Sèvre et Maine.

Around the Lac de Grand Lieu, southwest of Nantes, is a vast undulating landscape with vineyards "as far as the eye can see." Some 600 acres (240 ha) of this area were designated A.O.C. in 1994. The Côtes de Grand-Lieu produce a fuller style Muscadet. Feeding the lake is the Boulogne River, one of the "swallow tails" of vineyards, including extensive vineyards of the Gros Plant which produces a high-acid wine.

If there was ever a seashore grape it is the Muscadet. Its very freshness suggests the sea. It rivals Chablis as the accompaniment to oysters – oysters harvested within sight of the Muscadet vines. Although excellent with shellfish, Muscadet is really a wine for any time – before, during, or after a meal. It is said that it is not necessary to be a connoisseur to appreciate the virtues of a Muscadet, just drink and enjoy it.

Wine Brotherhoods of the Loire

Nine wine co-fraternities are dedicated to spreading the word of Loire wines in various ways – wine fairs and holidays, appearances in their colorful costumes, etc. They extend their advocacy by selective induction of lovers of Loire wine from around the world. Names of some confréries are as intriguing as their costumes are colorful.

Vouvray's Confrérie des Chevaliers de la Chantpleure is patterned after the winemakers' societies of the Middle Ages, the name suggesting the squeak of the tap is a song of tearful joy.

The Confrérie des Chevaliers du Sacavin, based in Angers, is one of the oldest in France, dating from 1604. The name comes from the Sac à Vin, the barrel in the cellar handy to the tippler. Candidates at their invitation ceremonies swear to follow the example and philosophies of François Rabelais:

"Quand mon verre sera plein,	("When my glass is full,
je le videray.	I'll empty it.
Et quand il sera vide,	When it is empty
je le pleindray."	I'll feel sorry for it, I'll fill it.")

Les Entonneurs Rabelaisiens of Chinon is a prestigious group which also extols the philosophy of Rabelais and the fame of Chinon wines.

L'Ordre des Chevaliers Bretvins is the fourth oldest wine order in the world. It is dedicated to promoting the wines of the Nantais and to maintaining Breton folklore and traditions. The popularity of Muscadet helps in this promotion.

Epilogue

Countless visitors from over the world travel to see the châteaux of the Loire. The Route des Châteaux and Route du Vin in Touraine and Saumur are essentially coincident. The opportunities for "dégustation" are frequent. There is a wine for every taste and mood. The kings and nobles knew a good thing when they discovered the Loire. Learning the history and wines of the Loire is a pleasant and rewarding study.

9 The Kimmeridgian Chain: a band of chalky scarps

Like a set of nested dishes, the strata of the Paris Basin dip toward the center from all directions. The rim of one of these "dishes" along the southeastern part of the basin, the Kimmeridgian, is a remarkably uniform band of chalky marl, capped by a hard limestone called the Portlandian. For 200 miles (320 km), this classic cap-rock slope supports one wine area after another.

The wine areas are "islands" that are separated from the major regions with which they are traditionally associated: the Aube, 75 miles (120 km) southeast of the Marne Champagne; Chablis, the same distance north of the Côte d'Or; Pouilly-sur-Loire and Sancerre 80 miles (130 km) cross-country from Touraine-Anjou. Figure 9.1 outlines the geology and geography of this arc of wine islands.

Figure 9.1
General geology of the Kimmeridgian Chain
The Chablis and Sancerre–Pouilly-sur-Loire wine regions are mapped in greater detail as Figures 9.2 and 9.3

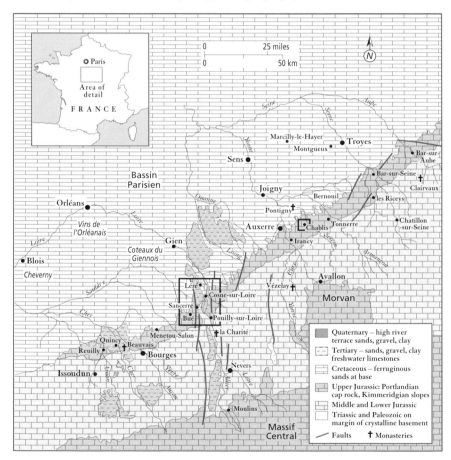

English names for French wine rocks
The British Isles are a part of the Euro-Asian landmass, and southeastern England was at one time an arm of the Paris Basin. Downwarping during the Ice Age allowed the North Sea to flood the land bridge that joined England and France. The English Channel thus severed the English arm of the Paris Basin.

The French geologist Alcide d'Orbigny, working in southern England in the mid-18th century, named the massive Jurassic limestone on the Isle of Portland, Dorset, the Portlandian. The Isle is not in fact an island but a pendant-like peninsula where limestones have been quarried since the Middle Ages.

Further eastward along the coast near Swanage, d'Orbigny named a dark marl below the Portlandian the Kimmeridgian. The marls in this area are petroliferous and when they were set fire by lightning or spontaneous combustion were known as the "burning cliffs."

The Kimmeridgian of France is relatively uniform chalky marl and thin marly limestone containing many lenses or banks of sea shells. The fossils and fragments of frost-shattered Portlandian help aerate the slopes and aid drainage. The marly soils develop good structure and water retention characteristics and are easily cultivated (*see* Color Plate 38). One of the fossils found in abundance is a small, comma-shaped oyster, *Exogyra virgula* (*see* Color Plate 39); *virgule* being French for comma. In the Aube region, the abundance of the oyster in the upper Kimmeridgian gives it the name "Virgulien."

The making of the archipelago

The Cretaceous and Jurassic strata were deposited in widespread seas. Sagging of the central Paris Basin during the late Tertiary and Quaternary allowed erosion to fashion the concentric bands of ridges and plains illustrated in the Champagne chapter (Figure 2.2, page 66). The stream courses of the Seine, Aube, Yonne, and Loire were well established before the Paris Basin began to sag. The tilting was sufficiently slow for the rivers to be able to downcut through the rising ridges, much the way a buzz saw "eats" into a board. The rivers thus cut the Kimmeridgian-Portlandian outcrop band into an archipelago of wine areas. Our discussion of the islands of the chain starts with the Aube and proceeds westward along the arc.

The Aube

Unjustly or not, the Aube bears the stigma of the *deuxième zone* of Champagne, a status largely brought on by the Aube's persistence at being included in *Champagne Viticole*. The controversy goes back before World War I when delimitation was being developed. Marne Champagne wanted to exclude the Aube, saying its soils were different – which is true. The Champenois of the Marne also claimed the Aube grapes did not participate in the development of champagne's reputation – which may have been the case. The Aube's contention was based on history, pointing out that Aube was part of the original county of Champagne and Troyes its first capital. Aube is now officially a part of Champagne, but, philosophically, not as a full partner. We offer here the Aube a home as a charter member of the Kimmeridgian Chain which is geologically where it belongs.

The Aube vineyards are on Kimmeridgian slopes of lateral streams of the Aube and Seine. The principal wine towns are Bar-sur-Aube and Bar-sur-Seine. The word "bar" is thought to be of Celtic or Gallo-Roman origin, meaning a height or promontory. Evidently the term indicates the portals or gateways where the two rivers cut through the massive Portlandian limestone.

The cap rock of the Kimmeridgian Chain has an impressive English pedigree. Sir Christopher Wren selected this stone for London's St.-Paul's Cathedral; it was the building stone for Westminster Abbey and Salisbury Cathedral. Along the Dorset coast, the massive limestone forms some of Europe's most spectacular coastal scenery.

The formations dip at a very low angle into the Paris Basin so that their erosional pattern is quite intricate. When I visited the Aube, the mayor of Colombé-le-Sec showed me the commune cadastre (land maps). Although the outcrops are very irregular, the Portlandian–Kimmeridgian contact on my geologic map coincided precisely with the appellation boundary – wine on the appropriate rocks.

It is reported that the chalky marls of the Jurassic Kimmeridgian do yield a wine of different character from the same grapes as wine from the Cretaceous chalk–Tertiary clastics combination of the Marne. Wines of the Aube tend to be a bit more golden (like Chablis), and the taste of the grape a bit more forward.

Under the *échelle des crus* classification (*see* page 73) the Aube communes rate a patronizing 80 percent – almost no market exists for grapes 75 percent or below. One wonders whether the Aube might have achieved a renown of its own similar to Chablis had it worked as hard at developing its own identity and style of wine rather than trying to join a family that clearly did not want it.

Despite all the controversy, the Aube is not without good credentials to its claim as an ancient wine area. In the 11th century, Count Thibaut IV of Blois designated the city of Troyes as the capital of the new county of Champagne. Fairs held in various towns attracted merchants from throughout western Europe. The red and white still wines of the Aube as well as those of the Marne regions became widely known – long before Dom Pérignon and fizzy wines.

In the 12th century, the Abbot Bernard (later St.-Bernard) from Burgundy founded his abbey, Clairvaux (clear valley). Bernard selected for his site the valley of the River Absinthe (meaning wormwood), south of Bar-sur-Aube. Quite understandably, the name Absinthe was later changed to Vallon de St.-Bernard. In addition to its apostolic work, the abbey became a great center of learning. Over 4,000 volumes from Clairvaux are preserved in the library at Troyes.

Whether or not it was the monks of Clairvaux who introduced the Pinot Noir, it currently comprises about 80 percent of the Aube planting. There is, however, little wine made into champagne in the Aube, most of it being sent to Reims or Epernay to be processed and blended by the major houses. One compelling reason for this is that there are no great chalk caverns and storage tunnels in the Aube as there are in the Cretaceous chalk.

Sometime in the distant past, Les Riceys built its fame on its "Rosé des Riceys," a very perfumed, still wine with a "nutty" flavor made from 100 percent Pinot Noir. It can only be made in the best, very ripe vintages – just three times in the past 15 years. The principal producer is the grower family of Alexandre Bonnet. Wine not used for Rosé des Riceys is used in the production of a very good, pink sparkling wine.

Ricey's vineyards lie along a ridge of Kimmeridgian southwest of Bar-sur-Seine overlooking a clutch of Les Riceys' hamlets along the little Saignes River.

Tonnerre-Epineuil

The road from Les Riceys westward to Tonnerre runs along the foot of the Kimmeridgian slope. In pre-phylloxera times, it was almost a continuous strip of vineyards. Now there is only the odd vineyard or two. At the Armançon River opposite Tonnerre, the outcrop band of Kimmeridgian opens into broad noses below the wine village of Epineuil.

The name Epineuil derives from *épine,* meaning thorn or prickle. Evidently in the early days, the "sticker-bushes" competed with grapevines for occupancy of the hillslope. Vineyards of the Epineuil area are Damnots, Côtes de Grisey, Les Fauconniers (the falconers), and Les Froherts (old French for *grillon,* "cricket").

The monks were quite involved in early-day development of viticulture in the area. The abbey of Môlesme, which the Abbot Robert left to found Cîteaux, built Petit Môlesme at Epineuil as a dormitory for its vignerons. The abbey of Quincy, from the distant Bourges area, also had a dormitory, Petit Quincy, which still stands on the northwest outskirts of Epineuil.

Patiently, the good Kimmeridgian soils waited for 100 years after the phylloxera devastation for rediscovery. It came in the form of André Durand, a former teacher and mayor of Epineuil. He and the mayor of Tonnerre, a former Minister of Agriculture, brought in outside capital and stimulated local pride in restoration of the region. Since around 1960 they have vigorously urged a policy of replanting with Pinot Noir and Chardonnay on the excellent Kimmeridgian sites south of Tonnerre and on the hillsides around Epineuil. The project is well along and more will be heard of Tonnerre in the future.

Bernouil, 5 miles (8 km) north of Tonnerre, is something of a viticultural relic. The village lies wholly within the sandy outcrops of the Lower Cretaceous. It is a known fact that phylloxera does not thrive in sandy soils. Consequently, phylloxera never got fully established at Bernouil. According to Rosemary George MW, the vines are not grafted but are growing on their own roots.

Chablis

Chablis is the "big island" of the Kimmeridgian Chain. Situated about half way between Paris and Beaune, a few miles east of the Autoroute du Soleil, the village is rather drab as wine villages go. But it is chief town of one of the most popular and most imitated wines in the world.

What makes Chablis so well known and highly regarded? To begin with, the Chardonnay, the grape of Chablis, is a perfect fit with the chalky marls of the Kimmeridgian. The crisp, greenish-gold wine is characterized by the distinct flavor of that grape.

Given that a good wine justifies itself, the popularity of Chablis may also be partially due to the simplicity of its name – short and easy to pronounce in most any tongue. This was sheer good fortune. What if the name had been, say, Auxerre? (The "x" has an "s" sound.) The simplicity of the Chablis name has also been a factor in the ease of imitation. As we shall see, earning a good reputation is one thing, protecting it is quite another.

There are seven Grands Crus "climats," about a dozen and a half Premiers Crus, and very many commune grade Chablis. (*Climat* is a term used especially in Burgundy referring to a specific vineyard.) The roughly circular appellation is bisected by the Serein, a lazy, gentle stream, perfect for picnics and fly fishing. Drainage, largely by intermittent waterways, has eroded the low-dipping strata into an intricate pattern of slopes and ridges (*see* Figure 9.2).

Facing the town of Chablis on the north side of the Serein is a classic cap-rock cuesta slightly over a mile long. This is the Grand Cru slope of Chablis. The inset map on Figure 9.2 and Color Plate 36 identify the seven *climats* of this

For several centuries, the Tonnerre area enjoyed active winegrowing, but then Tonnerre is not the vigorous wine town that it was in the 16th century when it was ravaged by fire, leaving only a few of its buildings standing. The hospital, a survivor of the fire, had been founded in 1293 by the Countess Marguerite, a native of Burgundy and widow of Charles, Count of Anjou. The Hôtel-Dieu (hospital) in Beaune, built 150 years later, has a ward-chapel ("Room of the Poor") that is an almost exact duplicate of the one in Tonnerre. Both hospitals are now museums, but due to their locations, Tonnerre sees few visitors, while the one at Beaune receives thousands each year.

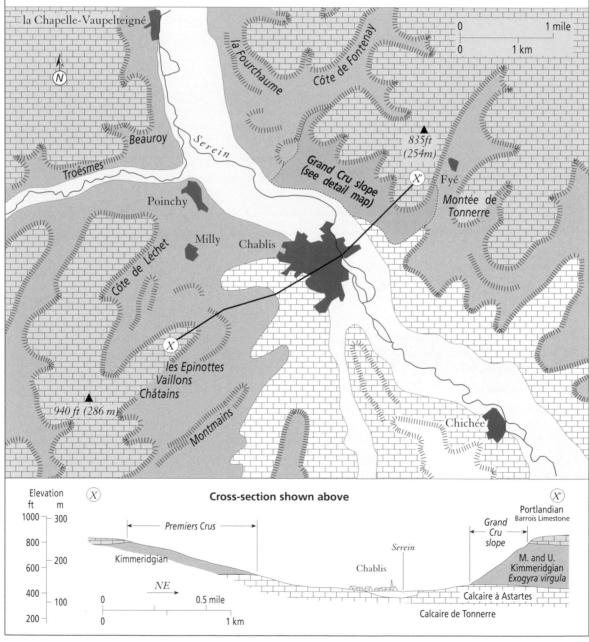

Figure 9.2
General geology and cross-section of Chablis
(after Tonnerre Sheet no. 97, 1966, by kind permission of Service de la Carte Géologique)

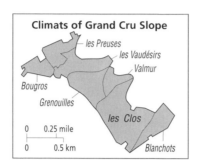

Climats of Grand Cru Slope

les Preuses
les Vaudésirs
Valmur
Bougros
Grenouilles
les Clos
Blanchots

0   0.25 mile
0   0.5 km

Portlandian – Calcaire de Barrois
Kimmeridgian
Calcaire à Astartes
Calcaire de Tonnerre
River alluvium

Climats are specifically named vineyards; it is the slope that is classified Grand Cru. Select Premiers Crus are shown by name on the map.

la Chapelle-Vaupelteigné

la Fourchaume

Côte de Fontenay

N

Beauroy

Serein

Troêsmes

835ft (254m)

Poinchy

X'

Fyé

Montée de Tonnerre

Milly

Chablis

Côte de Léchet

X

les Epinottes

Vaillons

Châtains

Chichée

940 ft (286 m)

Montmains

0   1 mile
0   1 km

Cross-section shown above

Elevation
ft   m

1000 — 300

800 — 200

600 —

400 — 100

200 —

X

Premiers Crus

Kimmeridgian

NE

0   0.5 mile
0   1 km

Serein

Chablis

Calcaire à Astartes

Calcaire de Tonnerre

Grand Cru slope

Portlandian
Barrois Limestone

M. and U. Kimmeridgian
Exogyra virgula

X'

Grand Cru slope. The total area of the Grand Cru slope is 245 acres (100 ha), with Les Clos the largest at about 55 acres (22 ha). The Chablis *climats* are erroneously referred to as "Grands Crus," but technically it was the geologic slope that was classified Grand Cru, not the individual terroirs. A minor matter, perhaps which the labels do nothing to clarify. For example, you may see: CHABLIS GRAND CRU "Les Clos."

A relic of early-day ownerships on the Grand Cru slope is the estate of La Moutonne. Although officially a *climat*, its wines are never found on the shelves of wine shops for the simple reason that no wine is produced under that label. Its 6 acres (2.4 ha) of vines are harvested, vinified, and the wine marketed with Les Preuses and Vaudésir.

Geologic conditions identical to the Grand Cru slope extend both northwest and southeast as shown in Figure 9.2, but the vineyards are classified only Premiers Crus. Experts are of the opinion that Premiers Crus such as Montée de Tonnerre, Mont de Milieu, and Fourchaume are every bit as good as those of the Grand Cru slope (*see* Color Plate 37).

On the opposite side of the Serein, long, Portlandian-capped finger-ridges extend northwestward. On the sunny, southeast side of the ridges are found the noted Premiers Crus of Côte de Léchet, Vaillons (Les Lys), Beauroy and Montmains (sometimes rendered as Monts Mains). The shady sides of the ridges support only sparse vineyards interspersed with other crops and woods.

It is not clear when vines were first brought to Chablis, but in the 9th century monks from St.-Martin of Tours cultivated vines in the area. During the 12th century the Cistercians of the abbey of Pontigny transacted for about 50 acres (20 ha) for winegrowing in the area. They also obtained a building known as Le Petit Pontigny which served as a press room, dormitory, and religious house. The little nondescript house still stands in Chablis. The ecclesiastical presence was important, but according to Professor Gérald Gilbank, by the end of the Middle Ages, the vineyards of Chablis were largely in the hands of local families, many of whose ownerships persist to this day.

Chablis grape varieties

With all the ruckus about what is a true Chablis, there is no question about the Chardonnay being the true grape. It is the exclusive, authorized variety for the Chablis appellation. Known locally as the Beaunois, the synonym suggests that the vine was probably brought from the Côte d'Or (Beaune), where it does so well on the calcareous marly soils of the Jurassic that is somewhat older than the Kimmeridgian. Other varieties are permitted adjacent to the Petit Chablis appellation, but they are looked upon by Chablis purists as misbegotten grapes.

The high-producing Sacy (or Tresallier) variety in earlier days competed with the noble Chardonnay – indeed almost usurped Chardonnay from the Chablis vineyards at the beginning of the 20th century. Sacy was presumably brought from Italy in the 13th century and adopted its name from a village south of the main Chablis area. Because of its high acidity, the Sacy is an important component in sparkling wine.

Whatever the grape or geologic formation, the vineyards of the Chablis region must contend with late frosts that are a constant threat.

Feuding about the true Chablis

Today Chablis is the most imitated white wine abroad and is the root of controversy at home. As early as the 19th century, it became imperative for the Chablis growers to protect a well-earned reputation by defining exactly what was Chablis. Far easier said than done.

The conflicts and problems in defining the true Chablis appellation read like feuds over fencing and water rights in the early American West rather than a classic French wine region. (So far there has been no shooting.) At the heart of the problem is the geology of the Kimmeridgian and Portlandian.

Although not precisely charted before the mid-19th century, the viticultural zones of Chablis were unofficially considered coincident with the outcrop of the Kimmeridgian. More specifically, what was thought to be easily and clearly identified was the geologic contact between the soft Kimmeridgian marl and the hard Portlandian cap rock. Geology became the problem when it was discovered that some wines being sold as Chablis actually came from marly beds inside the Portlandian outcrop. The marly "inlier" resembled the Kimmeridgian, but was it really that formation?

Such a stratigraphic anomaly is a fairly common phenomenon for near-shore deposition. Shifting shorelines create an interfingering of different facies. Throughout much of the Kimmeridgian Chain, the contact is clear-cut between the massive Portlandian limestone and the Kimmeridgian marl. This holds across most of Chablis, but apparently there was some interfingering of deposition.

In a seemingly brilliant and simple compromise solution of the "renegade Kimmeridgian" problem, it was agreed to delimit Chablis to the Kimmeridgian outcrop as would be defined by geology experts. But to everyone's dismay, the experts couldn't agree as to just where on the ground to draw the boundary.

A succession of commissions, syndicates, tribunals, and legislatures proposed various other definitions and delimitations for Chablis, but all proved to be deficient in one way or another. One proposal held that there should be no right to the name Chablis unless production had been by "loyal, constant, and local usage." Although the vineyards on the Kimmeridgian "inlier" fit the criteria, this solution was not acceptable to the "purists." Another proposal was to make historical plantation of the Chardonnay a qualifying condition. This sounded fine, until it was pointed out that some "true" Kimmeridgian vineyards had long been planted with the Sacy grape. If location on "true" Kimmeridgian was a prerequisite, would not those Sacy vineyards be Chablis? Again unacceptable, as the prolific, white Sacy produces a coarse wine – certainly not Chablis.

In one effort at compromise in 1923, the Tonnerre tribunal introduced the term Petit Chablis to cover all wine produced from the Chardonnay, but on soil other than Kimmeridgian. At first, this seemed like an acceptable solution, but here again, the limits of the Kimmeridgian were still in dispute. Neither legislation nor decree could make precise that which was geologically imprecise. Nevertheless, there are a surprising number of Petit Chablis vineyards identified on wine maps.

A one-man "posse" seeking to bring to justice violators of *les vrais Chablis* is William Fèvre. His rallying cry is "Kimmeridge forever!" In a well-documented pamphlet, Mr. Fèvre argues with fervor about the *les vrais* (true) Chablis and *les autres* (the others). Mr. Fèvre is the largest owner of vines on the Chablis Grand Cru slope. He condemns "abusive extensions of its [Chablis'] terroirs and usurpations of its name."

While the problem remains unresolved, entrepreneurs continue to create new sites within the current appellation that are questionably suitable as an honest-to-goodness Chablis. For buyers of "Chablis" from other than the seven *climats* of the Grand Cru slope or the Premiers Crus, *caveat emptor.*

Chablis, the frost capital

For some, not-very-evident reason, the pleasant little Serein River is notorious as "frost valley." Possibly it is cold air from the Barrois plateau that drains into the valley. In eight out of the twenty years immediately following the end of World War II, frost destruction was widespread in the Chablis vineyards. During the 1960s, however, overhead sprinkler systems began to be installed which helped to minimize frost threat.

An example of what can happen to vineyards weather-wise occurred in the spring of 1989 when night-time temperatures suddenly dropped into the mid-range of 20°F (about –4°C), affecting some 15 percent of the area. Hardest hit were the Premiers Crus located on the northerly-oriented finger ridges. The south-facing Grand Cru slope escaped damage, perhaps with the help of the spray system then in use in most of those vineyards. (The explanation of how the spray system protects the young buds is given on page 41.)

For frost protection, smoke pots or *chaufferettes* are still in use in a number of vineyards. About 100 *chaufferettes* are required per acre, and the expense of upkeep as well as initial cost is fairly high. These small heaters burn fuel oil and have to be lit by hand when there is threat of frost. This means in 1992, an operating cost in labor and fuel at about 1000 francs per acre per night or $180. Jet heaters are more effective than smoke pots, since they can be rotated and moved from place to place, but the capital cost for the equipment is also high.

The water spray method is being used more and more in Chablis, as it is not only the most reliable but the cheapest to operate: 50 acres (20 ha) can be sprayed at the same cost as one acre protected by smoke pots. However, the inevitable drawback is the significant capital investment required. Fortunately, Chablis has a cooperative for equipment installation and water supply, which reduce costs appreciably. The problem is getting all owners in a vineyard to participate.

Auxerre and the Yonne Valley

Auxerre is more noted today for its cathedral of St.-Etienne, its shady boulevards, and view of the Yonne Valley than as a wine town. But in the days before the railroads, it was the shipping port for wines of Chablis, Tonnerre, and the Yonne Valley. From Auxerre the wine shipments went downstream into the Seine, on to Paris, Rouen, and markets overseas. In the past, the river sometimes outdid itself in its eagerness to carry wine. There is the account that in 846, a sudden flood inundated the quay at Auxerre, floating barrels of wine to unscheduled points downriver.

The famed "sea of vines," which in the Middle Ages surrounded Auxerre, did not survive phylloxera. As most of the Auxerrois vineyards were on shallow soils of the Portlandian *Calcaire du Barrois*, they were replaced by orchards. Today only La Chainette and Clos de Migraine survive, neither on the Kimmeridgian. Clos de Migraine grows on Lower Cretaceous marls overlying the Portlandian; La Chainette is on an alluvial terrace of limestone pebbles and sand. Survival of the tiny La Chainette is undoubtedly due to its belonging to the Hôpital Psychiatrique de l'Yonne since soon after the Revolution.

Auxerre was already an important town when Clovis conquered it early in the 6th century. It was here that his Queen Clotilde – Burgundian princess and a Christian – established the Benedictine abbey of St.-Germain. Famed as a center of theology, the abbey counted among its students one who became the celebrated St.-Patrick of Ireland and another who became Pope Urban V. Only the abbey church, crypt, and conventional buildings, including the 14th-century wine cellar, remain of the original abbey. Auxerre's magnificent cathedral of St.-Etienne (St.-Stephen) was constructed between the 13th and 16th centuries using Portlandian limestone.

Roger Dion, the eminent wine historian, quotes a document from 680 in which the Bishop of Auxerre praises the wines of the Clos de Migraine. Sheltered among the buildings, the vineyard enjoys this man-made microclimate. It has often been said that migraine does not seem a very good advertisement for wine. Perhaps this wine was once prescribed as an antidote for such severe headache.

Other isles of the Yonne Valley

On either side of the Yonne, south of Auxerre, the Kimmeridgian outcrops in ridges and leaf-shaped basins. Southwest of Chablis between the Autoroute du Soleil and the Yonne are clustered the wine communes of Chitry, St.-Bris-le-Vineux, and Irancy. These areas have not become embroiled in the Chablis controversy but have kept about their own business. That business is rosés and red wines for Irancy and white wines for Chitry and St.-Bris.

Chitry is planted primarily with the Aligoté, but also Sacy, Chardonnay, and Sauvignon. Its white wines go mostly to the S.I.C.A.V.A. for making Crémant de Bourgogne. St.-Bris-le-Vineux, a very old wine town, lies in a stellate-shaped basin, pimpled with small, rounded Portlandian-capped hills. An assortment of grapes grow on these hillocks: Chardonnay, Sacy, Pinot Noir, Gamay, and the local César. A large number of small growers, in their own traditional family ways, produce several styles of wines. Of particular note is St.-Bris Aligoté regarded by some connoisseurs as rivaling that of Burgundy's Hautes Côtes.

Irancy is an amphitheater almost a mile across (*see* Color Plate 40). Aided by a favorable microclimate, Irancy produces some exceptional red wines from the Pinot Noir which are often blended with César and Tressot. Its most famous terroir is Palotte overlooking the Yonne. The wine styles of different growers vary with the amount of César used, which imparts high tannin and a deep color.

From the devastation of phylloxera, until after World War II, the vineyards of Irancy suffered serious neglect. But soon after the war, vineyards were systematically replanted with Pinot Noir; these efforts were rewarded with Irancy being given its own appellation in 1977.

One of Irancy's native sons, Jacques Germain Soufflot, is famous for having designed the Panthéon and the Hôtel de Ville in Paris. Soufflot honored his hometown by designing its parish church.

The vineyards of Coulanges-la-Vineuse lie along a Kimmeridgian slope facing Irancy across the Yonne. This commune is re-establishing its once fine reputation by emphasizing red wines from the Pinot Noir.

South of Coulanges and west of Avallon on a prominent hill overlooking the Cure Valley is Vézelay with its imposing basilica of Ste.-Marie Madeleine. Vines once covered the entire valley, but phylloxera and depopulation of the rural area all but spelled the end of viticulture in this area. For the past 20 years, however, it has been undergoing a slow but steady revival.

Joigny, 15 miles (24 km) down the Yonne from Auxerre, was in pre-phylloxera days an active winegrowing and shipping center. Today, only the small, 10-acre (4-ha) terroir of Côte St.-Jacques is in operation. Slope wash from a cap rock of Tertiary sands, gravel, and clays make a good soil mix with the underlying Cretaceous chalk. Although classed only Appellation Bourgogne, the label for its red and rosé wines is authorized to carry the name Côte St.-Jacques as a concession to its venerable history.

Westard from the Yonne to the Loire, there are no streams, no Portlandian scarp, and hence no vineyards. The undulating terrain is given to large field cultivation and the raising of cattle. This 35-mile (56-km) gap in the island chain separates two viticultural traditions – the Chardonnay and Pinot Noir to the east and the Sauvignon Blanc to the west.

The acronym is for the Société d'Intérêt Collectif Agricole du Vignoble Auxerrois. They are the exclusive makers and marketers of Crémant de Bourgogne in Auxerre.

Foundation of the abbey at Vézelay was consecrated in 878 by Pope John VIII, and St.-Bernard preached the Second Crusade there in 1146. A column of the basilica features Adam and Eve and the serpent. Eve is being tempted, not with an apple, but a bunch of grapes.

Pouilly-sur-Loire

The Portlandian and Kimmeridgian cuestas are exposed in a complex of faulting and overlapping deposition at the Loire, *see* Figure 9.3. The northward courses of the rivers Loire and Allier from deep within the Massif Central are guided by a rift system. Faulting apparently lowered the east bank of the Loire, preserving remnants of the Tertiary and Quaternary. These deposits cover portions of flat-lying Portlandian and Kimmeridgian. A long fault-block ridge in the Loire Valley is crowned by the town of Sancerre.

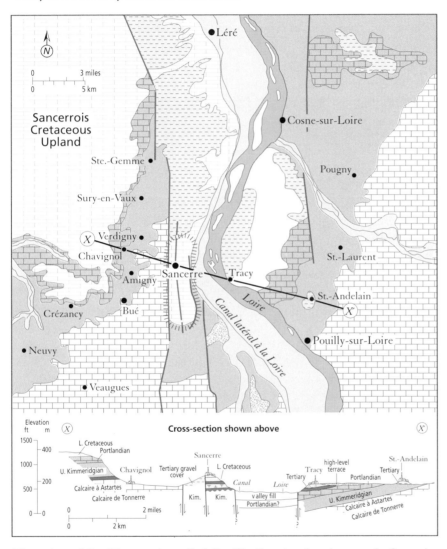

Figure 9.3
General geology of Sancerre–Pouilly-sur-Loire and cross-section of Sancerre
(after Bourges Sheet no. 18, 1968, by kind permission of Service de la Carte Géologique)

The wine of Pouilly may be called Pouilly-Fumé only when made from the Sauvignon Blanc. It is named *fumé*, French for smoked, which describes the characteristic "flinty" flavor of the Sauvignon Blanc grown in Pouilly. It is a pale, fresh, clean wine with a fruity bouquet. The variety of soils in Pouilly gives individual personality and character to its wines.

The typical Kimmeridgian slope has been altered by the faulting, so that the strata essentially lie flat. Just north of Pouilly is the 25-acre (10-ha) Château du Nozet, owned by Domaine de Ladoucette. The domaine also has vineyards in

Sancerre, Vouvray, Muscadet, and Chablis. The energetic and innovative Baron Patrick de Ladoucette uses a helicopter to run the widely separated properties.

St.-Andelain occupies a low hill of Kimmeridgian crowned by lower Tertiary strata whose flints, sands, and gravel mix with the chalky slopes to give St.-Andelain one of Pouilly's better vineyards. Further along the east bank of the Loire on patches of Tertiary sandy clays and Quaternary terrace conglomerates are the vineyards of Les Loges (*see* Color Plate 41), Côtes des Girames, and Tracy.

The better terroirs of Pouilly are always found where the calcareous Kimmeridgian is involved and planted to the Sauvignon. The old high-level river terraces, being more silicaceous (sandy), usually carry the Chasselas. Although a very old variety, the Chasselas has never come close to grape nobility. Locally, however, it is popular as a summer wine to be drunk young. Its plantation is diminishing, but the locals feel there will always be a place for the Chasselas in those areas where the Sauvignon does not do so well.

Wines of the big bend

Although not Kimmeridgian, the orphaned vineyards along the Loire from Cosne to below Orléans are included in the chain. Downstream from Cosne, the Kimmeridgian disappears under Cretaceous, Tertiary, and Quaternary strata. Soils are mostly sandy, and the Coteaux du Giennois and Vins de l'Orléanais are only mediocre quality. Production is from Pinots Noir and Meunier, Gamay, Cabernet Franc, Sauvignon, and Chardonnay, vinified entirely by cooperatives.

Before modern transportation, wines of Sancerre and Pouilly-sur-Loire had to compete with the down-river wines of Touraine-Anjou. Wines from above Orléans were often delayed by shipping disputes for such long periods that the wines turned to vinegar. Thus Orléans became the vinegar capital of France.

Sancerre

Sancerre is a sister wine to Pouilly-Fumé, but its bright crispness and floral bouquet contrast the "flinty" aftertaste of the Fumé from Pouilly-sur-Loire.

The town of Sancerre is perched on the summit of the central valley fault block (*see* Color Plate 42). Since Roman times, this hill-town has been of strategic importance, offering observation of the Loire Valley in all directions. A fault along the spine of the ridge places brush-covered gravel slopes on the west against Cretaceous and Kimmeridgian on the east. Vineyards on the east side are reasonably good, but Sancerre's quality vineyards are on classic Portlandian–Kimmeridgian slopes along the west side of the valley. The Portlandian has become thinner but, fortunately, ferruginous sandstones of the basal Cretaceous reinforce the cap rock. Weathering of the sandstones also contributes iron to the slope soils. The iron content may be a contributing factor to the smoky or flinty taste in Pouilly as well as Sancerre. In Pouilly, most of the ferruginous sandstones have been removed by erosion, but the iron may be residual in the soil.

The Kimmeridgian has developed three lithologic zones. The uppermost, known locally as the St.-Doulchard marl, weathers into the distinctive *terres blanches* (white earth). The St.-Doulchard, correlative with the Virgulien marl of the Aube, also contains numerous lenses of the comma-shaped oyster, *Exogyra virgula*. Intermittently, near the base of this zone, are thin beds of glauconite, a granular mica, rich in iron. (Recall that iron is most important in counteracting chlorosis, yellowing of leaves, common to plants grown in very calcareous soils.) Below the St.-Doulchard is the *Calcaire à Astartes*, a zone named for its fossil clam, *Astartes*. Astarte was the Phoenician goddess of love and fertility. Perhaps d'Orbigny, who named the Kimmeridgian, chose the name because of the vast reproduction of these bivalves as evidenced by the numerous banks of shells.

The *Calcaire de Tonnerre* at its type locality around Tonnerre is a very hard limestone. In Sancerre, the Tonnerre has become soft and porous – so vesicular (sponge-like), in fact, that it has been erroneously called a lava. The Astartes and Tonnerre limestones weather in combination to form a pebbly, calcareous soil known as *caillottes* (pebbles). Some Sancerre experts make much of the difference between wines grown on *terres blanches* and the *caillottes*. Wines of the former are generally judged to be fruitier and more delicate than the more robust and full-bodied wines from the *caillottes*.

From the commune of Ste.-Gemme-en-Sancerrois, northernmost of the Sancerre communes, the scarp of the western plateau curves southwest through Sury-en-Vaux and the celebrated communes of Verdigny, Amigny, Bué and Crézancy-en-Sancerre.

Bué is perhaps the better known of the Sancerre communes with its famous Clos du Chêne Marchand located on the *caillottes*. A companion terroir, Clos de la Poussie, originally belonging to the monks of the Abbey of Bué, is located partially on the *caillottes* and on the *terres blanches*. These Bué vineyards occupy a narrow cirque, where the upper slopes of *terres blanches* reach angles of 20–30 degrees. There is no terracing, and the vineyards were laboriously worked by hand until World War I when they were abandoned to acacia trees.

The Sancerre wines of Bué have many ardent admirers, among them Pierre Bréjoux, who observed that there are some Bué wines for which "one would like to have a throat as long as a swan's neck so as to taste them better." Other *terres blanches* terroirs of good reputation are Côte de Champtin, Clos du Roi, La Côte at Verdigny, Les Monts Damnés of Chavignol, and La Grande Côte of Amigny.

Although the "caillottes" of Amigny, Chavignol, and Verdigny produce wines of fine bouquet, they fade quickly. Grapes from the "caillottes" and the *terres blanches* are vinified together, resulting in a wine reputed to be superior to that from either soil alone. Sancerre's reputation was made on its white wine, but the rosé and red wines made from the Pinot Noir are also entitled to the appellation. With the better terroirs are planted to Sauvignon, the Pinot Noir is usually relegated to soils that do not bring out the best of its potential. Even so, some Pinot shows good progress has been made.

Menetou-Salon

The Sauldre, a tributary of the Cher, parallels the big bend of the Loire on a shorter radius. By headward erosion, it "backed" across the Kimmeridgian outcrop, separating Sancerre and Menetou-Salon. The thickness and strength of the Portlandian cap rock have greatly deteriorated in the Menetou area, but happily it is also shored up here by Lower Cretaceous ferruginous sandstones.

Some authorities report more charm of scent and taste in the wines of Menetou-Salon than in those of Sancerre. This may in part be due to the

Some years ago, Mr. Octave Crochet, whose great-grandfather acquired la Poussie following the Revolution, undertook replanting of his Bué vineyard. He installed a sled pulled by a windlass to replace the "hotte," a back-packed container into which the pickers dump their baskets. The success of this device encouraged reconstitution of other steep slopes of abandoned terres blanches in Bué, Chavignol, and adjacent communes.

additional iron from these ferruginous sandstones. Remember also, we are getting closer to the influence of the maritime climate (*see* Color Plate 3).

In the communes of Humbligny, Morogues, and Parassy the Kimmeridgian has eroded into numerous knolls and slopes, but surprisingly, we find few vineyards. Menetou-Salon has considerable future potential in its under-utilized Kimmeridgian slopes.

Around the village of Menetou-Salon and westward, the terrain becomes level to slightly undulating – more suited to cereals and orchards than vineyards. The region has such a varied history of conquest and reconquest, it is a wonder that winegrowing survived at all. Besides being somewhat isolated from the larger, more active wine areas, the region also begins to run out of good wine geology – we are nearing the end of the Kimmeridgian Chain.

Quincy and Reuilly

West from Menetou-Salon, the Portlandian barrier has broken down completely. Absence of this barrier allowed early Tertiary outwash sands from the Massif Central to spread into the big bend of the Loire. Remnants of these sands are found on the divides between the tributaries of the Cher. Although the Portlandian-Kimmeridgian sub-crops beneath the outwash, Quincy and Reuilly are not full-fledged Kimmeridgian islands.

These two appellations produce respectable wines, but they are practically unknown outside the immediate area. The historic city of Bourges on the Cher is the region's commercial and industrial center and principal market for these wines, as well as those of Menetou-Salon. Quincy and Reuilly suffer from limited production, shortage of labor, lack of interest in viticulture, and competition from larger established wine districts. At Quincy, Tertiary outwash of gravel, sands, and clays vary greatly in thickness. Except where the detrital cover is quite thin, it is unlikely that vineroots reach the Kimmeridgian.

The Sauvignon is still the principal grape in Quincy, although some red grapes (usually Gamay) are cultivated for local consumption. Maturity occurs about a week earlier than in Sancerre, perhaps due to a gravel-warmed soil plus the influence of the mild maritime climate.

The Cistercian monks from the former Quincy (Beauvais) monastery were probably the first to cultivate vines here in the 14th century – the soils are just the sort of sterile-looking ground that challenged Cistercian viticulturists. In spite of a long history of wine, Quincy was never a large producer. The flat land and sandy soils simply favor other crops.

Reuilly, situated on the Arnon, a tributary of the Cher, is the anchor-island at the western end of the Kimmeridgian Chain. A window of Kimmeridgian outcrops on the west bank of the Arnon, but the principal vineyards of Reuilly are on the upland surface of thin, Tertiary, sandy soils, as at Quincy. The Sauvignon is again the main grape, and its white wine is for what Reuilly is noted. However, a rosé from the Pinot Gris is given quite high marks, and both the Pinot Noir and Pinot Gris have a right to the A.O.C.

West of Reuilly, the Kimmeridgian disappears under the Lower Cretaceous, so ending the Kimmeridgian Chain and with it the wine islands – the end of a delightful wine odyssey.

Color Plate 30
Chenin Blanc thrives on the hard, blocky "yellow tuffeau" soils of Vouvray. The best is honey-like, dry, sweet or sparkling, and can reach a great age

Color Plate 31
Old vines in Touraine soil with chalk fragments: Clos de l'Echo, near Chinon

Color Plate 32
The chalky, well-drained slopes of St.-Nicolas de Bourgueil admirably suit the Cabernet Franc which here makes sturdy fruity red wines

Color Plate 33
The Roche aux Moines and its château, perched on southeast-facing slopes above the Loire, viewed from the Coulée de Serrant. The Roche aux Moines (monks again) has been producing wines since the 11th century

Color Plate 34
The Coteaux du Layon
(a tributary of the Loire)
excel at producing creamy
sweet wines. The Quarts
de Chaume vineyards are
sufficiently outstanding
to merit their own
appellation for this style
of white wine

Color Plate 35
Some of the best
Muscadets come from the
hilly terrain of Muscadet
de Sèvre et Maine where
granite has weathered to
produce deep loams and
clays. Scarcely an acre is
not planted with vines

Color Plate 36
The Chablis Grands Crus are a continuous, undulating escarpment with arbitrary boundaries between the *climats*; that is, there are no natural breaks

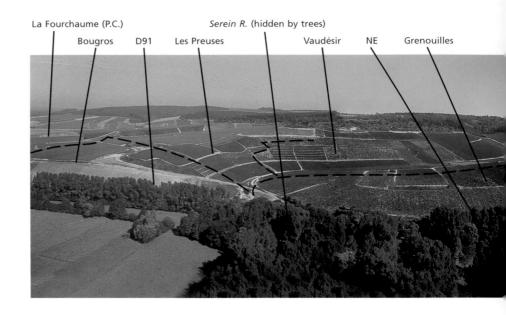

La Fourchaume (P.C.)   Serein R. (hidden by trees)

Bougros   D91   Les Preuses   Vaudésir   NE   Grenouilles

Color Plate 37
The Blanchots on the eastern end of the Grand Cru slope above Chablis village, viewed from the Premier Cru Montée de Tonnerre

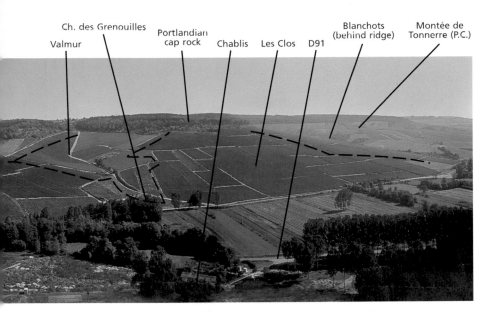

Valmur — Ch. des Grenouilles — Portlandian cap rock — Chablis — Les Clos — D91 — Blanchots (behind ridge) — Montée de Tonnerre (P.C.)

Color Plate 38
The Premier Cru Monts Mains, south of Chablis village, with the Grand Cru slopes beyond.
The soft Kimmeridgian limestone fragments present no problem in hand cultivation

Color Plate 39
Exogyra virgula, a small hooknosed oyster named for the French word for "comma," which it resembles. *Virgula* is the key fossil for the Upper Kimmeridgian. (The one-franc coin is about the size of a U.S. nickel)

Color Plate 40
Irancy is an unusual appellation on the Kimmeridge chain, producing red wines from the Pinot Noir, César, and Tressot grapes. The vineyards lie in an amphitheater which has a very favorable microclimate. It is the vestige of the once huge Auxerre vineyard

Color Plate 41
Les Loges, an excellent terroir north of Pouilly-sur-Loire, produces Pouilly-Fumé from the
Sauvignon grape. The wines are characteristically "flinty," fresh, and clean-tasting. The town
of Sancerre tops the hill in the distance

Color Plate 42
Sancerre perches on the top of a long fault-block ridge which has for centuries made it a strategic town (it has a magnificent view of the Loire valley from its Promenade de la Porte César). Its finest vineyards are on the western side, on classic Portlandian-Kimmeridgian slopes. The world knows Sancerre for its Sauvignon Blanc, but the locals also take delight in its pale Pinot Noir

10 Auvergne-Bourbonnais: a rift shadowed by volcanic peaks

As wines go, except for those of St.-Pourçain, Auvergne is better known for the inspiring volcanic scenery of the Puy de Dôme, the restorative baths and waters of Vichy, and the commercial business of Clermont-Ferrand – dominated by the mammoth Michelin tire factory. The Auvergne-Bourbonnais is seldom part of a wine tour, but the region has important history, interesting scenery and geology, and very respectable wines.

Landscape

The principal structural feature is a graben, but not as classical as the Rhine graben of Alsace. The floor of the graben is the wide, flat Limagne, flanked on the west by the volcanic plateaux and mountains of the Monts d'Auvergne (*see* Figure 10.1). The Auvergne rift system originates deep within the Massif Central and extends northward through the Pouilly-sur-Loire–Sancerre area, channeling the Loire and its tributary, the Allier. This rift system is genetically related to the Saône–Rhône crustal deformation.

Bourbonnais means "land of the Bourbons" – puzzling to Americans who think that land is Kentucky, but there is a link. The name actually comes from a Celtic god, Bou or Bor, protector of the local hot springs. The name was borrowed by the originally obscure lords of the castle of Bourbon L'Archambault, and the name was eventually shortened. From this rural beginning, the Bourbons became the ruling houses of France, Spain, and Italy. Admiration for the powerful French rulers prompted the state of Kentucky in the 19th century to name one of its counties Bourbon. Spirits distilled from fermenting corn mash became the famed "bourbon" whiskey.

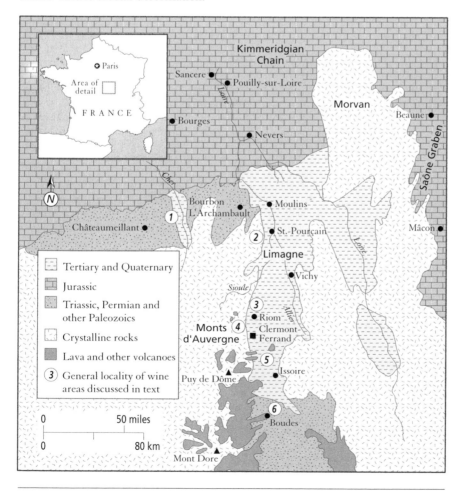

Figure 10.1
General geology of the Auvergne-Bourbonnais
(generalized from *Carte Géologique de la France*)

Legend:
- Tertiary and Quaternary
- Jurassic
- Triassic, Permian and other Paleozoics
- Crystalline rocks
- Lava and other volcanoes
- (3) General locality of wine areas discussed in text

0 50 miles
0 80 km

Rifting started in early Oligocene and continued until near the end of the Tertiary. As typical of grabens, the trenches filled with detritus about as fast as they sank. Streams spread alluvium over the valley floor, and in late Tertiary lakes formed along the western margin of the basin. Extensive reef-like mounds of travertine, a dense, finely crystalline, precipitated limestone, developed along the lake shore. The weathered travertine produced excellent vineyard sites and soils while the fresh rock was quarried for building stone.

About the time the graben was forming, the Massif Central had risen like a giant carbuncle. A deep lesion of the Massif crust tapped into molten rock. Cinder and ash spewed out as cones, and lava was bled in all directions as sheets and rivers. Tongues of lava spilled into the Limagne, often becoming interbedded with lake and river deposits. Lava formed cap rocks-plateaux of various sizes on which important vineyards were later developed. The weathered lava (basalt) provides excellent mineral nutrients, while broken pieces add coarse elements to the soil texture.

Although structural deformation ceased toward the end of the Tertiary, volcanic activity continued into the Quaternary. The Monts d'Auvergne became a land of fire and ice. The chain of "puys" (peaks of volcanic origin) are the most spectacular scenery of the Massif Central. The skyline of the volcanic landscape is irregular, its peaks reaching only 3000 feet (less than 1000 m), but the mountain range provides a moderately effective weather shield for the vineyards of the Limagne.

Appellations

Wines of Auvergne-Bourbonnais are classified V.D.Q.S. The main producing regions, indicated by the circled numbers on Figure 10.1, are as follows:

The Châteaumeillant vineyards (1) are scattered on slopes and hillocks along the Cher on soils from schists, granitic-like rocks, and Triassic sandstones on the north flank of the Massif Central. The wines are pale reds and rosés from the Gamay and Pinot Noir.

The St.-Pourçain-sur Sioule appellation (2) is certainly the best known of the region. Clear, dry, whites are made from the Sauvignon, Tressallier (local name for the Sacy of the Chablis region), Aligoté, and Chardonnay. The reds and rosés – the café wines of Vichy – are from the Gamay and Pinot Noir. The vineyards are on travertine reefs and a variety of Tertiary outwash and lake deposits.

The name is St.-Pourçain for a monk who led a group of monastic brothers in futile defense of Auvergne against Thierry, son of Clovis. The monks also started the vineyards which now cover only about 2000 acres (800 ha) which in pre-phylloxera covered almost ten times that amount in the 18th century. After the devastation, wine cultivation in the plains was given over to other crops.

V.D.Q.S. Côtes d'Auvergne is for reds and rosés made from Gamay and Pinot Noir and for a very light white, made from the Chardonnay. The appellation includes the following four districts. The vineyards of Châteaugay (3), south from St.-Pourçain toward Clermont-Ferrand, are found on a basalt-capped plateau with soils from a complex of marls, limestone, and granitic sands. The soils are "peppered" with granules of glassy lava and large fragments of vesicular (sponge-like) lava.

In the early part of the French Revolution, General Lafayette (of American Revolutionary fame) came to the area to meet with his friend the Marquis de Châteaugay. The two prepared governance reforms along the lines which Lafayette had seen put into practice following the American Revolution.

The soils of Chanturges (4) on the north outskirts of Clermont-Ferrand are very like those of Châteaugay but without the basalt "pepper." Just south of Clermont-Ferrand is the lava-capped plateau of Corent (5) with soils of marly-limestone and weathered basalt.

Some 20 miles (32 km) south of Clermont-Ferrand, the Limagne wedges out into the fault-splintered Massif Central. The wine district of Boudes (6) is on a low plateau with soils of slope wash of marl and clay with blocks of hard limestone and fragments of lava. The sub-soils are red and green clays from deeply weathered limestones.

Auvergne is a relatively small wine district and its vineyards are on plateau-like landforms. However, the variety of rocks, lava, schists, and granitic rocks, contribute valuable mineral nutrients to the soils. The weathered reef travertine, lake-bed marls, and basalt make excellent soils equally to the liking of the red Gamay and Pinot Noir, as well as the white Chardonnay and Sauvignon. Most of the wines are vinified by cooperatives and consumed locally with the aid of tourists, business visitors, and those taking cures at the spas.

Opportunities for expanding vineyards are very limited. Moreover, being somewhat isolated, there is little incentive to compete for markets outside the region. Nevertheless, this scenic, historical region proudly produces some of France's very interesting and satisfying wines.

The Auvergne wine area includes Roanne in the Loire Valley which, in earlier days was important for winegrowing. The industry suffered, like much of this part of central, rural France, from a population exodus – as well as a dearth of good vineyard slopes. The appellation here is V.D.Q.S. Côtes Rouannaises, a stronghold of Gamay in a style not unlike Beaujolais. Roanne is, however, more noted for its fine restaurants which offer a good selection of Auvergne's wines.

11 The Rhône and the Southeast: rootless mountains – shear geology

The smear of colors on the geologic map of the southeast sector of France (*see* Color Plate 1) is the picture of a collision – the collision of the Afro-Arabian and the Euro-Asian crustal plates. The Alps were the epicenter of this deformation. Crowning this scenic, awe-inspiring jumble of rocks is Mont Blanc. Guarding the high Alps are the Pre-Alps or sub-alpine ranges composed of bewildering geology with their own particular scenery. Collaring around these mountain masses to the north and west in a ripple-effect are the long, wrinkled ridges of the Jura. Framing this southeast sector of deformation is the Rhône–Saône graben, part of a rift system that cuts across western Europe from the Mediterranean, through the Rhine graben, and on out beneath the North Sea.

This chapter explains the mechanism by which mountain masses are piled high and moved for miles. It also explains how glaciation, another new geologic process, has affected the wine landscape of much of the region.

The geologic elements in mountain building are force, material, and time. The force in the southeast sector was the crustal collision, now essentially quiet except for a few seismic murmurs from time to time. Activity of the plate system, however, is still active in the Middle East where destructive earthquakes occur periodically in Iran.

Current plate movements are observable in the U.S. where the Pacific plate is side-swiping the North American plate along the San Andreas Fault. Rocks piled 3 miles (5 km) high in the Alps is ample evidence that crustal forces 150 million years ago in southeast France were enormous.

The significance to the new landscape architecture was that these forces were acting in a horizontal direction. The principal forces which we have dealt with up to now have been vertical – sagging of basins, domal uplift, tilting of strata, and downfaulting into the Rhine and Rhône–Saône grabens. If the principal stress is horizontal or at a low angle, the crustal strata will be bowed, buckled, overthrust, and possibly sheared. The actual style of deformation will depend on the nature of the basement rocks and the overlying strata.

The materials on which the compressive forces acted in the southeast sector was a thick sequence of Cretaceous and Jurassic limestones, dolomites, and marls totaling some 40,000 feet (12,000 m). Critical to the mountain-building process were the thick deposits of salt, anhydrite, and shales of the Triassic.

It may seem impossible that these thick beds could have been folded and contorted as now seen in the mountain landscapes. Several factors are involved in these structural phenomena. First, it should be recognized that these contortions occurred not up in the air but deep within the crust where the confining pressure was very great. Continuing pressure squeezed much of the deformed masses to the surface and raised it even higher. Another factor that helped the erstwhile "stiff" layers to be tightly folded was that they were interbedded with shales and marls. These "weak" rocks allowed a "slippage" in the bending, much as the smooth faces of playing cards slip when they are flexed for shuffling.

Perhaps the most significant, but little-known property of rocks is the way they behave under the heat and pressure at depth – salt, anhydrite, and shale become plastic – even marly limestones become malleable. These properties were determined by oil company research where the heat and pressure of the earth's depths were replicated in their laboratories. The plasticity of salt and shale is well demonstrated by the salt domes of the U.S. coastal plain and under the waters of the Gulf of Mexico, the Hannover Basin of Germany, and the Zagros Mountains of Iran. These salt plugs (diapirs) or blisters penetrate the overlying strata, doming it, and sometimes reaching the surface, creating "islands" e.g. Avery Island in south Louisiana, High Island on the Texas coast.

The part that plasticity plays in the geology of the southeast region is to provide "breakaway" zones where great slabs or rock units responding to the horizontal pressure broke away from the underlying sequence and were shoved distances often measured in miles. The salt or shale of the "breakaway" zone also greased the glide surface – the sole fault. Sometimes the overthrust element broke up, with sub-elements overriding each other – or imbricating. As the imbricating elements run out of "push" and "grease," they "stall-out" in the shape of ski tips, seen particularly in the Côtes du Jura.

Thick beds of salt in the Triassic and shale in the lower Jurassic meant that at depth the Alps were surrounded by an extensive breakaway zone. Nature did not overlook this unusual opportunity – the Subalpine ranges and the Jura were sheared off from the basement and these "rootless mountains" were moved several miles outward from the epicenter. The vineplants do not feel there is anything apologetic about these "rootless mountains" or their slopes and soils in the Côtes du Jura, Savoie-Bugey, Diois, Southern Rhône, and Provence.

Time is the third factor in development of the landscape – time for building, time for erosion. As discussed in Part One, some geologic processes such as earthquakes and beach erosion may happen while we watch; deposition of thick shales and limestones may take millions of years. Mountain-building is a creepy process; movements are by fits and starts. Erosion doesn't wait until the building is done before it starts, but the structures go up faster than they are worn down. The mountain-building quakes were undoubtedly of major magnitude – perhaps greater than any in recorded history.

As the Alps began to rise, the erosional sediments were finer grained shales and sands called flysch. As upthrusting became more rapid and the mountains higher, the sheetwash material became coarser – conglomerates, sands, clays, and marls – sediments known as molasse. The term is borrowed from the French word *mollasse*, meaning flabby or without body. These great aprons of molasse extending from the Alps to the Rhône were later cut into plateaux or redistributed in terraces on which numerous vineyard sites are located.

A sinuous and less spectacular crustal disturbance began a short time before the Alps. Actually, it was the rejuvenation of an ancient line of deformation known as the Hercynian trend. By the beginning of the Triassic, this once magnificent mountain chain composed of Paleozoic strata was worn to a "toothless plain" and covered by Jurassic and Cretaceous limestones. This Hercynian trend extends eastward beneath the Mediterranean from the Pyrenees to the Rhône delta where it is interrupted by the Rhône–Saône rift.

Along the Languedoc coast, the crustal stresses pushed thrust sheets of Jurassic and Cretaceous ashore like a tidal wave reaching to the flanks of the Corbières, the Montagne Noire, and the Massif Central. "Flotsam" of this tidal-like thrust are the klippen of La Clape, Frontignan et al. Eastward beyond the Rhône delta and Marseille, the Hercynian trend reappears east of the Maures and Esterel massifs. The Maures is composed of basement crystalline rocks, and the Esterel is a complex of Paleozoic strata. These old Hercynian rocks provide a variety of vineyard soils for Provence.

The island of Corsica is an unusually high bulge of the Hercynian trend that has been rotated approximately 90 degrees clockwise. The western two-thirds of the island is granite. East of a prominent band of thrust material, a coastal plain is composed of Tertiary and Quaternary deposits.

In southeast France in the latter part of the Tertiary, the collision forces quieted down and nature welded the crustal elements in place for today's landscape. This extraordinary period of building and moving mountains was followed by the unique Ice Age of the Quaternary Pleistocene.

Figure 11.1
General geology and wine areas of the Southeast

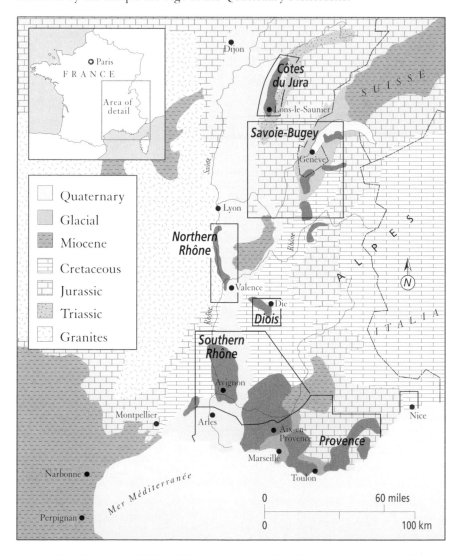

France itself was not under the continental glacier, but in the periglacial zone. A thick ice cap developed on the Alps in a wide arc from Nice to beyond Salzburg, Austria. The Ice Age lasted two million years with four cold periods separated by warm interglacials. Like topping on a cake, lobes and glacial fingers oozed down the mountain valleys. These valley glaciers acted as giant ice rasps scouring the sides and bottoms of the valleys into U-shaped profiles. The power of such glacial action is picturesquely illustrated by Half Dome in Yosemite National Park, California, where a Sierra Nevada valley glacier wore away half of a large granite knob. Most famous of the Alpine glaciers was the Rhône glacier which scooped out Lake Geneva (Lac Léman) and Lake Bourget, overrode the Jura, stopping just short of the Massif Central at Lyon.

When valley glaciers melted, they left a mess of broken and ground-up rock on the valley floor called till. Ridges of similar material shouldered aside or carried along by the rivers of ice were dumped as lateral moraines. Rock material bulldozed ahead by the glacier are called terminal moraines. Melt water and later floods rearranged some of these glacial residues as terraces for vineyard sites.

The geologic processes described above do not affect each of the following seven wine regions to the same degree or in the same way, but will serve to acquaint the reader with the mechanisms that have produced the particular landscapes of the areas outlined on Figure 11.1.

The Côtes du Jura
Unusual Geology, Unusual Wines

Chances are you've never had a glass of *vin jaune*, nor seen its peculiar long-necked, hunched-shouldered bottle. This yellow wine is not unusual because of the geology, but the geology is unusual. There are Jura reds, rosés, and whites too, but *vin jaune* is the "signature wine."

Chances are also very good that the visitor to Poligny or Arbois came across the Saône from the Côte d'Or. It is immediately apparent that the terrain of the Jura side of the valley is not a mirror image of the Côte d'Or. The Burgundy side is long ridges of cap rock-slopes. Those of the Jura are low, mound-like ridges backed by a wall of massive limestones. One may stand among the alien rocks in front of this wall and ponder whether the "rootless mountains" could possibly have been shoved several miles northward from their original place in the earth's crust. The proof of this mountain-moving mechanism is the borehole shown in the cross-section Figure 11.2 where older strata have been thrust out over young valley fill of the Saône graben. Layers of salt and anhydrite in the Lower Triassic composed the breakaway zone and greased the skid-plane over which the thrust sheet was moved.

The line labeled FS (frontal scarp) on Figure 11.2 is the wall of massive Jurassic limestone. The line labeled OE (outer edge) is the outermost line of the thrust sheets. The area between these two lines is the quality viticultural zone.

The grape varieties are as curious as the geology. The white Savagnin Blanc (not Sauvignon Blanc) from which the *vin jaune* is made is found only in this small corner of France. The Trousseau and Poulsard, the red grapes, are equally unfamiliar varieties.

Figure 11.2
The Côtes du Jura,
viticultural zone and
geologic cross-section
The more restricted A.O.C.s
of Etoile, Château-Chalon,
and Arbois-Pupillin
indicate the best vineyards
within the regional Côtes
du Jura appellation
(geology of cross-section
modified from 1:50,000
Poligny sheet no. 555 by
kind permission B.R.G.M.)

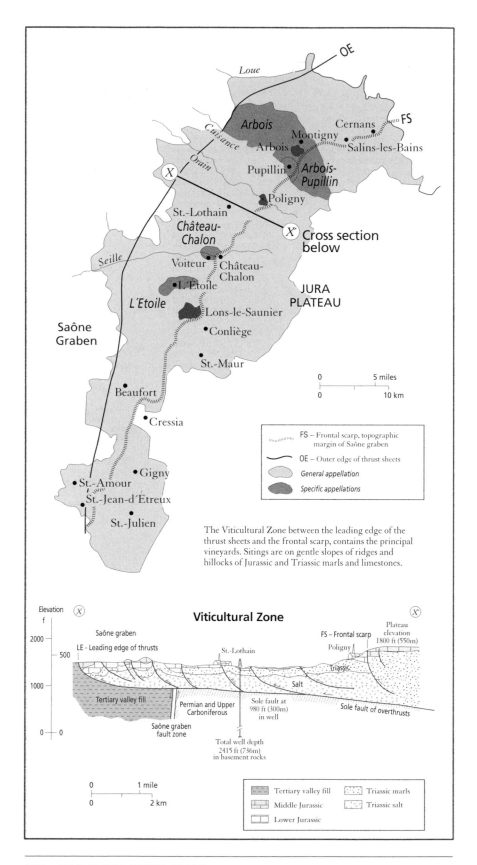

The Viticultural Zone between the leading edge of the
thrust sheets and the frontal scarp, contains the principal
vineyards. Sitings are on gentle slopes of ridges and
hillocks of Jurassic and Triassic marls and limestones.

The Côtes du Jura are almost like a land that time forgot. In fact, viticulture nearly became extinct as a result of the phylloxera devastation followed by World War I and an exodus of the labor-force after World War II.

The province in which the Côtes du Jura are located has a puzzling name, Franche-Comté. Origin of the name should stir Gallic admiration. Reynald III, a count of the 12th-century kingdom of Burgundy, refused to pay homage to the Emperor of East Germany, a holdover of Charlemagne's Holy Roman Empire. After 10 years of successfully defying subjugation, in 1127, Reynald was conceded to be a *franc-comte* or "free count" with his county known as Franche-Comté.

The landscape

The Côte d'Or and Côtes du Jura are alike but different somehow. The difference is the way the crustal beds are sliced – those of the Côte d'Or are sliced vertically. The Côtes du Jura are sliced horizontally. Vertical faulting of the Côte d'Or creates long scarps with classic cap-rock slopes. The Côtes du Jura are topped by a thick, blunt slice of limestone overlying thinner slices of wrinkled strata – the geology very much resembles the frontal scarp and "disturbed zone" of Glacier National Park in Montana in the U.S.

Vineyards of the Jura are on hillocks and ridges of the wine zone, *see* Figure 11.2. The small valleys cutting the Jura scarp are steep-walled, flat-bottomed "box canyons," in contrast with the sharp "V" combes of the Côte d'Or. In addition to plantations on the viticultural zone, vines are also draped along narrow slopes at the base of the frontal scarp and on the floors of the canyons.

The dark, multicolored shales and marls of the Liassic (Lower Jurassic) gave the name Black Jura to the Côtes du Jura and to its soils, the *terres noires*. These soils have good structure and water-retention characteristics so that the vines are seldom under stress. Successively younger Jurassic strata toward the Alps become lighter in color giving the names Brown Jura and White Jura.

Climate

The climate is essentially a mild version of the continental zone. Although the high, blunt escarpment is in the back of the viticultural zone, it deflects upward the approaching Westerlies and cold, north winds, giving a favorable micro-climate to the ridges and hills in front. The terrain offers many opportunities for southeast and southern exposures. The grapes are relatively late-ripening, exposing them to early frosts which are common. Warm, sunny days, however, generally extend well into autumn. Rainfall is adequate, averaging around 25 inches (630 mm) per year. On the limestone plateau, much of the rainfall quickly disappears into underground drainage, issuing as springs or full-born streams at the heads of many blind valleys or box canyons.

Unique grapes, unique wines

The red Poulsard, commonly referred to as the Arbois, goes by several other synonyms depending on the particular village: Ploussard, Plessard, Mâche, or Meythe. The grapes are pale red and yield a wine of about the same shade – almost a rosé. The wine has a freshness to the nose and a delightful bouquet. The other unique red, the Trousseau, is a very productive vine, and the grapes are

Derek V. Ager relates an interesting story regarding the underground drainage here. In 1901, a gentleman out for an early morning walk near the source of the Loue River east of Salins-les-Bains discovered that the otherwise clear, spring-fed stream had the color, odor, and taste of absinthe. It was learned that the previous night a fire broke out at a Pernod factory. (Pernod, an aromatic liqueur, used to be made from absinthe, wormwood but this is long since banned.) The fire caused a million liters of absinthe to be dumped into the Doubs River. The factory was over 7 miles (12 km) across the plateau from the source of the Loue. By dye-tracing, it was found that the waters of the Loue are actually from the Doubs River. Just downstream from the Pernod factory, a crevice in the river bed feeds an underground stream which issues as the "source" of the Loue.

well-colored. The wine, however, has an astringency which diminishes its character, but it keeps well. Jancis Robinson thinks the Trousseau is an incarnation of the Bastardo of Portugal, which is logical enough when one remembers that this area was once under the control of Spain. The grape could indeed have been imported from the Iberian Peninsula during that period. Comparing the Trousseau with the Poulsard, Robinson says that Trousseau is the iron fist for the velvet glove of Poulsard – a happy combination, as the two grapes are frequently blended.

The Savagnin Blanc, the *vin jaune* grape, is isolated to the northern Jura. According to Desmond Seward, the Savagnin's ancestor may have been the Traminer of the Alto Adige. (Recall from Part One Professor Dumay's theory of grapevines coming to Gaul from northern Italy via the Brenner Pass and the Upper Danube Basin.)

It is reported that the *vin jaune* was created by the Black Nuns of the abbey at Château-Chalon, a religious order reserved for ladies of the nobility. According to the story, in the 14th century one of the Abbess' vignerons ordered her laborers to pick the grapes as late as possible. The overripe grapes produced a must extremely high in sugar. *Vin jaune* was born. Fermentation by the nuns was done in vats hewn from the limestone on which Château-Chalon is located. The religious order was dissolved in 1790, and the abbey destroyed, but the winemaking process has continued – except for the rock-hewn vats.

Wherever *vin jaune* is produced, one bureaucratic idiosyncrasy is that just before the harvest, a commission visits each vineyard to check the quality of the grapes, sugar levels, etc., and fix its yield. If everything is not up to standard, the appellation designation may be denied for that year.

Photograph 11.1
Frontal scarp:
Château-Chalon
The blunt frontal scarp of massive Jurassic limestone is surmounted by Château-Chalon. The vineyards in front of the scarp are on imbrications from the sole fault on which these strata have ridden

Traditionally, harvest of the Savagnin for *vins jaunes* is delayed until after the first frost. Aging after fermentation goes on for six years in the same cask without topping-off to replace evaporation. Yeasts and fermentation products form a crust that prevents oxidation. In the six years, however, the wine loses a third of its volume. After this long period of aging, the amber wine has become like a light sherry, with a pleasant bouquet and a distinct nutty taste. It is bottled in the distinctive *clavelins*, with the long neck and hunched shoulders. It has learned to live alone, unattended, and will easily keep another 100 years.

The Savagnin is also the principal grape of another "cottage-industry" wine, the *vin de paille* of L'Etoile. The term *paille* has a double meaning: the first is that the grapes traditionally were dried on straw (*paille*) mats until they were almost raisins. The name also describes the golden straw color of this sweet, liqueur-like wine, which is quite high in alcohol. L'Etoile also makes *vins jaunes*, as well as conventional style whites from the Savagnin and Chardonnay.

The appellations and soils

Within the general A.O.C. of the Côtes du Jura appellations have been granted for Arbois, Arbois-Pupillin, Château-Chalon, and L'Étoile. South of L'Étoile, the viticultural zone extends some 20 miles (30 km) but gradually narrows and produces no exceptional wines.

From almost 46,000 acres (18,600 ha) in pre-phylloxera days, the area under vine is now less than one tenth that amount. The grower and merchant Henri Maire, who himself plants 20 percent of the current 3600 A.O.C. acres (1450 ha), has been a tireless force in rejuvenation of viticulture in the Jura and the promotion and marketing of its wines. Henri Maire is now a household name for all Jura appellation wines.

Although only 1700 acres (690 ha), Arbois and Arbois-Pupillin produce half of the A.O.C. wines of the Côtes du Jura. The Arbois district was approved in 1936, and the enclave of Arbois-Pupillin in 1970. Red and rosé wines made from the Trousseau grape are the principal products of these appellations. This grape does well on *terres noires* while the Poulsard prefers deeper, rich, well-exposed soils. Some white wines from the Savagnin Blanc are also produced. One of the first cooperative wineries in France was opened in Arbois in 1906.

Château-Chalon is the smallest of the four appellations at 125 acres (50 ha), mostly in the protected cove of the blind valley of the Seille River and along its terraces in the viticultural zone. The appellation is reserved for production of the famed *vins jaunes*. The appellation includes the valley villages of Menetru-le-Vignoble, Nerby, and Voiteur – all within hailing distance from the château on top of "the rock."

The 160-acre (64-ha) appellation of L'Etoile has good southerly exposures on the knobs and elongate hills. It is known for its white wines, especially *vins de paille*. The area also makes *vins jaunes* and other conventional style whites, both still and sparkling.

A thrust wedge of Middle Jurassic, *Calcaire à entroques*, the principal bedrock of Burgundy's Côte de Nuits, caps a small round hill on which sits the château at L'Etoile. The star-like cross-section of the fossilized head of the entroques ("sea lily") gives the name L'Etoile (star) to the village.

Out of the way for most English-speaking tourists, but if the many pleasures of the northern Jura beckon, Arbois and Château-Chalon are delightful places to start. The wines of Jura are little known outside France, but it is worth the diversion to meet them on their home ground. You will surely be able to say you have had a glass of *vin jaune*.

Savoie

It is said of Savoie wines that they do not to travel well and should be consumed in the region where they grow. What delightful advice! One may enjoy limitless panoramas of mountains and lakes while savoring some of the finest food in the world accompanied by a dry, light, fruity white or lively red Savoie wine. Some writers accord Savoie (or Savoy) as having only "local wines" of little interest or dismiss it altogether. What a shame! Provincial wines they may be, but they have pleased as wide a range of international palates as any wines of France, prestigious ones included.

Albertville, which hosted the 1992 Winter Olympics, lies only a few miles up the Isère Valley from the wine districts of Montmélian and Chambéry. A decade earlier, the same event was held at Grenoble, 30 miles (50 km) to the south. Geneva, over the border, is the diplomatic and business crossroad of the world. Add to this the year-round stream of international tourists visiting the French and Swiss Alps, and the tasting of Savoie wines has been truly Olympian.

Savoie is the oldest documented wine area of northern Gaul, being in part the land of the Celtic Allobroges which had been annexed to Rome's Transalpine Gaul, a century or more before Caesar. The mountainous terrain and complex geology mean the wine areas are scattered on good exposures not preempted by man for settlements and growing other crops. The vineyard soils are mostly lime-rich glacial material and scree along the base of mountain flanks. The largest production by far is white wine, but red wine is grown in places where favorable microclimates allow sufficient maturation of red grapes.

In this large scenic area there are only 4000 acres (1600 ha) of vines, vying with people for sunny sites and good soil. For example, the very popular eastern shore of Lake Bourget has only a few tiny vineyards, relics of a former "Eden" of Mediterranean vegetation – olive, fig, and almond as well as the grape.

The landscape

Savoie is a virtual textbook of structural geology and glaciation. Mont Blanc and the surrounding sky-piercing peaks form a scenic backdrop for the vineyards. The valleys provide surprisingly mild microclimates. Understanding the geologic processes that made the mountains only increases their wonder.

Origin of the Alps, sub-Alpine ranges, the Jura, and glaciation were explained in the introduction to this chapter. Figure 11.3 outlines the major tectonic features and the wine areas of Savoie and Bugey.

The Franco-Swiss Plain is a plain only in contrast to the mountains, for it is very hilly and bumpy. Forty miles (64 km) wide in the Zurich–Bern area, it narrows rapidly westward, pinching out between the Jura and Bauges south of Lake Geneva. During the mountain-building period, this lowland belt received great quantities of molasse – thick, soft sands, clays, marls, and conglomerates. It provided an easy pathway for the great Rhône valley glacier of the Quaternary Ice Age which over-deepened Lake Geneva and scooped out Lake Bourget, overriding the Jura, and reaching the buttress of the Massif Central at Lyon. Lateral moraines and till left by the glacier are composed of fragments and ground-up rock which became soils for the vineyards around Lake Geneva, Seyssel, and La Chautagne (a dried-up northward extension of Lake Bourget).

André Combaz, co-editor with Robert Lautel of *Terroirs et Vins de France*, has his second home in Albertville, and, of course, knows Savoie well. I asked him if he would work up Savoie for me. He did such a thorough and beautiful job that I urged him to have his report published as a book of his own in time for the 1992 Winter Olympiad, which he did. His excellent material has been invaluable in the preparation of this section on Savoie.

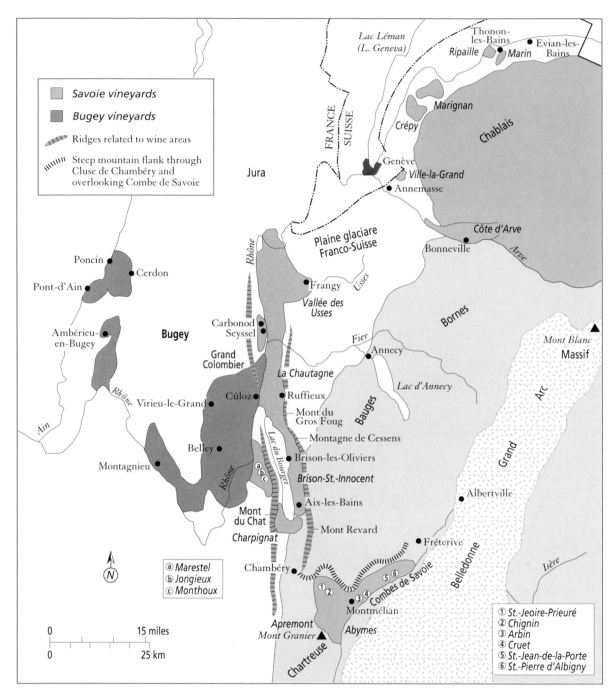

Figure 11.3
Wine areas of Savoie and Bugey

Poetically, mountains are extolled as the epitome of solidity; geologically, the Jura and sub-Alpine ranges are "rootless mountains." They have been sheared from their roots and moved several miles north and west. No cause for alarm; nature welded them to their present positions 10 million years ago when the mechanism ran out of "push" and "skid-grease."

The geology of the sub-Alpine ranges is sufficiently complex to excite any geologist to near apoplexy. Massive limestones of Cretaceous and Jurassic age have been folded, buckled, thrusted, and the folds overturned. Cut-away views of these highly complex structures are seen in the *cluses*, the regional term for the narrow valleys which cut across ridges at right angles (*see* Color Plate 47).

Ridges of tightly folded Jurassic limestone of the Jura swing around the north side of Lake Geneva and merge with the Bauges and Chartreuse built of Cretaceous limestones, *see* Figures 11.1 and 11.3. The massive limestones are of different ages, although the structural style and landscapes of these three mountain ranges are very similar. (Sands and shales of the Lower Cretaceous of the Paris Basin have given way to massive limestones in the Savoie region.) The long ridges of the Grand Colombiers and Mont du Chat of the Jura are paralleled by the sub-Alpine Mont du Gros Foug and Montagne de Cessens. Cores of the Cretaceous Subalpine folds are exposures of underlying Jurassic.

Counter-clockwise from the northeast, the four sub-Alpine massifs are: Chablais (not to be confused with Chablis), Bornes, Bauges, and Chartreuse. Chablais is a vastly complex jumble of Jurassic and Cretaceous folds and thrusts. The Bornes are somewhat less jumbled, and the Bauges begin a more orderly style of long fold-ridges that merge with those of the Chartreuse. The principal soils of vineyards along Lake Geneva, however, are related to glacial residues. The crystalline rocks of the Belledonne Grand Arc (*see* Figure 11.3) are not directly involved in Savoie viticulture, but have contributed to river gravel and glacial material.

Climate

In Savoie, winefields and snowfields may enjoy the same scenery. Skiers may look back down a valley where they passed workers harvesting grapes less than an hour ago. Although basically continental in character, the lakes Geneva, Bourget, and Annecy bring a Mediterranean mellowness to the region. Olive trees, the insignia of Mediterranean climate, thrive alongside vineyards at Brison-les-Oliviers on the east side of Lake Bourget.

The prevailing winds are the Westerlies which characteristically bring ample moisture at just under 40 inches (1000 mm) annually – much of it as snow. Summer and autumn sunshine is abundant, totaling some 1600 hours. The principal grain of the ridges is north–south, therefore southerly exposures are quite limited, and vineyards compete with fruit orchards and villages for the preferred exposure.

The grapes

The leading white grapes of Savoie are the Jacquère, Roussanne, and the Altesse, also known as Roussette. These are veritable botanical museum plants. Other white varieties include the Chasselas, especially for sparkling wine, and there are minor plantings of Chardonnay, Molette Blanche, Savagnin, and Aligoté.

The Jacquère is well adapted to the calcareous clay soils of the glacial till and scree slopes. It yields a pale yellow wine, which is fresh and discreetly fruity. Either the Roussanne was introduced into the area from the Northern Rhône, or it may have been the other way round. At any rate, the vineplant particularly likes the pebbly scree soils of Chignin. Its dry wines are high in alcohol, of exquisite aroma, and held by some connoisseurs to be one of the distinguished wines of France.

As proof of the moderate climate of Savoie, the famous nursery at Fréterive, down the Isère from Albertville in the Combe de Savoie, grows cuttings and rootstocks of various grape varieties for other regions of France as well as for the vineyards of Savoie.

The Altesse very possibly was brought from the island of Cyprus in 1366 by Count Vert, Amédée VI, on his return from a crusade. The variety likes the scree slopes, and gravelly white, marly soils with good exposures. The wine is supple, with a complex aroma and taste of several fruits.

The Chasselas, known in the Lake Geneva area as the Crépy, gives a delicate and light wine with a flowery to gun-flint taste. It is the basis of the wine industry in Seyssel and is made still and sparkling.

The red grapes are the lesser known Mondeuse Rouge, the Etraire, and the familiar Gamay and Pinot Noir. It is possible that the Mondeuse may be the "Allobroges" cultivated by the Celts and mentioned by the ancient historians Pliny the Elder and Columella. The Gamay and Pinot Noir are, of course, well known in Burgundy. It has been suggested that these two grapes may have been long-ago mutations of early vines in the Savoie region.

The wine areas

The wine districts of Savoie are quite scattered, but can be grouped geologically in eight areas. One is the southern end of Lake Geneva, which has four terroirs of note: Ripaille, Marin, Marignan, and Crépy. The first three are all A.O.C. Vins de Savoie; Crépy is recognized as an appellation in its own right. Ripaille is on the delta (alluvial cone) of the Dranse River built into Lake Geneva. Sands and gravel of the cone have grown to sufficient height to provide a reasonably thick growing zone for roots of the Chasselas well above the water table. Château de Ripaille is the highly regarded label for a dry, light, white wine.

Marin is on terraces eroded into a lateral moraine with soils of clays, sands, and lignitic material. The vineyards overlook Thonon-les-Bains and Evian-les-Bains. The brilliant white wine of Marin, also made from the Chasselas, rivals in clarity the Evian spring water of international fame.

Marignan is spread around the northeast slopes of Mont de Boissy, a low hill of molasse that was not completely ground away by the Rhône glacier. The soils are a mixture of clayey molasse and coarse sands derived from crystalline rocks of the high Alps. The principal area of production originally belonged to the abbey de Filly, founded in 930. The monks established a model farm at Tour de Marignan in the 14th century where clones of selected vines were cultivated and most likely distributed around the region.

Crépy, also part of the domain of the abbey de Filly, employs the vinification process used by the monks of simply bottling the wine without drawing it off its lees (sediment). This allows some fermentation to continue, giving the wine a *perlant* effect (very slightly sparkling). The label will indicate *sur lie*. Crépy's vineyards are on the southwest nose of the Mont de Boissy where the clayey molassic soils are similar to those of Marignan, but with better sun exposure.

Second, the vineyards of Côte d'Arve at Bonneville overlook the busy autoroute from Geneva to Chamonix and the Mont Blanc tunnel. The highway and parallel railroad follow the Arve River which rises in the Mont Blanc massif and joins the Rhône just as it exits Lake Geneva. At elevations nearing 1800 feet (550 m), the vines are close to the climatic limits for grape growing. The area has an average of 115 frost days in the year. However, exposures are to the south and are protected from north winds by the Chablais Massif, one of the "rootless mountain" masses that slid outward from the Mont Blanc region. Authorized as an appellation in 1944, these "Vins de Savoie," comprise three adjoining communes along the river front: la Côte d'Hyot, Ayze, and Marignier. The Arve River has cut its channel down into the molasse below the overriding detached massifs of Chablais and the Bornes. The soils of the appellation are thus a mixture of molasse, river terraces, and outwash from the Chablais.

After the phylloxera devastation, late-maturing plants were selected for adaptation to the climate of this area. These are the Gringet (local name for Savagnin), occupying about two-thirds of the planting, the Roussette d'Ayze, or Mondeuse Blanche, Grosse Roussette (Marsanne), and the Bon Blanc (Chasselas). A local method of fermentation called *fermentation spontanée* is used to produce a lightly sparkling wine bottled in a heavy black "champenoise" bottle. This "champagne Savoyard" exhibits a pleasant mountain hardiness described as making the tongue "sing in the palate."

The third area, the Vallée des Usses, a tributary of the Rhône between Geneva and Lake Bourget, was highly praised in ancient times. Becoming almost extinct following phylloxera crisis, the valley now contains scattered vineyards planted to the Roussette or Altesse grapes. Preferred locations are the south-facing slopes on pebbly clays mixed with underlying molasse. There has been a greatly renewed interest in cultivation of quality wine in the Usses Valley below Frangy.

The small but ancient vineyards of Seyssel lie on both sides of the Rhône north of Lake Bourget. They were developed in the 14th century by the Chartreuse monks and the now defunct order of the Chartreuse sisters. Seyssel wines gained recent fame as favorites of people taking cures at Aix-les-Bains and other spas along the eastern shore of Lake Bourget. Seyssel developed a naturally fizzy tendency into a fully fledged sparkling wine made by the classic method. The vineyards are on morainal clayey sands and gravel mixed with molasse. Roussette de Seyssel is a still white wine grown on the "brown soils" of the moraine; Seyssel Mousseux prefers the pebbly, sandy soils of the molasse.

From Seyssel southward along the western flank of the Mont du Gros Foug anticline to near the head of Lake Bourget lies the red-wine district of La Chautagne. The vineyards face westward overlooking marshlands which were formerly a northward extension of Lake Bourget. The soils are old lake terraces and slope wash from the Gros Foug. The principal vineyards are on a bench of molasse where a bed of calcareous glauconite mixes with limestone scree from the Gros Foug combining to make an excellent soil which gives the red wine a full-bodied structure with a rich, fruity taste. Chautagne wines are blends of about 70 percent Gamay, with the remainder Pinot Noir and Mondeuse. There are minor amounts of white wine made from the Jacquère and Aligoté.

Region six, the Val du Bourget, occupies the entire eastern shore of Lake Bourget, but today there are few vines. The beauty of the lake and the pleasant climate has attracted urban development that has replaced all but one commercial vineyard, Brison-St.-Innocent. This small surviving terroir is just north of Aix-les-Bains, on a bench of morainal sands and gravel. The reds of this ancient vineyard, made from the Gamay and particularly the Roussette, are aromatic and delightfully fresh.

It is suspected that it was along these slopes that the Celtic Allobroges cultivated their "Allobrogia" grapes. The first specific written account, however, of grape growing here is from the chronicles of Bérold de Chautagne in the 10th century, whose name is honored by the appellation. Wines from the Chautagne graced the tables of the Counts of Savoie in the 14th century.

Chautagne certainly enjoys an exceptional microclimate with an average annual temperature of 68°F (20°C). Plants characteristic of the Mediterranean: apricot, fig, almond, and olive share the limited growing space with the grape.

Bordering Lake Bourget tightly on the west is a long Jura ridge called the Mont du Chat, mountain of the cat. (The tunnel just before Chambéry on the autoroute from Lyon goes beneath the Mont du Chat.) One would never suspect that nestling in an embayment on the west side of this ridge are some of the most beautiful but seldom seen vineyards in Savoie.

Scree slopes from marly limestones of the Kimmeridgian provide the sites for these tucked-away vineyards. Where the scree is thin, vines are planted in the underlying rock with the help of a pick hammer. As André Combaz, in his report on Savoie for me, says, "here are vines *in*, not on the rocks" (*see* Color Plate 46). The noted terroirs on the slopes extending up to elevations of 1500 feet (450 m) are Jongieux, Marestel, and Monthoux. The Marestel vineyard owes its name to Claude Marestel, advisor to the Duke Emmanuel-Philbert in the 16th century. Marestel discovered the thin but favorable Kimmeridgian soils of the area and developed the early-day vineyards. A parallel ridge on the west shields the vineyards from the Westerlies, giving the area a favorable microclimate. About half the production of these three terroirs is white wine from the Altesse, along with the Jacquère and Chardonnay. The red grapes are the Mondeuse, Pinot Noir, and Gamay.

The final region, Cluse de Chambéry, is a deep valley separating the Bauges from the Chartreuse which extend southward. Although vineyards have lost out to urbanization on much of the desirable land elsewhere in Savoie, in the Cluse de Chambéry reasonable accommodation has been made between the two. For example, Monterminod, the most famous vineyard of the area whose reputation is 1000 years old, is in the very suburbs of Chambéry. The vineyard had all but disappeared during the middle of the 19th century, but was restored after phylloxera had been conquered.

In addition to Monterminod, St.-Jeoire-Prieuré, Chignin, and Montmélian are situated around the south-facing backslope of this huge syncline like the rounded end of a bathtub. The vineyards grow on slopes of morainal material over a substratum of marly limestone.

Southwestward across the *cluse* is Mont Granier and the Chartreuse range. Located in the shadow of this mountain are Apremont and Abymes de Myans on a large apron of rubble from Mont Granier. In the middle of the night on November 24, 1248, a mass on the north side of Mont Granier suddenly collapsed. The enormous slide of rock and mud buried the village of St.-André and several surrounding hamlets. Water from a period of excessive rain had seeped into fractures of a great mass of precariously perched strata, lubricating potential slide planes.

This shroud of 3000 acres (1200 ha) of chaotic rock material was left alone for almost five centuries and became overgrown with brushwood. Late in the 18th century, the people of Chambéry together with local inhabitants, decided they would honor the long-buried villages if they cleared the land and planted vineyards. Delimitation of the appellation is that of the Granier rock-slide, now planted with the Jacquère.

The Combe de Savoie is a continuation of the Cluse de Chambéry up the Isère Valley toward Albertville. (*Combe* is a word of Celtic origin meaning a sharp, deep valley.) The vineyards look down upon the "boulevard of the Alps,"

Chartreuse

Ten miles (16 km) north of Grenoble, in the fastness of the sharp-ridged Chartreuse, the austere order of Carthusian monks was founded in 1084. (Carthusian is a modification of the spelling of chartreuse.) Chartreuse is the mysterious yellow and green herbal liqueur originated by this austere order. It also became the name for that particular green color.

For the want of sufficient vineyard sites in the Chartreuse, wine-making by the order is now carried out in the Côte d'Or, the southern Rhône, and Bordeaux; the wineries for their Chartreuse, however, are located in the Rhône Valley.

the heavily traveled route to Albertville during both the ski and summer seasons. As in the Cluse de Chambéry, the vineyards are on scree slopes and *terres noires* of Jurassic dark limestones and black marls. In unbroken succession upstream from Montmélian are Arbin and Cruet, producing red wine; St.-Jean-de-la-Porte and St.-Pierre d'Albigny producing white. Historically, these wines have been some of the most highly regarded of Savoie. Just beyond St.-Pierre are the vineyards and nursery of Fréterive, providing plantlets and consultation to growers, not only to Savoie, but to other areas in France and Europe.

A bit of history

The French are proud of the Savoie vineyards, but Savoie did not officially become a part of modern France until April 1860, voted in by the local population. The kingdom of Sardinia to which the province belonged at the time was falling apart. It was agreed to return the territory of Savoie to France if the people living there approved. The vote was 130,833 "yeas" to 235 "nays." What a democratically peaceful solution! But the history of Savoie has not always been that peaceful and simple.

Savoie was originally part of the territory of the Celtic Allobroges. Half a century before Caesar came, the Romans had annexed Allobrogia to Transalpine Gaul which included Languedoc and Provence. Julius Caesar, as proconsul of Transalpine Gaul in the last century B.C., learned that the Celtic Helvetii of Switzerland were preparing to migrate across the territory of the Allobroges. He swiftly took action to prevent the violation of a Roman province by this aggressive tribe. Whether this threat was sufficient provocation for Caesar to invade and subjugate all of northern Gaul is a subject of historical debate, but, nevertheless, Gaul became Roman, then French.

In the 5th century, A.D., the Romans settled the Burgundians in the territory of Sapadia (Latin, Sabudia) part of the present-day Savoie. The name Savoie (rendered Savoy in English) is derived from the name of that original territory. In the next century, the Burgundians were conquered by the Franks, but for the next 300 years, the inhabitants of Savoie were left very much alone. The valleys and lake shores were cultivated and monastic communities were established. Most of the vineyards of Savoie today date from this period.

When the region was annexed to the Holy Roman Empire in 1032, Savoie became a county under Humbert I. Chambéry was the capital, and the nobles chose for their shield the white cross on a red background, the emblem of Savoie today.

In the 15th century, Savoie was elevated to a duchy, which suffered perpetual conflict between France and Italy. The Duchy extended from Geneva to Nice and on into Italy incorporating Genoa and Milan. From 1536 to 1559, Savoie was under France, then by treaty it was returned to the "House of Savoie." As things developed, mainly after 1860, it was the House of Savoie that made Italy an important nation and ruled it until 1946.

In the 16th and 17th centuries and then from 1792 to 1815, Savoie again came under French control. During more than a century of occupation, the cultural ties with France became strengthened in language, literature, and in spirit.

The former dukes of Savoie became Italian kings and sought to regain influence over Savoie. Many Savoyards, however, were migrating to France. Savoie was French by tongue, philosophy, and geography. So the outcome of the plebiscite in 1860, was of no great surprise.

In World War I, Alpine infantrymen of Savoie fought on all fronts with the Allies and lost four percent of its already sparse population. During the occupation of France by Germany in World War II, Savoie, ironically, was allowed to come under the control of Italy. But it was the Savoyard "Maquis" who really controlled the region.

Since World War II, Savoie has built a strong economy based on hydroelectric power and the electro-chemical industry. Its magnificent scenery attracts tourism year round. Savoie wines and food can satisfy the most discriminating palate, especially if consumed in the spectacular countryside of Savoie. The hotels of Savoie are well organized and planned for both the summer and ski seasons. The several spas of Aix-les-Bains, Evian, Thonon, and others have acquainted international visitors with both the comfort and cuisine of Savoie. "Savoy hotels" are found in many cities in Western Europe and North America. "Savoy" in a hotel name is meant to assure the guest comfort and luxury. You will find a "welcome mat" and a glass of its delightful wine awaiting you at the most modest chalet or finest hotel.

Bugey

The wines of Bugey are not great nor widely known wines, but in a neighborly gesture, without apology, are offered in the famous restaurants of Lyon, considered by some to be the gastronomic capital of France. Bugey wines were extensively developed during Roman times because Lyon was an important center on the great network of Roman roads. The wines remained important into the Middle Ages largely under the influence of several abbeys in the region. Bugey gradually began to lose importance as more accessible vineyards were developed in Burgundy and along the Rhône southward from Lyon.

The vineyards are mainly on slopes in the great loops of the Rhône as it works its way through the ridges of the Jura to be joined by the Saône at Lyon. The terrain means the vineyards are more disconnected, far less extensive, and of even lesser fame than those of Savoie. In these isolated vineyard areas, it was logical that winemaking traditions would develop differently. Perhaps the only unifying factor was that they used the same grapes.

The great Rhône glacier overrode this part of the Jura without materially modifying the valleys and soils. Where the Jura ridges plunge out southward east of Lyon, the Rhône glacier ground to a halt against the Massif Central. This terminal area is a patchwork of Miocene molasse and glacial till. It is not good grape land because water tables are shallow, slopes discontinuous, and soils poor.

The principal red grape varieties are Poulsard, locally called the Mèche, the Gamay, and the Mondeuse, all of which produce light red wines and rosés. White grapes include the Chardonnay, Altesse and Roussette.

In 1963, three areas were classified V.D.Q.S. and allowed to use their name along with Bugey: Cerdon, Manicle, and Montagnieu. Cerdon makes a sparkling wine from the Pinot Noir and Gamay which is appreciated as an aperitif. Manicle is a tiny area just southwest of Virieu-le-Grand, and was the home of the master epicure, Brillat-Savarin. Its white wines are made from the Chardonnay and Pinot Gris, and its reds are from the Pinot Noir. The exposures are on steep, south-facing slopes with soils from the limestones mixed with some glacial material. The Montagnieu vineyards stretch along slopes of the Rhône with good southeast exposures. The strongly perfumed white wines are made from the Altesse, or "Roussette du Bugey," and Mondeuse Blanc.

Diois

Diois, most famous for Clairette de Die, extends along the Drôme Valley for 35 scenic miles (over 50 km) through the heart of the Vercors, *see* Figure 11.1. The Vercors, one of the sub-Alpine ranges, has spectacular Lower Cretaceous limestone peaks framing an inner core of Jurassic marls and limestones. Die, Dea Augustus of the Romans, was the chief town of the Celtic tribe of the Voconti, or Voconci. This territory had been annexed as part of the Roman Transalpine province over 50 years before Caesar began his conquest of Northern Gaul. It is reported that the Voconci were making a naturally sweet, sparkling wine, probably from the Clairette and Muscat for some time before the Christian era. Tradition says many of the Roman vineyards were on slopes which were formerly winter grazing pastures of the Celtic Voconcis. Today, vines are planted on low-level river terraces in coves along the Drôme, on patches of ancient landslides (Celtic pastures), and in erosional basins of small side streams. The Drôme Valley was one of the routes leading to passes over the Alps. Supposedly this was the route of Hannibal's journey to attack Italy through the back door.

The reason the Drôme Valley became grapeland is geology. A clue to the geologic influence is the big U-shaped north loop of the Drôme. It is skirting the large up-faulted block (a horst) of Jurassic, the core of the Cretaceous Vercors. It is the dark marls of the Jurassic which weather to the excellent soils of *terres noires*, "black earth," so well suited to the Clairette and Muscat grapes.

During the Ice Age, freeze-thaw caused extensive local slumping (small landslides) of the massive Jurassic marls. The "plowing" effect of the slump areas hastened weathering of the *terres noires*, on whose soils pastures, orchards, and vineyards abound. Rock fragments in the *terres noires* contribute to good drainage and soil structure. The beige-colored irregular splotches labeled "E" on Figure 11.4, are the slump areas. ("E" is for *éboulis*, the French term for gravity slump material.) These little landslides, long since stabilized, vary in size from 50 acres (20 ha) to several square miles.

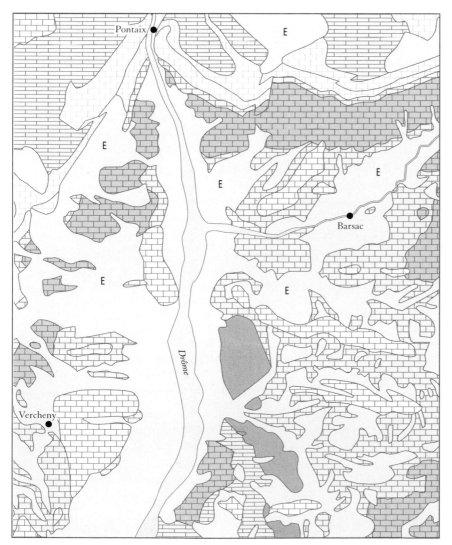

Figure 11.4
Geology of Diois
The sparkling wine Crémant de Die is now an appellation. Individual vineyards would be extremely difficult to pinpoint, owing to their small size and scattered nature, especially along the river. Many vineyards, however, are found on the *éboulis* (adapted from 1:50,000 Die sheet no. 843 by kind permission of B.R.G.M)

☐ Stabilized landslides composed of material from higher relief

▤ High terraces – limestone pebbles, sands and slope wash

▤ Basal Cretaceous – coloured marls and thin limestones

☐ Upper Jurassic, Portlandian massive limestone

▦ Upper and Middle Jurassic limestones and dark marls – *terres noires*

The small appellation of Châtillon-en-Diois is in the valley of the Bez, a tributary of the Drôme in the shadow of the Montagne de Glandasse. Wines are from the Gamay and a blend of Aligoté and Chardonnay. Further up the Drôme, at Luc-en-Diois, a landslide dammed the Drôme, causing a small lake and waterfall known as Le Claps. Upstream the valley narrows and vines begin to disappear.

Downstream from Die, the Drôme and the highway are squeezed into a narrow defile guarded by the medieval town of Pontaix. The defile is created by a transverse ridge of Tithonian limestone crossing the valley.

Barsac (same spelling as the appellation in the Graves of Bordeaux) is a wine village of great tradition in a picturesque little landslide basin. Its vineyards are on the "black earth" mixed with angular fragments of limestone.

The village of Vercheny is on the upper rim of an amphitheater where old, high-level alluvial terraces lap onto a large patch of *terres noires*. The upper part of the village known as Le Temple, is surrounded by a marvelous vineyard. The high ground gives an excellent view southeastward toward Barsac and the great temple-peaks of Tithonian limestone.

The wines of Diois are nearly all blends of the Muscat à Petits Grains and the Clairette Blanc, both ancient Mediterranean grapes. The Muscat is generally conceded to have been one of the grapes brought by the Greeks to Massalia (Marseille). The two grapes complement each other in traditional blending of the wine of Diois, as well as in the soils they prefer: the Muscat primarily on the *terres noires*, while the Clairette prefers the slopes of limestone scree.

The wine for which Diois is famous is its Clairette de Die Tradition, made, as the name suggests, in the same way for 2000 years. Its moderate fizz comes from being bottled before the original sugar of its Muscat grapes is fully fermented. A Brut is made solely from the Clairette by the classic method.

Because of the variation in soil and microclimates, Diois wines vary considerably in character along the valley. About two dozen growers bottle their own wines, the remainder of the production is from two cooperatives. Some wine areas in France are worth a side trip for their scenery, some for their wines. Diois is worth the trip for both reasons.

The Rhône Valley

The Rhône is born high in the Swiss Alps within yodeling distance of headwaters of two other of Europe's great rivers, the Rhine and Danube. The river starts as melt water at the foot of the Rhône glacier, still a spectacular view, although only ice-cube in size compared to the once-mighty valley glacier that ground and scraped its way to the buttress of the Massif Central. From the source of high meadows of Edelweiss and tinkling cow bells through its scenic course to the sea, the Rhône is seldom out of site of vineyards.

From youthful exuberance in the Alps, the Rhône enters a more quiet, diplomatic status in Lake Geneva where it is half French and half Swiss. Leaving the lake, the Rhône loops its way through the Jura to be joined by the Saône at Lyon. After a few twists and turns at Givois and Vienne, the full-flowing Rhône starts the final leg of its journey to the sea down a rift valley with a steep west wall of granite and a more open sloping side on the east. This is part of the rift system across western Europe (*see* the chapter on Alsace).

The steep wall is hung with terraces from Côte Rôtie to St.-Péray – the Northern Rhône. At Valence, the crystallines of the Massif Central veer southwest along the major Alès fault, opening into the Languedoc. The parallel Cévennes and Garrigues are terminated bluntly at the river by the rift zone. Eastward, the valley expands to the "rootless mountains" of the Baronnies and Lubéron. This large triangular area from the west bank to the foothills of the sub-Alpine ranges is the Southern Rhône.

Typical Mediterranean climate does not reach much north of Valence, but the Rhône is "sunshine valley" throughout – with a minimum of rainfall. It is the route of the infamous *mistral*, the north wind that blows when there is high pressure over northern France and low pressure in the western Mediterranean. Velocity of the wind is increased to speeds over 90 miles (140 km) per hour by the air mass being funneled between the Vercors and Massif Central. Its destructive force diminishes at Cornas as the winds spread into the inverted "V" below Valence and along the coastal area, particularly into Languedoc. In the mid-Rhône, vines are pruned low to strengthen them against the cyclonic velocity of the *mistral*; otherwise, they would suffer the same bending and battering as the olive trees illustrated in many of Van Gogh's paintings. Only occasionally does the *marin*, the moist sea wind riding the "vent du Midi," penetrate the Valence gateway to reach the Northern Rhône. Although the weather may vary from very hot to harshly cold, overall the Rhône Valley has a favorable climate for viticulture, producing some of France's most memorable wines.

The Northern Rhône

The steep vineyard terraces, almost continuous from Vienne to Valence, date from the Romans. Employing a craft developed for the steep, rocky slopes of the eastern Mediterranean, dry, packed-rock walls were built shoulder-high as sturdy and lasting as masonry.

The mineral-rich soils from the crystalline rocks of the Massif Central are particularly well suited to the Syrah. This red grape is well adapted to the very hot to harshly cold Rhône climate. There are four white grapes: the Marsanne, Roussanne, Roussette, and Viognier. The grapes grow at elevations of 500 feet (150 m) at valley level to 1000 feet (300 m) on the plateau.

Eight individual appellations are designated along the 40 miles (25 km) of steep bluffs, *see* Figure 11.5. Filling in the gaps between the A.O.C. vineyards are those of the general Côtes du Rhône.

A 6-mile (10-km) southwest course of the Rhône gives a full sun-baked exposure to the crystalline rocks of the Côte Rôtie, "roasted slope." The appellation is made up of numerous small parcels on choice exposures and soils.

Bedrock of the northeastern part of the scarp upstream from Ampuis is a schist containing both muscovite (white mica) and biotite (black mica). The rock weathers to dark brown which gave it the name Côte Brune (brown slope). Below Ampuis is a complex of schist and gneiss (a granitic-like, metamorphic rock), which weather to a grayish cast, the celebrated Côte Blonde (blonde slope). The white Viognier does well on Côte Blonde, while the Syrah is the grape of the Côte Brune. The two grapes used to be blended to give a good balanced wine and up to 20% Viognier is still permitted, though in practice it is less used now.

According to popular legend, the Seigneur of Ampuis had two daughters, one blonde, the other brunette. He gave each one a dowry of vineyards in the Côte Rôtie corresponding to her hair coloring. The legend says that is how Côte Brune and Côte Blonde came to be so named. But geology and weathering determined the color of the soils millions of years before there was a Seigneur with two daughters.

Figure 11.5
**Appellations of the
Northern Rhône**
Principal appellations are
along the granite walls of
the eastern flank of the
Massif Central

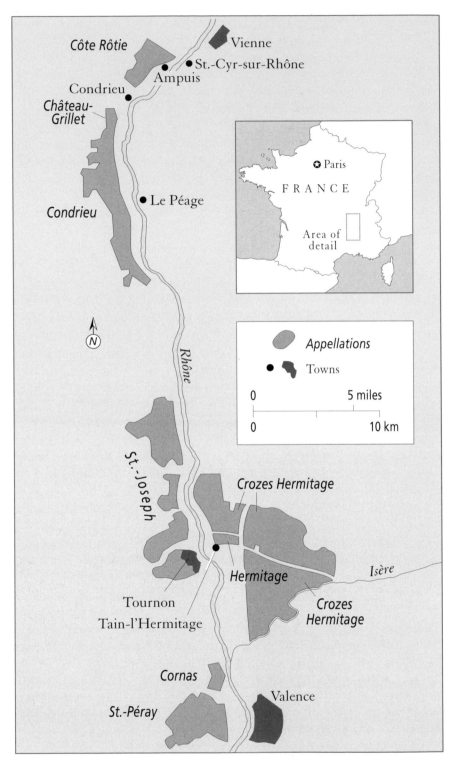

On my first visit to Condrieu, I went immediately to visit the steeply terraced vineyards. They are indeed steep. The climb up the pathway, slippery from a recent shower, was like trying to go up the down escalator. According to the local saying, Condrieu vignerons must have "bon dos, bon pied et bon oeil." I would add to "good back, good feet, and good eyes," that they need good lungs. When I pushed open a squeaky, old wooden entrance door to a terrace, I was met with a shock – there were only weeds and brush. I felt as if I was entering a haunted place or a graveyard. In a way they were both. The vineyards were left to die after the phylloxera and the loss of many vignerons in World War I – a graveyard of unfulfilled dreams. Happily for Viognier, the fickle grape of this appellation, when the fashion swung towards white, especially dry, wines in the 1970s, Condrieu growers were encouraged to reconstruct their vineyards. With new investment, the appellation thrives again with 150 acres (60 ha) now planted (compared to less than 25 acres (10 ha) in the 1960s).

Granites, including those of Condrieu, are classified according to their texture and "accessory minerals" such as the micas. A geologic report of this area contained the term "granite hétérogine." This was translated by a non-geologist as an "incongruous granite." Perhaps some heterogenous granites such as this, with an odd mixture of minerals, do appear incongruous. As you will recall from Part One, micas and feldspars weather to clay. The abundance of micas in the heterogenous granites of Condrieu produces good clay binding for the gritty soils and may contribute to the suppleness which characterizes Condrieu wines with their delicate but elusive bouquet redolent of apricots and violets.

Château-Grillet, a 5-acre (2-ha) enclave within Condrieu is a "five-star" terroir. It is France's second smallest appellation – after Burgundy's La Romanée at just over 2 acres (0.8 ha). Grillet is also a monopole, a single ownership property, belonging to the Neyret-Gachet family since 1830. Small it may be, but the microclimate of this steeply terraced amphitheater helps the Viognier produce an exceptionally fine, white wine with a flowery bouquet.

It was rare good fortune to find Mr. André Neyret-Gachet, a gracious and fascinating man, at home when my daughter and I appeared there unannounced one October day. He discussed numerous aspects of Château-Grillet and the Côtes du Rhône. It was pointed out that vines on some of the terraces were almost 80 years old. Our host said the Château-Grillet soils are relatively uniform with little observable variations in the granite bedrock. Obviously he was proud of the unique terroir producing one of the finest white wines in the region. Mr. Neyret-Gachet called over to our hotel to ensure we had a bottle of Château-Grillet for dinner that night. I was saddened later to learn that he had died.

The appellation of St.-Joseph extends from Château-Grillet to Tournon, an ugly industrial sprawl. The bedrock is a granite containing very large crystals – like a plum pudding. The brown soil on slopes and terraces is deep and stony. A series of small side streams increases the number of good vineyard slopes. There are numerous points in the vineyards where the valley wall is almost vertical. The plateau above these bluffs offers scant growing opportunity, as the soils are thin and the moisture limited, although this did not stop vignerons from planting here and on the valley floor. Although the St.-Joseph vineyards are very old, the appellation itself dates only from 1956 and the delimited area was changed in 1992 to regain the emphasis on the slopes. Some of the slopes around Tournon are less precipitous, but terracing is still required.

Across the river from Tournon is Hermitage, one of the stars of the Northern Rhône. It is often hyphenated with Tain, wine capital of the region.

The hill mass of Hermitage above Tain is a curious combination of granite with Quaternary delta deposits and Pliocene clay plastered tightly to it on the eastern side. The Pliocene is a remnant of a marine arm of the Mediterranean. An erosional remnant of a fan-delta of the Isère overlies the Pliocene. Capping the hill are deposits of loess, containing calcareous "rock flour" whose slope wash "seasons" the coarse, infertile delta. The rock flour was ground in the Alps by valley glaciers and brought to the Rhône Valley by the Isère and other streams. The "seasoned" delta soils particularly favor the Syrah grape which produces about 80 percent of Hermitage wines. The number one terroir is generally conceded to be Les Bessards, situated entirely on the granite. Also on the granite is the small La Varogne terroir.

Forming an arc around the hill of Hermitage is the large appellation of Crozes Hermitage composed of three geologic terrains, each producing different quality wine. The narrow exposure of granite at Hermitage extends northward, producing Crozes' best red wines. Cultivation is dominated by the domaines of M. Chapoutier and Paul Jaboulet Aîné. East of Hermitage is a highly dissected, low plateau made up of a Pliocene clay at the base and a glacial terrace capped by a late Quaternary terrace splotched with loess. This mixture of sands, clays, and loessic soils seems ideally suited to the white grapes of Hermitage, Marsanne and Roussanne. The terrain southeast of Hermitage is a series of Quaternary terraces growing both red and white wines of only Côtes du Rhône appellation quality.

Geology and the Mediterranean climate combine to make Cornas what some consider to be the finest wine of the Northern Rhône. A narrow block of Jurassic limestone is downfaulted against granite of the Massif Central – the first limestones appearing in a vineyard south of Bas-Beaujolais. Although the slopes are only moderately steep, terracing is still needed. The mixture of limestone, marl, and sand with the granite soils gives Cornas wines a 1000-year-old tradition for great quality. The appellation is nearly 1360 acres (550 ha), though not all of it is planted. Wines in the southern part of the appellation where the soils are particularly sandy are well balanced and quick-aging.

The end of the journey down the Northern Rhône is celebrated with a sparkling wine, St.-Péray. The method is that of the Champenois but there is much individuality in styles due to a variety of soils and the number of growers. Soils weather from granite, old terrace deposits, and Jurassic limestones of the Cornas fault block. The different soils dominate certain patches influencing the character of the wine grown. The wines are a Marsanne–Roussanne blend, about one-fifth of which are still wines. The sparkling wines are fruity and somewhat heavier than other sparkling wines such as the Clairette de Die.

The Southern Rhône

Below Valence, the Rhône Valley opens into a topographic embayment with a variety of vineyard landforms (mountain-flank slopes, river terraces, molassic plateaux, and klippen, remnants of thrust sheets from the sub-Alpine ranges). The west bank of the Rhône continues to be steep as ridges of the Cretaceous Garrigues and Costières du Gard come right to the river front. The embayment is bounded on the east by foothills of the Subalpine ranges of the Baronnies and Lubéron, *see* Figure 11.6.

Interest in viticulture was greatly heightened by the papal presence in Avignon in the beginning of the 14th century. As an inducement to persuade the Holy See to move the papacy from Rome to Avignon the French offered a large tract of land called the Comtat Venaissin. The Comtat was a region of natural beauty north of the Dentelles, east of Orange. It remained an enclave of church property within France until it, like so many other estates, was confiscated at the time of the Revolution.

Winegrowing in the region was renewed briefly in the 19th century, only to be cut short by the phylloxera devastation. In 1953, a significant incentive for development was the authority given to a number of communes to use their names on their labels, provided they followed certain A.O.C. regulations. The 16 privileged villages are identified in Figure 11.6 by squares. The viticultural stars are indicated by that symbol on the map.

Development of the landscape

In the late Cretaceous there was no Rhône; the area was a dismal mix of dry land, lakes, marshes — and strange beasts. In the early Tertiary, a trough-like depression developed in the location of the Rhône Valley. As the Alps began to rise, great quantities of molasse were shed across the area to the young Rhône. The downwarp became more acute as the Rhône–Saône rift formed a crease along the margin of the Massif Central. During the Pliocene, an arm of the Mediterranean invaded the valley and adjacent low areas to the east, leaving thin deposits of clay and sand.

In the later phases of Alpine mountain building, the "rootless" Baronnies, Ventoux, and Lubéron were thrust west and southwest. Sheets (nappes) of Cretaceous limestones were pushed almost to the Rhône. Subsequent erosion left remnants of the sheets as klippen, limestone islands which became vineyard sites.

West of the Rhône, a major fault trending northeast–southwest through Alès separates the crystalline Cévennes, an element of the Massif Central, from the Cretaceous Garrigues. The terminal hills of the Garrigues overlooking the Rhône provide slopes for Tavel, Lirac, and general appellation wines. On the eastern side, floods of the Ice Age reworked molasse, adding debris of their own to build extensive terraces and gravel plateaux, providing many vineyard sites.

The wine areas

There are three groups of wine areas (*see* the legend in Figure 11.6). The stars of the Southern Rhône are Châteauneuf-du-Pape, Gigondas, Tavel, Lirac, and now Vacqueyras. Châteauneuf is unquestionably the flagship appellation. Bear in mind, however, that there is no one Châteauneuf, as numerous growers in the appellation make their own style of that wine. The vines grow on a small plateau almost 300 feet (100 m) above the Rhône Valley, surrounded by Quaternary and Recent alluvium. Elevation of the plateau provided a welcome relief for the popes from the hot, humid summers of Avignon.

Wine from the Châteauneuf plateau would have achieved more than local fame on its own merits, but association with papal majesty gave this deep red wine a special prestige — and its name. Almost three-quarters of this highly acclaimed wine is exported.

The photogenic trademark of Châteauneuf-du-Pape is its big round stones, viewed by many as "touchstones" for quality. These stream-rolled cobbles are part of the Miocene molasse derived from the Alpine region. They are difficult to walk on and even harder on mechanical equipment. The stones do absorb heat during the day to be radiated to the underside of the plant during the evening, but heat is really not a problem in this climate.

The secret of Châteauneuf is not the stones, but the subsoil of red clay and ferruginous sands of the underlying molasse. Moreover, good Châteauneuf is produced where there are no stones, but vineyards without stones do not get a second look by tourists. Another popular notion that Châteauneuf wines are made from 13 grapes is only half true — most of the 500 growers use only half a dozen of the permitted grape varieties. I cannot imagine what a wine blended of 13 grapes would be like!

Most Châteauneuf is composed of the Grenache (red and white varieties), Syrah, Mourvèdre, Cinsault, Clairette, and Roussanne. In general, the wines are about 80 percent Grenache. Not enough white wine is used to affect the deep red color for which Châteauneuf is noted. (These days white varieties are often used to make a white Châteauneuf du Pape.) The proportions of the various grapes used are the individual vintner's choice, hence there is no one Châteauneuf-du-Pape. However, all are dark in color, high in alcohol, with plenty of aroma.

Orange

Just north of the Châteauneuf plateau is Orange, wine capital of the region. This is where the delightful fruit got its name, a name now given to states, counties, and cities. A fruit tree imported long ago from Asia did well in this part of the Rhône Valley. The name of the fruit was derived from "Arausio," a Celtic god, evolving to "orange."

In the 16th century, Orange was the capital of a small Dutch principality whose first lord was William, Count of Nassau. William returned to his native land to lead a revolt against its Spanish overlords. He was dubbed the "Prince of Orange". When William became the first king of the Netherlands, his House of Nassau became popularly known as the "House of Orange."

Gigondas, lesser known than Châteauneuf-du-Pape, is one of the premier wines of the Southern Côtes. The name Gigondas derives from the Latin jocunditas, meaning "merry city." The village is said to be anything but lively except at harvest time. Merry or not, the town is in a picturesque setting: the lush Ouvèze Valley in the foreground bordered by tall Florentine cypress with the Dentelles de Montmirail as a scenic backdrop. The Dentelles is a vertical slab of Jurassic limestone that has weathered into a mesh-like lace, French *dentelle*. Gigondas is the senior of more than half a dozen villages which cluster around the Dentelles that will be discussed later.

The vineyards are on soils of an upper terrace of the Quaternary Ice Age enhanced by slope wash from Cretaceous marls and Jurassic limestones. The very dark red "block-buster" wine is made from the Grenache with additions of Mourvèdre and Syrah.

Vacqueyras, southwest around the hill from Gigondas, gained appellation status in 1990. Its wines are often compared in style with Gigondas — they are both emphatically *vins de garde*. In the 14th century, the Bishops of Orange had encouraged development of vineyards and olives in this area. Severe frost in 1956 destroyed most of the ancient olive trees, after which grapes gained in a big way.

The last two of the "starred" appellations are Tavel and Lirac, west across the Rhône from Châteauneuf-du-Pape. These two areas produce perhaps the most famed rosés of France. One wonders why Tavel and Lirac decided to make rosé rather than red. Climate and geology may have had something to do with why.

The west bank of the Rhône is somewhat higher and drier than Châteauneuf-du-Pape on the east side. The calcareous, sandy soils originally cultivated on the lower levels produced a lighter wine than either Châteauneuf or vineyards upstream. Perhaps Tavel growers decided that rather than compete at a disadvantage with the solid reds, they would make rosés.

Figure 11.6
Appellations of the Southern Rhône
Vineyards of this widened Southern Rhône Valley are distributed on klippen and around the margins of rootless mountain masses

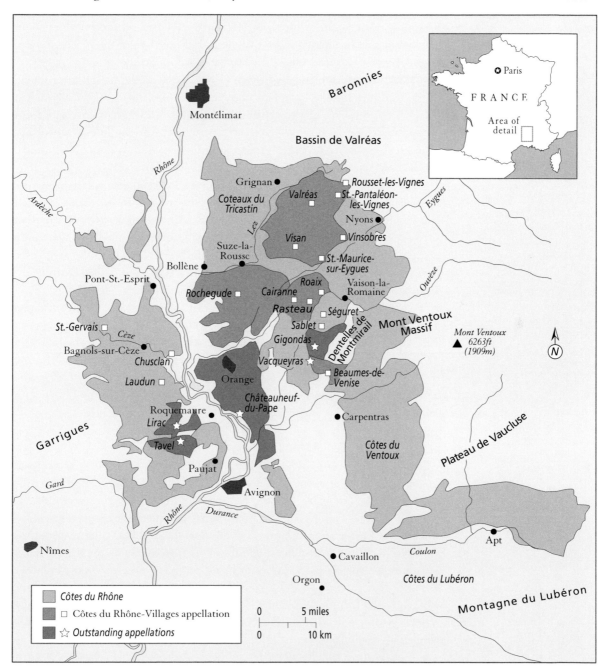

However it came about, Tavel and Lirac produce some of the best rosés going. Made from the same red Grenache as Châteauneuf and Gigondas, the wine is blended with Clairette, and some Cinsault. The particular style of Tavel and Lirac comes from the addition of small amounts of the white Piquepoul and Bourboulenc for flavor. Proportions are not to exceed 60 percent Grenache with a required minimum of 15 percent Cinsault.

In many areas it was the monks who led the way in viticulture. At Tavel it was the farmers who taught an order of monks about wine. Near the end of the 19th century, monks of Ste.-Famille, an order for those taking vows later in life, came to the hamlet of Manissay near Tavel. The farm they bought included vineyards. The order, which originated in Holland, knew nothing about growing grapes or making wine. Obliging neighbors taught them. The monks' former property is now some of the best vineyard in Tavel.

Tavel has the dubious distinction of being one of the places from which phylloxera spread. In the latter part of the 19th century, a grower in the village of Pujaut known for his grape experimentation, received some rooted vines from America. Neither he nor his benefactor knew that a deadly little creature (and probably eggs) had come along on the roots of the vines. The story of the spread, devastation, and eventual control of phylloxera is told in Part One.

Lirac, adjoining Tavel on the north, is much larger in area, but its wines are less well known. The geology is the same, but the atmosphere of Lirac is polluted much of the time with smoke from steelworks to the north, delaying maturation of the grapes by a week or more. Lirac remained a quiet, traditional winemaking area until the early 1960s when an outsider brought new life to the area. This time it was an airplane rather than a bulldozer. Again it is Livingston-Learmonth and Masters to credit with the story (*see* margin feature).

On the Rhône opposite Châteauneuf-du-Pape is Roquemaure, which was for several hundred years before the coming of the railroad, a busy shipping port. The major fault through Nîmes that separates the Garrigues and the Costières du Gard extends through Roquemaure and across the Rhône. The faulting dislevels the bedrock in the river creating a shallows which was a ford in the early days. History points to this as Hannibal's crossing-point of the Rhône with his elephants on his way to attack Rome.

The "-Villages" appellations

The -Villages appellations, next in hierarchy below the "stars," may be grouped in four geologic areas: the Valréas Basin, Dentelles de Montmirail, the area around Bollène, and villages on the west bank of the Rhône.

The Valréas Basin is a topographic embayment with the town of Valréas at the hub, *see* Figure 11.6. The basin is walled on the north and east by upturned Cretaceous, massive limestones of the Baronnies. On the south, the Aigues River separates the Valréas Basin from the Dentelles, a frontal element of the Mont Ventoux geologic complex. The Valréas was a shallow depositional basin in the Miocene, collecting molassic sands, clays, and conglomerates. In the Pliocene, the Valréas became a shallow marine embayment leaving thin deposits of sands and clays. The resulting terrain is undulating with two hill-masses formed by cap rocks of cemented conglomerates.

Nine of the sixteen -Villages appellations are located in this basin: Valréas, Visan, St.-Pantaléon-les-Vignes, Rousset, Vinsobres, St.-Maurice-sur-Eygues, Cairanne, Rasteau, and Roaix.

Valréas, wine capital of the area, was the chief town of the Comtat Venaissin, the papal enclave. It is on a low hill surrounded by rich, fertile land supporting a polyculture. The vines, however, prefer the slopes of the nearby hills with soils of pebbly, chalky clay. The better vineyards of the village of Visan are located on slopes of the northernmost molassic hill-mass.

The vineyards of Vinsobres dating at least from the 4th century, extend from slopes of the hill-mass several miles upstream on terraces along the Eygues. A short distance downstream from Vinsobres is St.-Maurice-sur-Eygues whose vines on gentle, south-facing slopes of molasse overlook the Eygues Valley.

Rousset is at the base of the steep front of the Baronnies, but its vineyards, with those of St.-Pantaléon, are on gently sloping terrain on gravelly soils and clay mixed with limestone outwash at the base of the mountain front.

The Dentelles de Montmirail stand like a cockscomb back of Gigondas. Around the slopes west and south of this detached mass from Mont Ventoux are five of the other identified wine villages: Roaix, Rasteau, Séguret, Sablet, and Beaumes-de-Venise.

The "rootless" Baronnies and Dentelles rode on a sole fault greased by beds of Triassic salt and anhydrite. Two small salt diapirs were squeezed out to the surface. (Diapirs are "blisters" of deep, plastic material which break through the overburden.) It was sulfurous springs for medical purposes that first attracted the Romans to the Dentelles. These springs came from a solution of anhydrite (calcium sulfate). The hills rising abruptly over 1500 feet (450 m) above the surrounding plain provide pleasant microclimates. Springs of pure as well as sulfurous water and the nearby vineyards brought the Avignon popes to the area.

Roaix is an attractive medieval village whose vineyards are on terraces along the Ouvèze. Roaix wine, made from the Grenache, grows on stony, limestone soils along with fields of lavender.

Rasteau produces a little-known *vin doux naturel* (naturally vinified sweet wine), one of the Côtes du Rhône's most unusual wines, and also continues to make a hearty red. The vineyards of Rasteau adjoin those of Cairanne at the southwest corner of the southern hill-mass. This village feels the full brunt of the enervating *mistral*, but its vineyards are in the lee of the hill-mass on soils of clay and sandy clay.

Sablet and Séguret are twin medieval towns less than 2 miles (3 km) apart. Vineyards of these appellations extend from the villages on soils of Miocene molasse and terraces of the Ouvèze.

On the south slope of the Dentelles is Beaumes-de-Venise, the historical center of the region. Beaumes is an old Provençal word for grotto, while Venise is derived from *Venaissin*, old French, meaning church property. Beaumes has the distinction of being the only place in the Côtes du Rhône where the Muscat is grown – the same grape as the Muscat de Frontignan in Languedoc. But the Muscat is susceptible to diseases and pests that abound in the southern Rhône climate, requiring a great deal of care. The vineyards of Beaumes rival those of Gigondas in size but not in quality.

Lirac and the airplane

A French winegrower from Algeria, Charles Pons-Mure, came to the Southern Rhône to find a new start. He was a pilot and reconnoitered much of the lower Rhône Valley from the air. Lirac was selected as having undeveloped possibilities. Pons-Mure and his wife bought and cleared brush-covered slopes and started their vineyard.

Later the Pons-Mures entered some of their rosé at the wine fair at Mâcon where it took prizes. At the time, they were living in a tumbled-down small house, and as something of a whimsy, put on their label Castel Analow, which means "castle, there is no" in Provençal. Later, label officials paid them a visit and asked to see the castle. Madame Pons-Mure told the inspectors there was no castle, the one on the label she had sketched from the story of Snow White and the Seven Dwarfs. The officials were not amused and required that a cross be printed over the castle on the label. Castel Analow has gained in popularity, but still bears its cross.

South of Bollène, located on one of the "islands" of Cretaceous limestone, are the villages of Rochegude and Cairanne. This klippe has in large part been weathered down to a low relief and is covered with vines. Rochegude backs on to a resistant ridge of limestone of the Bollène "island" with vineyards sweeping northward toward Suze-la-Rousse. In addition to its wine, Rochegude is noted for its pottery made from clay derived from the deeply weathered rocks.

The fourth area of village appellations is on the west bank of the Rhône north of Lirac: it includes Laudun, Chusclan, and St.-Gervais. As the Garrigues approach the Rhône, the scrubby ridges become plateau-like, and the soils more arable. These three villages, as do Tavel and Lirac, produce primarily rosés, but with some red and some white wines.

Laudun, on the slopes of the Plateau du Camp de César, extends down to the River Cèze. It is a very old wine village where amphorae dating 100 years or more B.C. have been found in archeological excavation. In the 18th century, Chusclan wines were more widely appreciated than either Tavel or Lirac. The presence of a Benedictine priory assured good-quality wines, while their popularity was assured by the counts of Grignan who owned the properties. Chusclan's east-facing vineyards overlook the Rhône. St.-Gervais was awarded its appellation in 1974, but is still not very well known. The terrain is almost flat, with little protection from the drying winds of the *mistral*.

The regional appellations

Regional and V.D.Q.S. appellations surround the "stars" and the special -Villages making an almost solid cape of vineyards (*see* Figure 11.6). Unfortunately, large volumes of bulk wine of low quality, especially from the catch-all A.O.C. Côtes du Rhône, stigmatize the Southern Rhône.

West of the Rhône, north of Chusclan, is the large appellation of Côtes du Vivarais, better known for its trout streams than its wines. Most of its red and rosé wines are consumed locally by the seasonal visitors.

South of Tavel, additional general appellation vineyards are found on terraces of the Gard River adjoining Languedoc. Coteaux de Tricastin, on the east side of the Rhône, on a dissected plateau of Miocene molasse, produces about one tenth of the wine of the Southern Rhône. Some vineyards on the plateau alternate with fields of lavender, but there are better vineyards on terraces of the late Ice Age composed of gray to yellowish sandy, marly clay with numerous limestone pebbles.

The Côtes du Ventoux vineyards are on alluvial aprons and terraces around the western front of the large Vaucluse molassic plateau. The soils are of sandstones, greenish-gray marls and gravel from the Eocene and Miocene molasse. Overall, wines of the Côtes du Ventoux are of reasonably good character, but the variability of the soils and lack of consistency in adaptation of grape to soil, places the area in the bulk wine category. However, some growers have proved that there are sites capable of producing excellent wine.

Vineyards of the large Côtes du Lubéron are scattered in the valleys and along the lower slopes of the Cretaceous Montagne du Lubéron. This general appellation is sometimes included in Provence, but we have taken the Durance as the arbitrary boundary between the two provinces.

Provence

At the time of the ancients Provence was something of a staging area for emigration and travel up the Rhône corridor into northern Gaul, supplying vineplants to the Allobrogia of the Savoie region and perhaps beyond. Provence could thus claim to be the cradle of French viticulture. Why then, is it not a premier wine province today?

Some say it is the sun – too much of it. Some complain that there are too many grape varieties. Some suggest the province lacks physiographic continuity (where there is a physiographic continuity, growers feel attached to the land as they do in Burgundy, Alsace, and the Médoc). Elsewhere in France adaptation of vineplant to a variety of soils and landforms has been a way of life for the vigneron. Only in recent times has it become a serious effort in Provence because for too long the captive audience on a holiday budget was a disincentive to making individual, quality wines.

I suggest that the problem is a combination of the sun, the sea, and the geology. While the beaches are limited, the sun and the sea have attracted a growing population to the area. Good vineyard sites have been preempted by man for other uses except for a few, such as Cassis and Bandol.

There is indeed a lack of physiographic continuity or structural style to the land. The geology of Provence is confusing as it represents the meeting ground of three tectonic influences. Discontinuity of the geology of Provence may be one of its faults, but at the same time it contributes to the interest of the landscape. And it was three crustal deformations during the Tertiary which gave variety to its landscape.

The landscape

The first of the three crustal deformations was associated with the Pyrenees, creating the Provençal ranges. The second period of deformation was the Alpine, which left the Provençal and Maritime Alps. And the pressures of the Alpine deformation resulted in a third phase which rejuvenated the old Hercynian trend with the thrusting ashore of crystalline rocks of the Maures and the Paleozoic rocks of the Esterel. These three trends create a dichotomy of interesting landscape:physiographic discordance.

Climate

Overall, the Mediterranean climate is most conducive to the growth of flowers, trees, and fruits, including grapevines. What is good for crops is good for people. A number of years ago, Provence, and the Côte d'Azur in particular, replaced Biarritz on the Atlantic coast as the most popular sun and sea vacation land of northwest Europe.

Although warm and sunny most of the year, rainy periods seasonally occur in the spring, followed by a long, hot, dry summer. The long, dry spell leading into the grapes' maturation period makes moisture-holding soil and water storage in the bedrocks very critical. The drying winds of the *mistral* are strongly felt from Marseille and west into Languedoc. In addition to the *mistral*, the mountains–sea relationship generates eight winds that blow from all directions of the compass (*see* Color Plate 3).

Special and regional appellations

Recognizing the poor reputation of Provence wines, in 1931 a syndicate of growers in the Côtes de Provence began the bid to resurrect pride in quality and confidence by the consumer. In cooperation with the I.N.A.O. (the regulatory body for the entire quality wine industry, founded in 1932) resurgence was firmly based on geology, hydrology, and microclimate to identify the most favorable viticultural areas and the most suitable grapes. The growers themselves provided strict tastings and analyses to verify quality. These efforts were interrupted by World War II, but in 1953, the Côtes de Provence was awarded V.D.Q.S. status.

Palette, Cassis, and Bandol, which had for a number of years been recognized as terroirs of distinction, had already been given A.O.C. status. Within Provence, these three small distinguished appellations represent less than 2 percent of the total area under vines. In 1977, the entire Côtes de Provence, which covers a diversity of geology and wines, was raised to appellation status. The outstanding and general (regional) appellations of Provence are outlined on the map opposite, Figure 11.7.

For the last few decades, Provence's reputation has been largely based on light, easy quaffing wines (80 percent is rosé) which pair easily with the classic Mediterranean fare. The rosés are generally blends of Grenache and Carignan; the reds are from Cinsault, Syrah, and Mourvèdre, with some Cabernet Sauvignon, especially in the north. The whites (less than 5 percent of total production) are primarily Ugni Blanc and Clairette, with frequent additions of Rolle, Sémillon, Sauvignon Blanc, and Chardonnay.

The large area of Coteaux d'Aix-en-Provence is composed of three zones: Coteaux des Baux, Etang de Berre, and Aix.

The Coteaux des Baux is at the foot of the Alpilles, a highly deformed Cretaceous limestone massif. On the northeast flank of the Alpilles, the promontory of Baux rises abruptly some 1300 feet (400 m) above the Rhône Valley. The now abandoned ancient village of Les Baux is on a spectacular spur overlooking St.-Rémi and vineyards in soils of limestone scree and terrace deposits. Excellent Cabernet Sauvignon blends and reasonable Chardonnays are being made here. Efforts by local growers have led to appellation status for the reds and rosés, which now go under the name Côtes des Baux de Provence. However, those which have more than 20 percent Cabernet in the blend, including some of the best, can only be sold as *vins de pays*.

Bauxite, a compact, earthy mineral is named for Les Baux where it was discovered in 1822. Bauxite is the chief source of the metal aluminum. Being composed primarily of aluminum oxide, it is the product of long and thorough weathering of certain clays. Some surface mining operations are still active in this ancient quarry.

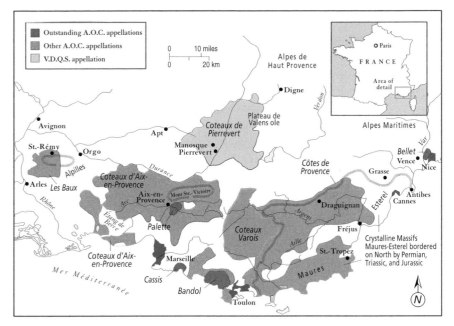

Figure 11.7
Appellations of Provence
The distribution and diverse trends of the several geologic provinces emphasize the lack of continuity of Provence vineyards

The Etang de Berre was at one time a bay which became a lagoon when sandbars closed all but a narrow outlet to the sea. The flanks of east–west trending, Cretaceous limestone ridges on the north and south of the lagoon support vineyards in soils of deeply weathered limestone scree.

Vineyards of the Aix-en-Provence zone are on small plateaus and slopes of the strongly deformed east-west trending Montagne Ste.-Victoire. Some estates on these slopes were the first to prove that Provence can produce very good wines. Sharp ridges of the Montagne often appear in Cézanne's landscapes. The strata are limestones of the Tertiary, Cretaceous, and Jurassic. Someone aptly described the limestone surfaces as where the rocks are always ready to tear a hole in the thin top soil.

In the eastern suburb of Aix-en-Provence is the appellation of Palette. It was given special appellation status in 1948 in recognition of the distinctive limestone outcrop. In a country where ancient is commonplace, this small terroir was planted only about 500 years ago by the Carmelites of Aix. (The Carmelites originated as hermits on Mt. Carmel in the Holy Land.) The principal vineyards, now belonging to Château Simone, one of the pioneers of quality wines, are on northwest-facing terraces overlooking the Route de Cézanne.

The soils are pebbly, calcareous slope wash from a ridge of Tertiary limestone. Viticulturists have declared that the secret of Palette's quality is the microclimate of its northern exposure which moderates the intensity of the summer sun. Red, white, and rosé wines are produced from the traditional grape varieties of the region: Grenache, Cinsault, Clairette, Syrah, Bourboulenc, and Mourvèdre. The vignerons attempt to match these varieties with their preferences of the local variations of soil.

Coteaux Varois, a new (1993) A.O.C. was delimited to accommodate the vineyards on various limestone terrains of the Triassic-Jurassic plateaux between the Coteaux d'Aix-en-Provence and the main Côtes de Provence. The Cabernet Sauvignon has been quite successful on these limy-clay soils.

Along the coastal bluffs between Marseille and Toulon are two of Provence's top appellations, Cassis and Bandol, noted for white and red wines respectively.

The small fishing port of Cassis and its equally small appellation are threatened by urbanization from Marseille. The spectacular sea-cliffs are massive Upper Cretaceous limestones composed of large elongate fossil oysters called rudists. Ridges of rudist limestone shed scree to mix with the gravelly soils of the 375-acre (150-ha) Cassis vineyards. A large colony of rudists form the mound-like Mont de Saoupe, dominant topographic feature of the Cassis plateau. Exposed below the cap rock of the cliff is a thick bed of clean sand which supplies a narrow, but well-protected, popular beach.

Cassis wines are principally made from the Clairette, Marsanne, Ugni Blanc, and Sauvignon Blanc. These wines are ideal complements to the catch by the village fishermen.

About 20 twisting, scenic miles (32 km) east of Cassis along the headlands is Bandol, the largest of Provence's special appellations. The 1500 acres (600 ha) of vineyards are fitted into protected coves in craggy hills of Jurassic limestones, sandstones, and conglomerates. Bandol produces red, white, and rosé wines, with reds being undoubtedly the best of Provence. They can have a tannic firmness that has traditionally been rare in this region, some capable of maturing for 10 years and more. Many producers make Bandol with 100 percent Mourvèdre.

The best areas of production are on soils of slope-wash from calcareous sandstones of the Upper Cretaceous. Lesser areas of production are found on stony, red clay soil and scree from the Triassic and Jurassic hills. Although slightly acidic, the sandy soil has good water retention, a quite important characteristic as there is very little precipitation from May to September. The Mourvèdre, the principal grape of Bandol, likes deep, well-drained, but moisture-holding soil. As at Cassis, the moist sea air moderates the dry heat of mid-summer, aiding proper maturation of the grapes.

The extensive appellation of Côtes de Provence produces some 80 percent of Provence wine, on three different geologic sub-provinces: the Maures-Esterel crystalline complex, the intricately eroded plateau of Jurassic-Permo-Triassic, and the outer zone of dissected Jurassic-Cretaceous limestones. The geologic differences of each are reflected in grape preferences and wine styles.

The crystalline rocks of the Maures-Esterel massif form a ragged highland along the coastline from Toulon through Fréjus to Antibes. The rocks of the Maures province are light-colored, micaceous crystalline schists along with dark, slate-like schists containing crystals of quartz.

The name Maures is derived from a Provençal word, *Maouro*, meaning dark forests, describing the pine-covered ridges. The Maures reaches heights of 2000 feet (600 m) only 10–15 miles (15–25 km) inland. It was the maritime pines from this coastal area that were planted to arrest the migrating dunes of Les Landes that threatened to overwhelm the Médoc vineyards of Bordeaux.

The Argens and Gapeau rivers have eroded wide valleys skirting the resistant core of the Maures providing excellent vineyard slopes and terraces in a complexity of faulting and rock types. Deeper within the massif, terraced vineyards are tucked in amongst the trees on soils of multi-colored schists and deeply weathered granite.

A thesis study of the soils and growing conditions of Bandol by Suzanne Baeltz was kindly provided by Mr. Lucien Peyraud of Domaine Tempier.

The Esterel complex contains Tertiary volcanic rocks extruded at the time of Hercynian rejuvenation. The dense lava contains large crystals (phenocrysts) of various colors, red, green, yellow, purple, and gray. Stone from quarries east of Fréjus were fashioned by the Romans into shafts of columns for many of their buildings in Provence (generally, they preferred rocks with blue phenocrysts). In recent decades forest fires have denuded many of the hills. New vineyard plantings have been made along with a reforestation program.

The Permo-Triassic-Jurassic strata are intricately faulted with crystalline rocks in an arc bordering the north side of the Maures massif. Soils of this steeply terraced zone are dark red, sandy, and pebbly. This terrain and soil provide a variety of good vineyard sites.

The outer plateau of Cretaceous-Jurassic limestone is intricately meshed by erosion with the zone of older strata. Further away from the complexities of the massifs, the terrain becomes more gentle with large estates of extensive vineyards, many producing bulk wines.

In the coastal region toward the Italian border, the north–south ridges of the Maritime Alps come right to the seas. There are no vines to speak of until Nice but there are flower farms in abundance. The town of Grasse is internationally famous for its perfume made from these extensive acres of cultivated flowers.

In the environs of Nice, we find the small 75-acre (30-ha) special appellation of Bellet, struggling for survival in the urban area. Planting is on very steeply terraced slopes of the Serre hills overlooking the Var River. The gravelly, sandy clay soils are weathered from Permian puddingstones (small gravel in a limy-clay matrix). The very existence of Bellet is threatened by commercial flower nurseries and other developments. Viticulturists credit Bellet's quality to a microclimate – the cooling effect of sea breezes during the day and cool air funneled down the Var Valley from the Maritime Alps during the night. Up the Var, there are also a few isolated wine areas found tucked away in side valleys.

For such a small area, an amazing variety of grapes is used to make red, white, and rosé wines. In addition to the traditional grapes of Provence, there are exotic varieties from neighboring Italy that give interesting flavors to Bellet wines. The white wine is the most remarkable, being made principally from the Rolle (known as the Vermentino in Corsica) which is grown nowhere else in France. Blended with it are the Roussanne de Var, Mayorquin, and lesser quantities of Clairette and Muscat. The Fuella Nera (Folle Noire), the Braquet, Cinsault and Grenache are used for the rosés and red wines.

The narrow beaches east of Toulon are backed by cliffs except at the head of the Gulf of St.-Tropez, where the terrain inland is relatively gentle. This was the site of the Allied amphibious landing in August, 1944 as a "second front" in the liberation of France. From this beachhead, aided by airborne troops, Toulon and Marseille were taken from the land side.

The wine brotherhoods

In Provence, as in every wine producing area of France, fraternal associations have been formed to promote knowledge and appreciation of their local wines. They all encourage growers and négociants to improve quality.

One of the first bacchanalian orders in France was organized by the Naval Governor of Toulon in 1690. It was the Societé des Frères de Méduse, revived in 1951 as the Ordre Illustre des Chevaliers de Méduse.

The Confrérie des Echansons de Vidauban was organized in Vidauban in 1970 which, in the Triassic-Jurassic zone north of the Maures, enthusiastically champions Provence's wines. But it will be some time yet before the wine-buying public can erase the notion that the wines are ordinary and mostly rosés. Be that as it may, increasing numbers of growers in this region are estate bottling and establishing individual reputations for quality.

The large V.D.Q.S. of Coteaux de Pierrevert is located on both sides of the wide valley of the upper Durance. The north–south course of the river is controlled by the extension of the Aix fault. Vineyards to the west occupy protected slopes of the Lubéron chain and the Vaucluse plateau and yield Rhône-style wines.

On foothills of the Provençal Alps, more extensive sitings are found on terraces and ridges of a large apron of Miocene molasse. These hinterland wines are all vinified by cooperatives, largely as bulk wines.

Urban development has effectively preempted opportunities for more enclaves like Bandol or Cassis along the coast, but there are certainly many good inland areas of Provence that could develop vineyards of V.D.Q.S. and A.O.C. status. These areas would of necessity be patchy, for the lack of geologic continuity is, unfortunately, a permanent affliction.

Corsica

From the air, Corsica appears like a spiny-backed monster half risen from the sea. Corsica and its larger island companion, Sardinia, are indeed strange creatures geologically. They are high-standing, buckled remnants of the ancient Hercynian belt rejuvenated during the Alpine mountain-building.

The western two-thirds of this mini-continent, Ajaccio Corsica (Ancient Corsica) is composed of basement granite and Paleozoic rocks penetrated in several places by Permian lava vents. These old rocks form the stegosaurus-like backbone of the island. Mont Cinto, the highest point on Corsica, rises to 8,891 feet (2700 m) high, only 15 miles (24 km) from the coast.

The northeast part of the island, Bastia Corsica (Alpine Corsica), comprises two zones – metamorphic *schistes lustrés* and Tertiary deposits of a coastal plain. The metamorphic zone is akin to the Maritime Alps around Monaco. The *schistes lustrés* are very fine-grained, calcareous mudstones with lenses of dark green serpentine, chlorite, and other dark minerals. Heat and pressure of Alpine deformation gave the mudstone a silky sheen or luster, hence the name.

The bony, finger-like peninsula of Cap (cape) Corse points to Genoa on the Italian coast, 100 miles (160 km) to the north. This is metaphorically a reminder that Corsica was once controlled by the city-states of Genoa and Pisa. Most of the Corsican place-names and many of the grapes are of Italian origin.

Diagonally across Corsica, a band of *schistes lustrés* separates the granite and the coastal element. The band is a thrust zone of nappes onto the granite mass of the Hercynian complex. Vines and other crops abound in the valley which developed along the *schistes lustrés,* these being far less resistant than the granite. Flooding of the desert-like Miocene basin developed a coastal plain on the east side of Corsica. Quaternary outwash obscures much of these Tertiary deposits.

Climate

Corsica's mountainous backbone helps create a very pleasant climate. Air rising over the peaks condenses moisture from the Westerlies, generating abundant rainfall, particularly on the western or granite side of the island. The mountains also influence thermal conditions, creating a sea breeze during the day and a land breeze at night. The surrounding sea, of course, moderates the overall climate. Corsica is sunnier than mainland France, and the north is hotter than the south.

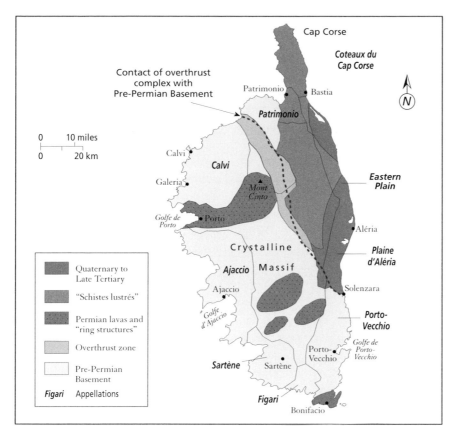

Figure 11.8
General geology and wine areas of Corsica
The western two-thirds of the island is granite; the eastern part is composed of a coastal plain of Tertiary and Quaternary deposits separated from the granite by a narrow overthrust band and the *schistes lustrés*

Despite the clemency of the climate, opportunities for cultivation of any kind on Corsica are quite limited. Citrus and olive groves, vines, and market products hug the coast. At higher elevations there are pastures. The largest vineyard areas are found on the eastern coastal plain, from Bastia to Solenzara. Those on the granite side are on slopes of inlets and old outwash fans.

The grape varieties

Given Corsica's long history of Italian control, many of the grapes are of that nationality. Grapes of the western areas are the Vermentino (white) and four red grapes, the Nielluccio (Italy's Sangiovese), Nebbiolo, and Sciacarello, which may be unique to the island. Reflecting later occupation by the French, the vineyards of the plains use grapes identified with Provence – Grenache, Cinsault, Carignan, Syrah, Mourvèdre, and increasingly, Cabernet Sauvignon, Merlot, Chardonnay and Chenin Blanc.

The appellations

Vineyards of Corsica are found on soils of three origins: granites, the *schistes lustrés,* and sedimentary rocks of the coastal plain. The granitic soils, typically sandy and stony, are generally acidic and poor in organic matter.

Accessory minerals of the *schistes lustrés,* serpentine and chlorite, provide abundant important nutrients, but the soils tend to be heavy. The Quaternary gravel, sands, and silts of the eastern coastal plain yield light, loamy soils, but, unfortunately, they are often heavily leached.

The appellation Vin de Corse was identified in 1976. Of more interest are the "Crus" of Vin de Corse and the more limited appellations of Patrimonio and Ajaccio which identify the island's best vineyards. Those of Patrimonio bordering the Gulf of St.-Florent are on calcareous clayey soils from the *schistes lustrés*. Here the red Nielluccio grape produces a wine high in color and rich in bouquet. Ajaccio's vineyards are on slopes of pink granites producing wines of long-standing reputation from the Vermentino and Sciacarello.

The "Crus" are Coteaux de Cap Corse, Calvi, Sartène, Porto-Vecchio, and Figari. The Coteaux de Cap Corse are the pride of Corsica. Clos Nicrosi, at the extreme northeast tip, yields its best and most expensive white, although other growers have abandoned the hard-to-work terraces on Silurian schist-like rocks and moved to the alluvial plain. A Cap Corse red, made in the style of Muscat, is called Rappu. There is an appellation for muscat made entirely from Muscat Blanc à Petits Grains. Calvi, on the northwest coast, and Sartène on the southwest coast, which has the biggest proportion of appellation wines, are both on the granite hill slopes. Porto-Vecchio and Figari, on the southern end of the island, have seen considerable experimentation with grape varieties. The eastern coastal plain has no specific appellations and is classified Vin de Corse. Both production and quality vary considerably, although increasingly improving *vins de pays* derive from this region and form the island's biggest export.

Limited growing space and geology and tradition considerably reduce the potential for development of wines in Corsica. The Corsicans seem in no great hurry to improve the island's reputation as a producer of bulk wine, most of it consumed locally by the Corsicans and tourists.

A bit of history

The strategic maritime value of Corsica and its ports has been recognized since the times of the Greeks, Etruscans, Carthaginians, and, of course, the Romans. Later it was the city-states of Pisa and Genoa that controlled Corsica. The Italian grape names, particularly the "hill grapes" on the granite side, reflect the seven centuries under Italian rule.

When the French came, they were interested only in the ports and the easy-to-work eastern coastal plain. The interior was too rugged and forbidding. As a consequence, the granite-dwellers were left to develop their own society based fundamentally on the traditional Italian "extended family." It also meant that their viticulture was developed very much in isolation. Several of the grapes varieties with Italian names, probably mutations of some unidentified grape, are found nowhere else in the world.

In the early 18th century, a rebellion against the Genoese resulted in an independent Corsica, but was annexed to France in 1769 – the year Napoleon Bonaparte was born in Ajaccio. Napoleon entered the French military academies at an early age. Much of his later military success can be credited to a developed sense of terrain and maneuver, having grown up in the rugged hills of granite Corsica.

Color Plate 44
The ancient monastic vineyards of Seyssel above Corbonod are on a glacial moraine on the west side of the Rhône

Color Plate 45
Jongieux in the Savoie is surrounded by appellation vineyards, with the best parcels entitled to the more precise classification of Roussette de Savoie Marestel. Snow is a frequent visitor in these parts.

Color Plate 46 Of more concern to the vigneron, the marly limestones of the Jurassic Kimmeridgian require a pick hammer to loosen the stony soil to get young plants started

Color Plate 47
The vineyards of Chignin in the Cluse de Chambéry were the "optima vini" of the 11th century. Each year vines are pushed a little higher up the slopes toward the massive limestones of the Upper Jurassic that make the Combes de Savoie

Plate 48
The valley of Barsac, in the Diois, home of Clairette de Die. The *terres noires* are usually covered by a veneer of broken rock with the "black earth" underneath

307

Color Plate 49
The steep, narrow terraces of the Côte Rôtie must be worked by hand. Reflection from the barren crystalline rocks truly makes a "roasted slope"

Color Plate 50
The Viognier grape produces some of France's most costly white wines on the terraced slopes of Condrieu in the northern Rhône. The terroir of Château-Grillet, a tiny enclave within Condrieu, is a steep amphitheater with a particular microclimate capable of producing a sublime golden wine of concentrated bouqet

Color Plate 52
In the searing heat of the Châteauneuf-du-Pape vineyards the mighty Syrah and up to a dozen other varieties mature to make a deep-colored, intensely concentrated wine that must age for a decade or more to tame its strength and flavors. The ruined summer palace of the Avignon popes dominates the skyline

Color Plate 53
One of France's best, and indisputably the greatest red wine of Provence, is Bandol, grown along a 10-mile (16-km) coastal stretch west of Toulon. The principal grape here is the Mourvèdre for which the combination of sun, sea, and craggy calcareous sandstone slopes is a winner

Color Plate 54
The massive ocher-colored limestone of the lower Cretaceous at the edge of the Lubéron Mountains east of Avignon, Provence

Color Plate 55
Mas de Daumas Gassac in the Herault, north of Montpellier was one of the first to show that the Coteaux du Languedoc has terroirs capable of producing fine quality wines. The profile shows the unique red glacial soils of the domaine. Vineyards were cut from the garrigue (native Mediterranean shrubs and herbs), and have yielded extraordinary Cabernet Sauvignon

Color Plate 56
The medieval fortifications of Carcassonne with vines on Eocene molasse in the foreground

Color Plate 57
Vines and soils in the A.O.C. Banyuls, abutting the Spanish border, almost fall into the sea, such is the steepness of the slopes

Color Plate 58
Corsica's mountainous backbone limits winegrowing to the coastal margins, but the island has interesting wines and indigenous grapes. Patrimonio remains one of its best appellations

12 Languedoc-Roussillon: battered rocks, relentless sun

The wines of Languedoc-Roussillon grow on some of the most battered rocks in France and indeed on some of the oldest and some of the youngest of geologic formations. The irregularity of colors on the geologic map (*see* Color Plate 1) gives a clue to the geologic complexity of this coastal province.

Languedoc-Roussillon was also one of the oldest, if not the oldest, civilized and grape-producing areas in Gaul, being Galli-Narbonensis, a part of the Roman province of Transalpine Gaul.

But it was climate, not geology, that attracted man to Languedoc-Roussillon – that and a long, sweeping, accessible coastal zone. The coastal trade route between the eastern Mediterranean and Spain undoubtedly brought adventurers of the very early days to the area, but it was the Romans who left impressive legacies of their presence: the great amphitheater at Arles, the portal of St.-Gilles, and the Pont du Gard north of Nîmes. This was Rome's retirement "sun belt" for veterans of its legions – the Sixth at Alès and the famous Tenth Legion at Narbonne. These disciplined soldiers and engineers contributed materially to the development of these cities.

Grapes, along with other Mediterranean fruits and vegetables, were a natural for the soils and climate of Languedoc-Roussillon. Except for the periods of occupation by the Visigoths and Muslims after the demise of the Roman Empire, wine has been grown in Languedoc-Roussillon since long before the Christian era.

The landscape

Landscape and geology, while incredibly complex, developed more systematically than paint flicked on a canvas as the colors on Color Plate 1 may suggest.

In the late Cretaceous, Languedoc-Roussillon was a dismal scene – lakes, rivers, and swamps inhabited by an assortment of wild creatures. There were no Pyrenees, no Aquitaine Basin, no Mediterranean, and the Massif Central was a low veldt. Seas of the Triassic, Jurassic, and early Cretaceous had extended across the region depositing strata of varying thicknesses. Soon the "Languedoc-Roussillon symphony" would begin: slow, rhythmic movements in the late Cretaceous, early Tertiary, building to a crashing crescendo in the Oligocene.

Also in the late Cretaceous, a crustal welt developed across the upper Iberian peninsula that would become the Pyrenees. As the narrow uplift grew during the Eocene, extensive sheets of molasse were shed northward, some reaching as far as the Rhône. As discussed in Chapter 11, the collision of the Afro-Arabian and Euro-Asian crustal plates caused deformation of the Pyrenees, Alps, and mountain chains extending eastward to the Himalayas.

As crustal compression intensified, the Pyrenees were squeezed upwards, blossoming into high mountains. Huge slabs of upthrust rocks broke away, sliding down and outward from the mountain slope to become the Mouthoumet Massif and a portion of the Corbières. The rejuvenated Hercynian trend, like an

Fig 12.1
General geology of
Languedoc-Roussillon
(geology based on *B.R.G.M.
Carte Géologique de France*
and reproduced by kind
permission of Editions du
B.R.G.M., France)

elongated piston, thrust strata northward along the coastal plain like a great tidal wave. This was a long and involved "movement" of the "Languedoc-Roussillon symphony" during which Jurassic, Cretaceous, and early Eocene strata were wrinkled, buckled and sometimes overturned. Erosion of this "symphony score" further confused by later sedimentation resulted in the geologic cacophony, the battered rocks of Languedoc-Roussillon, shown in Figure 12.1.

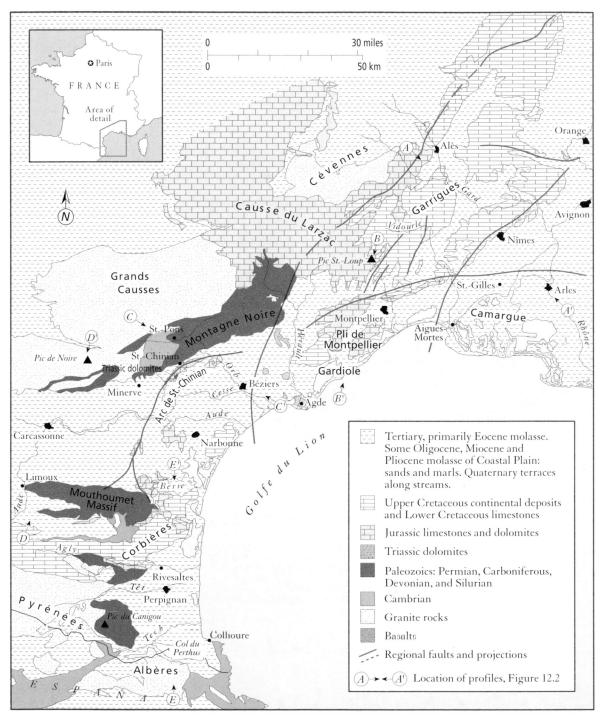

A portion of the stress created by the crustal blocks was relieved by a large fault trending northeast through Alès, shearing off the Cévennes from the Massif Central. A companion fault separates the Cévennes and the Garrigues.

The Nîmes fault extends northeastward across the Rhône in the area of Châteauneuf-du-Pape. It dislevels the rocks in the bed of the stream creating a ford which was reputedly used by Hannibal's forces in crossing the river.

The Montagne Noire, which hangs like a pendant on the southern part of the Massif Central possibly had some outward as well as vertical movement. Caught in the cross fire between these crustal deformations, is it any wonder the rocks of Languedoc-Roussillon are shattered and battered?

The panel of cross-sections, Figure 12.2, illustrates the geologic complexity of the surface and hence the soils. The main structural phase was completed

Figure 12.2
Geologic profiles
Geologic interpretations of the profiles are generalized and somewhat diagrammatic, particularly as to the Paleozoics and other deformed strata (compiled from various sources)

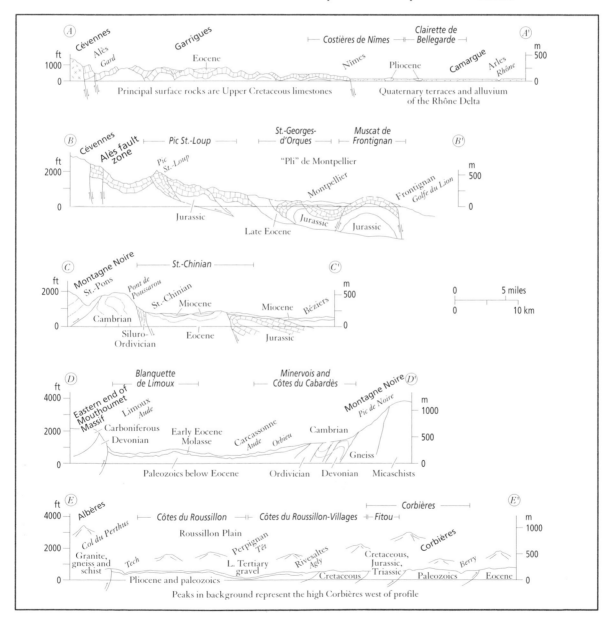

during the Oligocene which included leaving the Mediterranean basin as a desert-like depression in the Miocene. During the Pliocene, the sill between Gibraltar and Morocco which had held back the waters of the Atlantic was breached, allowing the basin to be filled, creating the azure blue Mediterranean. Even today the submerged sill damps the tidal effect from the Atlantic so that the tidal range in the Mediterranean is only a few feet. This new sea invaded the Rhône Valley as far as Valence, as well as shallow embayments along the Languedoc-Roussillon coast.

The reborn Mediterranean had barely accommodated itself to the landscape when the Quaternary Ice Age began. An ice cap formed on the Pyrenees and snow fields on the Massif Central. Languedoc-Roussillon, however, was not in the periglacial zone; the principal affects of the Ice Age were torrential rains and floods that built terraces along the streams leading from the mountains to the sea. These terraces are the site of some of the region's best vineyards.

Although the Mediterranean sea level was lowered to some extent it was not sufficient to induce the digging of a flume-like channel, as did the Gironde. Consequently, when the sea level returned to normal, the mouth of the Rhône did not become a deep-water estuary. On the contrary, the river began to "silt-up." When a river approaches the sea, it begins to lose its velocity and starts to drop its load of sand and silt, choking the mouth of the river. This caused the Rhône to break its banks and find a new, less obstructed way to the sea. As this process continues, the "distributaries" build a delta, named for the triangular-shaped Greek letter. The modern département covering this area is appropriately named Bouches-du-Rhône, mouths of the Rhône.

Imagine the number and length of trains that would be required to haul 20 million cubic yards of sand, silt, and gravel (the metric equivalent is not much less). That is the load that the Rhône dumps into the Mediterranean each year. Over the centuries this sand and silt has been swept southwestward by the onshore currents, redepositing it as longshore bars created which have created *étangs* (brackish-water lagoons) and large shallow lakes.

The delta itself is a land of sandy plains, marshes, and fresh-water lakes known as the Camargue. The lakes and marshes are wildlife refuges. More habitable areas are famous for breeding farms of black, fighting bulls – and enormous mosquitoes as vicious as the bulls. Surprisingly, some very good wines are produced in the sandy soils from which most of the salt has been leached (*see* feature below). Phylloxera does not proliferate in sandy soils, so the delta was largely unaffected by that crisis.

Photograph 12.1
Under the tradename Listel the Salins du Midi is producing some extraordinary wines grown in reclaimed sand-dunes

Vins des Sables du Golfe du Lion

The hugely wealthy Salins du Midi is a vast salt company, which now has the biggest wine estate in France, largely in the sand dunes of the Gulf of Lions. This improbable-sounding venture was begun in the mid-19th century, as the Domaines Viticoles des Salins du Midi. The company's considerable profits were used to pioneer vines in the sandy soils which remained phylloxera-free throughout the period when the bug devastated the wine economy of France. The sands are both stabilized and fertilized by a crop of winter cereals, and a system of dykes ensures that seawater does not invade the vineyards (similar to the polders of the Netherlands and the palus of the Médoc-Gironde). The wines can only be sold as *vins de pays* but such are the standards here that the estate is viewed almost as an appellation in its own right. Research into rootstocks best adapted to these sandy soils is also carried out.

Climate

The Mediterranean climate is as one a unifying element and an affliction. Vines will grow most anywhere in Languedoc-Roussillon, and do. In such heat grapes mature rapidly with little acidity – excellent for sweet wines and for reds from rustic grape varieties. Throughout its history the region naturally focused on these two styles of wine. In this land of easygoing viticulture, it was quite normal that wine would be produced in great volumes. When quantity dominates, quality suffers. Until the late 1960s Languedoc was viewed almost universally as a great reservoir of cheap wine. Its reputation as the source of the "plonk" of the French "Poilu" of World War I was difficult to live down. But the south of France woke from its slumbers the same time as California. Recent outside interest in the region and investment in modern viticultural and winemaking techniques has encouraged the normally conservative vignerons to look beyond their traditions and realize the vast potential of their soils and climates. Languedoc in particular is earning recognition and respect by producing wines – dry whites included – in controlled areas where particular grapes do best.

During the 1970s, hostility by growers of quality wines had reached the point of violence toward fraudulent négociants and participating producers of cheap wine. Whereupon the government, in conjunction with local agencies, developed a master plan to improve the quality and marketability of Languedoc-Roussillon wines. The plan called for significant restructuring of many of the existing vineyards, emphasizing consideration of geology, soils, and terrain for the delimitation of areas which had the potential for quality improvement. Evaluation took into account slope, exposure, depth, and type of soil, water reserves, drainage, and vegetation already in place. Considering tradition as far as possible, the best fit of grape to select locations was urged. Strangely, many vineyards with north-facing slopes which would give a lesser sun-angle in this hot climate were declassified.

The program required consolidation and exchange of properties and replanting with quality vines. Delays in income were inevitable as were legal and psychological problems. The French vigneron may be traditional, proud and stubborn, but he also has a pocketbook. Many planters eventually saw the economic merit to the program. The designation of special or sub-appellations was initiated; there are now 33. Extensive beach-front development of tourist accommodation and winter homes attests to the desirable climate of the Mediterranean coast. Mild winters favor agriculture as well as delight tourists. Nearness of mountains to the sea enhances the landscape, but also triggers violent thunderstorms, which account for much of the annual rainfall.

The sunshine and temperature graphs in Figure 1.5 (*see* page 36) show that Languedoc leads the other French wine regions in both categories. The Ecole Nationale Supérieure d'Agronomie at Montpellier has studied the bioclimate of the Languedoc grape varieties and related them to the Amerine-Winkler zonation of degree-days discussed in Part One. (Recall that degree-days are the total number of hours the temperature is above 50° Fahrenheit (10°C) for the growing season from mid-May to mid-October.) Developed from their research in California, Amerine and Winkler recognized five zones beginning with 2,500 degree-days for Zone I, the coolest. The scale increases in increments of 500

Montpellier, the wine capital of Languedoc, was an ancient university city with a school of law founded in 1160, and a school of medicine in 1289. Today, its Ecole Nationale Supérieure Agronomie is foremost among the French wine institutes, and is especially noted for its research on phylloxera.

degree-days for each succeeding zone, up to 4,500 degree-days for Zone V. Utilizing the concept, the Ecole researchers have worked out a grape-to-zone chart as a guide for replanting vineyards in Languedoc. For an area reputed to have such a hot climate, it is surprising that according to the authorities Zone V, the hottest (as in California's Central Valley), does not exist in Languedoc.

Although there is a great variety of soils on the complex geology, it would seem that a grape:soil preference guide such as Professor Claude Sittler and Robert Marocke prepared for Alsace would also be useful.

California's Napa Valley is relatively warm, comprising both Zones II and III with the Cabernet Sauvignon doing well in both zones. In Languedoc, however, the Cabernet Sauvignon is recommended only for the coolest zone under all soil conditions, but restricted to dry soils in the warmer zones. To take another example, the workhorse grape the Carignan is apparently quite sensitive to cooler temperatures, as it is advised against use in Zones I and only in Zone II under certain conditions. It is recommended for Zone III, provided the soil is poor and dry; for Zone IV it is recommended under all conditions.

The cold, dry, north wind of the famous *mistral*, coming down the Rhône Valley, spreads out along the coast as far as Béziers. It often displaces the warm, moist *marin* blowing from the sea whose lingering humidity too often promotes gray rot (not the noble sort). At other times, the *marin* gives welcome relief to the land heat. Consequently, the *mistral* and *marin* are alternatively blessed or damned by the vignerons, depending on the service rendered at the time. In the Roussillon, the *tramontane* and the *cers* are the dry winds off the Pyrenees making coastal Roussillon the driest area in France.

On the northeast coastal belt, from the Rhône delta to the vicinity of Agde, rainfall is irregular and poorly distributed, coming mostly in early spring and the autumn. Frequent periods of drought occur in the summer, making water retention of the soils extremely important.

Microclimates or subclimates found in upland valleys and along the flanks of the massifs were important factors in selection of the A.O.C. sub-appellations. Vines thrive up to altitudes of over 2000 feet (600 m) with the threat of frost minimal, and rainfall generally more dependable. Appellation boundaries are generously extended into the mountainous areas both to encompass vineyards in isolated valleys and to encourage further development of the quality potential. As plantings take advantage of the cooler microclimates of the mountain valleys, more white wines are likely to result. The vignerons of the Val d'Orbieu in the Aude département are already producing good examples.

The French "New World"

The shift from quantity to quality wines commenced about twenty years ago in Languedoc-Roussillon, hence its relatively nascent appellations. Both new and old varieties of red and white grapes are strictly regulated for A.O.C. vineyards, which produce about 13 percent of an unbelievable total of nearly three billion bottles a year. In fact Languedoc has shown itself to be the most anarchic wine region in France, with many growers thumbing their noses at the permitted appellation varieties and choosing to go the *vin de pays* route. This is the land of experimentation – with the Cabernet Sauvignon, Merlot, Sauvignon Blanc, Chenin Blanc, even the so-called fickle Viognier, and of course Chardonnay producing some very acceptable *vins de pays* and a few extraordinary ones, led by the Mas de Daumas Gassac (*see* Color Plate 55).

Grape varieties

Languedoc-Roussillon's long history of growing grapes means there was without doubt considerable trial and error to fit the grapes to the region's complex soils. It is a pity that there is no record as to the identity of the varieties grown in the pre-Christian era. In more recent times the highest-yielding varieties took hold and without the spur of competition for markets, laissez-faire attitudes prevailed.

Today, the largest percentage of the red and rosé wines (which constitute the bulk of the production of Languedoc-Roussillon) are still made from three traditional varieties: Cinsault, Grenache Noir, and Carignan (a Spanish import). Two other red grapes which probably did much to give the entire region its poor reputation, the Aramon and the Alicante Bouchet, are likely to disappear entirely in the drive toward improvement. Other red varieties of quality that have been more recently introduced are Syrah, Mourvèdre, and now the Bordeaux trio: Cabernet Franc, Cabernet Sauvignon, and Merlot. Because the climate promotes early maturation, it is said that blending of varieties is necessary to achieve balance in these wines.

Despite the predominance of red and sweet wines throughout the region, a number of white grapes are also found: two being white varieties of traditional reds Grenache Blanc and Carignan Blanc. The Clairette, known from the Diois (*see* page 284), is the grape of two sub-appellations – Clairette de Bellegarde and Clairette du Languedoc – but the variety does far better on the "black earth" terraces of the Diois than on the hotter coastal plain. The Picpoul Blanc or Picpoul de Pinet is the grape of the sub-appellation by the latter name. Blanquette (or Mauzac), is used in Blanquette and Crémant de Limoux. The white felting on the underside of the leaf accounts for the name "blanquette," blanket. Other white grapes are the Terret Gris, Ugni Blanc, and Bourboulenc, local name for the Malvoisie (the ancient Greek Malvasia), and the Muscat, which is discussed next under *vins doux naturels*. The latest, increasingly planted, introductions are the Sauvignon Blanc, Chardonnay, Chenin Blanc and Viognier.

Vins doux naturels

Sweet wines have been traditional in Languedoc-Roussillon since the 13th century. They are the easy, logical product of this hot climate. The sweet wines are called *vins doux naturels* (V.D.N.) which is something of a misnomer as the sweetness is not altogether natural, but is brought about by addition of alcohol during fermentation, which stops spontaneous action of the yeast thus retaining some of the natural sugars.

Vins doux naturels appellations use only quality varieties: the Grenache, Maccabéo, and Tourbat (the local name in Roussillon for the Malvoisie). A small percentage of Carignan is also permitted. The Maccabéo is thought to be of Middle Eastern origin, which accounts for its adaptability to dry climates. The four V.D.N. appellations in Roussillon are Banyuls Grand Cru, Grand Roussillon, Maury, and Rivesaltes.

There are several Muscat appellations using either the Muscat à Petits Grains, the variety with the small seeds, or the Muscat d'Alexandrie. The appellations using the Muscat include it in the name such as Muscat de Frontignan and Muscat de Rivesaltes (*see* Figure 12.3).

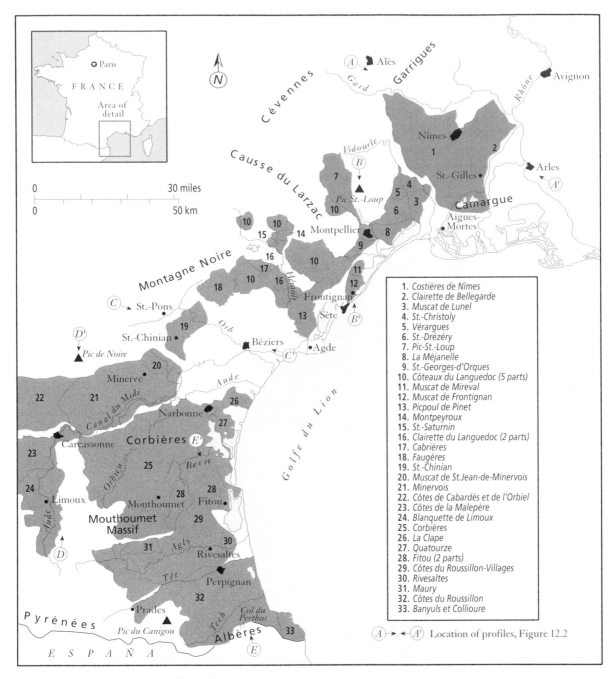

Figure 12.3
The appellations of
Languedoc-Roussillon

1. *Costières de Nîmes*
2. *Clairette de Bellegarde*
3. *Muscat de Lunel*
4. *St.-Christoly*
5. *Vérargues*
6. *St.-Drézéry*
7. *Pic-St.-Loup*
8. *La Méjanelle*
9. *St.-Georges-d'Orques*
10. *Côteaux du Languedoc (5 parts)*
11. *Muscat de Mireval*
12. *Muscat de Frontignan*
13. *Picpoul de Pinet*
14. *Montpeyroux*
15. *St.-Saturnin*
16. *Clairette du Languedoc (2 parts)*
17. *Cabrières*
18. *Faugères*
19. *St.-Chinian*
20. *Muscat de St.Jean-de-Minervois*
21. *Minervois*
22. *Côtes de Cabardès et de l'Orbiel*
23. *Côtes de la Malepère*
24. *Blanquette de Limoux*
25. *Corbières*
26. *La Clape*
27. *Quatourze*
28. *Fitou (2 parts)*
29. *Côtes du Roussillon-Villages*
30. *Rivesaltes*
31. *Maury*
32. *Côtes du Roussillon*
33. *Banyuls et Collioure*

(A) ▸ ◂ (A') Location of profiles, Figure 12.2

The wine areas

The vineyards of Languedoc-Roussillon are found on rocks of the entire geologic column. Much of the battered rocks are hidden by extensive deposits of the Tertiary and Quaternary, *see* Figure 12.1. By far, the largest vineyards are cultivated as flat-land crops on soils of Tertiary and Quaternary along the coastal plain. This is not to say they produce the best wines, only the greatest volume. Many of the very good wines, such as the Muscat de Frontignan and those of La Clape, are produced on or around "islands" or klippen, the flotsam of the Hercynian tidal wave of Jurassic and Cretaceous. Good terroirs occur in sub-appellations along the flanks of the Montagne Noire, on crystalline and Paleozoic rocks, between the Mouthoumet Massif and the higher Pyrenees and the complex geology of the Corbières. It is impossible to say where the best wines are produced – best what? Rosés, reds or whites, *vins doux naturels*, Muscats?

In general, soils of the Tertiary-Quaternary are red, pebbly clays and gravel; those of the Jurassic and Cretaceous are calcareous, loamy soils with limestone fragments, while those of the Paleozoic and crystalline basement are gritty, sandy or schistose-clayey soils.

It is difficult to group appellations under geologic categories as few of the delimitations lie wholly within a single geologic unit. The logical approach, therefore, is to discuss the appellations in the order in which they appear in Figure 12.3. The numbers after the appellation names in the text correspond to the numbered outlines on Figure 12.3.

The large Costières de Nîmes (1) lies primarily in the Camargue on old alluvium of the Rhône delta, and its reds and rosés are made in Rhône style. The scarp of the major fault zone of Nîmes limits growth of the delta on the northwest, *see* Profile A, Figure 12.2. Only a small portion of the Costières extends northwest across this fault into the Garrigues as the soils of that limestone province are thin and decalcified. The stony ridges of Cretaceous limestone support only tangled brush and dwarfed trees such as the Kermès oak. The name Garrigue, incidentally, derives from "garric", which is Occitan (the language of the Pays d'Oc) for oak.

The small white-wine appellation Clairette de Bellegarde (2) is on delta alluvium interspersed with irregular deposits of Pliocene marls.

Coteaux du Languedoc (10) was a large appellation from which a dozen sub-appellations of special quality were later carved, leaving only scattered pieces of the original appellation. The largest of these pieces is situated on Tertiary marls, sandstones, and gravel southwest of Montpellier. The geology of the other scattered pieces is essentially associated with the adjacent sub-appellations. The Coteaux and its sub-districts produce mainly reds and rosés.

Photograph 12.2
The Pont du Gard northeast of Nîmes, a major attraction for photographic-minded tourists, engineers, and archeologists, was part of an amazing aqueduct system of tunnels, siphons, and bridges built in 19 B.C. to bring fresh, mountain water to the aristocratic Roman city of Nîmes. Make no mistake, the citizens of Nîmes liked their wine as well as fresh water. It was easily obtainable from the numerous wine areas lying north and west of Nîmes which today produce some of the best wines in Langudeoc.

The grouping of the small sub-appellations of Muscat de Lunel (3), St.-Christoly (4), Vérargues (5), and St.-Drézéry (6), is on a complex of Cretaceous limestones interspersed with Eocene and Oligocene gravel and clay. The Grenache, Syrah and Mourvèdre thrive particularly on the gravel terraces and ridges in pebbly, red clay soils.

Pic-St.-Loup (7) vineyards are on slopes of pebbly, red soil derived from marly Cretaceous limestone. The Pic is a sharp pyramid of Jurassic limestone that was caught up in a confusion of highly buckled Cretaceous limestones, *see* Profile B, Figure 12.2.

La Méjanelle (8) and St.-Georges-d'Orques (9) are located on the "Pli de Montpellier," where the overthrust nappe above the sole fault was warped into a low, faulted domal feature, again *see* Profile B, Figure 12.2. Vineyard soils of red clay are mixed with limestone scree washed down from the Garrigues. Like most of the Coteaux du Languedoc, this is red (and rosé) wine country, although one of La Méjanelle's top producers also makes a white blend of Grenache Blanc, Roussanne, and Marsanne.

The vineyards of Muscat de Mireval (11) and Muscat de Frontignan (12) are spread around the flanks of the Montagne de la Gardiole. This Jurassic limestone "island" was buckled into a steep-sided, faulted anticline within the nappe itself, *see* Profile B, Figure 12.2. Soils are the typical red clay-limestone scree mix.

The geology of Montpeyroux (14), St.-Saturnin (15) (both for red wines), Clairette du Languedoc (16) (a rather dull white), and Cabrières (17) (good for rosé) is similar to the Pic St.-Loup section of Profile B, except the vineyards extend into the Paleozoics of the Montagne Noire. The principal exposures of these older rocks are Permian red schists which weather into excellent soils that seem to suit the Syrah. The main area of Clairette du Languedoc is on Miocene calcareous clays and lacustrine limestone laced with rivulets of Quaternary basalt. The basalts emerge through a zone of southeast-trending fractures and culminate in a volcanic plug, the hill of Agde, a coastal headland. (You will recall that basalts weather to exceptionaly good soils.)

Picpoul de Pinet (13) lies in the angle between the Hérault River and the Thau Basin, largest of the *étangs* along the coast. Picpoul is the alternate spelling for the grape Piquepoul Blanc, and produces a pleasant dry white. (The name should not be confused with "Piquepoul," the "lip stinger" grape of Armagnac and Cognac which is the local name there for the Folle Blanche.) The Picpoul de Pinet grows on relatively flat Cretaceous limestone and marls on the Pli de Montpellier. Soils include red and yellow clays and conglomerates of the Eocene and Pliocene. The lower part of the appellation is on terraces of Quaternary gravel from the Montagne Noire along the Hérault.

Profile C in Figure 12.2 shows that undisturbed late Eocene, Miocene, and Pliocene strata cover much of the inner Arc de St.-Chinian thrust sheet from Béziers to just above St.-Chinian. (The Miocene is a marine molasse composed of fossiliferous limestones and conglomerates, which together with Eocene marls and conglomerates weather to deep, red-colored soils.) Faugères (18), St.-Chinian (19), and Muscat de St.-Jean-de-Minervois (20) are on these Tertiary formations and variegated shales of the Triassic. Vineyards also extend across the frontal thrust fault well into the Paleozoics of the Montagne Noire.

Just beyond the village of St.-Chinian, the foothills of the Montagne Noire begin where a major fault throws up a wall of Cambrian (Paleozoic) limestones. Into the Montagne, the country quickly becomes quite hilly with numerous small vineyards on the schistose soils of the Paleozoic Ordovician.

The Minervois (21) and its westward extension Côtes de Cabardès et de l'Orbiel (22) are on the belt of non-thrusted strata skirting the Montagne Noire in the plains of the Carcassonne Gateway (or Seuil de Carcassonne). The Gateway is the meeting place of Atlantic, Mediterranean, and Pyrenean climates (*see* Color Plate 3), resulting in abundant sunshine and a good distribution of rainfall. Some Orbiel vineyards extend back into valleys of the Montagne, *see* Profile D, Figure 12.2. The plains are floored with undisturbed Eocene molasse comprised of limestones and clays with some conglomerates. The Paleozoic Cambrian, Ordovician, and Silurian of the Montagne Noire are composed of shales, sandstones, quartzites, limestones, and schists. Semi-officially the Minervois is divided into five zones, based on terroir and microclimate. Cabardès and Orbiel districts produce notably different wines to the others of Languedoc-Roussillon. Being the most westerly extension, the climatic influence here is from the Atlantic rather than the Mediterranean, and the Cabardès and Orbiel vineyards are planted with Atlantic as well as Mediterranean grapes.

Opposite the Orbiel district, southward across the Canal du Midi and the Fresquel, a tributary of the Aude, is the Côtes de la Malepère (23). Malepère, which means "bad stone," probably refers to the rugged ridge of cemented conglomerate which is covered by the Bois de Malepère. The vineyards are on less consolidated conglomerates of the upper Eocene molasse interbedded with soft sand and minor amounts of clay. The conglomerates, derived from the Pyrenees, contain an interesting variety of pebbles consisting of granite, limestone, quartzites, and marbleized limestone. Weathering of the molasse produces good viticultural soils aiding Malepère to V.D.Q.S. appellation status. It too is influenced by the Atlantic weather systems and has the Bordeaux grape trilogy in its vineyards.

Blanquette de Limoux (24) is reputed to be France's oldest sparkling-wine area. There is also an appellation for *crémant*, made by the classic method. The principal grape variety of Blanquette de Limoux is the Mauzac with auxiliary grapes being the Chenin Blanc and Chardonnay. It has lately been eclipsed in the marketplace by Crémant de Limoux, which has a greater proportion of Chardonnay and Chenin in the blend. The principal vineyards are on lower Eocene molasse similar to the Malepère, but extend southward into the rugged foothills of the Mouthoumet Massif. Conglomerates, lacustrine limestones, sandstones, and ocher-colored marls of the molasse are wrinkled into long, chevron-like open folds oriented east–west.

Corbières (25) is the largest of the Roussillon appellations. Like Minervois it has recognized zones, based on its terroirs. Its topography seems to have been just thrown together – a fairly apt description for this jumble of "rootless mountains." Nappes of the eastern Corbières were thrust westward over 10 miles (16 km) by the rejuvenated Hercynian deformation. Later, erosion left klippen of Triassic, Jurassic, and Cretaceous. The western Corbières become more rugged and collar around the Mouthoumet Massif of Paleozoic rocks.

The wine district of Minervois, collaring around the southern projection of the Montagne Noire, takes its name from the old Roman city of Minerve, perched on an Eocene limestone prominence overlooking the Cesse River.

The historical city of Carcassonne occupies a strategic location in the low pass between the Aquitaine Basin and the Mediterranean coast. It was the Roman fort-city of Corcaso, improved in the Middle Ages to an almost impregnable fortress. The old cité is high on an Eocene limestone butte overlooking the Aude (*see* Color Plate 56) and the modern city which has developed on the left bank.

Elevations of the coastal zone of the Corbières reach 1000 feet (300 m) only a few miles from the sea. Slopes of the principal vineyards of the coastal zone face east toward the Mediterranean while the more northerly vineyards look toward the Carcassonne Gateway. The better sites are found on Jurassic and Cretaceous limestones, but very good vineyards are also on Eocene molasse of the coastal plain and Carcassonne Gateway. Wines of the Corbières are 90 percent red with the remainder divided between rosé and white – including some excellent examples. For long Carignan dominated the reds, but the grape is now limited to 60 percent, with Grenache, Mourvèdre, and Syrah making up the blend.

The sub-appellation of La Clape (26) surrounds the Montagne de la Clape, an "island" of Cretaceous limestone lying along the coast east of Narbonne. Origin of this steep-sided anticline is similar to La Gardiole, being a part of the overthrust sheet which apparently buckled during the thrusting. The backbone of the anticlinal ridge overlooking the Mediterranean reaches an elevation of 700 feet (200 m). Vineyards around the base of the "island" on weathered limestone scree produce red, white, and rosé wines from the traditional Midi grape varieties. Unusually, the whites and rosés are reputed to be better than its reds.

On the southern outskirts of Narbonne is the tiny appellation of Quatourze (27) on a pebbly Pliocene plateau about 100 feet (30 m) above sea level. The Pliocene limestone is deeply weathered to a rust-colored soil containing limestone fragments and white quartz pebbles. The red, white, and rosé wines from this small appellation are of local fame only.

Fitou (28), the oldest established red-wine A.O.C. in Languedoc (1948), is in two parts: a coastal sector and a western portion within the Corbières. Nine of its communes make Muscat and V.D.N. Rivesaltes. The seacoast portion is situated on a klippe of Jurassic limestone overlooking the Etang de Lucate. The light-colored soils are derived from Miocene molasse and a small klippe of Jurassic and Cretaceous limestones. The better wines, however, come from the hill-country sector around Tuchan on soils developed from a klippen complex of Cretaceous, Jurassic, Triassic, and Paleozoic strata, *see* Profile E, Figure 12.2.

The Côtes du Roussillon-Villages (29) are in the Plaine du Roussillon where the valleys of the Agly, Têt, and Tech converge. The vineyards, on Quaternary gravel terraces and Pliocene marls, share space with orchards and truck (market) gardens for which the area is famous.

Perpignan, capital of Roussillon, has a long and complicated history, having paid homage alternately to France or to the Spanish Aragons, depending on who won the last local war. It is principally a trade center for wine, and particularly for fruit and vegetables whose early ripening brings premium prices in Paris.

Vineyards extend back into the small valleys opening off the Agly and Têt in the Mouthoumet Massif whose Precambrian gneisses, granites, and Silurian schists yield soils supporting quality vineyards.

Rivesaltes (30) is an enclave of the Côtes du Roussillon-Villages appellation, situated on a high-level rocky Quaternary terrace some 100 feet (30 m) above the coastline. The gravel soil is quite deep and contains abundant limestone pebbles. It is quick to heat, providing excellent maturation conditions for Grenache, Maccabéo and a little Malvoisie and Muscat. A portion of the area is Muscat de Rivesaltes, biggest of the V.D.N. appellations. This sweet brown wine is made from the Muscat à Petits Grains and the Muscat d'Alexandrie; the former showing a preference for the relatively cooler sites and calcareous soils. The latter is grown because it ripens later and resists drought.

West of the Roussillon-Villages appellation are the sweet-wine vineyards of Maury (31) lying in the valley of the Ruisseau de Maury, a tributary of the Agly. The stream runs on an outcrop band of Cretaceous limestone, one of the slabs of the overbuilt Pyrenees which slid down the mountainside. Maury wines are 100 percent Grenache Noir.

The Côtes du Roussillon (32) are in the rugged country between the Plaine du Roussillon and the Albères range, the easternmost part of the Pyrenees. Known locally as the Aspres wine region, it extends westward from the coast to the foothills of the Massif du Canigou with its dominating Pic du Canigou.

Every prominent hill of the region, and there are many, seems to be surmounted by an ancient chapel or shrine with a vineyard mantling the lower slopes. The principal vineyards are on the same Quaternary gravel terraces and Pliocene marls as the Villages Côtes except they are also found in valleys which reach back into the Paleozoics and crystalline rocks of the Albères and Canigou. Côtes de Roussillon reds are made from the Carignan, an old Catalan variety, together with Grenache and Syrah. Many smaller producers around Perpignan and up the Agly and Tet valleys are making some formidable wines, the best stiffened with Syrah and Mourvèdre.

In addition to the regular red wines typical of the region, the town of Thuir, southwest of Perpignan, produces the aperitifs Dubonnet and the lesser known but well-named Byrrh. These products are prepared in the fashion of V.D.N.s with a herbal flavoring added at the point of blending.

Near the eastern end of the Albères on the border with Spain is the Col du Perthus. Just under 900 feet (270 m) in elevation, the pass carries the Autoroute Catalane into Spain, paralleling the old RN9. (There are no rail connections between France and Spain.) Perthus was also the pass over which Hannibal in 219 B.C. brought his elephants from Spain into Gaul. This was the incredible flanking route to attack Rome from across the Alps.

Banyuls (33) and its sweet wine is perhaps the best known of Languedoc's sub-appellations, certainly its finest V.D.N., even though just four communes are entitled to use it. It also has its own Grand Cru for wines which have 75 percent Grenache Noir in the blend. The twisty coastal road from Collioure (a tiny appellation for intensely concentrated reds) through Banyuls to the Spanish border gives rapidly alternating views between the Mediterranean and steep vineyard terraces (*see* Color Plate 57). These ancient terraces are so steep and narrow (to prevent the thin soils from being washed away by violent storms) they can be worked only by man and mule.

Outcroppings along the steep slopes facing the sea are Cambrian sandstones and shales, while capping the ridges are overthrust slabs of Precambrian schists and gneisses. The soils contain abundant chlorite, a greenish mica which weathers to montmorillonite clay with its high cation-exchange capacity for the soil. These thin soils can only support "rustic" grapes, mainly old Grenache vines, and the yields are meager. The torrid heat, however, means the crop is literally bursting with sugar – perfect for sweet and concentrated wines.

A colorful idiom for viticulture in Languedoc is *Wine from where the Mistral Blows,* the title of a little book by J. M. Weston. The author gives an engaging account of Languedoc's history, wine, and people. Freda White's book, *West of the Rhône*, also gives a personal narrative of this interesting land and its people.

Languedoc-Roussillon deserves an objective "second chance," having now become more serious about its quality potential. Unlike the other French wine regions which long ago matched grape varieties with terroirs, Languedoc-Roussillon, with the help of geologists, soil experts, and climatologists, continutes in the search for the best grape–terroir combination.

Vins de Pays

Languedoc-Roussillon is also France's largest producer of *vins de pays*, indicative of fresh thinking among growers, cooperatives included, who, frustrated by the limits on varieties imposed by the regulations of their youthful appellations, rightly believe the wine in their bottles is more important than the label. Cooperatives were instrumental in stabilizing the production and marketing in the depressed period between the two world wars. These same cooperatives are now responsible for wines that are comparable with the top individual growers who bottle their own wines.

Epilogue

Terroir has taken us on a viticultural odyssey through a diversity of scenic landscapes and powerful history. We have figuratively excavated the French vineyards to reveal why the great wines grow where they do. The answers are not in one or two elements but in the totality of the elements of the vineyard habitat – the very essence of terroir.

Bibliography

Leon Adams, *The Wines of America* (New York: McGraw-Hill, 1973).

Derek V. Ager, *The Geology of France* (New York: John Wiley & Sons, 1980).

M. A. Amerine and A. J. Winkler, "Composition and quality of must and wines of California grapes," *Hilgardia* 15, 1944: 493–675.

M. A. Amerine and P. M. Wagner, "The vine and its environments," Part III–1 in *Book of California Wine*, D. Muscatine, M. A. Amerine, and B. Thompson, eds (Berkeley, CA: University of California Press/ Sotheby Publications, 1984).

Jacques Beauroy, *Vins et Société à Bergerac* (Saratoga, CA: Anma Libri, 1976).

Olivier Bernier, *Words of Fire, Deeds of Blood* (Boston: Little, Brown, 1989).

H. Berr, *The Greatness and Decline of the Celts* (London: Constable, 1987).

Suzanne Blanchett, *Les Vins du Val de Loire* (Paris: Edns JEMA, 1982).

Pierre Bréjoux, *Revue du Vin de France*, no. 208 (1966): 37.

Pierre Bréjoux, *Les Vins de Loire* (Paris: Société Française d'Editions Vinicoles, 1974).

Pierre Bréjoux, "Le terroir et le cépage," *Revue du Vin de France*, no. 264 (1977): 14.

Georges Chappaz, *Le Vignoble et le Vin de Champagne*, esp. ch. 4, "Le sol et le sous-sol des vignobles de Champagne," (Paris: Louis Larmat, 1955).

Gabriel Chevalier, *Clochemerle*, Eng. trans. J. Godefroi (London: Secker & Warburg, 1936).

Jean Clavell and Robert Baillaud, *Histoire et Avenir des Vins en Languedoc* (Toulouse: Edns Privat), 1985.

André Combaz, *Les Vins des Terroirs de Savoie* (Suresnes: Jean-Pierre Taillandier, 1992).

Christopher Cope, *The Lost Kingdom of Burgundy, a Phoenix Frustrated* (New York: Dodd Mead, 1987).

J. L. Delpal, *The Valley of the Loire* (no place, no date of pub., Edns J.A.).

Roger Dion, *Histoire de la Vigne et du Vin en France* (Paris: Flammarion, 1977).

J. Dreyer, "The wines of Alsace at the Colmar Regional Fair," *Revue du Vin de France*, vol. 226 (Jan.–Feb. 1970): 43.

Joseph Dreyer, "The wines of Alsace," *Le Grand Livre du Vin* (New York & Cleveland: World Publishing Co., 1970).

Philippe Duchaufour, *Pedology*, English trans. T. R. Paton (London: Allen & Unwin, 1982, first published Masson, Paris: 1977).

Hubrecht Duijker, *The Loire, Alsace, and Champagne* (London: Mitchell Beazley 1981; New York: Crescent Books).

Hubrecht Duijker, *The Great Wines of Burgundy* (London: Mitchell Beazley, 1983; New York: Crescent Books).

Raymond Dumay, *La Mort du Vin* (Paris: Stock, 1976).

Jacky Dupont, "Les Problèmes de l'adaption de la vigne dans le vignoble de Chinon" (Poitiers: Université de Poitiers, 1978 thesis): 38–66.

Henri Enjalbert, *Les Grands Vins de St. Emilion, Pomerol, et Fronsac* (Paris: Edns Bardi, 1983).

Nicholas Faith, *Château Margaux* (London: Christie's, 1980).

Nicholas Faith, "Wine survey, a difficult vintage," *The Economist*, Dec. 24, 1983: 90.

Henry Faul and Carol Faul, *It Began with a Stone* (New York: Wiley, 1983).

Edward Féret, *Bordeaux and Its Wines* (Bordeaux: Edns Féret et Fils, 1986).

William Fèvre, *Les Vrais Chablis et les Autres* (Chablis: published privately by Fèvre, 1978).

William J. Flagg, *Three Seasons of European Vineyards* (New York:Harper & Bros, 1869).

Snowden D. Flora, *Hailstorms of the United States* (Norman, OA: University of Oklahoma Press, 1956).

T. Bedford Franklin, *Climate in Miniature* (New York: Philosophical Library, 1955).

Patrick Forbes, *Champagne, the Wine, the Land and the People* (New York: William Morrow & Co., 1967).

Pierre Forgeot, *Guide de L'Amateur de Bourgogne* (Paris: PUF, 1967).

Rolande Gadille, *Le Vignoble de la Côte Bourguignonne* (Paris: Belles Lettres, 1967).

P. Galet, *Cépages et Vignobles de France* (2nd edn, Montpellier: Pierre Galet, 1990).

Rudolf Geiger, *The Climate Near the Ground*, trans. Milroy N. Stewart and others (Boston: Harvard University Press, 1957).

Rosemary George, *The Wines of Chablis* (London: Sotheby's in association with the Wine Appreciation Guild, 1984).

Gérald Jack Gilbank, *Les Vignobles de Qualité du Sud-Est du Bassin Parisien* (Bagnolet/ Paris: published privately by Gilbank, 1981).

S. S. Goldich, "A study in rock weathering," *Journal of Geology*, vol. 46, 1936: 17–58.

M. Guilloux, J. Duteau, and G. Seguin, "Les grands types de sols viticoles de Pomerol et St. Emilion," *Connaissance de la Vigne et du Vin*, no. 3 (Talence: Institut d'Oenologie, University of Bordeaux, 1978): 141–65.

Ernest Hornickel, *The Great Wines of Europe* (New York: G. P. Putman's Sons, 1965).

Pierre Huglin, "Primauté des cépages," *Le Vin d'Alsace* (Montalba, 1978).Thomas Henry Huxley, *Autobiography and Selected Essays*, the Riverside Literature Series (New York: Houghton Mifflin, 1909).

Hugh Johnson, *Vintage: The Story of Wine* (London: Mitchell Beazley; New York: Simon & Schuster, 1989).

Hugh Johnson, *The Wine Atlas of France*, 4th edition (London: Mitchell Beazley; New York: Simon & Schuster, 1997)

J. M. Jouanneau and C. Latouche, "The Gironde estuary," *Sedimentology*, nos. 10–20. (Stuttgart: E. Sweizerbart'sche Verlagsbuchhandlung, 1981.)

Camille Jullian, "Histoire de la Gaule," *L'Agriculture* (Paris: Librairie Hachette, 1920).

W. M. Kliewer, *Grapevine Physiology*, Leaflet no. 21231 (University of California, Davis, Division of Agricultural Sciences, 1981).

Matt Kramer, *Making Sense of Burgundy* (New York: William Morrow, 1989).

Lillian Langseth-Christensen, "Alsace," *Gourmet*, August issue, 1974: 67.

Larousse, *Wines and Vineyards of France* (New York: Arcade Publishing, 1990).

Victor Lemoine, "La vigne en Champagne," from *Communication, Les Temps Géologiques*, 1886. (Reproduction from the Bibliotheque Communale, Epernay, provided by Professor H. Guérin.)

N. Leneuf, R. Clemet-Dels, G. Callot, *Occurrence of Smectite in Cracks of Tectonized Granites in Beaujolais* (Granada, Spain: International Symposium on Geochemistry of the Earth's Surface, Session E, Ref. #14, 1986).

E. Le Roy Ladurie, *Histoire du Climat Depuis L'An Mil* (Paris: Flammarion, 1983).

John Livingston-Learmonth and Melvyn C. H. Masters, *The Wines of the Rhône* (London and Boston: Faber & Faber, 1978).

Jean-Jacques Macaire, *The Wines and Winelands of France* (London: Robertson McCarta, 1989).

Avery McClurg, "The Texan who saved the French vineyards," *Journal of the International Wine and Food Society*, vol. 4, no. 2, Nov. 1977: 13–17.

André Maurois, *A History of France* (London: Jonathan Cape, 1952).

B. S. Meyer, D. B. Anderson, R. H. Bohning, D. G. Fratianne, *Introduction to Plant Physiology* (New York: D. Van Nostrand, 1973).

Tage Nilsson, "The Pleistocene," *Geology and Life of the Quaternary Ice Age* (Dordrecht, Holland/Boston, U.S.A.: D. Riedel, 1983).

George Ordish, *The Great Wine Blight* (London: J. M. Dent, 1972).

Robert M. Parker, Jr., *The Wine Advocate*, issue 92, April 30, 1994 (Parkton, Maryland: Robert Parker).

René Pijassou, *Le Médoc* (Paris: Librairie Jules Tallandier, 1980).

Daniel Querre, "Le Terroir," *Revue du Vin de France*, no. 232, March–April, 1971.

Cyril Ray, *Mouton-Rothschild* (London: Christie's, 1980).

Jancis Robinson, *Vines, Grapes and Wines* (London: Mitchell Beazley/New York: Alfred A. Knopf, 1986).

Bruno Roncarati, *Viva Vino, D.O.C. Wines of Italy* (London: Wine & Spirit Publications, 1978).

Jean and Georges Samalens, *Armagnac* (London: Christie's, 1980): 21.

Gérard Seguin "'Terroirs' and pedology of wine growing," *Experimenta* 42, 1986 (Basel: Birkhäuser-Verlag): 861.

Gérard Seguin "Influence des facteurs naturels sur les caractères des vins", *Science et Techniques de la Vigne*, fig. 11.1, p. 683 (Paris, Dunod, 1971).

Desmond Seward, *Monks and Wine* (London: Mitchell Beazley 1979).

André L. Simon, *The Noble Grapes and The Great Wines of France* (New York: McGraw-Hill, 1968). *André Simon's Wines of the World*, 2nd edn, ed. Serena Sutcliffe (New York: McGraw-Hill, 1987).

Claude Sittler and Robert Marocke, "Géologie et oenologie en Alsace: sols et terroirs – cépages et spécificité des vignes," *Sciences Géologiques*, Tome 34, Fasc. 3, 1981: 171.

Bruno Stehle, *Leiden und Freuden der Weinbauern in Ober-Elass* [Sorrows and joys of the winegrowers of Upper Alsatia] (Strasbourg: Geib & Mundel, 1899): 9.

Tom Stevenson, *Champagne* (Paris: Sotheby's in association with the Wine Appreciation Guild; U.S. distribution through the Wine Appreciation Guild, 1986).

Pamela Vandyke Price, *Alsace Wines* (London: Sotheby's, 1984).

Terroirs et Vins de France, Itinéraires oenologiques et géologiques, under the direction of Charles Pomerol, co-edited by André Combaz and Robert Lautel (Orléans and Paris: Edns du B.R.G.M.–Total Edition-Presse, 1984.)

J. M. Weston, *Wine from Where the Mistral Blows* (London: Wine & Spirit Publications, 1981).

Freda White, *West of the Rhône* (New York: W. W. Norton, 1981).

William Younger, *Gods, Men and Wine* (London: Wine and Food Society in association with World Publishing Co., 1966): 234.

Acknowledgments

Terroir would not have been possible without the excellent maps and publications available from the Bureau de Recherches Géologiques et Minières (B.R.G.M.) and the Institut Géographique National (I.G.N.). I thank them for their kind permission to use certain materials in the book.

It took the assistance of many people of varied talents to bring to book-form how geology and wine are related. I gratefully acknowledge the indirect as well as the direct help of the many experts. Sincere appreciation is expressed to Professor Charles Pomerol, under whose direction the geologic guide *Terroirs et Vins de France* was published, with Robert Lautel and André Combaz as co-editors. It was an extremely useful book during my years of research and field study. I am indebted to Dr. Lautel for his varied and valuable assistance in review of the general geology, obtaining many permissions for copyright material, and for his photographic work – including a last-minute dash to Château Chalon for a replacement photograph.

Especial thanks to Hugh Johnson, the patron saint of *Terroir,* for his encouragement from the time my idea for this book was a "seedling," through years of slow and uncertain growth, to the writing of his gracious Foreword.

At an early stage, Professor Noël Leneuf demonstrated to me that geology and soil did indeed influence the character of wine. Catherine Ponsot-Jacquin undertook fieldwork and photography in Burgundy. André Combaz provided an exceptional and complete study in Savoie. In the Upper Rhône, Anne Lesvignes provided very useful material. In Champagne, Professors Hubert Guérin and Michel Laurain rendered expert assistance in reviewing my geologic interpretations and supplying key photography. Professor Claude Sittler in Alsace was a cordial mentor, providing geologic and historical review and field guidance. Also in Alsace, thanks to Dr. Georges Hirleman for his field guidance and to Robert Maroque for his discussion on soil–vine preferences. In Bordeaux, Professor Michel Vigneaux thoughtfully arranged for field excursions with Professors Louis Pratviel, Emile Peynaud, Gérard Seguin, and J. C. Dumon, and for Dora Morel to accompany us as translator. In the Loire, Professor Romain Brossé, Drs. J. Salette, and R. Morlat provided helpful field guidance, discussions, and publications. I acknowledge too my grateful appreciation of Charles Froucht for many miles of safe driving and acting as interpreter.

Special mention is due to Dr. Peigi Wallace for giving the first public paper on geology and wine, presented in 1971 at the World Geologic Congress in Montreal, Canada. When the Congress met in Paris in 1980, field excursions were offered to Burgundy and Bordeaux. Over-subscription for these trips attested to the growing interest in geology and wine.

For a broader understanding on the role of soil in viticulture, I consulted with several authorities in the U.S.: Dr. George Ray McEachern, Dr. Thomas Tieh, Texas A&M University, Dr. Gordon R. Dutt, University of Arizona, Armand N. Kasimatis and Gene Begg, consultants in Davis, California. I was also privileged to have a most interesting discussion with the late A. J. Winkler, Professor Emeritus at Davis.

An enormous amount of resource material required translations effectively done by Dr. Virginia Hill Martinson, Irene Sclavenitis, Bernard Rudloff, and John Sullivan. From the early inception of this book, Lev Ropes, now with LCT Graphics, consulted with the author regarding the artwork. Jon Haven of LCT skillfully converted rough sketches and drawings into computer graphics. Patti Cahill did the early hand-drafting and the creative hand of Carol Jarecke was effective in the reprography. Linda Gruber helped organize notes and edit early drafts. Julianne Griffin offered professional advice. Ruth Echols edited some early chapters. I am grateful to them all.

As the manuscript grew, editing became a serious problem. Happily, the solution was found within the family. Daughter Elizabeth employing her experience in writing and editing immediately focused on the rigid format and helped reorganize and rewrite sections of the manuscript to stress the geologic interpretation and capture reader interest. My wife, Elloie, who with infinite patience visited vineyards on end and had endured countless, lonely days while I worked on the book, then volunteered to read and help edit the growing text. There were numerous disagreements, but the marriage lasted. Daughter Judith Grant was an arbiter for questions of grammar and word usage.

Marguerite Bradford, for over a decade, produced reams of drafts and redrafts through four generations of computer upgrades. At times when spirits were low she was encouraging, scolding on others, but semper fidelis. Thanks, Marguerite.

Sincere thanks to Sue Jamieson at Mitchell Beazley for consideration of my manuscript and for carrying it through to its acceptance for publication. When it came to the final editing, I could not have been more fortunate than to have had Stephanie Horner assigned to my book. Her attention to detail was amazing. Her supplementary suggestions, formating, and updating of information were gratefully welcomed. Her sense of humor made the whole process enjoyable. Thanks also to Fiona Knowles for her assiduous review of the artwork and for her overall design. I wish to acknowledge the wonderful work of the in-house team that behind the scenes "put the book together."

Robert Lautel and Noël Leneuf
André Combaz, Claude Sittler,
R Morlat, Gérard Seguin, Michel
Vigneaux and J.-C. Dumon

Index

Indexer's note: page references in italic refer to color plate captions

Photographic credits